Survival Communications
in Hawaii

John E. Parnell, KK4HWX

10 ISBN 1478199105
13 ISBN 978- 1478199106

Cover design by:
Lynda Colón
FREELANCE GRAPHIC DESIGN &
MARKETING COMMUNICATIONS
www.hirelynda.webs.com

I do wish to acknowledge the hard work of **Angie Shirley** in putting together the database required for this book. Without her efforts, this book could not have been done.

Titles available in this series:

Survival Communications in Alabama
Survival Communications in Alaska
Survival Communications in Arizona
Survival Communications in Arkansas
Survival Communications in California
Survival Communications in Colorado
Survival Communications in Connecticut
Survival Communications in Delaware
Survival Communications in Florida
Survival Communications in Georgia
Survival Communications in Hawaii
Survival Communications in Idaho
Survival Communications in Illinois
Survival Communications in Indiana
Survival Communications in Iowa
Survival Communications in Kansas
Survival Communications in Kentucky
Survival Communications in Louisiana
Survival Communications in Maine
Survival Communications in Maryland
Survival Communications in Massachusetts
Survival Communications in Michigan
Survival Communications in Minnesota
Survival Communications in Mississippi
Survival Communications in Missouri

Survival Communications in Montana
Survival Communications in Nebraska
Survival Communications in Nevada
Survival Communications in New Hampshire
Survival Communications in New Jersey
Survival Communications in New Mexico
Survival Communications in New York
Survival Communications in North Carolina
Survival Communications in North Dakota
Survival Communications in Ohio
Survival Communications in Oklahoma
Survival Communications in Oregon
Survival Communications in Pennsylvania
Survival Communications in Rhode Island
Survival Communications in South Carolina
Survival Communications in South Dakota
Survival Communications in Tennessee
Survival Communications in Texas
Survival Communications in Utah
Survival Communications in Vermont
Survival Communications in Virginia
Survival Communications in Washington
Survival Communications in West Virginia
Survival Communications in Wisconsin
Survival Communications in Wyoming

The above titles are available from your favorite online or brick-and-mortar bookstore or directly from the publisher at Tutor Turtle Press LLC, 1027 S. Pendleton St. – Suite B-10, Easley, SC 29642.

TABLE OF CONTENTS

Appendix A – Hawaii Ham Radio Clubs

ARRL Affiliated Amateur and Ham Radio Clubs – By City

Appendix B – Hawaii Ham Licensees by City

Survival Communications in Hawaii

Perhaps you have prepared for WTSHTF or TEOTWAWKI with respect to food, water, self-defense and shelter. But what about communication?

Whenever there is a disaster (hurricane, earthquake, economic collapse, nuclear war, EMF, solar eruption, etc.), the normal means of communication that we're all reliant upon (cell phone, land line phone, the Internet, etc.) will probably be, at best, sporadic and at worst, non-existent.

As this author sees it, short of smoke signals and mirrors, there are three options for communication in "trying times": (1) GMRS or FRS radios; (2) CB radios; and (3) ham or amateur radio. Let's consider each of these options to come up with the most acceptable one.

GMRS (General Mobile Radio Service) / FRS (Family Radio Service)

GMRS (General Mobile Radio Service) / FRS (Family Radio Service) radios work optimally over short distances where there is minimal interference. Originally designed to be used as pagers, particularly inside a building or other such confined area, these radios are low-cost and convenient to carry. Unfortunately their small size and light weight comes with a trade-off – short range and short battery life. These radios are supposed to be able to communicate for up to 25-30 miles. Right. That's on level terrain, without buildings or trees getting in the way. While battery life technology is constantly improving, you will need spare batteries to keep communicating or someway of recharging the ones in the radio. In this author's opinion, GMRS/FRS radios are not first choice when concerned with medium or long range communication.

CB (Citizens Band)

CB (Citizens Band) radios operate in a frequency range originally reserved for ham or amateur radio operation. Because of the overwhelming number of people wishing quick, low-cost, regulation-free communication, the FCC (Federal Communication Commission) split off a portion of the frequency spectrum and allowed anyone to purchase a CB radio and start communicating. No test. No license. Just personal/business communication. Today, CB radios are readily available in such outlets as eBay and Craigslist. This author has seen them at yard/garage/tag sales and at flea markets.

CB radios come in a variety of "flavors." Fixed units, sometimes referred to as base units are intended for home use. For the most part, they derive their power from the utility company. In the event of loss of electricity, most base units can also be connected to a 12-volt battery, like that in your car/truck. If you choose to obtain a fixed unit, make sure you know how to connect the unit to the battery – ahead of time. Trying to figure this out when you're under extra stress is not a good situation.

A second type of CB radio is designed to be mobile, that is, installed in your car/truck. It gets its power from the vehicle's battery. You can either attach an antenna permanently to the vehicle or have a removable, magnetic type antenna.

The third type of CB radio is designed for handheld use. They are small and light. Most weigh less than a pound and operate on batteries. Yes, using batteries in a CB poses the same limitations as those by the GMRS/FRS radios, but have the added advantage that most handheld units come with a cigarette lighter adapter. Comes in handy when you are on the move and wish to be able to communicate both from a vehicle and also when you have to abandon it.

While they have a greater range than GMRS/FRS radios, CB radios are, legally, limited to operate on 40 channels, with a power rating of four (4) watts or less. Yes, it is possible to alter CB radios to get around these limitations, but not legally,

Ham/Amateur Radio

Ham/Amateur radio is very appealing. With a ham radio, you are not limited to less than 50 miles, but can communicate with anyone in the world (who also has access to a ham radio, of course).

Standardized Amateur Radio Prepper Communications Plan

In the event of a nationwide catastrophic disaster, the nationwide network of Amateur Radio licensed preppers will need a set of standardized meeting frequencies to share information and coordinate activities between various prepper groups. This Standardized Amateur Radio Communications Plan establishes a set of frequencies on the 80 meter, 40 meter, 20 meter, and 2 meter Amateur Radio bands for use during these types of catastrophic disasters.

Routine nets will not be held on all of these frequencies, but preppers are encouraged to use them when coordinating with other preppers on a routine basis. Routine nets may be conducted by The American Preparedness Radio Net (TAPRN) on these or other frequencies as they see fit. However, TAPRN will promote the use of these standardized frequencies by all Amateur Radio licensed preppers during times of catastrophic disaster. The promotion of this Standardized Amateur Radio Communications Plan is encouraged by all means within the prepper community, including via Amateur Radio, Twitter, Facebook, and various blogs.

Standardized Frequencies and Modes
80 Meters – 3.818 MHz LSB (TAPRN Net: Sundays at 9 PM ET)
40 Meters – 7.242 MHz LSB
40 Meters Morse Code / Digital – 7.073 MHz USB (TAPRN: Sundays at 7:30 PM ET on CONTESTIA 4/250)
20 Meters – 14.242 MHz USB
2 Meters – 146.420 MHz FM

Nets and Network Etiquette

In times of nationwide catastrophic disaster, the ability of any one prepper to initiate and sustain themselves as a net control may be limited by the availability of power and other resource shortages. However, all licensed preppers are encouraged to maintain a listening watch on these frequencies as often as possible during a catastrophic disaster. Preppers may routinely announce themselves in the following manner:

• This is [Your Callsign Phonetically] in [Your State], maintaining a listening watch on [Standard Frequency] for any preppers on frequency seeking information or looking to provide information. Please call [Your Callsign Phonetically]. Preppers exchanging information that may require follow up should agree upon a designated time to return to the frequency and provide further information. If other stations are utilizing the frequency at the designated time you return, maintain watch and proceed with your communications when those stations are finished. If your communications are urgent and the stations on frequency are not passing information of a critical nature, interrupt with the word "Break" and request use of the frequency.

For More Information

Catastrophe Network: http://www.catastrophenetwork.org or @CatastropheNet on Twitter The American Preparedness Radio Network: http://www.taprn.com or @TAPRN on Twitter

© 2011 Catastrophe Network, Please Distribute Freely

In order to use a ham radio, legally, one must be licensed to do so by the FCC (other countries have analogous governmental bodies to regulate ham radio). To obtain a license is quite easy – take a test and pay your license fee. There are currently three classes of license – Technician, General, and Amateur Extra. With each of these licenses come specific abilities.

Technician class is the beginning level. The exam consists of 35 multiple choice questions randomly drawn from a pool of 395 questions. The question pool is readily available online for free downloading (http://www.ncvec.org/downloads/Revised%20Element%202.Pdf) or in such publications at *Ham Radio License Manual Revised 2nd Edition* (ISBN 978-0-87259-097-7). The current Technician pool of questions is to be used from July 1, 2010 to June 30, 2014. Be sure the question pool you are studying from is current. You will need to score at least 26 correct to pass. (Do not worry, Morse Code is no longer on the test, although many ham operators use it anyway.) You do not need to take a formal class in order to qualify to take the exam. You can learn the material on your own. Most people spend 10-15 hours studying and then successfully take the exam. The cost of taking the exam is under $20. The exam is given in MANY locations throughout the US. Usually the exam is given by area ham clubs. You do not have to belong to the club to take the exam. Check Appendix A for a listing of clubs in South Carolina.

Topics for the Technician License in Amateur Radio

The Technician license exam covers such topics as basic regulations, operating practices, and electronic theory, with a focus on VHF and UHF applications. Below is the syllabus for the Technician Class.

Subelement T1 – FCC Rules, descriptions and definitions for the amateur radio service, operator and station license responsibilities

[6 Exam Questions – 6 Groups]

T1A – Amateur Radio services; purpose of the amateur service, amateur-satellite service, operator/primary station license grant, where FCC rules are codified, basis and purpose of FCC rules, meanings of basic terms used in FCC rules

T1B – Authorized frequencies; frequency allocations, ITU regions, emission type, restricted sub-bands, spectrum sharing, transmissions near band edges

T1C – Operator classes and station call signs; operator classes, sequential, special event, and vanity call sign systems, international communications, reciprocal operation, station license licensee, places where the amateur service is regulated by the FCC, name and address on ULS, license term, renewal, grace period

T1D – Authorized and prohibited transmissions

T1E – Control operator and control types; control operator required, eligibility, designation of control operator, privileges and duties, control point, local, automatic and remote control, location of control operator

T1F – Station identification and operation standards; special operations for repeaters and auxiliary stations, third party communications, club stations, station security, FCC inspection

---

Subelement T2 – Operating Procedures

[3 Exam Questions – 3 Groups]

T2A – Station operation; choosing an operating frequency, calling another station, test transmissions, use of minimum power, frequency use, band plans

T2B – VHF/UHF operating practices; SSB phone, FM repeater, simplex, frequency offsets, splits and shifts, CTCSS, DTMF, tone squelch, carrier squelch, phonetics

T2C – Public service; emergency and non-emergency operations, message traffic handling

---

Subelement T3 – Radio wave characteristics, radio and electromagnetic properties, propagation modes

[3 Exam Questions – 3 Groups]

T3A – Radio wave characteristics; how a radio signal travels; distinctions of HF, VHF and UHF; fading, multipath; wavelength vs. penetration; antenna orientation

T3B – Radio and electromagnetic wave properties; the electromagnetic spectrum, wavelength vs. frequency, velocity of electromagnetic waves

T3C – Propagation modes; line of sight, sporadic E, meteor, aurora scatter, tropospheric ducting, F layer skip, radio horizon

Subelement T4 - Amateur radio practices and station setup

[2 Exam Questions – 2 Groups]

T4A – Station setup; microphone, speaker, headphones, filters, power source, connecting a computer, RF grounding

T4B – Operating controls; tuning, use of filters, squelch, AGC, repeater offset, memory channels

Subelement T5 – Electrical principles, math for electronics, electronic principles, Ohm's Law

[4 Exam Questions – 4 Groups]

T5A – Electrical principles; current and voltage, conductors and insulators, alternating and direct current

T5B – Math for electronics; decibels, electronic units and the metric system

T5C – Electronic principles; capacitance, inductance, current flow in circuits, alternating current, definition of RF, power calculations

T5D – Ohm's Law

Subelement T6 – Electrical components, semiconductors, circuit diagrams, component functions

[4 Exam Groups – 4 Questions]

T6A – Electrical components; fixed and variable resistors, capacitors, and inductors; fuses, switches, batteries

T6B – Semiconductors; basic principles of diodes and transistors

T6C – Circuit diagrams; schematic symbols

T6D – Component functions

Subelement T7 – Station equipment, common transmitter and receiver problems, antenna measurements and troubleshooting, basic repair and testing

[4 Exam Questions – 4 Groups]

T7A – Station radios; receivers, transmitters, transceivers

T7B – Common transmitter and receiver problems; symptoms of overload and overdrive, distortion, interference, over and under modulation, RF feedback, off frequency signals; fading and noise; problems with digital communications interfaces

T7C – Antenna measurements and troubleshooting; measuring SWR, dummy loads, feedline failure modes

T7D – Basic repair and testing; soldering, use of a voltmeter, ammeter, and ohmmeter

Subelement T8 – Modulation modes, amateur satellite operation, operating activities, non-voice communications

[4 Exam Questions – 4 Groups]

T8A – Modulation modes; bandwidth of various signals

T8B – Amateur satellite operation; Doppler shift, basic orbits, operating protocols

T8C – Operating activities; radio direction finding, radio control, contests, special event stations, basic linking over Internet

T8D – Non-voice communications; image data, digital modes, CW, packet, PSK31

Subelement T9 – Antennas, feedlines

[2 Exam Groups – 2 Questions]

T9A – Antennas; vertical and horizontal, concept of gain, common portable and mobile antennas, relationships between antenna length and frequency

T9B – Feedlines; types, losses vs. frequency, SWR concepts, matching, weather protection, connectors

Subelement T0 – AC power circuits, antenna installation, RF hazards

[3 Exam Questions – 3 Groups]

T0A – AC power circuits; hazardous voltages, fuses and circuit breakers, grounding, lightning protection, battery safety, electrical code compliance

T0B – Antenna installation; tower safety, overhead power lines

T0C – RF hazards; radiation exposure, proximity to antennas, recognized safe power levels, exposure to others

Once your name and call sign are available in the FCC database, you have the privilege of operating on all VHF (2 m) and UHF (70 cm) frequencies above 30 megahertz (MHz) and HF frequencies 80, 40, and 15 meter, and on the 10 meter band using Morse code (CW), voice, and digital mode. For a Technician license in Hawaii, your call sign will consist of a two-letter prefix beginning with AH, KH, NH, or WH, then either of the numbers six (6) or seven (7), and a three-letter suffix. The single digit number in the call sign is determined according to which area of the US you obtain your first license. Even though you may move to another state, you keep this number in your call sign. This is also true should you upgrade to a higher license and get a new call sign. The numeral portion of your call sign stays the same.

Call Sign Numbers

Below is a chart showing the various numbers and the state(s) in which you would obtain the number.

Call Sign Number	State(s)
0	CO, IA, KS, MN, MO, NE, ND, SD
1	CT, ME, MA, NH, RI, VT
2	NJ, NY
3	DE, DC, MD, PA
4	AL, FL, GA, KY, NC, SC, TN, VA
5	AR, LA, MS, NM, OK, TX
6	CA
7	AZ, ID, MT, NV, OR, WA, UT, WY
8	MI, OH, WV
9	IL, IN, WI

Residents of Alaska may have any of the following call sign prefixes assigned to them: AL0-7, KL0-7, NL0-7, or WL0-7. Likewise, residents of Hawaii may have the prefix AH6-7, KH6-7, NH6-7, or WH6-7 assigned.

Once you obtain your Technician license, do not stop there. Go and get your General license.

General is the second of three ham license classes. Like the Technician license, to get a General license, you merely have to take a 35-question multiple choice exam and pay your license fee. Passing is still at least 26 correct answers and the fee is the same (less than $20). Again the question pool is available for free online (http://www.ncvec.org/page.php?id=358). It is also available in such print publications as *The ARRL General Class License Manual 7th Edition* (ISBN 978-0-87259-811-9). The current General pool of questions is to be used from July 1, 2011 to June 30, 2015. Be sure the question pool you are using is current. Being a bit more comprehensive than the Technician license, the General license usually requires 15-20 hours of study to learn the material. Check Appendix A for a listing of clubs in Hawaii where you might take your exam. Once your name and NEW call sign is listed in the FCC database, you're good to go. For a General license in Hawaii, your call sign will consist of a two-letter prefix beginning with AH, KH, NH, or WH, either of the numbers six (6) or seven (7), and a three-letter suffix.

Topics for the General License in Amateur Radio

The General license exam covers regulations, operating practices and electronic theory. Below is the syllabus for the General Class.

Subelement G1 – Commission's Rules

(5 Exam Questions – 5 Groups)
G1A – General Class control operator frequency privileges; primary and secondary allocations
G1B – Antenna structure limitations; good engineering and good amateur practice, beacon operation; restricted operation; retransmitting radio signals
G1C – Transmitter power regulations; data emission standards
G1D – Volunteer Examiners and Volunteer Examiner Coordinators; temporary identification
G1E – Control categories; repeater regulations; harmful interference; third party rules; ITU regions

---

Subelement G2 – Operating procedures

(5 Exam Questions – 5 Groups)
G2A – Phone operating procedures; USB/LSB utilization conventions; procedural signals; breaking into a OSO in progress; VOX operation
G2B – Operating courtesy; band plans, emergencies, including drills and emergency communications

---

G2C – CW operating procedures and procedural signals; Q signals and common abbreviations; full break in
G2D – Amateur Auxiliary; minimizing interference; HF operations
G2E – Digital operating; procedures, procedural signals and common abbreviations

Subelement G3 – Radio wave propagation

(3 Exam Questions – 3 Groups)
G3A – Sunspots and solar radiation; ionospheric disturbances; propagation forecasting and indices
G3B – Maximum Usable Frequency; Lowest Usable Frequency; propagation
G3C – Ionospheric layers; critical angle and frequency; HF scatter; Near Vertical Incidence Sky waves

Subelement G4 – Amateur radio practices

(5 Exam Questions – 5 Groups)
G4A – Station Operation and setup
G4B – Test and monitoring equipment; two-tone test
G4C – Interference with consumer electronics; grounding; DSP
G4D – Speech processors; S meters; sideband operation near band edges
G4E – HF mobile radio installations; emergency and battery powered operation

Subelement G5 – Electrical principles

(3 Exam Questions – 3 Groups)
G5A – Reactance; inductance; capacitance; impedance; impedance matching
G5B – The Decibel; current and voltage dividers; electrical power calculations; sine wave root-mean-square (RMS) values; PEP calculations
G5C – Resistors; capacitors and inductors in series and parallel; transformers

Subelement G6 – Circuit components

(3 Exam Questions – 3 Groups)
G6A – Resistors; capacitors; inductors
G6B – Rectifiers; solid state diodes and transistors; vacuum tubes; batteries
G6C – Analog and digital integrated circuits (ICs); microprocessors; memory; I/O devices; microwave ICs (MMICs); display devices

Subelement G7 – Practical circuits

(3 Exam Questions – 3 Groups)
G7A – Power supplies; schematic symbols
G7B – Digital circuits; amplifiers and oscillators
G7C – Receivers and transmitters; filters, oscillators

Subelement G8 – Signals and emissions

(2 Exam Questions – 2 Groups)

G8A – Carriers and modulation; AM; FM; single and double sideband; modulation envelope; overmodulation

G8B – Frequency mixing; multiplication; HF data communications; bandwidths of various modes; deviation

Subelement G9 – Antennas and feed lines

(4 Exam Questions – 4 Groups)

G9A – Antenna feed lines; characteristic impedance and attenuation; SWR calculation, measurement and effects; matching networks

G9B – Basic antennas

G9C – Directional antennas

G9D – Specialized antennas

Subelement G0 – Electrical and RF safety

(2 Exam Questions – 2 Groups)

G0A – RF safety principles, rules and guidelines; routine station elevation

G0B – Safety in the ham shack; electrical shock and treatment, safety grounding, fusing, interlocks, wiring, antenna and tower safety

With a General license, you can use all VHF and UHF frequencies and most of the HF frequencies. You would have access to the 160, 30, 17, 12, and 10 meter bands and access to major parts of the 80, 40, 20, and 15 meter bands. Of course, this is in addition to all bands available to Technician license holders.

Amateur Extra is the third of three ham license classes. Like the Technician and General classes, you merely have to pass a test and pay your fee to get your Amateur Extra license. This class of license is more comprehensive than the lower license classes. The exam is longer – 50 questions – and the minimum passing score is higher – 37. However, once you get your Amateur Extra license, all ham frequencies, VHF, UHF and HF are available for your enjoyment. The Extra exam covers regulations, specialized operating practices, advanced electronics theory, and radio equipment design.

Like for the other license classes, the question pool for the Amateur Extra license is available online for downloading (http://www.ncvec.org/downloads/Final%202008%20Extra.pdf or http://www.ncvec.org/downloads/REVISED%202012-2016%20Extra%20Class%20Pool.doc). It is also available in print form in such publications as *The ARRL Extra Class License Manual Revised 9th Edition* (ISBN 978-0-87259-887-4).

Topics for the Extra License in Amateur Radio

Subelement E1 – Commission's Rules

[6 Exam Questions – 6 Groups]

E1A – Operating Standards: frequency privileges; emission standards; automatic message forwarding; frequency sharing; stations aboard ships or aircraft

E1B – Station restrictions and special operations: restrictions on station location; general operating restrictions, spurious emissions, control operator reimbursement; antenna structure restrictions; RACES operations

E1C – Station control: definitions and restrictions pertaining to local, automatic and remote control operation; control operator responsibilities for remote and automatically controlled stations

E1D – Amateur Satellite service: definitions and purpose; license requirements for space stations; available frequencies and bands; telecommand and telemetry operations; restrictions, and special provisions; notification requirements

E1E – Volunteer examiner program: definitions, qualifications, preparation and administration of exams; accreditation; question pools; documentation requirements

E1F – Miscellaneous rules: external RF power amplifiers; national quiet zone; business communications; compensated communications; spread spectrum; auxiliary stations; reciprocal operating privileges; IARP and CEPT licenses; third party communications with foreign countries; special temporary authority

Subelement E2 – Operating procedures

[5 Exam Questions – 5 Groups]

E2A – Amateur radio in space: amateur satellites; orbital mechanics; frequencies and modes; satellite hardware; satellite operations

E2B – Television practices: fast scan television standards and techniques; slow scan television standards and techniques

E2C – Operating methods: contest and DX operating; spread-spectrum transmissions; selecting an operating frequency

E2D – Operating methods: VHF and UHF digital modes; APRS

E2E – Operating methods: operating HF digital modes; error correction

Subelement E3 – Radio wave propagation

[3 Exam Questions – 3 Groups]

E3A – Propagation and technique, Earth-Moon-Earth communications; meteor scatter

E3B – Propagation and technique, trans-equatorial; long path; gray-line; multi-path propagation

E3C – Propagation and technique, Aurora propagation; selective fading; radio-path horizon; take-off angle over flat or sloping terrain; effects of ground on propagation; less common propagation modes

Subelement E4 – Amateur practices

[5 Exam Questions – 5 Groups]

E4A – Test equipment: analog and digital instruments; spectrum and network analyzers, antenna analyzers; oscilloscopes; testing transistors; RF measurements

E4B – Measurement technique and limitations: instrument accuracy and performance limitations; probes; techniques to minimize errors; measurement of "Q"; instrument calibration

E4C – Receiver performance characteristics, phase noise, capture effect, noise floor, image rejection, MDS, signal-to-noise-ratio; selectivity

E4D – Receiver performance characteristics, blocking dynamic range, intermodulation and cross-modulation interference; 3rd order intercept; desensitization; preselection

E4E – Noise suppression: system noise; electrical appliance noise; line noise; locating noise sources; DSP noise reduction; noise blankers

Subelement E5 – Electrical principles

[4 Exam Questions – 4 Groups]

E5A – Resonance and Q: characteristics of resonant circuits: series and parallel resonance; Q; half-power bandwidth; phase relationships in reactive circuits

E5B – Time constants and phase relationships: RLC time constants: definition; time constants in RL and RC circuits; phase angle between voltage and current; phase angles of series and parallel circuits

E5C – Impedance plots and coordinate systems: plotting impedances in polar coordinates; rectangular coordinates

E5D – AC and RF energy in real circuits: skin effect; electrostatic and electromagnetic fields; reactive power; power factor; coordinate systems

Subelement E6 – Circuit components

[6 Exam Questions – 6 Groups]

E6A – Semiconductor materials and devices: semiconductor materials germanium, silicon, P-type, N-type; transistor types: NPN, PNP, junction, field-effect transistors: enhancement mode; depletion mode; MOS; CMOS; N-channel; P-channel

E6B – Semiconductor diodes

E6C – Integrated circuits: TTL digital integrated circuits; CMOS digital integrated circuits; gates

E6D – Optical devices and toroids: cathode-ray tube devices; charge-coupled devices (CCDs); liquid crystal displays (LCDs); toroids: permeability, core material, selecting, winding

E6E – Piezoelectric crystals and MMICs: quartz crystals; crystal oscillators and filters; monolithic amplifiers

E6F – Optical components and power systems: photoconductive principles and effects, photovoltaic systems, optical couplers, optical sensors, and optoisolators

Subelement E7 – Practical circuits

[8 Exam Questions – 8 Groups]

E7A – Digital circuits: digital circuit principles and logic circuits: classes of logic elements; positive and negative logic; frequency dividers; truth tables

E7B – Amplifiers: Class of operation; vacuum tube and solid-state circuits; distortion and intermodulation; spurious and parasitic suppression; microwave amplifiers

E7C – Filters and matching networks: filters and impedance matching networks: types of networks; types of filters; filter applications; filter characteristics; impedance matching; DSP filtering

E7D – Power supplies and voltage regulators

E7E – Modulation and demodulation: reactance, phase and balanced modulators; detectors; mixer stages; DSP modulation and demodulation; software defined radio systems

E7F – Frequency markers and counters: frequency divider circuits; frequency marker generators; frequency counters

E7G – Active filters and op-amps: active audio filters; characteristics; basic circuit design; operational amplifiers

E7H – Oscillators and signal sources: types of oscillators; synthesizers and phase-locked loops; direct digital synthesizers

Subelement E8 – Signals and emissions

[4 Exam Questions – 4 Groups]

E8A – AC waveforms: sine, square, sawtooth and irregular waveforms; AC measurements; average and PEP of RF signals; pulse and digital signal waveforms

E8B – Modulation and demodulation: modulation methods; modulation index and deviation ratio; pulse modulation; frequency and time division multiplexing

E8C – Digital signals: digital communications modes; CW; information rate vs. bandwidth; spread-spectrum communications; modulation methods

E8D – Waves, measurements, and RF grounding: peak-to-peak values, polarization; RF grounding

Subelement E9 – Antennas and transmission lines

[8 Exam Questions – 8 Groups]

E9A – Isotropic and gain antennas: definition; used as a standard for comparison; radiation pattern; basic antenna parameters: radiation resistance and reactance, gain, beamwidth, efficiency

E9B – Antenna patterns: E and H plane patterns; gain as a function of pattern; antenna design; Yagi antennas

E9C – Wire and phased vertical antennas: beverage antennas; terminated and resonant rhombic antennas; elevation above real ground; ground effects as related to polarization; take-off angles

E9D – Directional antennas: gain; satellite antennas; antenna beamwidth; losses; SWR bandwidth; antenna efficiency; shortened and mobile antennas; grounding

E9E – Matching: matching antennas to feed lines; power dividers

E9F – Transmission lines: characteristics of open and shorted feed lines: 1/8 wavelength; 1/4 wavelength; 1/2 wavelength; feed lines: coax versus open-wire; velocity factor; electrical length; transformation characteristics of line terminated in impedance not equal to characteristic impedance

E9G – The Smith chart

E9H – Effective radiated power; system gains and losses; radio direction finding antennas

Once your new call sign is listed in the FCC database, you are good to go. For a Amateur Extra license in Hawaii, your call sign will consist of a single letter prefix beginning with AH6-7, KH6-7, NH6-7, or WH6-7, then (7) either of the numbers six (6) or seven (7), and a two-letter suffix, or a single letter prefix beginning with A, N, K or W, then either of the numbers six (6) or seven (7), and a one-letter suffix, or a single letter prefix beginning with A, then either of the numbers six (6) or seven (7), and a two-letter suffix.

Ham radio equipment can be expensive or you can do it "on the cheap." The cost will run from a couple hundred dollars to well in the thousands, depending on what you have available. eBay, and Craigslist are good places to start looking. Most ham clubs do some sort of hamfest annually wherein club members or others are willing to part with older equipment. See Appendix A for a list of clubs in Hawaii.

Another excellent source of equipment, as well as advice on setting the equipment up and how to use it properly, is current ham operators. In Appendix B, the author has listed all the FCC licensed ham operators in Hawaii, listed by city, and then sorted by street and house number on the street. Who knows, maybe someone who lives close to you is a ham operator. Be a good neighbor, stop by and have a chat with him/her.

Like CB radios, ham radios come in three formats – base, mobile, and handheld. They can use the electric company for power, or operate off a car battery. In the opinion of this author, in spite of the slightly higher cost of the equipment and having to take a test to legally use the equipment, ham radio is the way to go when concerned about communication during times of crisis.

Canadian Call Sign Prefixes

Because of our proximity to Canada, many times ham contact is made with our northern neighbors. Below is a chart showing the origin of Canadian call sign prefixes.

Call Sign Prefix	Provence or Territory
CY0	Sable Island
CY9	St. Paul Island
VA1, VE1	New Brunswick, Nova Scotia
VA2, VE2	Quebec
VA3, VE3	Ontario
VA4, VE4	Manitoba
VA5, VE5	Saskatchewan
VA6, VE6	Alberta
VA7, VE7	British Columbia
VE8	North West Territories
VE9	New Brunswick

VO1	Newfoundland
VO2	Labrador
VY0	Nunavut
VY1	Yukon
VY2	Prince Edward Island

Common Radio Bands in the United States

Certain radio bands are more popular with ham radio enthusiasts than others. Below is a chart showing these bands and when they are most popular.

	Band (meter)	Frequency (MHz)	Use
HF	160	1.8 – 2.0	Night
	80	3.5 – 4.0	Night and Local Day
	40	7.0 – 7.3	Night and Local Day
	30	10.1 – 10.15	CW and Digital
	20	14.0 – 14.350	World Wide Day and Night
	17	18.068 – 18.168	World Wide Day and Night
	15	21.0 – 21.450	Primarily Daytime
	12	24.890 – 24.990	Primarily Daytime
	10	28.0 – 29.70	Daytime during Sunspot highs
VHF	6	50 – 54	Local to World Wide
	2	144 – 148	Local to Medium Distance
UHF	70 cm	430 – 440	Local

Common Amateur Radio Bands in Canada

160 Meter Band - Maximum bandwidth 6 kHz
1.800 - 1.820 MHz - CW
1.820 - 1.830 MHz - Digital Modes
1 830 - 1.840 MHz - DX Window
1.840 - 2.000 MHz - SSB and other wide band modes

80 Meter Band - Maximum bandwidth 6 kHz
3.500 - 3.580 MHz - CW
3.580 - 3.620 MHz - Digital Modes
3.620 - 3.635 MHz - Packet/Digital Secondary
3.635 - 3.725 MHz - CW
3.725 - 3.790 MHz - SSB and other side band modes*
3.790 - 3.800 MHz - SSB DX Window
3.800 - 4.000 MHz - SSB and other wide band modes

40 Meter Band - Maximum bandwidth 6 kHz
7.000 - 7.035 MHz - CW
7.035 - 7.050 MHz - Digital Modes

7.040 - 7.050 MHz - International packet
7.050 - 7.100 MHz - SSB
7.100 - 7.120 MHz - Packet within Region 2
7.120 - 7.150 MHz - CW
7.150 - 7.300 MHz - SSB and other wide band modes

30 Meter Band - Maximum bandwidth 1 kHz

10.100 - 10.130 MHz - CW only
10.130 - 10.140 MHz - Digital Modes
10.140 - 10.150 MHz - Packet

20 Meter Band - Maximum bandwidth 6 kHz

14.000 - 14.070 MHz - CW only
14.070 - 14.095 MHz - Digital Mode
14.095 - 14.099 MHz - Packet
14.100 MHz - Beacons
14.101 - 14.112 MHz - CW, SSB, packet shared
14.112 - 14.350 MHz - SSB
14.225 - 14.235 MHz - SSTV

17 Meter Band - Maximum bandwidth 6 kHz

18.068 - 18.100 MHz - CW
18.100 - 18.105 MHz - Digital Modes
18.105 - 18.110 MHz - Packet
18.110 - 18.168 MHz - SSB and other wide band modes

15 Meter Band - maximum bandwidth 6 kHz

21.000 - 21.070 MHz - CW
21.070 - 21.090 MHz - Digital Modes
21.090 - 21.125 MHz - Packet
21.100 - 21.150 MHz - CW and SSB
21.150 - 21.335 MHz - SSB and other wide band modes
21.335 - 21.345 MHz - SSTV
21.345 - 21.450 MHz - SSB and other wide band modes

12 Meter Band - Maximum bandwidth 6 kHz

24.890 - 24.930 MHz - CW
24.920 - 24.925 MHz - Digital Modes
24.925 - 24.930 MHz - Packet
24.930 - 24.990 MHz - SSB and other wide band modes

10 Meter Band - Maximum band width 20 kHz

28.000 - 28.200 MHz - CW
28.070 - 28.120 MHz - Digital Modes

28.120 - 28.190 MHz - Packet
28.190 - 28.200 MHz - Beacons
28.200 - 29.300 MHz - SSB and other wide band modes
29.300 - 29.510 MHz - Satellite
29.510 - 29.700 MHz - SSB, FM and repeaters

160 Meters (1.8-2.0 MHz)

1.800 - 2.000 CW
1.800 - 1.810 Digital Modes
1.810 CW QRP
1.843-2.000 SSB, SSTV and other wideband modes
1.910 SSB QRP
1.995 - 2.000 Experimental
1.999 - 2.000 Beacons

80 Meters (3.5-4.0 MHz)

3.590 RTTY/Data DX
3.570-3.600 RTTY/Data
3.790-3.800 DX window
3.845 SSTV
3.885 AM calling frequency

40 Meters (7.0-7.3 MHz)

7.040 RTTY/Data DX
7.080-7.125 RTTY/Data
7.171 SSTV
7.290 AM calling frequency

30 Meters (10.1-10.15 MHz)

10.130-10.140 RTTY
10.140-10.150 Packet

20 Meters (14.0-14.35 MHz)

14.070-14.095 RTTY
14.095-14.0995 Packet
14.100 NCDXF Beacons
14.1005-14.112 Packet
14.230 SSTV
14.286 AM calling frequency

17 Meters (18.068-18.168 MHz)

18.100-18.105 RTTY
18.105-18.110 Packet

15 Meters (21.0-21.45 MHz)

21.070-21.110 RTTY/Data
21.340 SSTV

12 Meters (24.89-24.99 MHz)

24.920-24.925 RTTY
24.925-24.930 Packet

10 Meters (28-29.7 MHz)

28.000-28.070 CW
28.070-28.150 RTTY
28.150-28.190 CW
28.200-28.300 Beacons
28.300-29.300 Phone
28.680 SSTV
29.000-29.200 AM
29.300-29.510 Satellite Downlinks
29.520-29.590 Repeater Inputs
29.600 FM Simplex
29.610-29.700 Repeater Outputs

6 Meters (50-54 MHz)

50.0-50.1 CW, beacons
50.060-50.080 beacon subband
50.1-50.3 SSB, CW
50.10-50.125 DX window
50.125 SSB calling
50.3-50.6 All modes
50.6-50.8 Nonvoice communications
50.62 Digital (packet) calling
50.8-51.0 Radio remote control (20-kHz channels)
51.0-51.1 Pacific DX window
51.12-51.48 Repeater inputs (19 channels)
51.12-51.18 Digital repeater inputs
51.5-51.6 Simplex (six channels)
51.62-51.98 Repeater outputs (19 channels)
51.62-51.68 Digital repeater outputs
52.0-52.48 Repeater inputs (except as noted; 23 channels)
52.02, 52.04 FM simplex
52.2 TEST PAIR (input)
52.5-52.98 Repeater output (except as noted; 23 channels)
52.525 Primary FM simplex
52.54 Secondary FM simplex
52.7 TEST PAIR (output)
53.0-53.48 Repeater inputs (except as noted; 19 channels)
53.0 Remote base FM simplex

53.02 Simplex
53.1, 53.2, 53.3, 53.4 Radio remote control
53.5-53.98 Repeater outputs (except as noted; 19 channels)
53.5, 53.6, 53.7, 53.8 Radio remote control
53.52, 53.9 Simplex

2 Meters (144-148 MHz)

144.00-144.05 EME (CW)
144.05-144.10 General CW and weak signals
144.10-144.20 EME and weak-signal SSB
144.200 National calling frequency
144.200-144.275 General SSB operation
144.275-144.300 Propagation beacons
144.30-144.50 New OSCAR subband
144.50-144.60 Linear translator inputs
144.60-144.90 FM repeater inputs
144.90-145.10 Weak signal and FM simplex (145.01,03,05,07,09 are widely used for
    packet)
145.10-145.20 Linear translator outputs
145.20-145.50 FM repeater outputs
145.50-145.80 Miscellaneous and experimental modes
145.80-146.00 OSCAR subband
146.01-146.37 Repeater inputs
146.40-146.58 Simplex
146.52 National Simplex Calling Frequency
146.61-146.97 Repeater outputs
147.00-147.39 Repeater outputs
147.42-147.57 Simplex
147.60-147.99 Repeater inputs

1.25 Meters (222-225 MHz)

222.0-222.150 Weak-signal modes
222.0-222.025 EME
222.05-222.06 Propagation beacons
222.1 SSB & CW calling frequency
222.10-222.15 Weak-signal CW & SSB
222.15-222.25 Local coordinator's option; weak signal, ACSB, repeater inputs, control
222.25-223.38 FM repeater inputs only
223.40-223.52 FM simplex
223.52-223.64 Digital, packet
223.64-223.70 Links, control
223.71-223.85 Local coordinator's option; FM simplex, packet, repeater outputs
223.85-224.98 Repeater outputs only

70 Centimeters (420-450 MHz)

420.00-426.00 ATV repeater or simplex with 421.25 MHz video carrier control links and
    experimental

426.00-432.00 ATV simplex with 427.250-MHz video carrier frequency
432.00-432.07 EME (Earth-Moon-Earth)
432.07-432.10 Weak-signal CW
432.10 70-cm calling frequency
432.10-432.30 Mixed-mode and weak-signal work
432.30-432.40 Propagation beacons
432.40-433.00 Mixed-mode and weak-signal work
433.00-435.00 Auxiliary/repeater links
435.00-438.00 Satellite only (internationally)
438.00-444.00 ATV repeater input with 439.250-MHz video carrier frequency and repeater links
442.00-445.00 Repeater inputs and outputs (local option)
445.00-447.00 Shared by auxiliary and control links, repeaters and simplex (local option)
446.00 National simplex frequency
447.00-450.00 Repeater inputs and outputs (local option)

33 Centimeters (902-928 MHz)

902.0-903.0 Narrow-bandwidth, weak-signal communications
902.0-902.8 SSTV, FAX, ACSSB, experimental
902.1 Weak-signal calling frequency
902.8-903.0 Reserved for EME, CW expansion
903.1 Alternate calling frequency
903.0-906.0 Digital communications
906-909 FM repeater inputs
909-915 ATV
915-918 Digital communications
918-921 FM repeater outputs
921-927 ATV
927-928 FM simplex and links

23 Centimeters (1240-1300 MHz)

1240-1246 ATV #1
1246-1248 Narrow-bandwidth FM point-to-point links and digital, duplex with 1258-1260.
1248-1258 Digital Communications
1252-1258 ATV #2
1258-1260 Narrow-bandwidth FM point-to-point links digital, duplexed with 1246-1252
1260-1270 Satellite uplinks, reference WARC '79
1260-1270 Wide-bandwidth experimental, simplex ATV
1270-1276 Repeater inputs, FM and linear, paired with 1282-1288, 239 pairs every 25 kHz, e.g. 1270.025, .050, etc.
1271-1283 Non-coordinated test pair
1276-1282 ATV #3
1282-1288 Repeater outputs, paired with 1270-1276
1288-1294 Wide-bandwidth experimental, simplex ATV
1294-1295 Narrow-bandwidth FM simplex services, 25-kHz channels

1294.5 National FM simplex calling frequency
1295-1297 Narrow bandwidth weak-signal communications (no FM)
1295.0-1295.8 SSTV, FAX, ACSSB, experimental
1295.8-1296.0 Reserved for EME, CW expansion
1296.00-1296.05 EME-exclusive
1296.07-1296.08 CW beacons
1296.1 CW, SSB calling frequency
1296.4-1296.6 Crossband linear translator input
1296.6-1296.8 Crossband linear translator output
1296.8-1297.0 Experimental beacons (exclusive)
1297-1300 Digital Communications

2300-2310 and 2390-2450 MHz

2300.0-2303.0 High-rate data
2303.0-2303.5 Packet
2303.5-2303.8 TTY packet
2303.9-2303.9 Packet, TTY, CW, EME
2303.9-2304.1 CW, EME
2304.1 Calling frequency
2304.1-2304.2 CW, EME, SSB
2304.2-2304.3 SSB, SSTV, FAX, Packet AM, Amtor
2304.30-2304.32 Propagation beacon network
2304.32-2304.40 General propagation beacons
2304.4-2304.5 SSB, SSTV, ACSSB, FAX, Packet AM, Amtor experimental
2304.5-2304.7 Crossband linear translator input
2304.7-2304.9 Crossband linear translator output
2304.9-2305.0 Experimental beacons
2305.0-2305.2 FM simplex (25 kHz spacing)
2305.20 FM simplex calling frequency
2305.2-2306.0 FM simplex (25 kHz spacing)
2306.0-2309.0 FM Repeaters (25 kHz) input
2309.0-2310.0 Control and auxiliary links
2390.0-2396.0 Fast-scan TV
2396.0-2399.0 High-rate data
2399.0-2399.5 Packet
2399.5-2400.0 Control and auxiliary links
2400.0-2403.0 Satellite
2403.0-2408.0 Satellite high-rate data
2408.0-2410.0 Satellite
2410.0-2413.0 FM repeaters (25 kHz) output
2413.0-2418.0 High-rate data
2418.0-2430.0 Fast-scan TV
2430.0-2433.0 Satellite
2433.0-2438.0 Satellite high-rate data
2438.0-2450.0 WB FM, FSTV, FMTV, SS experimental

3300-3500 MHz
3456.3-3456.4 Propagation beacons

5650-5925 MHz
5760.3-5760.4 Propagation beacons

10.00-10.50 GHz
10.368 Narrow band calling frequency 10.3683-10.3684 Propagation beacons
10.3640 Calling frequency

Now that you have your license (you do, don't you?), and your equipment, you are ready to go live. Below is a suggested start.

1) Assuming you have the HT set up to the appropriate frequency, and offset, press the mic button on the HT and say, "KK4HWX listening." Replace the KK4HWX with your own call sign, the one assigned to you by the FCC (it's the law). If no one responds to your call, you may wish to try again. Hopefully someone will respond to your call.

2) Once you get a response, it will be in the form of something like, "KK4HWX this is ??1??? in Eastport returning. My name is Florence. Back to you. ??1???" then a tone. Let us examine the response more closely. She first acknowledged your call sign (KK4HWX), then identified hers (??1???). From the 1 in her call sign, you know that she first got her license in Region 1, meaning she got it while a resident of CT, ME, MA, NH, RI, or VT. She then told you where she's transmitting from (Eastport). The term "returning" means that she is returning your call. Her name is Florence. The phrase, "Back to you" indicates that she is turning over the conversation to you. She then repeats her call sign. The tone indicates to you that it is okay to proceed with your response. BTW if she had used the term "Over" instead of "Back to you," it would mean the same thing, just fewer words.

3) At this point, press the mic button and continue with the conversation. You should restate your call sign often during the conversation (perhaps every 10 minutes or less and whenever you begin transmitting). Don't forget to say, "Over" or "Back to you" whenever you are giving Florence control of the conversation again.

4) When you are ready to stop the conversation, you should say goodbye or use the phrase "73", meaning "best wishes." Your conversation would end something like, "??1??? 73, this is KK4HWX clear and monitoring." The "clear and monitoring" indicates that you are going to continue to monitor the frequency. If you are not going to continue monitoring, you may wish to end the conversation with Florence with, "clear and QRT" instead. The QRT means that you are stopping transmissions.

Call Sign Phonics

Because of different accents of various people, sometimes it is difficult to understand call sign letters when spoken. For this reason, most ham operators verbalize their call sign using phonics. Below is a table listing the accepted phonics for letters and numbers.

A = ALFA
B = BRAVO
C = CHARLIE
D = DELTA
E = ECHO
F = FOXTROT
G = GOLF
H = HOTEL
I = INDIA
J = JULIETT
K = KILO
L = LIMA
M = MIKE
N = NOVEMBER
O = OSCAR
P = PAPA (PA-PA')
Q = QUEBEC (KAY-BEK')
R = ROMEO

S = SIERRA
T = TANGO
U = UNIFORM
V = VICTOR
W = WHISKEY
X = X-RAY
Y = YANKEE
Z = ZULU (ZED)
1 = ONE
2 = TWO
3 = THREE (TREE)
4 = FOUR
5 = FIVE (FIFE)
6 = SIX
7 = SEVEN
8 = EIGHT
9 = NINE (NINER)
0 = ZERO

The words in parentheses are the pronunciation or the alternate pronunciations for the words or numbers, but you will hear both used. With the letter Z, (ZED) is by far the most commonly used. With the number 9, NINER is the most common and easiest to understand ON THE AIR.

If you wish to use Morse code (CW) instead of voice communication, the "conversation" would follow the same steps, with a few modifications. To type out each word would require a lot of typing and translating. If you are like this author, more means more, i.e., more typing means more typos are likely. To help with this situation, CW enthusiasts have developed a language all their own – they use abbreviations for common phrases. Below is a chart showing some of these abbreviations.

Abbreviation	Use
AR	Over
de	From or "this is"
ES	And
GM	Good Morning
K	Go
KN	Go only
NM	Name

QTH	Location
RPT	Report
R	Roger
SK	Clear
tnx	Thanks
UR	Your, you are
73	Best Wishes

Morse Code and Amateur Radio

If you wish to use CW, but are concerned about accuracy, you might consider purchasing a Morse code translator. This is an electronic device that you place in front of your speakers. It takes the CW sounds and translates them into English and displays the transmission on an LCD display. For the reverse, you can pick up a CW keyboard. With the keyboard, you type in your message and it converts the text to Morse code. The translator does not need to be attached to your ham equipment, whereas the keyboard would.

For your convenience, below is a table showing the Morse code signals and their meaning.

Character	Code
A	· —
B	— · · ·
C	— · — ·
D	— · ·
E	·
F	· · — ·
G	— — ·
H	· · · ·
I	· ·
J	· — — —
K	— · —
L	· — · ·
M	— —
N	— ·
O	— — —
P	· — — ·
Q	— — · —
R	· — ·
S	· · ·
T	—
U	· · —
V	· · · —
W	· — —
X	— · · —

Y	— · — —
Z	— — · ·
0	— — — — —
1	· — — — —
2	· · — — —
3	· · · — —
4	· · · · —
5	· · · · ·
6	— · · · ·
7	— — · · ·
8	— — — · ·
9	— — — — ·
Ampersand [&], Wait	· — · · ·
Apostrophe [']	· — — — — ·
At sign [@]	· — — · — ·
Colon [:]	— — — · · ·
Comma [,]	— — · · — —
Dollar sign [$]	· · · — · · —
Double dash [=]	— · · · —
Exclamation mark [!]	— · — · — —
Hyphen, Minus [-]	— · · · · —
Parenthesis closed [)]	— · — — · —
Parenthesis open [(]	— · — — ·
Period [.]	· — · — · —
Plus [+]	· — · — ·
Question mark [?]	· · — — · ·
Quotation mark ["]	· — · · — ·
Semicolon [;]	— · — · — ·
Slash [/], Fraction bar	— · · — ·
Underscore [_]	· · — — · —

An advantage of using Morse Code is that when broadcasting CW, you are using reduced power, thereby saving your battery. Your battery is used only while actually transmitting or receiving.

International Call Sign Prefixes

As was stated earlier, all ham radio call signs begin with letters (or numbers) taken from blocks assigned to each country of the world by the *ITU - International Telecommunications Union,* a body controlled by the United Nations. The following chart indicates which call sign series are allocated to which countries.

Call Sign Series	Allocated to
AAA-ALZ	**United States of America**
AMA-AOZ	Spain

APA-ASZ	Pakistan (Islamic Republic of)
ATA-AWZ	India (Republic of)
AXA-AXZ	Australia
AYA-AZZ	Argentine Republic
A2A-A2Z	Botswana (Republic of)
A3A-A3Z	Tonga (Kingdom of)
A4A-A4Z	Oman (Sultanate of)
A5A-A5Z	Bhutan (Kingdom of)
A6A-A6Z	United Arab Emirates
A7A-A7Z	Qatar (State of)
A8A-A8Z	Liberia (Republic of)
A9A-A9Z	Bahrain (State of)
BAA-BZZ	China (People's Republic of)
CAA-CEZ	Chile
CFA-CKZ	Canada
CLA-CMZ	Cuba
CNA-CNZ	Morocco (Kingdom of)
COA-COZ	Cuba
CPA-CPZ	Bolivia (Republic of)
CQA-CUZ	Portugal
CVA-CXZ	Uruguay (Eastern Republic of)
CYA-CZZ	Canada
C2A-C2Z	Nauru (Republic of)
C3A-C3Z	Andorra (Principality of)
C4A-C4Z	Cyprus (Republic of)
C5A-C5Z	Gambia (Republic of the)
C6A-C6Z	Bahamas (Commonwealth of the)
C7A-C7Z	World Meteorological Organization
C8A-C9Z	Mozambique (Republic of)
DAA-DRZ	Germany (Federal Republic of)
DSA-DTZ	Korea (Republic of)
DUA-DZZ	Philippines (Republic of the)
D2A-D3Z	Angola (Republic of)
D4A-D4Z	Cape Verde (Republic of)
D5A-D5Z	Liberia (Republic of)
D6A-D6Z	Comoros (Islamic Federal Republic of the)
D7A-D9Z	Korea (Republic of)
EAA-EHZ	Spain
EIA-EJZ	Ireland
EKA-EKZ	Armenia (Republic of)
ELA-ELZ	Liberia (Republic of)
EMA-EOZ	Ukraine
EPA-EQZ	Iran (Islamic Republic of)
ERA-ERZ	Moldova (Republic of)
ESA-ESZ	Estonia (Republic of)

ETA-ETZ	Ethiopia (Federal Democratic Republic of)
EUA-EWZ	Belarus (Republic of)
EXA-EXZ	Kyrgyz Republic
EYA-EYZ	Tajikistan (Republic of)
EZA-EZZ	Turkmenistan
E2A-E2Z	Thailand
E3A-E3Z	Eritrea
E4A-E4Z	Palestinian Authority
E5A-E5Z	New Zealand - Cook Islands (WRC-07)
E7A-E7Z	Bosnia and Herzegovina (Republic of) (WRC-07)
FAA-FZZ	France
GAA-GZZ	United Kingdom of Great Britain and Northern Ireland
HAA-HAZ	Hungary (Republic of)
HBA-HBZ	Switzerland (Confederation of)
HCA-HDZ	Ecuador
HEA-HEZ	Switzerland (Confederation of)
HFA-HFZ	Poland (Republic of)
HGA-HGZ	Hungary (Republic of)
HHA-HHZ	Haiti (Republic of)
HIA-HIZ	Dominican Republic
HJA-HKZ	Colombia (Republic of)
HLA-HLZ	Korea (Republic of)
HMA-HMZ	Democratic People's Republic of Korea
HNA-HNZ	Iraq (Republic of)
HOA-HPZ	Panama (Republic of)
HQA-HRZ	Honduras (Republic of)
HSA-HSZ	Thailand
HTA-HTZ	Nicaragua
HUA-HUZ	El Salvador (Republic of)
HVA-HVZ	Vatican City State
HWA-HYZ	France
HZA-HZZ	Saudi Arabia (Kingdom of)
H2A-H2Z	Cyprus (Republic of)
H3A-H3Z	Panama (Republic of)
H4A-H4Z	Solomon Islands
H6A-H7Z	Nicaragua
H8A-H9Z	Panama (Republic of)
IAA-IZZ	Italy
JAA-JSZ	Japan
JTA-JVZ	Mongolia
JWA-JXZ	Norway
JYA-JYZ	Jordan (Hashemite Kingdom of)
JZA-JZZ	Indonesia (Republic of)
J2A-J2Z	Djibouti (Republic of)
J3A-J3Z	Grenada

J4A-J4Z	Greece
J5A-J5Z	Guinea-Bissau (Republic of)
J6A-J6Z	Saint Lucia
J7A-J7Z	Dominica (Commonwealth of)
J8A-J8Z	Saint Vincent and the Grenadines
KAA-KZZ	**United States of America**
LAA-LNZ	Norway
LOA-LWZ	Argentine Republic
LXA-LXZ	Luxembourg
LYA-LYZ	Lithuania (Republic of)
LZA-LZZ	Bulgaria (Republic of)
L2A-L9Z	Argentine Republic
MAA-MZZ	United Kingdom of Great Britain and Northern Ireland
NAA-NZZ	**United States of America**
OAA-OCZ	Peru
ODA-ODZ	Lebanon
OEA-OEZ	Austria
OFA-OJZ	Finland
OKA-OLZ	Czech Republic
OMA-OMZ	Slovak Republic
ONA-OTZ	Belgium
OUA-OZZ	Denmark
PAA-PIZ	Netherlands (Kingdom of the)
PJA-PJZ	Netherlands (Kingdom of the) - Netherlands Antilles
PKA-POZ	Indonesia (Republic of)
PPA-PYZ	Brazil (Federative Republic of)
PZA-PZZ	Suriname (Republic of)
P2A-P2Z	Papua New Guinea
P3A-P3Z	Cyprus (Republic of)
P4A-P4Z	Netherlands (Kingdom of the) - Aruba
P5A-P9Z	Democratic People's Republic of Korea
RAA-RZZ	Russian Federation
SAA-SMZ	Sweden
SNA-SRZ	Poland (Republic of)
SSA-SSM	Egypt (Arab Republic of)
SSN-STZ	Sudan (Republic of the)
SUA-SUZ	Egypt (Arab Republic of)
SVA-SZZ	Greece
S2A-S3Z	Bangladesh (People's Republic of)
S5A-S5Z	Slovenia (Republic of)
S6A-S6Z	Singapore (Republic of)
S7A-S7Z	Seychelles (Republic of)
S8A-S8Z	South Africa (Republic of)
S9A-S9Z	Sao Tome and Principe (Democratic Republic of)
TAA-TCZ	Turkey

TDA-TDZ	Guatemala (Republic of)
TEA-TEZ	Costa Rica
TFA-TFZ	Iceland
TGA-TGZ	Guatemala (Republic of)
THA-THZ	France
TIA-TIZ	Costa Rica
TJA-TJZ	Cameroon (Republic of)
TKA-TKZ	France
TLA-TLZ	Central African Republic
TMA-TMZ	France
TNA-TNZ	Congo (Republic of the)
TOA-TQZ	France
TRA-TRZ	Gabonese Republic
TSA-TSZ	Tunisia
TTA-TTZ	Chad (Republic of)
TUA-TUZ	Côte d'Ivoire (Republic of)
TVA-TXZ	France
TYA-TYZ	Benin (Republic of)
TZA-TZZ	Mali (Republic of)
T2A-T2Z	Tuvalu
T3A-T3Z	Kiribati (Republic of)
T4A-T4Z	Cuba
T5A-T5Z	Somali Democratic Republic
T6A-T6Z	Afghanistan (Islamic State of)
T7A-T7Z	San Marino (Republic of)
T8A-T8Z	Palau (Republic of)
UAA-UIZ	Russian Federation
UJA-UMZ	Uzbekistan (Republic of)
UNA-UQZ	Kazakhstan (Republic of)
URA-UZZ	Ukraine
VAA-VGZ	Canada
VHA-VNZ	Australia
VOA-VOZ	Canada
VPA-VQZ	United Kingdom of Great Britain and Northern Ireland
VRA-VRZ	China (People's Republic of) - Hong Kong
VSA-VSZ	United Kingdom of Great Britain and Northern Ireland
VTA-VWZ	India (Republic of)
VXA-VYZ	Canada
VZA-VZZ	Australia
V2A-V2Z	Antigua and Barbuda
V3A-V3Z	Belize
V4A-V4Z	Saint Kitts and Nevis
V5A-V5Z	Namibia (Republic of)
V6A-V6Z	Micronesia (Federated States of)
V7A-V7Z	Marshall Islands (Republic of the)

V8A-V8Z	Brunei Darussalam
WAA-WZZ	**United States of America**
XAA-XIZ	Mexico
XJA-XOZ	Canada
XPA-XPZ	Denmark
XQA-XRZ	Chile
XSA-XSZ	China (People's Republic of)
XTA-XTZ	Burkina Faso
XUA-XUZ	Cambodia (Kingdom of)
XVA-XVZ	Viet Nam (Socialist Republic of)
XWA-XWZ	Lao People's Democratic Republic
XXA-XXZ	China (People's Republic of) - Macao (WRC-07)
XYA-XZZ	Myanmar (Union of)
YAA-YAZ	Afghanistan (Islamic State of)
YBA-YHZ	Indonesia (Republic of)
YIA-YIZ	Iraq (Republic of)
YJA-YJZ	Vanuatu (Republic of)
YKA-YKZ	Syrian Arab Republic
YLA-YLZ	Latvia (Republic of)
YMA-YMZ	Turkey
YNA-YNZ	Nicaragua
YOA-YRZ	Romania
YSA-YSZ	El Salvador (Republic of)
YTA-YUZ	Serbia (Republic of) (WRC-07)
YVA-YYZ	Venezuela (Republic of)
Y2A-Y9Z	Germany (Federal Republic of)
ZAA-ZAZ	Albania (Republic of)
ZBA-ZJZ	United Kingdom of Great Britain and Northern Ireland
ZKA-ZMZ	New Zealand
ZNA-ZOZ	United Kingdom of Great Britain and Northern Ireland
ZPA-ZPZ	Paraguay (Republic of)
ZQA-ZQZ	United Kingdom of Great Britain and Northern Ireland
ZRA-ZUZ	South Africa (Republic of)
ZVA-ZZZ	Brazil (Federative Republic of)
Z2A-Z2Z	Zimbabwe (Republic of)
Z3A-Z3Z	The Former Yugoslav Republic of Macedonia
2AA-2ZZ	United Kingdom of Great Britain and Northern Ireland
3AA-3AZ	Monaco (Principality of)
3BA-3BZ	Mauritius (Republic of)
3CA-3CZ	Equatorial Guinea (Republic of)
3DA-3DM	Swaziland (Kingdom of)
3DN-3DZ	Fiji (Republic of)
3EA-3FZ	Panama (Republic of)
3GA-3GZ	Chile
3HA-3UZ	China (People's Republic of)

3VA-3VZ	Tunisia
3WA-3WZ	Viet Nam (Socialist Republic of)
3XA-3XZ	Guinea (Republic of)
3YA-3YZ	Norway
3ZA-3ZZ	Poland (Republic of)
4AA-4CZ	Mexico
4DA-4IZ	Philippines (Republic of the)
4JA-4KZ	Azerbaijani Republic
4LA-4LZ	Georgia (Republic of)
4MA-4MZ	Venezuela (Republic of)
4OA-4OZ	Montenegro (Republic of) (WRC-07)
4PA-4SZ	Sri Lanka (Democratic Socialist Republic of)
4TA-4TZ	Peru
4UA-4UZ	United Nations
4VA-4VZ	Haiti (Republic of)
4WA-4WZ	Democratic Republic of Timor-Leste (WRC-03)
4XA-4XZ	Israel (State of)
4YA-4YZ	International Civil Aviation Organization
4ZA-4ZZ	Israel (State of)
5AA-5AZ	Libya (Socialist People's Libyan Arab Jamahiriya)
5BA-5BZ	Cyprus (Republic of)
5CA-5GZ	Morocco (Kingdom of)
5HA-5IZ	Tanzania (United Republic of)
5JA-5KZ	Colombia (Republic of)
5LA-5MZ	Liberia (Republic of)
5NA-5OZ	Nigeria (Federal Republic of)
5PA-5QZ	Denmark
5RA-5SZ	Madagascar (Republic of)
5TA-5TZ	Mauritania (Islamic Republic of)
5UA-5UZ	Niger (Republic of the)
5VA-5VZ	Togolese Republic
5WA-5WZ	Samoa (Independent State of)
5XA-5XZ	Uganda (Republic of)
5YA-5ZZ	Kenya (Republic of)
6AA-6BZ	Egypt (Arab Republic of)
6CA-6CZ	Syrian Arab Republic
6DA-6JZ	Mexico
6KA-6NZ	Korea (Republic of)
6OA-6OZ	Somali Democratic Republic
6PA-6SZ	Pakistan (Islamic Republic of)
6TA-6UZ	Sudan (Republic of the)
6VA-6WZ	Senegal (Republic of)
6XA-6XZ	Madagascar (Republic of)
6YA-6YZ	Jamaica
6ZA-6ZZ	Liberia (Republic of)

7AA-7IZ	Indonesia (Republic of)
7JA-7NZ	Japan
7OA-7OZ	Yemen (Republic of)
7PA-7PZ	Lesotho (Kingdom of)
7QA-7QZ	Malawi
7RA-7RZ	Algeria (People's Democratic Republic of)
7SA-7SZ	Sweden
7TA-7YZ	Algeria (People's Democratic Republic of)
7ZA-7ZZ	Saudi Arabia (Kingdom of)
8AA-8IZ	Indonesia (Republic of)
8JA-8NZ	Japan
8OA-8OZ	Botswana (Republic of)
8PA-8PZ	Barbados
8QA-8QZ	Maldives (Republic of)
8RA-8RZ	Guyana
8SA-8SZ	Sweden
8TA-8YZ	India (Republic of)
8ZA-8ZZ	Saudi Arabia (Kingdom of)
9AA-9AZ	Croatia (Republic of)
9BA-9DZ	Iran (Islamic Republic of)
9EA-9FZ	Ethiopia (Federal Democratic Republic of)
9GA-9GZ	Ghana
9HA-9HZ	Malta
9IA-9JZ	Zambia (Republic of)
9KA-9KZ	Kuwait (State of)
9LA-9LZ	Sierra Leone
9MA-9MZ	Malaysia
9NA-9NZ	Nepal
9OA-9TZ	Democratic Republic of the Congo
9UA-9UZ	Burundi (Republic of)
9VA-9VZ	Singapore (Republic of)
9WA-9WZ	Malaysia
9XA-9XZ	Rwandese Republic
9YA-9ZZ	Trinidad and Tobago

Third-Party Communications and Amateur Radio

If all of this information about ham radios is somewhat intimidating, do not despair.
"You" can still use ham radios for communications without being a licensed operator.
Yes, you do have to have a ham license in order to legally transmit by ham equipment (or
be under the direct supervision of someone else who is licensed), but there is an alterna-
tive – third-party communication.

Third-party communications occur when a licensed operator sends either written or verbal messages on behalf of unlicensed persons or organizations. There are two "controls" on third-party communication.

First, the communication must be noncommercial and of a personal nature. Asking a ham operator to contact another ham operator located in an area just hit by tornados and, because of being without power, phones do not work in Grandma Sally's city so you can check up on her, is okay. Asking a ham to send a message out that you have an old Chevy for sale would not be okay.

Second, the message must be going to a permitted area. Transmitting from a US location to another US location is okay, but transmitting from the US to another country may not. Because third-party communications bypass a country's normal telephone and postal systems, many foreign governments forbid such communications. In order to transmit from one country to another, the other country must have signed a third-party agreement with the US. What follows is a list of those countries that do have third-party a communications agreement with the US.

V2	Antigua / Barbuda
LU	Argentina
VK	Australia
V3	Belize
CP	Bolivia
T9	Bosnia-Herzegovina
PY	Brazil
VE	Canada
CE	Chile
HK	Colombia
D6	Comoros (Federal Islamic Republic of)
TI	Costa Rica
CO	Cuba
HI	Dominican Republic
J7	Dominica
HC	Ecuador
YS	El Salvador
C5	Gambia, The
9G	Ghana
J3	Grenada
TG	Guatemala
8R	Guyana
HH	Haiti
HR	Honduras
4X	Israel
6Y	Jamaica
JY	Jordan

EL	Liberia
V7	Marshall Islands
XE	Mexico
V6	Micronesia, Federated States of
YN	Nicaragua
HP	Panama
ZP	Paraguay
OA	Peru
DU	Philippines
VR6	Pitcairn Island
V4	St. Christopher / Nevis
J6	St. Lucia
J8	St. Vincent and the Grenadines
9L	Sierra Leone
ZS	South Africa
3DA	Swaziland
9Y	Trinidad / Tobago
TA	Turkey
GB	United Kingdom
CX	Uruguay
YV	Venezuela
4U1ITUITU	Geneva
4U1VICVIC	Vienna

Remember, before TSHTF, keep your pantry well stocked, your powder dry, and your batteries fully charged. 73

APPENDIX A

American Radio Relay League

Affiliated Amateur Radio Clubs in

Hawaii

ARRL Affiliated Club	**Honolulu Amateur Radio Club**
City:	Aiea, HI
Call Sign:	KH6WO
Section:	PAC
Links:	www.pdarrl.org

ARRL Affiliated Club	**Honolulu DX Club**
City:	Aiea, HI
Call Sign:	WH6DCO
Section:	PAC

ARRL Affiliated Club	**Hawaii QRP Club**
City:	Hilo, HI
Call Sign:	KH6AA
Section:	PAC
Links:	hiqrpclub.homestead.com

ARRL Affiliated Club	**Hilo Amateur Radio Club (Hilo ARC)**
City:	Hilo, HI
Call Sign:	KH6CC
Section:	PAC

ARRL Affiliated Club	**Hawaii DX Association**
City:	Hilo, HI
Section:	PAC
Links:	hawaii.dx.tripod.com/

ARRL Affiliated Club	**Big Island Amateur Radio Club**
City:	Hilo, HI
Call Sign:	KH6EJ
Section:	PAC
Links:	www.biarc.net

ARRL Affiliated Club	**Waikiki Amateur Radio Club**
City:	Honolulu, HI
Call Sign:	KH6CO
Section:	PAC

ARRL Affiliated Club	**Emergency Amateur Radio Club**
City:	Honolulu, HI
Call Sign:	WH6CZB
Section:	PAC
Links:	www.earchi.org

ARRL Affiliated Club	**Maui Amateur Radio Club**
City:	Kahului, HI
Call Sign:	KH6RS
Section:	PAC
Links:	www.kh6rs.org/

ARRL Affiliated Club	**Kona Amateur Radio Society**
City:	Kailua Kona, HI
Call Sign:	WH6DEW
Section:	PAC
Links:	www.cfht.hawaii.edu/~veillet/hwars.html

ARRL Affiliated Club	**Kohala Hamakua Radio Club**
City:	Kamuela, HI
Call Sign:	KH6KCC
Section:	PAC

ARRL Affiliated Club	**Koolau Amateur Radio Club**
City:	Kaneohe, HI
Call Sign:	KH6J
Section:	PAC
Links:	www.karc.net

ARRL Affiliated Club	**Pacific Radio Amateur Transmitting Society**
City:	Kaneohe, HI
Call Sign:	KH6JHM
Section:	PAC

ARRL Affiliated Club	**Kauai Amateur Radio Club**
City:	Kapaa, HI
Call Sign:	KH6E
Section:	PAC
Links:	KauaiARC.org

APPENDIX B

Amateur Radio License Holders

in

Hawaii
(by City)

FCC Amateur Radio License in Aiea

Call Sign: AH6JX
Sadao Ueda
99 1387 Aiea Heights Dr
Aiea HI 96701-3019

Call Sign: AH6NA
Spencer S Ueda
99 1387 Aiea Heights Dr
Aiea HI 96701-3019

Call Sign: AH6UM
Spencer S Ueda
99 1387 Aiea Heights Dr
Aiea HI 96701-3019

Call Sign: KH6JZ
Spencer S Ueda
99 1387 Aiea Heights Dr
Aiea HI 96701-3019

Call Sign: NH6A
Spencer S Ueda
99 1387 Aiea Heights Dr
Aiea HI 96701-3019

Call Sign: KH7XJ
Issac Veal
99 1440 Aiea Heights Dr
Aiea HI 96701-2902

Call Sign: KH7UF
John B Wesley
99 954 Aiea Heights Dr
Aiea HI 96818

Call Sign: KH7PD
Jorge B Bonilla Jr
99-1005 Aiea Heights Dr
Aiea HI 96701

Call Sign: KH6WM
Warren W Munro

99-1266E Aiea Heights Dr
Aiea HI 96701

Call Sign: WH7SY
Evelyn B Delgado
99-1329 Aiea Heights Dr
Aiea HI 96701

Call Sign: NH6OY
Edson P S Loo
99-1341 Aiea Heights Dr
Aiea HI 96701

Call Sign: WB5ZOV
Keith H Hollenbeak
99-1701 Aiea Heights Dr
Aiea HI 96701

Call Sign: WH7EK
Keith H Hollenbeak
99-1701 Aiea Heights Dr
Aiea HI 96701

Call Sign: NH7OT
Vernon L Enriques
99-405 Aiea Heights Dr
Aiea HI 96701

Call Sign: NH6HK
Michael C Koga
98-803 Ainanui Loop
Aiea HI 96701

Call Sign: WH6BMW
Doreen F Koga
98-803 Ainanui Loop
Aiea HI 96701

Call Sign: KH6BB
Battleship Missouri
Amateur Radio Club
981547 Akaaka St
Aiea HI 96701-3051

Call Sign: K1ER

John D Peters
98 1547 Akaaka St
Aiea HI 96701

Call Sign: KA4DPW
Joan E Peters
98 1547 Akaaka St
Aiea HI 96701

Call Sign: KH6KH
Honolulu Chapter 206
Qcwa
98 1547 Akaaka St
Aiea HI 96701-3051

Call Sign: WH6DHN
Honolulu Chapter 206
Qcwa
98 1547 Akaaka St
Aiea HI 96701-3051

Call Sign: AH6SO
Mome Dimovski
98 1559 Akaaka St
Aiea HI 96701

Call Sign: AH6ZM
Mome Dimovski
98 1559 Akaaka St
Aiea HI 96701

Call Sign: W6ECG
Echo Charlie Golf Club
98 1559 Akaaka St
Aiea HI 96701

Call Sign: WH6DNV
Coconut Wireless Dx Club
98 1559 Akaaka St
Aiea HI 96701

Call Sign: WH6DPY
Echo Charlie Golf Club
98 1559 Akaaka St
Aiea HI 96701

Call Sign: AH6SF
Paul Granger
98 1559 Akaaka St
Aiea HI 96701

Call Sign: WH7S
Paul Granger
98 1559 Akaaka St
Aiea HI 96701

Call Sign: NH7FS
Nathan F Stickel
98-1283 Akaaka St
Aiea HI 96701

Call Sign: NH7QV
Jeffrey N Stickel
98-1283 Akaaka St
Aiea HI 96701

Call Sign: WB8GNF
Mark F Radke
98-1420 Akaaka St
Aiea HI 96701

Call Sign: KA3CGD
Clinton H Ng
98-1503 Akaaka St
Aiea HI 96701

Call Sign: KH6WO
Honolulu Amateur Radio
Club
98-1547 Akaaka St
Aiea HI 96701-3051

Call Sign: WH6DCO
Honolulu Dx Club
98-1547 Akaaka St
Aiea HI 96701-3051

Call Sign: WH6DGG
Battleship Missouri
Amateur Radio Club

98-1547 Akaaka St
Aiea HI 96701-3051

Call Sign: AH6TK
Masaki Nakanishi
98-1559 Akaaka St
Aiea HI 96701

Call Sign: KI6KWD
Takuya Yoshihori
98-1559 Akaaka St
Aiea HI 96701

Call Sign: KK6EJ
Mitsunobu Koiso
98-1559 Akaaka St
Aiea HI 96701

Call Sign: AA8JA
Yukihiro Itoh
98-1559 Akaaka St
Aiea HI 96701

Call Sign: AH6KY
Masatoshi Shimizu
98-1559 Akaaka St
Aiea HI 96701

Call Sign: AH6ST
Yukihiro Itoh
98-1559 Akaaka St
Aiea HI 96701

Call Sign: AH6TH
Soichi Obe
98-1559 Akaaka St
Aiea HI 96701

Call Sign: AH6TJ
Shoji Nakanishi
98-1559 Akaaka St
Aiea HI 96701

Call Sign: AH6TL
Toru Kurosawa

98-1559 Akaaka St
Aiea HI 96701

Call Sign: AH6TN
Kiyoshi Sato
98-1559 Akaaka St
Aiea HI 96701

Call Sign: AH6TR
Kazuo Yoshikawa
98-1559 Akaaka St
Aiea HI 96701

Call Sign: AH6TZ
Toshiaki Nakamura
98-1559 Akaaka St
Aiea HI 96701

Call Sign: AH6XX
Coconut Wireless Contest
Club
98-1559 Akaaka St
Aiea HI 96701

Call Sign: AH7C
Tetsuo Tanaka
98-1559 Akaaka St
Aiea HI 96701

Call Sign: KH6AX
Hiromi Hirai
98-1559 Akaaka St
Aiea HI 96701

Call Sign: KH6BU
Akira Kogure
98-1559 Akaaka St
Aiea HI 96701

Call Sign: KH6ECG
Soichi Obe
98-1559 Akaaka St
Aiea HI 96701

Call Sign: KH6GX

Rf Hill Contest Club
98-1559 Akaaka St
Aiea HI 96701

Call Sign: KH6JGX
Ydxc Hawaii
98-1559 Akaaka St
Aiea HI 96701

Call Sign: KH7CW
Coconut Wireless Contest
Club
98-1559 Akaaka St
Aiea HI 96701

Call Sign: KH7XX
Coconut Wireless Contest
Club
98-1559 Akaaka St
Aiea HI 96701

Call Sign: KY1I
Yukihiro Itoh
98-1559 Akaaka St
Aiea HI 96701

Call Sign: N2MI
Masahiro Hirano
98-1559 Akaaka St
Aiea HI 96701

Call Sign: NH7Z
Prof Dr Achim Rogmann
98-1559 Akaaka St
Aiea HI 96701

Call Sign: WH6DHE
Rf Hill Contest Club
98-1559 Akaaka St
Aiea HI 96701

Call Sign: WH6DHW
Ydxc Hawaii
98-1559 Akaaka St
Aiea HI 96701

Call Sign: WH6DHZ
Coconut Wireless Contest
Club
98-1559 Akaaka St
Aiea HI 96701

Call Sign: WH6DSB
Shoji Tarasawa Sr
98-1559 Akaaka St
Aiea HI 96701

Call Sign: WH6DUT
Akira Kogure
98-1559 Akaaka St
Aiea HI 96701

Call Sign: WH6DUU
Hiromi Hirai
98-1559 Akaaka St
Aiea HI 96701

Call Sign: WH6DUZ
Toshiaki Nakamura
98-1559 Akaaka St
Aiea HI 96701

Call Sign: WH6DXL
Yoshiaki Oishi
98-1559 Akaaka St
Aiea HI 96701

Call Sign: WH6DXM
Kazuteru Kimura
98-1559 Akaaka St
Aiea HI 96701

Call Sign: WN1Y
Masatoshi Shimizu
98-1559 Akaaka St
Aiea HI 96701

Call Sign: KD1N
Yuichi Yoshida
98-1559 Akaaka St

Aiea HI 96701-3051

Call Sign: KH7ERI
Eri Shimizu
98-1559 Akaaka St
Aiea HI 96701-3051

Call Sign: WH6DWK
Hitoshi Mochizuki
C/O Kiyoshi Mizoguchi
98-1559 Akaaka St
Aiea HI 96701

Call Sign: WH6DWP
Yuichiro Sakai
C/O Kiyoshi Mizoguchi
98-1559 Akaaka St
Aiea HI 96701

Call Sign: WH7ZJ
Eri Shimizu
C/O T Tanaka 98-1559
Akaaka St
Aiea HI 96701

Call Sign: WH6DQQ
Kazuo Yoshikawa
C/O Tetsuo Tanaka 98-
1559 Akaaka St
Aiea HI 96701

Call Sign: NZ2F
Toru Kubokawa
T Tanaka 98-1559 Akaaka
St
Aiea HI 96701

Call Sign: WH7PF
Toru Kubokawa
T Tanaka 98-1559 Akaaka
St
Aiea HI 96701

Call Sign: WH6DMK
Masaki Nakanishi

Tetsuo Tanaka 98-1559
Akaaka St
Aiea HI 96701

Call Sign: WH6DOF
Shoji Nakanishi
Tetuo Tamaka 98 1559
Akaaka St
Aiea HI 96701

Call Sign: KH6BK
Kiyoshi Mizoguchi
98-1559 Akaaka St
Aiea HI 96701

Call Sign: NH6YF
James G Mc Kee
98-1643 Apala Lp
Aiea HI 96701

Call Sign: AF6CC
Mome Dimovski
98 1559 Auaaka St
Aiea HI 96701

Call Sign: NH6NW
Craig K Park
98 686 Aupunimoi Pl
Aiea HI 96701

Call Sign: WH7FV
Leslie A Munro
99-1266 East Aiea Heights
Dr
Aiea HI 96701

Call Sign: NH6GW
Roy R Kuroda
99-452 Fernridge Pl
Aiea HI 96701

Call Sign: WH6CYO
Erin Rose N Ebia
99 434 Hakina St
Aiea HI 96701

Call Sign: KH7HR
Michael S Tsuhako
98 1713 Halakea St
Aiea HI 96701

Call Sign: KF4IBW
Lauren P Rodier
99-605 Halawa Dr
Aiea HI 96701

Call Sign: KF4JLZ
Richard W Rodier
99-605 Halawa Dr
Aiea HI 96701

Call Sign: WH7YQ
Richard W Rodier
99-605 Halawa Dr
Aiea HI 96701

Call Sign: WH7YR
Lauren P Rodier
99-605 Halawa Dr
Aiea HI 96701

Call Sign: KH6BSI
Harold K Y Yee
99-711 Halawa Dr
Aiea HI 96701

Call Sign: KH6ON
Martin G Luna
99-719 Halawa Hgts Rd
Aiea HI 96701

Call Sign: WH6DTN
Martin G Luna
99-719 Halawa Hgts Rd
Aiea HI 96701

Call Sign: WH6DQU
John V Parker
98-263 Hale Momi Pl
Aiea HI 96701-4411

Call Sign: KD7KFT
John V Parker
98-263 Hale Momi Pl
Aiea HI 96701

Call Sign: WH6FL
Christopher J Jacoby
98-1689 Hapaki St
Aiea HI 96701

Call Sign: KH6R
Norman K Funamura
98-1879 Hapaki St
Aiea HI 96701

Call Sign: WH6BKZ
Kent K Funamura
98-1879 Hapaki St
Aiea HI 96701

Call Sign: WH7FU
Lindsey J Kimura
98-2016 Hapaki St
Aiea HI 96701

Call Sign: KH6AGK
John E Felmet
99-139A Heen Way
Aiea HI 96701

Call Sign: WA5EIC
Neil H Fleming
98 1972 Hoala St
Aiea HI 96701

Call Sign: KH7BZ
Roger K Nakata
99 644 Hoio St
Aiea HI 96701

Call Sign: WH6DSO
Julie M Yamashita
99-638 Hoio St
Aiea HI 96701

Call Sign: WH7MY
Edward M Nagamine Jr
99-715 Holoai St
Aiea HI 96701

Call Sign: KH6EX
Rodney H Morimoto
98-676 Holopuni St
Aiea HI 96701

Call Sign: NH6CS
Katherine Y Morimoto
98-676 Holopuni St
Aiea HI 96701

Call Sign: NH7SD
Anpeter H Nguyen
98-167 Honomanu St
Aiea HI 96701

Call Sign: WH6ASV
Stanley M Gapol
98-869A Iho Pl
Aiea HI 96701

Call Sign: AH6BM
Charles J Hartman
98-715 Iho Pl 4304
Aiea HI 96701

Call Sign: WH6CQL
Douglas C Gerding
98-869 Iho Pl Apt C
Aiea HI 96701

Call Sign: WH6DBK
Carly N Shriver
99 273 Iini Way
Aiea HI 96701

Call Sign: AH6D
Paul W Blankmann
98-823 Iliee St
Aiea HI 96701

Call Sign: KH6BIX
Herbert T Tao
98-1736 Ipuala Lp
Aiea HI 96701

Call Sign: WH7YM
Laura S Burgess
98-1451 Kaahumamu St
Apt C
Aiea HI 96701

Call Sign: KH7NN
Apolei K Bargamento
98 1465 B Kaahumanu St
Aiea HI 96701

Call Sign: WH7H
Starcomm Amateur Radio
Club
98-1631 Kaahumanu St
Aiea HI 96701

Call Sign: NH7QD
Jeff R Mccall
98-1277 Kaahumanu St
330
Aiea HI 96701

Call Sign: WH7YN
Brandon J Burgess
98-1451 Kaahumanu St
Apt C
Aiea HI 96701

Call Sign: NH6LQ
David K Shak
98-1871 Kaahumanu St
Apt C
Aiea HI 96701

Call Sign: KH6FGX
Harold K Y Shak
98 1036 Kaamilo St
Aiea HI 96701

Call Sign: KH6DB
Roy M Suzuki
98-437 Kaamilo St
Aiea HI 96701

Call Sign: NH6MM
Teresa N Suzuki
98-437 Kaamilo St
Aiea HI 96701

Call Sign: WH6CPZ
Nicole T Desaulniers
98-839 Kaamilo St
Aiea HI 96701

Call Sign: KH7XC
Paul K Takamiya
98 819 Kahaea Pl
Aiea HI 96701

Call Sign: KH6P
Bernard D Greeson
98-1145 Kahapili St
Aiea HI 96701

Call Sign: KH6CXB
Jose A Bumanglag
99-607 Kahema Pl
Aiea HI 96701-3317

Call Sign: KH6CIZ
Robert J Terry
99 531 Kaholi Pl
Aiea HI 96701-3319

Call Sign: NH6SH
Kevin M Nishida
99 920 Kalamoho Pl
Aiea HI 96701-3060

Call Sign: KH6HR
Michael K Nishida
99-920 Kalamoho Pl
Aiea HI 96701

Call Sign: KD6PHD
Hiroshi Mano
99-920 Kalamoho Pl
Aiea HI 96701

Call Sign: NH7IF
Wayne K Ohashi
310 Kamehameha Hwy
228
Aiea HI 96701

Call Sign: WH6DSR
Elton E Johnson Jr
98-139 Kanuku St Apt 109
Aiea HI 96701

Call Sign: WH7PD
Ralph L Miranda
98-135 Kanuku St Apt G
Aiea HI 96701

Call Sign: WH6ASW
Ramon E Fabre
98 1092 Kaonohi St
Aiea HI 96701

Call Sign: WH6SS
Charles H Moser
98 801 B Kaonohi St
Aiea HI 96701-2439

Call Sign: KH6CM
Andrew I Miyasato
98-1433 Kaonohi St
Aiea HI 96701

Call Sign: NH6CU
Carol S Miyasato
98-1433 Kaonohi St
Aiea HI 96701

Call Sign: KH7PS
Emmett H Helms
98 312 Kaonohi St 1

Aiea HI 96701

Call Sign: KC8KSS
Richard C Lane Sr
98-602 Kaonohi St Apt E
Aiea HI 96701-2416

Call Sign: NH7TW
Richard C Lane Sr
98-602 Kaonohi St Apt E
Aiea HI 96701-2416

Call Sign: WH6GO
Richard C Lane Sr
98-602 Kaonohi St Apt E
Aiea HI 96701-2416

Call Sign: WH6DKF
Eric Mendonca
98-670 Kaonohi St B
Aiea HI 96701

Call Sign: WH7JG
Russell R Watanabe
98-679 Kapukapu Pl
Aiea HI 96701

Call Sign: KH6RN
Warren J Tsuruda
98-690 Kapukapu Pl
Aiea HI 96701

Call Sign: KH7JV
Raymond B De Smet
99 060 Kauhale St 402
Aiea HI 96701

Call Sign: WH6CJR
Louisa K Kaaihue
99-060 Kauhale St 807
Aiea HI 96701

Call Sign: WH6DNL
Peter S Purcell
98-1965 Kaulahao St

Aiea HI 96701

Call Sign: WH6RM
Theodore R Rhea Jr
99-005 Kaupili Pl
Aiea HI 96701

Call Sign: WH6BZS
Norma M Greenleaf
99446 Kekoa Pl
Aiea HI 96701

Call Sign: KH6JLX
Ernest Y Miyashiro
99-422 Kekoa Pl
Aiea HI 96701

Call Sign: KH7EL
Anthony R Padayhag
98 352 Kilihe Way
Aiea HI 96701

Call Sign: NH7VU
Milo D Huempfner
98-405 Kilihea Way
Aiea HI 96701-2136

Call Sign: K2BBV
Thomas R Howes
98-1849 Kilika Pl
Aiea HI 96701

Call Sign: KH7HV
Christopher M Blasque
98 426 Kilinoe St 302
Aiea HI 96701

Call Sign: NH7VB
Paul E Long
98629 Kilinoe St Apt 2F1
Aiea HI 96701

Call Sign: WH6BXJ
Barbara K Simmons
98-483 Kilipohe St

Aiea HI 96701

Call Sign: N4ZIW
Margaret R Davis
98-487 Kipaepae
Aiea HI 96701

Call Sign: N6PJQ
James E Davis Jr
98-487 Kipaepae
Aiea HI 96701

Call Sign: WH6Q
James E Davis Jr
98-487 Kipaepae
Aiea HI 96701

Call Sign: KE4UXQ
James E Davis IIII
98 487 Kipaepae St
Aiea HI 96701

Call Sign: KH7RC
William R Ramiscal
98 533 Kipaepae St
Aiea HI 96701-2160

Call Sign: KC0GFG
Kingsley A Swanson Jr
98-450 Koauka Loop 1503
Aiea HI 96701

Call Sign: WH6CYF
Emergency Response
Radio System Honolulu
98-500 Koauka Loop 19M
Aiea HI 96701-4547

Call Sign: KH7JZ
Arlene Thomas
98 402 Koauka Loop 2111
Aiea HI 96701

Call Sign: WH6DHT

Oahu D-Star Amateur
Radio Club
98-402 Koauka Loop 413
Aiea HI 96701

Call Sign: N3RPI
Andrew Salamone
98-402 Koauka Loop Apt
1608
Aiea HI 96701

Call Sign: NH6OE
Cecil L Hendricks
98-410 Koauka Loop Apt
1F
Aiea HI 96701

Call Sign: NH7QH
Christopher S Colquhoun
98-402 Koauka Loop Apt
413
Aiea HI 96701

Call Sign: NH7FX
Lurenzia Robinson Jr.
98-410 Koauka Loop Apt
5H
Aiea HI 96701

Call Sign: WH7RI
Dan L Carl
98-450 Koauka Loop Apt
601
Aiea HI 96701

Call Sign: NH6DK
Chris Honsberger
98 487 Koauka Loop
B1104
Aiea HI 96701

Call Sign: NH7BF
Chris Honsberger
98 487 Koauka Loop
B1104

Aiea HI 96701

Call Sign: KH6GMB
Edward K Stanwood
98-500 Koauka Lp 12J
Aiea HI 96701

Call Sign: KH6JFT
John J Roche
98-487 Koauka Lp 907
Aiea HI 96701

Call Sign: WH6HG
William C Davies
98-487 Koauka Lp B1701
Aiea HI 96701

Call Sign: WH6CZZ
Phillip W T Kam
98 1077 A Komo Mai Dr
Aiea HI 96701

Call Sign: KH6XA
Joseph J Kaanapu Jr
98 1250 Kuawa St
Aiea HI 96701

Call Sign: KH6BOG
Nobuyoshi Komoda
98 1320 Kulawai St
Aiea HI 96701

Call Sign: KH6FDS
James T Shiroma
98-1025 Kupukupu Pl
Aiea HI 96701

Call Sign: WH7YK
Frank E Chandler Jr
98-1725 Kupukupu St
Aiea HI 96701

Call Sign: KH7P
Craig T Arakaki
98-1795 Kupukupu St

Aiea HI 96701

Call Sign: AH6PB
Stephen C I Pang
99 925 Lalawai Dr
Aiea HI 96701

Call Sign: KH7QC
Cynthia Y Pang
99 925 Lalawai Dr
Aiea HI 96701

Call Sign: KH7QD
Ryan K Pang
99 925 Lalawai Dr
Aiea HI 96701

Call Sign: KH6HPY
William P Kuntz Jr
99-1021 Lalawai Dr
Aiea HI 96701

Call Sign: KH6CG
Richard H Booth
99-856 Lalawai Dr
Aiea HI 96701

Call Sign: WH6DCR
Cub Scout Pack 181
99-925 Lalawai Dr
Aiea HI 96701

Call Sign: KH7QE
Jonelle S Pang
99-925 Lalawai Dr
Aiea HI 96701-3323

Call Sign: WH6DCQ
Boy Scout Troop 181
99-925 Lalawai Dr
Aiea HI 96701-3323

Call Sign: NH6DC
Gary M Miyata
98-641 Lania Pl

Aiea HI 96701

Call Sign: WH6BYI
Kazuto Tomoyasu
98 1211 Lauhulu St
Aiea HI 96701

Call Sign: WH6DHC
Koa Contest Club
98-838 Leihulu Pl
Aiea HI 96701

Call Sign: KH7RK
Eric W Tom
98 130 Lipoa Pl
Aiea HI 96701

Call Sign: WH7ZY
Billie A Zupan
98 142 Lipoa Pl 212
Aiea HI 96701

Call Sign: KG6ETW
Seth Miller
98 135 Lipoa Pl Apt 406
Aiea HI 96701

Call Sign: KH7L
Rodney Y Y Tom
98-125 LipoaPl
Aiea HI 96701

Call Sign: WH7JD
Mitchell D Seavey
99-040 Lohea Pl
Aiea HI 96701

Call Sign: KH6AKW
Robert H Pearson
99-060 Lohea Pl
Aiea HI 96701

Call Sign: NH7L
Richard C Beaman Jr
99-213 Mahiko Pl

Aiea HI 96701-3936

Call Sign: NH7L
Richard C Beaman Jr
99-213 Mahiko Pl
Aiea HI 96701-3936

Call Sign: WV4M
Richard C Beaman Jr
99-213 Mahiko Pl
Aiea HI 96701-3936

Call Sign: KH7TQ
Joseph M Mallare
2885 A Makuu Loop
Aiea HI 96701

Call Sign: AH6OY
James O De Tour
98 1108 Malualua St
Aiea HI 96701

Call Sign: WH6DSK
Donald I Tenney
642 McGrew Loop
Aiea HI 96701

Call Sign: KH6KPM
Kapi Olani Med Cntr At
Pali Momi Rad Grp
98-1079 Moanalua Rd
Aiea HI 96701

Call Sign: KC7HOG
Michael P Bellando
98 945 Moanalua Rd 1004
Aiea HI 96701

Call Sign: AH7N
Christian Sack
98-941 Moanalua Rd 904
Aiea HI 96701

Call Sign: WH6DOE
Ken Yamashita

98-688 Naalii St
Aiea HI 96701

Call Sign: WH6DBR
Tracie M Tomita
98 1774 Nahele St
Aiea HI 96701

Call Sign: NH6XG
Kevin Y Uyehara
98-1664 Nahele St
Aiea HI 96701

Call Sign: WH7GH
Shane C Kaopua
98-1746 Nahele St
Aiea HI 96701

Call Sign: WH6CDQ
Misuzu Fukeda
98-1808 Nahele St
Aiea HI 96701

Call Sign: WH6CDS
Sueki Fukeda
98-1808 Nahele St
Aiea HI 96701

Call Sign: WH7LE
Dennis D Dugay
99-119 Ohiakea St
Aiea HI 96701

Call Sign: KH6GI
Ted Chernin
98 878 Olena St
Aiea HI 96701

Call Sign: WH7IW
Stewart K Bell Jr
98-854 Olena St
Aiea HI 96701

Call Sign: NH6DX
Isabelo S Mendoza Jr

99-076 Olopana St
Aiea HI 96701

Call Sign: KH7MJ
Cassandra C Shepherd
98 988 Palula Way
Aiea HI 96701

Call Sign: KH7MK
Johnnie L Shepherd
98 988 Palula Way
Aiea HI 96701

Call Sign: N6QGT
John H Vorbau
98-1066 Palula Way
Aiea HI 96701

Call Sign: WH7LA
Jonathan J Serrao
99-1/3 Pamoho Pl
Aiea HI 96701

Call Sign: KH6IHY
Clarke S Vaughn
98-1527 Piki Pl
Aiea HI 96701

Call Sign: KH6UR
Glenn Y Arakaki
98-1718 Piki St
Aiea HI 96701

Call Sign: KH6CDS
Stanley H Tsutsumi
99-426 Poaha Pl
Aiea HI 96701

Call Sign: WH6DLC
Stephen H Adams
99-576 Pohue St
Aiea HI 96701

Call Sign: WH6DSP
Les K Chock

98-349 Pono St
Aiea HI 96701

Call Sign: KH6EDW
Calvin P F Ching
98-468 Pono St
Aiea HI 96701

Call Sign: KH6JQC
Lagrimas R Lee
98 346 Ponohale St
Aiea HI 96701

Call Sign: KH6JNN
William K Lee
98-346 Ponohale St
Aiea HI 96701

Call Sign: WH6BKC
Curtis P Wilmington Jr
98-346 Ponohale St
Aiea HI 96701

Call Sign: KH6MA
Glenn M Funamura
98-514 Puaalii St
Aiea HI 96701-2219

Call Sign: KI6TV
Glenn M Funamura
98-514 Puaalii St
Aiea HI 96701-2219

Call Sign: KH6GMM
John R Wine
98-28J Ualo St Unit T1
Aiea HI 96701

Call Sign: KH7AE
Randall W Mack
98 099 Uao Pl
Aiea HI 96701-5009

Call Sign: WH7HE
Victor S Trombley Jr

98-099 Uao Pl 3003
Aiea HI 96701

Call Sign: KH7PZ
Arthur W Neilson III
98 099 Uao Pl 706
Aiea HI 96701

Call Sign: AH6PZ
Arthur W Neilson IIII
98-099 Uao Pl 706
Aiea HI 96701

Call Sign: WH7N
Arthur W Neilson IIII
98-099 Uao Pl 706
Aiea HI 96701

Call Sign: KH6IE
Arthur T Lausten
99-126 Ululaau Pl
Aiea HI 96701

Call Sign: WH6TW
Russell K Kikuta
99 359 Ulune St
Aiea HI 96701

Call Sign: AH6JQ
Greg H Hiyakumoto
Aiea HI 96701

Call Sign: KH6HAM
John H Vorbau
Aiea HI 96701

Call Sign: KH6JAM
Gail Silva
Aiea HI 96701

Call Sign: NH7JI
Mark A Wade
Aiea HI 96701

Call Sign: NH7RK

Tadashi M Mitsuoka
Aiea HI 96701

Call Sign: KH3AF
Richard D Giles
Aiea HI 96701-0062

Call Sign: KH6RH
Gareth H Chang
Aiea HI 96701-0662

Call Sign: KH7Y
John C Magin
Aiea HI 96701-0756

Call Sign: WH6BQE
Leland T Gray Jr
Aiea HI 96701

FCC Amateur Radio License in Anahola

Call Sign: NH6GS
Saint M Kaluahine
Anahola HI 96703

Call Sign: NH7CJ
Saint M Kaluahine
Anahola HI 96703

Call Sign: NH7CR
Kaimana P Kuahiwinui
Anahola HI 96703

Call Sign: WH7SQ
Abilynn Rita
Anahola HI 96703

Call Sign: WH7SV
Donald A Thornburg
Anahola HI 96703

Call Sign: KH6QN
Samuel S Okami Jr
Anahola HI 96703-0490

FCC Amateur Radio License in Camp H M Smith

Call Sign: KH6SP
Mwr Fund Naval
Submarine Base
Camp H M Smith HI
96861-4020

Call Sign: KA4SBE
Robert T Godlewski
Cmdr Us Cincpac Attn J47
Camp H M Smith HI
96861-4020

Call Sign: KX6RTG
Robert T Godlewski
Cmdr Us Cincpac Attn J47
Camp H M Smith HI
96861-4020

Call Sign: KH6UL
Us Nav Cmptr & Tlcmn
Area Mstr Sta E Pac
Co Cdr Uscincpac J42
Camp H M Smith HI
96861

FCC Amateur Radio License in Captain Cook

Call Sign: NH7DR
James H Layton
82 - 969 Aka Ala St
Captain Cook HI 96704

Call Sign: NH7AO
Linda A Hall
88-1512 Eha Ave
Captain Cook HI 96704

Call Sign: WH7CD
James H Hall Jr

88-1512 Eha Ave
Captain Cook HI 96704

Call Sign: KG4HVM
Lynne E Houston
88-1543 Elima Ave
Captain Cook HI 96704

Call Sign: AH6SJ
William C Krumlinde
88-1546 Elima Ave
Captain Cook HI 96704

Call Sign: KF6PQE
William C Krumlinde
88-1546 Elima Ave
Captain Cook HI 96704

Call Sign: KH6OW
Geraldine A Mc Ternan
88-1546 Elima Ave
Captain Cook HI 96704

Call Sign: NH7DN
Lynne M Reynolds
89 785 Huanui Rd
Captain Cook HI 96704

Call Sign: KH6SKY
Jim Sky
89-720 Lani Kona Rd
Captain Cook HI 96704

Call Sign: KH7SU
Kay A Varela
87 2442 A Mamalahoa
Hwy
Captain Cook HI 96704

Call Sign: KD7UV
Bradley G Berman
82-5780 Napoopoo Rd
Captain Cook HI 96704

Call Sign: KD6HFW

Charles R Whitson
Captain Cook HI 96704

Call Sign: KH0HL
Nicholas Novick
Captain Cook HI 96704

Call Sign: NH7QG
Paul M Gibson
Captain Cook HI 96704

Call Sign: NH7QK
Danny B Patel
Captain Cook HI 96704

Call Sign: NH7YH
Kele H Fergerstrom
Captain Cook HI 96704

Call Sign: WA3ZLB
Mark A Shultise
Captain Cook HI 96704

Call Sign: WH6BAO
Rozemaryn Van Der Horst
Captain Cook HI 96704

Call Sign: WH6WT
Howell M Nagatori
Captain Cook HI 96704

Call Sign: WH7H
Nicholas A Daddis
Captain Cook HI 96704

Call Sign: AH6KH
Anita Broennimann
Captain Cook HI 96704

Call Sign: WB6PZF
James O Johnston
Captain Cook HI 96704

Call Sign: WH6FP
John D Bess

Captain Cook HI 96704

Call Sign: W6MFB
Ronald R Herr
Rr 1 Box 63 ~C4
Captain Cook HI 96704

FCC Amateur Radio License in Eleele

Call Sign: KB7FBM
Phillip A Tanner
767 Laulea St
Eleele HI 96705-0391

Call Sign: K0QDK
John R Wells
550 Leipapa Pl
Eleele HI 96705

Call Sign: N2EOW
Thomas W Cheney
Eleele HI 96705

Call Sign: NH6ST
Edieson B Lazaro
Eleele HI 96705

Call Sign: NH7EG
Jonathan M Rowe
Eleele HI 96705

Call Sign: NH7PG
Thomas W Cheney
Eleele HI 96705

Call Sign: WH6AIL
Brian D De La Cruz
Eleele HI 96705

Call Sign: WH6DBD
Laurelle D Riola
Eleele HI 96705

Call Sign: WH6DOO

Jodi S Kimura
Eleele HI 96705

Call Sign: WH7HS
Kalei P Lewis
Eleele HI 96705

Call Sign: WH7PV
Aleksander David L Josue
Eleele HI 96705

Call Sign: KH6NV
Toshio T Matsuda
Eleele HI 96705

Call Sign: WH6CIW
Helen N Kaneakua
Eleele HI 96705

Call Sign: WH6JI
Kenneth L Vicente
Eleele HI 96705

Call Sign: KH6ESP
Ming Wha Chun
Box 397
Eleele HI 96705

FCC Amateur Radio License in Ewa Beach

Call Sign: KF4ZLA
Jessica A Smith
6738A 108Th St
Ewa Beach HI 96706

Call Sign: KH6XI
Rodney A Rodrigues
91-1154 Aawa Dr
Ewa Beach HI 96706

Call Sign: WH7UA
Stewart M Choi
91-1166 Aawa Dr
Ewa Beach HI 96706

Call Sign: WH7YV
Thomas L Koontz
91-1202 Aawa Dr
Ewa Beach HI 96706

Call Sign: KH6GRT
Peter A Wokoun Sr
91 1023 Ahona St
Ewa Beach HI 96706

Call Sign: KH6FHQ
Sylvia T Humphreys
91-526 Aikanaka Rd
Ewa Beach HI 96706

Call Sign: N6FMB
James M Gause
92-603 Akaula St
Ewa Beach HI 96707

Call Sign: WH7IU
Kevin T Akagi
91-1032 Ama Ama St
Ewa Beach HI 96706-3507

Call Sign: KH6OT
Janna M Arakaki
91-030 Amio St
Ewa Beach HI 96706

Call Sign: WH6DNK
Janna M Arakaki
91-030 Amio St
Ewa Beach HI 96706

Call Sign: WH7RK
Edward J Fuller
91-1042 Anaunau St
Ewa Beach HI 96706

Call Sign: WH6BD
Kerry K Kartchner
92731 Aoloko Pl
Ewa Beach HI 96707

Call Sign: KH6CY
Elpidio C Barroga
91 1666 Auwaha St
Ewa Beach HI 96706

Call Sign: WH6CXG
Ohana Amateur Radio
Club
91 1666 Awwaha St
Ewa Beach HI 96706

Call Sign: KA1LFM
Douglas H Olson
5525 Bittern Ave
Ewa Beach HI 96706

Call Sign: WH6BVY
Romel G Marcelino
91-1729 Bond St
Ewa Beach HI 96706

Call Sign: KF4PRM
Lewis R Hagler
91-1025 D Manaolana St
Ewa Beach HI 96706-5900

Call Sign: KF4WGX
Katrina R Hagler
91-1025 D Manaolana St
Ewa Beach HI 96706-5900

Call Sign: AC6MS
Henry B Adams Jr
4855-D East Eha Way
Ewa Beach HI 96706

Call Sign: NH6PM
James E Richardson Jr
4938B Eono Way
Ewa Beach HI 96706

Call Sign: WH6CUC
Maile C Panerio
91 140 Ewa Beach Rd

Ewa Beach HI 96706

Call Sign: WH6O
Ronald C Jay
91-180 Ewa Beach Rd
Ewa Beach HI 96706

Call Sign: WH6D
Marcus E Reed
91-258 Ewa Beach Rd
Ewa Beach HI 96706

Call Sign: WH6CU
John M Roper
91-1100 F La Aulu St
Ewa Beach HI 96706

Call Sign: WH6DLT
Daniel T Yamamura
91-2106 Fort Weaver Rd H
Ewa Beach HI 96706

Call Sign: NH6BA
David L Creek
91-393 Ft Weaver Rd
Ewa Beach HI 96706

Call Sign: K4WEM
William D Michel
5952 Gannet Ave
Ewa Beach HI 96706

Call Sign: KH6BM
William D Michel
5952 Gannet Ave
Ewa Beach HI 96706

Call Sign: NH6RF
William D Michel
5952 Gannet Ave
Ewa Beach HI 96706

Call Sign: NH6WM
William D Michel
5952 Gannet Ave

Ewa Beach HI 96706

Call Sign: WH6BUM
James C Minnis
5914B Gannet Ave
Ewa Beach HI 96706

Call Sign: NH6RF
Roderick C S Au
91 1144 Haiwa Pl
Ewa Beach HI 96706

Call Sign: NH6RG
Joann C Au
91 1144 Haiwa Pl
Ewa Beach HI 96706

Call Sign: WH6DBC
Melissa P Mamasig
91 866 Halalii St
Ewa Beach HI 96706

Call Sign: NH7RA
Andrew T Key
91-1012 Hamoula St
Ewa Beach HI 96706

Call Sign: WH6AR
Marc S J Cooper
91-1010 Hanakahi St
Ewa Beach HI 96706

Call Sign: KB5OFW
Jon P Mahony
91 242 Hanapouli Circle
Ewa Beach HI 96706

Call Sign: NH2HR
Danilo Carino
91-1111 Hapua St
Ewa Beach HI 96706

Call Sign: NH6CD
Danilo Carino
91-1111 Hapua St

Ewa Beach HI 96706

Call Sign: WH6BUD
Tivadar J Horzsa
6073B Heron Ave
Ewa Beach HI 96706

Call Sign: KH6JPL
William Gomban Jr
91-1475 Hoano St
Ewa Beach HI 96706

Call Sign: KH6WP
Verna M Gomban
91-1475 Hoano St
Ewa Beach HI 96706

Call Sign: WH7IX
Scott R Boatwright
91-1012 Hooilo Pl
Ewa Beach HI 96706

Call Sign: WH7TO
Raymond T Ae
91-332 Hoomalule Pl
Ewa Beach HI 96706

Call Sign: WH6CHU
Gregorio Debutiaco
91-1313 Hoopio St
Ewa Beach HI 96706

Call Sign: KH6FQI
Robert C Short
91 1045 Huliau St Apt K
Ewa Beach HI 96706-4958

Call Sign: WH6DMP
Justin M Wagner
6273 Ibis Ave
Ewa Beach HI 96706

Call Sign: NH6CZ
Robert E Stalcup Sr
6377 Ibis Ave

Ewa Beach HI 96706

Call Sign: NH6SL
Mark A Mummert
6329B Ibis Ave
Ewa Beach HI 96706

Call Sign: KC8LAS
Christopher G Wall
5072A Iroquois Ave
Ewa Beach HI 96706

Call Sign: WH6DJN
Cornelius Nugent
91-1022 Kahiuka St
Ewa Beach HI 96706

Call Sign: KE6CVL
Michael L Frazee
91 1099 Kaihi St
Ewa Beach HI 96706

Call Sign: KF6UPQ
John R Belcher
91-1014 Kaihoi St
Ewa Beach HI 96706

Call Sign: N1CFD
Stephen J Putnoki
91-1060 Kaileolea Dr B1
Ewa Beach HI 96706

Call Sign: WH7YH
Rodney Y Ichimura
91-1124 Kaileonui St
Ewa Beach HI 96706

Call Sign: KJ4HUH
Robert W Collester Jr
91-1023 Kaimona St
Ewa Beach HI 96706

Call Sign: KB6OLD
Mitchell L Gildea
91 982 Kaiohee St

Ewa Beach HI 96706-5000

Call Sign: WH7PQ
Dale I Kamauu
91-2055 Kaioli St Apt
3904
Ewa Beach HI 96706

Call Sign: WB3HZF
Carl E Kaleugher
95 1005 Kaipalaoa St 105
Ewa Beach HI 96706

Call Sign: KH6JWI
Juanita Rose
91-1026 Kalapu
Ewa Beach HI 96706

Call Sign: KH7HZ
Jessica M Ah Loo
91 955 Kalapu St
Ewa Beach HI 96706

Call Sign: WH6BPZ
David B M Rose
91-1026 Kalapu St
Ewa Beach HI 96706

Call Sign: WA6STM
Daniel W Barrows
91-316 Kamaehu Pl
Ewa Beach HI 96706

Call Sign: NH6WP
Melvin P Vendiola
91-1394 Kamahoi St
Ewa Beach HI 96706

Call Sign: KB7JHB
David A Morris
91-2194 Kanela St
Ewa Beach HI 96706

Call Sign: KH7DO
Michael K Maeda

91-2188 Kanela St
Ewa Beach HI 96706

Call Sign: KH7NM
Miles M Watanabe
91 6523 Kapolei Park Way
Ewa Beach HI 96706

Call Sign: WH7MT
Daniel E Harris
91-345 Kaukolu Way
Ewa Beach HI 96706

Call Sign: WH6PD
George K Stender
91-204 Kaulona Pl
Ewa Beach HI 96706

Call Sign: WH6LB
Tony S Montoya
91-1041 Kaunolu St
Ewa Beach HI 96706

Call Sign: KE5PGX
David J Christison
91-1001 Kauoha St
Ewa Beach HI 96706

Call Sign: AH6QL
William D Michel
91 1161 Keaalii Pl
Ewa Beach HI 96706

Call Sign: KH7NH
Julio R Reyes Jr
91 1200 Keaunui Dr 602
Ewa Beach HI 96706

Call Sign: KB9EHR
Michael W Morton
91-1200 Keaunui Dr Apt
408
Ewa Beach HI 96706

Call Sign: WH6CTY

Stanley Peter Jr
91-228 Keonekapu Pl
Ewa Beach HI 96706-4600

Call Sign: WH7XZ
James D Roswell
91-1015 Keoneula Blvd
A3
Ewa Beach HI 96706

Call Sign: KH6MSH
Malcolm S Higa
91-1039 Keoneula Blvd
D1
Ewa Beach HI 96706

Call Sign: NH6OS
Malcolm S Higa
91-1039 Keoneula Blvd
D1
Ewa Beach HI 96706

Call Sign: WH6CLW
Heidi S Jackson
91-613 Kilaha St 75
Ewa Beach HI 96706

Call Sign: WH6CDN
Sumatala I Tauiliili
91-658 Kilaha St D5
Ewa Beach HI 96706

Call Sign: KH6IBH
Roland M J Wongwai
91 821 Koalipehu Pl
Ewa Beach HI 96706

Call Sign: WH6AFI
Manuel Viernes
91-741 Koalipehu St
Ewa Beach HI 96706

Call Sign: WH6DLX
Ryan R Hashiro
91-521 Koihala Pl

Ewa Beach HI 96706

Call Sign: KA2WXU
Robert E Maguire
91-1561 Kuhiawaho Pl
Ewa Beach HI 96706

Call Sign: WH7AQ
John C Cayapan
91-1028 Kuhina St
Ewa Beach HI 96706

Call Sign: KH6PV
Anthony R Schena
91-1037 Kuhina St
Ewa Beach HI 96706

Call Sign: WH6APT
Lora A Schena
91-1037 Kuhina St
Ewa Beach HI 96706

Call Sign: WH6BWT
Juliana E Malasig
91-613 Kulana Pl R5
Ewa Beach HI 96706

Call Sign: WH6BWU
Ryan E Malasig
91-613 Kulana Pl R5
Ewa Beach HI 96706

Call Sign: KH6SAT
Richard G Dittmer Sr
91-206 Kuloihi Pl
Ewa Beach HI 96706

Call Sign: NH7DE
Robert P Dalbec
91 1000 Kupekala St
Ewa Beach HI 96706

Call Sign: WH6BVS
Abel C Aiona
92-365 Laahaina Pl

Ewa Beach HI 96707

Call Sign: WH6BVW
Norina L Aiona
92-365 Laahaina Pl
Ewa Beach HI 96707

Call Sign: WH7AK
Elliott W Ross
91-1064 Laaulu St 20C
Ewa Beach HI 96706-3866

Call Sign: KI6FPL
Nicholas J Mendes
91-1039 Laaulu St 23D
Ewa Beach HI 96706

Call Sign: KB6UGR
Sandra M Mitchell
91-796 Launahele St
Ewa Beach HI 96706

Call Sign: N6QIH
Larry J Mitchell
91-796 Launahele St
Ewa Beach HI 96706

Call Sign: K7PGR
Phillip G Rosser
91-740 Launahele St
Ewa Beach HI 96706

Call Sign: W0UNX
Billy R Guthrie
91 1674 Laupai St
Ewa Beach HI 96706

Call Sign: KH7DG
Lester R Martinez
91 828 Lawalu Pl
Ewa Beach HI 96706

Call Sign: KH6GOZ
Carl L Mc Kean
92-770 Maalili Pl

Ewa Beach HI 96706

Call Sign: WH6BWN
Curtis L Gomer
92-695 57 Makakilo Dr
Ewa Beach HI 96707

Call Sign: WH6CBU
Ida L Prange
92-950 Makakilo Dr 82
Ewa Beach HI 96707

Call Sign: WH7VC
Victor M Torres
91 353 Makalea St
Ewa Beach HI 96706

Call Sign: KH6TDM
Terry D Moore
91-708 Makalea St
Ewa Beach HI 96706

Call Sign: N6IKX
Terry D Moore
91-708 Makalea St
Ewa Beach HI 96706

Call Sign: NH7ZJ
Joseph B Valoroso
91 521 Maohaka Pl
Ewa Beach HI 96706

Call Sign: KH7EW
Albert D Garcia Jr
91-1210 Mikohu St 43D
Ewa Beach HI 96706

Call Sign: WH7ZT
John J Novosel III
91-1119 Mikohu St Apt 28
C
Ewa Beach HI 96706

Call Sign: NH7Q
Arthur J Margerison

91-002 Nalomeli Pl
Ewa Beach HI 96706

Call Sign: NH6KR
Ellen L F Rumbaugh
92-756 Newa Pl
Ewa Beach HI 96707

Call Sign: WH7AT
Virgilio Ordillas
91 1052 Niolo St
Ewa Beach HI 96706

Call Sign: WH6T
Jennifer A Fuchikami
91-1038 Niolo St
Ewa Beach HI 96706

Call Sign: WH7AW
Jennifer A Fuchikami
91-1038 Niolo St
Ewa Beach HI 96706

Call Sign: WH7QI
Kevin R Fuchikami
91-1038 Niolo St
Ewa Beach HI 96706

Call Sign: WH7TJ
Kristi A Fuchikami
91-1038 Niolo St
Ewa Beach HI 96706

Call Sign: WH7TK
Jonathan W Fuchikami
91-1038 Niolo St
Ewa Beach HI 96706

Call Sign: WH7TR
Laura Fuchikami
91-1038 Niolo St
Ewa Beach HI 96706

Call Sign: WH6C
Gary R Fuchikami

91-1038 Niolo St
Ewa Beach HI 96706

Call Sign: KH7DF
Susan K L W Fuchikami
91-1038 Niolo St
Ewa Beach HI 96706

Call Sign: NH2CQ
Vivencio J Pasco
91 219 Niuhiwa Pl
Ewa Beach HI 96706

Call Sign: WH6VP
Vivencio J Pasco
91 219 Niuhiwa Pl
Ewa Beach HI 96706

Call Sign: KH6AZ
Mark Fajardo
91-219 Niuhiwa Pl
Ewa Beach HI 96706

Call Sign: KH6DAL
Dominador A Lubong
91-219 Niuhiwa Pl
Ewa Beach HI 96706

Call Sign: NH2HF
Dominador A Lubong
91-219 Niuhiwa Pl
Ewa Beach HI 96706

Call Sign: KH7INC
Scan International Hawaii
Chapter 2
91 219 Niuhiwa Pl 83
Ewa Beach HI 96706

Call Sign: WH6DHR
Scan International Hawaii
Chapter 2
91 219 Niuhiwa Pl 83
Ewa Beach HI 96706

Call Sign: WH6DRX
Rod L Bruno
91 219 Niuhiwa Pl 83
Ewa Beach HI 96706

Call Sign: NH6PW
Robert Y Ito
91 1188 Pohahawai St
Ewa Beach HI 96706

Call Sign: WH7YJ
Dennis Drake
91-1514 Pukanala St
Ewa Beach HI 96706

Call Sign: WH7WR
Rolando F Halili
91-921 Nohoihoewa Pl
Ewa Beach HI 96706

Call Sign: NH7VX
Linford M Ramos
91-711 Pohakupuna Rd
Ewa Beach HI 96706

Call Sign: KH6HJ
Richard G Vanderford
91-453 Pupu St
Ewa Beach HI 96706

Call Sign: WH6DLU
Jonathan S Durrett
91-1004 Okupe St
Ewa Beach HI 96706

Call Sign: WH6ZU
Ronie M Bautista
91-823 Poowai Pl
Ewa Beach HI 96706

Call Sign: WH6CAJ
Chad J Ingalls
91-633 Pupu St
Ewa Beach HI 96706

Call Sign: WH6BVU
Donald G Hall Sr
91-861 Paaloha St
Ewa Beach HI 96706

Call Sign: W6BYP
Jay B Cabautan
91 940 Puahala St 39 D
Ewa Beach HI 96706

Call Sign: WH6CHV
Nelson Manzanillo
91-1347 Puuhala St
Ewa Beach HI 96706

Call Sign: WH6BWQ
Shelly M Hall
91-861 Paaloha St
Ewa Beach HI 96706

Call Sign: KH7CU
Marilyn L Stafford
91 1050 Puamaeole 8E
Ewa Beach HI 96706

Call Sign: WH6CIP
Nelson L Manzanillo
91-1347 Puuhala St
Ewa Beach HI 96706

Call Sign: WH6DVJ
Teofilo S Rellesiva
91-426 Papipi Dr
Ewa Beach HI 96706

Call Sign: KH7YF
William A Chur
91 589 Puamaeole St
Ewa Beach HI 96706

Call Sign: WH6CJW
Clyde E Cabillon
91-1347 Puuhala St
Ewa Beach HI 96706

Call Sign: KH6HB
Harold K Buckle
91 1165 Pohahawai Pl
Ewa Beach HI 96706-1823

Call Sign: WH7ZZ
David Williams
91 1059 Puaniu St 21 R
Ewa Beach HI 96706

Call Sign: AH6QJ
William R Chur
91-589 U Puamaeole St
Ewa Beach HI 96706

Call Sign: WH6MD
Harold K Buckle
91 1165 Pohahawai Pl
Ewa Beach HI 96706-1823

Call Sign: WH6CWV
William J Schadt
91 104 Puhilaumilo Pl
Ewa Beach HI 96706

Call Sign: WH6ON
Gina A Wass
92-1315 Vahanai St
Ewa Beach HI 96707

Call Sign: NH6PV
Gloria Ito
91 1188 Pohahawai St
Ewa Beach HI 96706

Call Sign: KA3IGK
Carol K Kaiwi
91 327 Pukanala Pl
Ewa Beach HI 96706

Call Sign: WH7HD
James A Walker
91-1031 Waihuna Pl
Ewa Beach HI 96707

Call Sign: WH6DRB
Donna L Cruz
91-1065 Waikapuna St
Ewa Beach HI 96706

Call Sign: NH6AB
William L Mc Garry Jr
4802 West Ekolu Way Apt
B
Ewa Beach HI 96706

Call Sign: NH7VT
Curtis Leggett
Ewa Beach HI 96706

Call Sign: WH6DSA
Michael J Marcum
Ewa Beach HI 96706

Call Sign: WH7QV
Scott J Bradshaw
Ewa Beach HI 96706

Call Sign: WH6CJT
Phillip A Pellowski
Ewa Beach HI 96706

FCC Amateur Radio License in Fort Shafter

Call Sign: WH6CHF
Simon G Wall
1214C Hase Dr
Fort Shafter HI 96819

FCC Amateur Radio License in Haiku

Call Sign: KH6IPZ
Edward M Saphore
999 E Kuiaha Rd
Haiku HI 96708

Call Sign: WH7EY
Robie Price

1100 Haiku Rd
Haiku HI 96708

Call Sign: WH7NH
Diane M Bryant
810 Haiku Rd Ste113 Pmb
406
Haiku HI 96708

Call Sign: KH6QQ
Frederic H Martini
5071 Hana Hwy
Haiku HI 96708

Call Sign: NH6RI
Gene C Hughes Jr
101A Kahiapo Pl
Haiku HI 96708

Call Sign: WH6SA
Donald E Weiss II
1260 Kauhikoa Rd
Haiku HI 96708

Call Sign: NH6EV
John G Bruce
1299 Kauhikoa Rd
Haiku HI 96708

Call Sign: N8HAP
Wade A Alvarado
390 Kaupakalua Rd
Haiku HI 96708-0691

Call Sign: KH6UU
William R Heyde
2512 Kaupakalua Rd
Haiku HI 96708-6024

Call Sign: WD6M
Wayne Y Sakamoto
2548 Kaupakalua Rd
Haiku HI 96708

Call Sign: WH6SG

Anthony J Martyn
328 Kokomo Rd
Haiku HI 96708

Call Sign: KF6JRA
Christine E Diekman
1125 Kokomo Rd
Haiku HI 96708

Call Sign: WH7RU
Christine E Diekman
1125 Kokomo Rd
Haiku HI 96708

Call Sign: WH6BWI
Phillip O Meyer
1308 Kokomo Rd
Haiku HI 96708

Call Sign: KC5NZR
Richie L Allen
525A Kulike Rd
Haiku HI 96708

Call Sign: WH6DWH
B R Stoner
160 Laeanani St
Haiku HI 96708

Call Sign: WH6GD
David S Ferguson
795 107 Lanikai Pl
Haiku HI 96708

Call Sign: WH6DMF
Robert M Vickers Jr
2580 Lemi Pl
Haiku HI 96708

Call Sign: KD7FND
Noriyuki Yoshizumi
Maeda 44 ~Uakoko Pl
Haiku HI 96708

Call Sign: WH7UV

Perry H Tuttle
16A Makaio Pl
Haiku HI 96708

Call Sign: KH6IQO
Glen W Ashley Jr
7 Maluaina Pl
Haiku HI 96708

Call Sign: WH7XT
Christopher R Gedrites
201 Oili Rd
Haiku HI 96708

Call Sign: WH6DNX
Rhonda M Pico
2533 Poko Pl
Haiku HI 96708

Call Sign: WH6VF
Martin Ph Vollert
998 Puu Koa Pl
Haiku HI 96708

Call Sign: KH6EKB
Kenneth C Prince
400 Ulumalu Rd
Haiku HI 96708

Call Sign: KH6JKE
Melissa B Prince
400 Ulumalu Rd
Haiku HI 96708

Call Sign: AH6OH
David Dantes
4320 Une Pl
Haiku HI 96708

Call Sign: NH6SU
Averett W Higbee
321 W Kuiaha Rd
Haiku HI 96708

Call Sign: KH7ZS

Gerard W Franco
415 W Kuiaha Rd
Haiku HI 96708

Call Sign: NH7RN
Thomas M Nakagawa
490 W Kuiaha Rd
Haiku HI 96708

Call Sign: WH7AB
Matthew S Minford
1164 W Kuiaha Rd
Haiku HI 96708

Call Sign: NH6IA
Steven M Higbee
375 35 W Kuiaha Rd
Haiku HI 96708

Call Sign: KH6PO
Diane M Bryant
4415 Waha Pl
Haiku HI 96708

Call Sign: KE6OSE
Jan E Mullen
Haiku HI 96708

Call Sign: WH6CTW
Norman E Burkhart III
Haiku HI 96708

Call Sign: WH6CYE
Gregory J Putnam
Haiku HI 96708

Call Sign: WH6DIX
Theresa Kearney
Haiku HI 96708

Call Sign: WH6DIY
Joseph Kyllo
Haiku HI 96708

FCC Amateur Radio License in Hakalau

Call Sign: KH6RL
Robert C Lile
Hakalau HI 96710

Call Sign: KH6UO
Masaichi Chinen
Hakalau HI 96710

Call Sign: WH6DLI
Gerard P Lono Jr
Hakalau HI 96710

Call Sign: AH6RF
Claude R Fontaine Jr
Hakalau HI 96710-0365

Call Sign: KL7XT
John K Smith
Hakalau HI 96710-0387

Call Sign: NL7AW
Pamela G Smith
Hakalau HI 96710-0387

FCC Amateur Radio License in Haleiwa

Call Sign: WH6DNA
Aaron A Asato
59-615 Alapio Rd
Haleiwa HI 96712

Call Sign: WH7PS
Kevin Asato
59-615 Alapio Rd
Haleiwa HI 96712

Call Sign: NH7LO
Casey A Cummings
59-482 Aukauka Rd
Haleiwa HI 96712

Call Sign: KH6CV
Kin Leong
59-007 Hoalua St
Haleiwa HI 96712

Call Sign: KB8JMZ
Samantha L Metheney
66 545 Kam Highway Unit
C
Haleiwa HI 96712

Call Sign: WH6DBJ
Larry R Luehrs
59 790 Kam Hwy
Haleiwa HI 96712

Call Sign: WH7LD
Michael W Krzywonski
59-048 B Kam Hwy
Haleiwa HI 96712

Call Sign: KH6OR
Fred L Mason
61 259 Kam Hwy
Haleiwa HI 96712

Call Sign: NH6ZX
Patricia L Pettigrew
61-691 Kam Hwy
Haleiwa HI 96712

Call Sign: WH7TG
Hannah L Joachim
59-790 Kamahamaha Hwy
B
Haleiwa HI 96712

Call Sign: KH6YY
Alexander E Benton
59 768 Kanalani Pl
Haleiwa HI 96712

Call Sign: WH6EW
Roger W Hall
59-774 Kapuhi Pl

Haleiwa HI 96712

Call Sign: KH6ANF
John W Vollrath
59-654 Kawoa Pl
Haleiwa HI 96712-9567

Call Sign: KH6SC
Dennis C Vollrath
59-654 Kawoa Pl
Haleiwa HI 96712-9567

Call Sign: K7UUV
Douglas J Marr
66-498 Kilioe Pl
Haleiwa HI 96712

Call Sign: KH6KV
William D Osborn
58-041 Maika Pl
Haleiwa HI 96712

Call Sign: WH6CQW
Karl R Sandbo
66-127 Naoiwi Ln
Haleiwa HI 96712

Call Sign: WH6CQX
Larry R Sandbo
66-127 Naoiwi Ln
Haleiwa HI 96712

Call Sign: AH6DQ
William Anderson
66-477 Paalaa Rd Apt 313
Haleiwa HI 96721

Call Sign: KH6IOM
Paul J Taggart
66-457 Pikai St
Haleiwa HI 96712

Call Sign: WH6CJE
Paul R Heuchling
61-569 Pohaku Loa Way

Haleiwa HI 96712

Call Sign: KG6IGY
Angela De Vargas
59-456 Pupukea Rd
Haleiwa HI 96712

Call Sign: KH7TH
Christopher L Peck
58 138 Wehiwa Pl
Haleiwa HI 96712

Call Sign: KH6FC
Charles H Fisel
59-335 Wilinau Rd
Haleiwa HI 96712

Call Sign: KH6JKG
James H Connell V
59-335 Wilinau Rd
Haleiwa HI 96712

Call Sign: NH6BY
Pamela F Connell
59-335 Wilinau Rd
Haleiwa HI 96712

Call Sign: K6WSB
Robert A Miller Jr
Haleiwa HI 96712

Call Sign: KH6ET
Al K Abe
Haleiwa HI 96712

Call Sign: NH7QZ
John D Kim
Haleiwa HI 96712

Call Sign: WH6DPD
Donald A Bunnell Jr
Haleiwa HI 96712

Call Sign: WH6DUG
Andy M Morishita

Haleiwa HI 96712

Call Sign: KB3CQ
Edward A Abbot
Haleiwa HI 96712-0550

Call Sign: WH6CYP
Abraham B Barbero
Haleiwa HI 96712-1248

Call Sign: KH6LJ
Benjamin Ballesteros
Haleiwa HI 96712

Call Sign: WH6CLG
Larry L Diego Jr
Haleiwa HI 96712

Call Sign: WH6CLK
Epifania Ballesteros
Haleiwa HI 96712

Call Sign: WH6CNZ
Paul R Diego
Haleiwa HI 96712

Call Sign: WH6COF
Marlene D Diego
Haleiwa HI 96712

FCC Amateur Radio License in Hana

Call Sign: KH6VA
William M Conner
4045 Hana Highway
Hana HI 96713-0251

Call Sign: AH6SG
Alastair N Couper
Hc 181
Hana HI 96713

Call Sign: NH7O
Alastair N Couper

Hc 181
Hana HI 96713

Call Sign: WH7JO
Gale D Notestone
1525 Lower Nahiku Rd
Hana HI 96713

Call Sign: WH6ATR
Robert C Howell
Star Route 133
Hana HI 96713-0177

Call Sign: KH6HD
Tama L Starr
Star Route Box 181
Hana HI 96713

Call Sign: KH6T
Helen F Nielsen
Star Route Box 182
Hana HI 96713

Call Sign: KH6X
Jonathan A Starr
Star Route Box 182
Hana HI 96713

Call Sign: WH6BLE
Rosemary L Howell
Star Rt 133
Hana HI 96713

Call Sign: WH6BZJ
Gale D Notestone
Hana HI 96713

Call Sign: AH6IQ
John S Chitwood
Hana HI 96713

FCC Amateur Radio License in Hanalei

Call Sign: WH6BFD

Stephen B Ives
Box 3455 ~Pcs
Hanalei HI 96722

Call Sign: NH6GB
Mark A Weaver
Hanalei HI 96714

Call Sign: NH6OO
Edwin R Pollock
Hanalei HI 96714

Call Sign: NH6ZV
Stan Godes
Hanalei HI 96714

Call Sign: NH7CB
Mark A Weaver
Hanalei HI 96714

Call Sign: NH7EK
Jonathan G Wichman
Hanalei HI 96714

Call Sign: NH7US
Elizabeth A Kendall
Hanalei HI 96714

Call Sign: NH7YQ
John H Gordon
Hanalei HI 96714

Call Sign: WH7HW
Leimomi M Spencer-
Gacusan
Hanalei HI 96714

Call Sign: WH7PX
Robert S Sommer
Hanalei HI 96714

Call Sign: AH6EC
Alan E Faye Jr
Hanalei HI 96714

Call Sign: KH6SN
Toshio Okinishi
4721 Kane Rd
Hanapepe HI 96716

Call Sign: KH6IKV
Solomon W Kekoa
3750 Kuiloa Rd
Hanapepe HI 96716

Call Sign: KH6CKW
Peter A Kanekiyo
Hanapepe HI 96716

Call Sign: KH6DXO
George R Susterich
Hanapepe HI 96716

Call Sign: KH6HU
Gerald W Hill
Hanapepe HI 96716

Call Sign: KH6LG
Hawaii Chapter Quarter
Century Wireless Assoc
Hanapepe HI 96716

Call Sign: WH6DVO
Jei-Nhy K Quirantes
Hanapepe HI 96716

Call Sign: WH7SO
Eric L Nordmeier
Hanapepe HI 96716

Call Sign: WA6CJE
Tyge E Legier
Hanapepe HI 96716

Call Sign: WH6CCT
Jason M Sunada
Hanapepe HI 96716

Call Sign: WH6CNP
Darren K N Iese
54-185 Hanaimoa St
Hauula HI 96717

Call Sign: WH6CPB
Thomas J Faustino
54-124 Hauula Park Pl
Hauula HI 96717

Call Sign: WH6CSY
Benjamin P Richards
54-015 Kahikole Pl
Hauula HI 96717-0651

Call Sign: WH6UF
Ivan K Richards
54-015 Kahikole Pl
Hauula HI 96717-0855

Call Sign: WH6CYA
Gail L Draper
53-549 Kam Hwy 402
Hauula HI 96717

Call Sign: WH6CUY
Thad N Draper
53-549 Kamehameha Hwy
402
Hauula HI 96717

Call Sign: WH6CXP
Michael S Tuia
54152 Kawaewae Pl
Hauula HI 96717

Call Sign: KH7UX
Tyler D Silva
54 265 Kawaihemo Pl
Hauula HI 96717

Call Sign: KH7UW
Thomas I Ako
54 289 Kawaipuna Pl
Hauula HI 96717

Call Sign: KH7TM
Cheril C Carrington
54 134 Kawaipuna St
Hauula HI 96717-9515

Call Sign: WH6PS
Anthony M Vincent
54 170 Kawaipuna St
Hauula HI 96717

Call Sign: WH6CLM
Gordon K Dela Cerna
54-210 Keala Rd
Hauula HI 96717

Call Sign: WH6DWU
Peter Maneha
53-889 Pokiwai Way
Hauula HI 96717

Call Sign: WH7DX
Stephanie Y Pressman
54 126 Puuowaa St
Hauula HI 96717

Call Sign: KH7RO
Hyrum K Nihipali
54-148 Puuowaa St
Hauula HI 96717

Call Sign: WH6BOG
Larry K Nihipali
54-148 Puuowaa St
Hauula HI 96717

Call Sign: WH6CPC
Jacob K Nihipali
54-148 Puuowaa St
Hauula HI 96717-9610

Call Sign: WH6CNS
Jonathan M Taurua
54-050B Waikulama St
Hauula HI 96717

Call Sign: KE0TU
Ronald E Garrick
Hauula HI 96717

Call Sign: KH6RG
Ronald E Garrick
Hauula HI 96717

Call Sign: WH6DWN
Larry K Nihipali
Hauula HI 96717

Call Sign: WH7WB
Gregory S Gatioan
Hauula HI 96717

Call Sign: KH7XU
Robert S Rushforth
Hauula HI 96730

Call Sign: WH6DBM
David K Kinolau Jr
Hauula HI 96717-0432

Call Sign: KH7TI
Jason J Gonsalves
Hauula HI 96717-0913

FCC Amateur Radio License in Hawaii

Call Sign: KA2IXG
Satoshi Yabuki
Volcano Village
Hawaii HI 96785

Call Sign: AH6TG
Satoshi Yabuki
Volcano Village
Hawaii HI 96785

FCC Amateur Radio License in Hawaii National Park

Call Sign: AH6TQ
Darryl A Koon
Hawaii National Park HI
96718

Call Sign: KH6SX
Arthur K Seto
Hawaii National Park HI
96718

Call Sign: NH7WR
Patty L Connally
Hawaii National Park HI
96718

Call Sign: NH7WS
Weston W Connally
Hawaii National Park HI
96718

Call Sign: WH6DPL
Tahzay Jones
Hawaii National Park HI
96718

Call Sign: WH6DTA
Wyatt K Koon
Hawaii National Park HI
96718

Call Sign: WH6DTB
Denise M Koon
Hawaii National Park HI
96718

Call Sign: WH6DXE
Donna Z Grabow
Hawaii National Park HI
96718

Call Sign: WH7BR
Paul M Ducasse
Hawaii National Park HI
96718

Call Sign: WH7DK
Karl Halemano
Hawaii National Park HI
96718

Call Sign: WH7DL
Stacy M Okada Halemano
Hawaii National Park HI
96718

Call Sign: WH6DQ
William F Cullen
Hawaii National Park HI
96718-0058

Call Sign: W4EIN
Frank W Smith
Hawaii National Park HI
96718-0207

Call Sign: KH6SIX
The Kh6 Meter Group
Hawaii National Park HI
96718

Call Sign: WH6QO
Paul W Sturm
Hawaii National Park HI
96718

FCC Amateur Radio License in Hawi

Call Sign: KB7LPW
Len S Winkler
General Delivery
Hawi HI 96719

Call Sign: AH6EM
Norman T Knudson

Hawi HI 96719

Call Sign: KD5PIU
James H Berg Dr
Hawi HI 96719

Call Sign: KH7LW
Len S Winkler
Hawi HI 96719

Call Sign: KH7WB
Joe F Sheetz II
Hawi HI 96719

Call Sign: WH6DJP
Ronald E Volz
Hawi HI 96719

Call Sign: WH6DNS
Jacob S Takata
Hawi HI 96719

Call Sign: WH6VP
Jonjason P Lavea
Hawi HI 96719

Call Sign: KH7VZ
Joseph F Sheetz
Hawi HI 96749

Call Sign: AH6AB
John E Fernandez
Hawi HI 96719-0382

Call Sign: KH6TJ
Toni Withington
Hawi HI 96719

FCC Amateur Radio
License in Hickam AFB

Call Sign: WH6DNM
Devin M Bryant
1854 Maysey Hall 81Or
Hickam AFB HI 96853

FCC Amateur Radio
License in Hilo

Call Sign: NH6NY
Matsu Uehara
1920 A Pe Epe E Pl
Hilo HI 96721-5968

Call Sign: KH7XM
Reef L Tauati Jr
922 Ahuna Rd
Hilo HI 96720

Call Sign: NH7GV
Germaine K Tauati
922 Ahuna Rd
Hilo HI 96720

Call Sign: NH7GW
Reif K Tauati
922 Ahuna Rd
Hilo HI 96720

Call Sign: NH7HB
Javen K Tauati
922 Ahuna Rd
Hilo HI 96720

Call Sign: NH6TR
Martin D Kimball
2309 Ainakahele St
Hilo HI 96720

Call Sign: KH7VH
Charmaine U Felipe
2315 Ainakahele St
Hilo HI 96720

Call Sign: KH7VP
Geronimo G Felipe
2315 Ainakahele St
Hilo HI 96720

Call Sign: WH6BR

Collins K Tomei
467 Ainalako Rd
Hilo HI 96720

Call Sign: WH6CYT
Manuel A Moniz
1090 Ainaola Dr
Hilo HI 96720

Call Sign: NH7HJ
Kini K Burke
1265 Ainaola Dr
Hilo HI 96720

Call Sign: AL0HA
Coconut Island Dx
Association
2058 Ainaola Dr
Hilo HI 96720-3638

Call Sign: KH6AA
Hawaii Qrp Club
2058 Ainaola Dr
Hilo HI 96720-3638

Call Sign: KH6AC
Tropical Amateur Radio
Club
2058 Ainaola Dr
Hilo HI 96720-3638

Call Sign: KH6B
Dean W Manley
2058 Ainaola Dr
Hilo HI 96720-3638

Call Sign: KH6CC
Hilo Amateur Radio Club
2058 Ainaola Dr
Hilo HI 96720-3638

Call Sign: KH6GP
Hilo Amateur Radio Club
2058 Ainaola Dr
Hilo HI 96720-3638

Call Sign: KH6IN
Hilo Amateur Radio Club
2058 Ainaola Dr
Hilo HI 96720-3638

Call Sign: KH6OA
Coconut Island Dx Assn
2058 Ainaola Dr
Hilo HI 96720-3638

Call Sign: KH7EA
Ireneusz Lochert
2058 Ainaola Dr
Hilo HI 96720-3638

Call Sign: NQ6RP
Hawaii Qrp Club
2058 Ainaola Dr
Hilo HI 96720-3638

Call Sign: W8FGB
Digital City Amateur
Radio Club
2058 Ainaola Dr
Hilo HI 96720-3638

Call Sign: WH6DDC
Hawaii Chapter Qcwa
2058 Ainaola Dr
Hilo HI 96720-3638

Call Sign: WH6DDD
Hawaii Chapter Qcwa
2058 Ainaola Dr
Hilo HI 96720-3638

Call Sign: WH6DDE
Hawaii Chapter Qcwa
2058 Ainaola Dr
Hilo HI 96720-3638

Call Sign: WH6DFH
Coconut Island Dx
Association

2058 Ainaola Dr
Hilo HI 96720-3638

Call Sign: WH6DFI
Coconut Island Dx
Association
2058 Ainaola Dr
Hilo HI 96720-3638

Call Sign: WH6DFJ
Coconut Island Dx
Association
2058 Ainaola Dr
Hilo HI 96720-3638

Call Sign: WH6DFY
Hilo Amateur Radio Club
2058 Ainaola Dr
Hilo HI 96720-3638

Call Sign: AH6TF
Oleg V Borodin
2058 Ainaola Dr
Hilo HI 96720-3638

Call Sign: KH6OB
Oleg V Borodin
2058 Ainaola Dr
Hilo HI 96720-3638

Call Sign: KH7BQ
Roger W Carvalho
2644 Ainaola Dr
Hilo HI 96720

Call Sign: WH7JQ
Reiny Carvalho Sr
2644 Ainaola Dr
Hilo HI 96720

Call Sign: KH6ATQ
Noboru L Iwami
245 Aipuni St
Hilo HI 96720

Call Sign: KH6AUB
Pete T Okumoto
15 Akepa St
Hilo HI 96720-4906

Call Sign: AH6KQ
John Toth Jr
1732 Akolea Pl
Hilo HI 96720

Call Sign: NH7NT
Daina N Saiki
220 Akolea Rd
Hilo HI 96720

Call Sign: NH7HQ
Patricia Dunn
1480 Ala Kula St
Hilo HI 96720

Call Sign: WH6CCJ
Edward Victorino
102 Alaloa Rd
Hilo HI 96720

Call Sign: KB5HVJ
Dean S Kozel
557 Alawaena St
Hilo HI 96720

Call Sign: NH7ZH
Elena A Cornwell
111 Alawaena Way
Hilo HI 96720

Call Sign: WH6MA
Sterling T Cornwell
111 Alawaena Way
Hilo HI 96720

Call Sign: WH6VV
Julie S Tamura
1438 Alu St
Hilo HI 96720

Call Sign: WH6GE
Rachel J Okura
211 Amauulu Rd
Hilo HI 96720

Call Sign: NH7GS
Amy F Okura
211 Amauulu Rd
Hilo HI 96720

Call Sign: NH7GT
Nancy L Okura
211 Amauulu Rd
Hilo HI 96720

Call Sign: NH7GU
Sanford K Okura
211 Amauulu Rd
Hilo HI 96720

Call Sign: NH7EW
Kaui K Respicio
99 Andrews Ave
Hilo HI 96720

Call Sign: NH7HE
Robert L Kepaa
128 Andrews Ave
Hilo HI 96720

Call Sign: WH7BT
Kaleo W Aki
155 Andrews Ave
Hilo HI 96720

Call Sign: WH7BU
Liane M Aki
155 Andrews Ave
Hilo HI 96720

Call Sign: WH6DGA
Tetsuo Tanaka
213 Anela St
Hilo HI 96720

Call Sign: NH7IA
Vilsima Pedro
246 Anela St
Hilo HI 96720

Call Sign: KH6G
Chester S Zynel
101 Aupuni St Apt 908
Hilo HI 96720

Call Sign: KE5UZN
Lotis Jane A King
Aupuni Street
Hilo HI 96720

Call Sign: NH7UD
Aric T Matsubara
12 Awapuhi St
Hilo HI 96720

Call Sign: KG6CJA
John D Cruz
19 Awapuhi St
Hilo HI 96720

Call Sign: KG6CJK
Ivy F Kudo
19 Awapuhi St
Hilo HI 96720

Call Sign: NH7HT
Nancy N Okinishi
497 Awela St
Hilo HI 96720

Call Sign: NH7HZ
Stanley M Okinishi
497 Awela St
Hilo HI 96720

Call Sign: WH6BBK
John Kapuni Jr
317 Baker Ave
Hilo HI 96720

Call Sign: NH7LK
Eldred K Pea
30 Baker St
Hilo HI 96720

Call Sign: AH6SW
Clifton L Leonard
175 Banyan Dr Apt 201
Hilo HI 96720

Call Sign: KH6XJ
Clifton L Leonard
175 Banyan Dr Rm 211
Hilo HI 96720

Call Sign: KH6IBA
Carlo R Giacomini
Box 10520
Hilo HI 96721

Call Sign: NH7EO
Starr K Ritte Camara
238B Chong St
Hilo HI 96720

Call Sign: NH7LG
Mark C Wagoner
53 Desha Ave
Hilo HI 96720

Call Sign: NH7LE
Blaine K Marantan
100 Desha Ave
Hilo HI 96720

Call Sign: KH7XK
Kihei A Ahuna
287 Desha Ave
Hilo HI 96720

Call Sign: NH7EP
Richard K Kagawa
360 Desha Ave
Hilo HI 96720

Call Sign: NH7EQ
Shaun K Kagawa
360 Desha Ave
Hilo HI 96720

Call Sign: NH7ER
Shirley Kagawa
360 Desha Ave
Hilo HI 96720

Call Sign: NH7JY
Gretchen L Kamai
249 E Kahaopea
Hilo HI 96720-5368

Call Sign: NH7JZ
Roy J Kamai
249 E Kahaopea
Hilo HI 96720-5368

Call Sign: WH6VW
Janice Geronimo
187 E Kinai Pl
Hilo HI 96720

Call Sign: NH7HW
Darciann L Raffipiy
304 E Lanikaula St
Hilo HI 96720

Call Sign: NH6TT
Michael T Nakamura
24 E Ohea St
Hilo HI 96720

Call Sign: NH7GP
Celeste N Manuia
225 E Palai St
Hilo HI 96720

Call Sign: NH7GQ
Eva S Manuia
225 E Palai St
Hilo HI 96720

Call Sign: NH7GR
Corona V Morris
225 E Palai St
Hilo HI 96720

Call Sign: NH7HF
Walter K Manuia
225 E Palai St
Hilo HI 96720

Call Sign: NH7JF
Nelson N Nobriga
225 E Palai St
Hilo HI 96720

Call Sign: NH7MD
Eveliga V Kapeli
225 E Palai St
Hilo HI 96720

Call Sign: NH7MO
Pikake K Kupihea
225 E Palai St
Hilo HI 96720

Call Sign: N6ABW
Kevin D Cornwell
111 E Puainako St Ste 585
169
Hilo HI 96720

Call Sign: NH7LM
Kamuela K Kupihea
225 East Palai St
Hilo HI 96720

Call Sign: NH7UE
Matthew C Wung
864 Edena St
Hilo HI 96720

Call Sign: KH7ZR
Polly A Varize
393 A Ehehene St
Hilo HI 96720

Call Sign: NH7EN
Leonahenahe K Aina
1633 Elama Rd
Hilo HI 96720

Call Sign: NH7JQ
Candace H Aina
1633 Elama Rd
Hilo HI 96720

Call Sign: NH7JR
Daniel K Aina Jr
1633 Elama Rd
Hilo HI 96720

Call Sign: NH7EV
Cheyenne Makaokalani
57 Ewaliko Ave
Hilo HI 96720

Call Sign: NH7IN
Cody K Makaokalani
57 Ewaliko Ave
Hilo HI 96720

Call Sign: NH7IO
John K Makaokalani II
57 Ewaliko Ave
Hilo HI 96720

Call Sign: NH7IP
Roberta L Makaokalani
57 Ewaliko Ave
Hilo HI 96720

Call Sign: KH6CHK
Richard A Jaentsch
130 Ewaliko Ave
Hilo HI 96720

Call Sign: NH7LD
John K Makaokalani
57 Ewalino St
Hilo HI 96720

Call Sign: KH7VK
Leonard S Tanaka
1259 Haihai St
Hilo HI 96720

Call Sign: NH6CX
Harvey H K Keliikoa
458 Hilinai St
Hilo HI 96720

Call Sign: NH7XE
Brandon T Kaku
27 Hokupaa St
Hilo HI 96720

Call Sign: NH7WZ
David G Worth
285 Haili St 103
Hilo HI 96720

Call Sign: NH7BB
Harvey H K Keliikoa
458 Hilinai St
Hilo HI 96720

Call Sign: WH6BV
Kurt W Garbo
1270 Honua St
Hilo HI 96720

Call Sign: KH6FKG
Harry K Nishiyama
1990 Hale Hooko St
Hilo HI 96720

Call Sign: WH6BTZ
Albert Bungula
547 Hinano St
Hilo HI 96720

Call Sign: WH6CRY
Robert S Hill
3 Ho'Ohoaloha St
Hilo HI 96720

Call Sign: WH6AG
Sue Tsuyuko Nishiyama
1990 Hale Hooko St
Hilo HI 96720

Call Sign: NH7NU
Dan H Straight
594B Hinano St
Hilo HI 96720

Call Sign: WH6DCN
Erin S H Hill
3 Ho'Ohoaloha St
Hilo HI 96720

Call Sign: NH6IZ
David N Ahia
50 Hale Nani St
Hilo HI 96720

Call Sign: NH7HS
Allison L Mayeda
432 Hoaka Rd
Hilo HI 96720

Call Sign: NH6ES
Dominic A Uyetake Sr
36 Ho'Ohoaloha St
Hilo HI 96720

Call Sign: KH6FOO
Russel T Sakai
1776 Hale O Kea St
Hilo HI 96720

Call Sign: KH7VG
Duane L De Lima
925 Hoaka Rd
Hilo HI 97620

Call Sign: WH6CWL
Greg M Wagner Sr
193 Hoohua
Hilo HI 96720

Call Sign: WX6X
John C Sanders
25-178 Hana St
Hilo HI 96720

Call Sign: NH6TD
Stephen T Butler
870 Hoalauna Way
Hilo HI 96720

Call Sign: NH6MO
Guillerma G Sumera
129 Hookano St
Hilo HI 96720

Call Sign: WH7GA
Karla K Simmons
15 Hanohano St
Hilo HI 96720

Call Sign: WH6CDJ
Kelly S Minami
90 Hoaloha St
Hilo HI 96720

Call Sign: NH6MP
Herman Sumera Jr
129 Hookano St
Hilo HI 96720

Call Sign: NH6CK
Donald B Marks
Hc-01 Stainback Hwy
Hilo HI 96720

Call Sign: K6GHW
George N Suzuki
89 Hoku St
Hilo HI 96720

Call Sign: NH6PG
Charles H Sumera
129 Hookano St
Hilo HI 96720

Call Sign: WH6AWH
David F Shearer
495 Hookina Pl
Hilo HI 96720-6000

Call Sign: KH6AVF
William S Beckstrom
833 Hoolala Pl
Hilo HI 96720

Call Sign: WH6DAY
Larry E Walter
766 Hoolaulea St
Hilo HI 96720

Call Sign: KH6HGL
Michael K T Tong
43 Hoomana St
Hilo HI 96720-2028

Call Sign: NH6FO
Albert S Cabango
80 Hoonani Pl
Hilo HI 96720

Call Sign: WH6BM
Vernon A Ito
1042 Huaka Pl
Hilo HI 96720

Call Sign: KA6KMJ
Blake M Barton
400 Hualani St 10196
Hilo HI 96720

Call Sign: KH6AUA
Scott S Maeda
400 Hualani St 386
Hilo HI 96720

Call Sign: NH7NX
Jordan L Olds
416 Huali Pl
Hilo HI 96720

Call Sign: KH7JM
Sandra K Anderson
702 Hueu Pl
Hilo HI 96720

Call Sign: KF6FAY
James A Anderson
702 Hueu Pl
Hilo HI 96720-6026

Call Sign: AA7SH
Margaret A Alexander
333 Iliahi St
Hilo HI 96720-2399

Call Sign: AA7SU
Lawrence H Alexander
333 Iliahi St
Hilo HI 96720-2399

Call Sign: KH6AQU
Noboru Okamoto
519 Iwalani St
Hilo HI 96720-5568

Call Sign: N7CSJ
Clifford P Livermore
16 Kaaponi Loop
Hilo HI 96720

Call Sign: NH7LV
Kyle N Keamo
4 Kaapuni Lp
Hilo HI 96720

Call Sign: KH0AI
Patrick B Moore
1244 Kahoa Rd
Hilo HI 96720

Call Sign: WH6CSP
Marvin H Kitchen
86 Kaikuono
Hilo HI 96720

Call Sign: WH6BTV
Tracey M Nakayama
752 Kaima Pl
Hilo HI 96720

Call Sign: WB6PIO
Paul B Walp
266 Kaiulani St
Hilo HI 96720

Call Sign: WA8COZ
Stanley Fortuna Jr
96 Ka'Iulani St
Hilo HI 96720

Call Sign: NH7UC
Brad P Higa
590 Kaiwiki Rd
Hilo HI 96720

Call Sign: WH7HP
John R True
1991 Kaiwiki Rd
Hilo HI 96720

Call Sign: NH7LQ
Susan B O Neill
2390 Kaiwiki Rd
Hilo HI 96720

Call Sign: WH6BTT
Bruce M Sakamoto
2250A Kaiwiki Rd
Hilo HI 96720

Call Sign: NH7GH
Wanda E Cardines
1034 Kalanianaole Ave
Hilo HI 96720

Call Sign: KH7NT
Chad L Ahia
1846 Kalanianaole Ave
Hilo HI 96720-4918

Call Sign: NH6FK
Audrey L Pakani
2417 Kalanianaole Ave
Hilo HI 96720

Call Sign: NH7BT
Audrey L Pakani
2417 Kalanianaole Ave
Hilo HI 96720

Call Sign: NH7HL
John T Hilsher
1365 Kalanianaole Ave
205
Hilo HI 96720

Call Sign: NH7HM
Theresa S Hilsher
1365 Kalanianaole Ave
205
Hilo HI 96720

Call Sign: NH7LI
Al K Kaula
1365 Kalanianaole Ave
Apt 110
Hilo HI 96720

Call Sign: NH7HK
Patrick J Cardines
1034 Kalanianaole St
Hilo HI 96720

Call Sign: WH6BL
Nelson L Ahia
1846 Kalanianaole St
Hilo HI 96720

Call Sign: WH6CMB
Stanward S Oshiro
769A Kalanikoa St
Hilo HI 96720

Call Sign: WH6MJ

Milton A C Lee
347 Kalili St
Hilo HI 96720

Call Sign: WH6DPU
Scott S Maeda
51 Kalo St
Hilo HI 96720

Call Sign: KJ6CKZ
Christine Y Matsuno
69 Kamalii St
Hilo HI 96720

Call Sign: W6TUS
Paul J Agamata
69 Kamalii St
Hilo HI 96720

Call Sign: WH6FM
Paul J Agamata
69 Kamalii St
Hilo HI 96720

Call Sign: WH6KBR
Christine Y Matsuno
69 Kamalii St
Hilo HI 96720

Call Sign: KH6ATT
Kenichi Yamamoto
145 Kamana St Apt C3
Hilo HI 96720

Call Sign: NH7UF
Brian N Koge
315 Kamanelo Pl
Hilo HI 96720

Call Sign: NH6AH
Robert E Oliver III
94 Kamehameha Ave Ste 7
Hilo HI 96720

Call Sign: WH6XO

John K Endriss III
56 Kaneelani St
Hilo HI 96720

Call Sign: KE4WXJ
Matthew C Dinkins
200 Kanoelehua 232
Hilo HI 96720

Call Sign: KB8PBF
Chuen Shing N Yu
200 Kanoelehua Ave Pmb
332
Hilo HI 96720

Call Sign: W6MLD
Maria L Dunham
200 Kanoelehua Ave Pmb
332
Hilo HI 96720

Call Sign: W7MUX
Jerry R Dunham
200 Kanoelehua Ave Pmb
332
Hilo HI 96720

Call Sign: NH6VI
Emily J Souza
35 Kapiolani St Apt 18
Hilo HI 96720

Call Sign: KH6AN
Hawaii Chapter Quarter
Century Wireless
270 Kapualani
Hilo HI 96720

Call Sign: W6ORS
C E Kirk Jr
270 Kapualani
Hilo HI 96720

Call Sign: NH7GN
Mildred U Lyons

79 Kauhane Ave
Hilo HI 96720

1878 Kaumana Dr
Hilo HI 96720

485F Kaumana Dr
Hilo HI 96720

Call Sign: NH7GY
Sean K Lyons
79 Kauhane Ave
Hilo HI 96720

Call Sign: NH7LZ
Paula Pea
1914 Kaumana Dr
Hilo HI 96720

Call Sign: KH7ZM
Clayton M Morante
758 B Kaumana Dr
Hilo HI 96720

Call Sign: NH7GZ
Shane K Lyons
79 Kauhane Ave
Hilo HI 96720

Call Sign: NH7NW
Jon K Pea
1914 Kaumana Dr
Hilo HI 96720

Call Sign: WH6DTC
Roy H Veloria
1614 Kaunala Pl
Hilo HI 96720

Call Sign: NH7HU
Mark S Naumu
23 Kaulana St
Hilo HI 96720

Call Sign: KH6UA
Roger S Horie
2071 Kaumana Dr
Hilo HI 96720

Call Sign: WH7FY
Dawnelle K Forsythe
1581 Kaunala Way
Hilo HI 96720

Call Sign: KH6AT
Bryce A Carr
65 Kaulana St
Hilo HI 96720

Call Sign: KH7BR
Kent T Tsutsui
485 B Kaumana Dr
Hilo HI 96720

Call Sign: NH7XI
Robert R Kanemitsu
519 Kehaulari St
Hilo HI 96720

Call Sign: WH7BV
Iosefa K Trainer
433 Kaumana Dr
Hilo HI 96720

Call Sign: NH7NQ
Brandon K Meyers
485 F Kaumana Dr
Hilo HI 96720

Call Sign: AH6EB
James A Boetcher
1974 Keo St
Hilo HI 96720

Call Sign: WH7BW
Jeffrey J Trainer
433 Kaumana Dr
Hilo HI 96720

Call Sign: NH7LY
Bruce K Meyers
485 F Kaumana Dr
Hilo HI 96720

Call Sign: KH7WD
Derek B Kalima Sr
529 Keonaona St
Hilo HI 96720

Call Sign: WH7BX
Michalann Rae K Trainer
433 Kaumana Dr
Hilo HI 96720

Call Sign: NH7NR
Bruce Meyers III
485F Kaumana Dr
Hilo HI 96720

Call Sign: KH7WE
Youline K Kalima
529 Keonaona St
Hilo HI 96720

Call Sign: KH7VO
Eldred K Kalehua
839 Kaumana Dr
Hilo HI 96720-1818

Call Sign: NH7NS
Joelle I Meyers
485F Kaumana Dr
Hilo HI 96720

Call Sign: NH7IZ
Leeron M Kuamoo
546 Keonaona St
Hilo HI 96720

Call Sign: NH6FM
Blaine Y Oyama

Call Sign: NH7NO
Tammy Meyers

Call Sign: WH7IK
Tina M Mendiola

599 Keonaona St
Hilo HI 96720

1920 Kilavea Ave
Hilo HI 96720

420 King Ave
Hilo HI 96720

Call Sign: NH7XD
Darrick Iida
1227 Kihonua Pl
Hilo HI 96720

Call Sign: NH6WW
Don H Bartron Sr
1484 Kilikina St
Hilo HI 96720

Call Sign: NH7JB
Sean K Benito
420 King Ave
Hilo HI 96720

Call Sign: NH7GX
Derek F Cabarloc
1560 Kikaha St
Hilo HI 96720

Call Sign: NH6WX
Myrtle M Bartron
1484 Kilikina St
Hilo HI 96720

Call Sign: NH7UL
Gary K Kihara
547 Kinoole St
Hilo HI 96720

Call Sign: NH7TY
Chad T Fujiyama
1537 Kilaha St
Hilo HI 96720

Call Sign: NH7MS
Douglas C Rhodes
1605 Kilikina St
Hilo HI 96720

Call Sign: AH6S
Glenn W Nakano
1332 Kinoole St
Hilo HI 96720

Call Sign: KH6GZ
Howard Y Atebara
830 Kilauea Ave
Hilo HI 96720

Call Sign: AH6LZ
Douglas A Miller
1611 Kilikina St
Hilo HI 96720

Call Sign: WH6XN
Glenn Nakano
1332 Kinoole St
Hilo HI 96720

Call Sign: WH6XT
Justin T Okano
1284 Kilauea Ave
Hilo HI 96720

Call Sign: KH6DJF
Wallace T Oki
1635 Kilikina St
Hilo HI 96720

Call Sign: KH6BFB
Wayne M Canevali
1960 Kinoole St
Hilo HI 96720

Call Sign: NH7HX
Agnes L Pung
1752 Kilauea Ave
Hilo HI 96720

Call Sign: NH6DW
Steven N Noah Sr
159 King Ave
Hilo HI 96720

Call Sign: KH6TQ
Sam A Canevali
1960 Kinoole St
Hilo HI 96720

Call Sign: NH6EN
Jeremy K Burgess
1875 Kilauea Ave
Hilo HI 96720

Call Sign: WH6BDK
Margo K Noah
159 King Ave
Hilo HI 96720

Call Sign: NH6WV
Kiku Kaneshiro
1642A Kinoole St
Hilo HI 96720

Call Sign: NH7BM
Jeremy K Burgess
1875 Kilauea Ave
Hilo HI 96720

Call Sign: NH7QM
Phoebe I Anderson
326 King Ave
Hilo HI 96720

Call Sign: WH6BFF
Dave S Okamura
344 Kipuni St
Hilo HI 96720

Call Sign: WH6CXO
Barr M Canario

Call Sign: KH7XL
Clarence A Benito

Call Sign: WH6CAA
Steven Anicas

1022 Komohana St
Hilo HI 96720

Call Sign: WH6CQA
Harold T Yoshikawa
1393 Komohana St
Hilo HI 96720

Call Sign: KH9AB
David C Nardini
1421 Komohana St
Hilo HI 96720

Call Sign: KH7CN
Jeremy K Punsalan
1509 Komohana St
Hilo HI 96720

Call Sign: WH6PB
Thomas O Fletcher
822 Komomala Dr
Hilo HI 96720

Call Sign: NH7ES
Caycee John Matsuyama
99 Krauss Ave
Hilo HI 96720

Call Sign: NH7ET
Chelsie Matsuyama
99 Krauss Ave
Hilo HI 96720

Call Sign: NH7EU
Reece Matsuyama
99 Krauss Ave
Hilo HI 96720

Call Sign: NH7IY
Jonah U Kelekolio
99 Krauss Ave
Hilo HI 96720

Call Sign: NH7JS
Denise K Kelekolio

99 Krauss Ave
Hilo HI 96720

Call Sign: NH7JU
Maile Aina
178 Krauss Ave
Hilo HI 96720

Call Sign: NH7LF
Nathaniel K Paulino
178 Krauss Ave
Hilo HI 96720

Call Sign: WH6CWJ
Marqwaan E M Riedel
169 Kuakahi Pl
Hilo HI 96720

Call Sign: NH7LW
John K Mcbride
199 Kualua Pl
Hilo HI 96720

Call Sign: NH7LX
Lesli Mcbride
199 Kualua Pl
Hilo HI 96720

Call Sign: WH6XL
Andrew M Subica
314 Kuhilahi Pl
Hilo HI 96720

Call Sign: KH7VI
Hina H Sewell
314 Kuhilani Pl
Hilo HI 96720

Call Sign: KH7VJ
Olani H Sewell
314 Kuhilani Pl
Hilo HI 96720

Call Sign: WH6DHK

Hawaii Internet-Remote
Amateur Radio Club
85 Kuikahi St
Hilo HI 96720

Call Sign: WH6DLJ
Donald L Nithan
1470 Kuleana Pl
Hilo HI 96720

Call Sign: KH6JAF
Hideo Gushiken
1148 Kumukoa St
Hilo HI 96720-4032

Call Sign: KH6SD
Alejandro Baxa
36 Kupulau Pl
Hilo HI 96720

Call Sign: WH6DLH
Celeste A Baxa
36 Kupulau Pl
Hilo HI 96720

Call Sign: NH6VO
Carisa P Wong
811 Kupulau Rd
Hilo HI 96720

Call Sign: NH7ZN
Jason D Hardman
1396 Kuulei St
Hilo HI 96720-3228

Call Sign: WH6ND
Robert M Atebara
1573 Lanihan Pl
Hilo HI 96720

Call Sign: WH6NK
Earl A Sagucio
33 Laula Rd
Hilo HI 96720

Call Sign: KH6BV
Ivan V Faxon Jr
127 Laula Rd
Hilo HI 96720

Call Sign: KD4KNF
Don W Oelze
46 Lono St
Hilo HI 96720

Call Sign: WH7FQ
Shane S Shigematsu
1345 Makani St
Hilo HI 96720

Call Sign: AH6IL
Francis L Brown Sr
8 Leihala Dr
Hilo HI 96720

Call Sign: WH6LO
Harry P Riedel Jr
292 Lyman Ave
Hilo HI 96720

Call Sign: KH7RR
Roger W Kuntemeyer
1329 Malawaina St
Hilo HI 96720

Call Sign: NH6RW
Francis L Brown Jr
8 Leihala Dr
Hilo HI 96720-5013

Call Sign: NH7LA
Cynthia M Kapu
323 Lyman Ave
Hilo HI 96720

Call Sign: WH7HJ
Michael W Clarke
25-191 Malumalu St
Hilo HI 96720

Call Sign: WH6BGY
June L Ngaden
8 Leihala Dr
Hilo HI 96720-5013

Call Sign: NH7LB
Eugene K Kapu
323 Lyman Ave
Hilo HI 96720

Call Sign: WH6CHQ
Daniel Waeger
600 Manono St
Hilo HI 96720

Call Sign: NH6NV
Grant A Torigoe
14 Leihala St
Hilo HI 96720

Call Sign: KH6LE
Curtis T Nakayama
1514 Mailani St
Hilo HI 96720

Call Sign: NH6NZ
Wesley L Smith Sr
844A Manono St
Hilo HI 96720

Call Sign: KH6PC
R Keith Spencer
81 Likeke St
Hilo HI 96720

Call Sign: NH6RV
Suzanne T Nakayama
1514 Mailani St
Hilo HI 96720

Call Sign: AH6GD
Ted A Ross
270 Mohala Pl Apt 102
Hilo HI 96720

Call Sign: WH7QC
Michelle J Bauer
147 Likeke St
Hilo HI 96720

Call Sign: KH6AFQ
Kenneth K Bell Sr
167 Makani Cir
Hilo HI 96720

Call Sign: KH6IAA
Alfred Pacheco
20 Mokuhonua Ln
Hilo HI 96720

Call Sign: WH7DH
Roy G Bauer
147 Likeke St
Hilo HI 96720

Call Sign: KH6KB
Makani Arc
167 Makani Cir
Hilo HI 96720

Call Sign: NH7HP
Adi K Akiona
1429 Mona Loop
Hilo HI 96720

Call Sign: WH6NB
John Iswan
137 Lit Pl
Hilo HI 96720

Call Sign: NH6XB
Clara L Bell
167 Makani Cir
Hilo HI 96720

Call Sign: WH7FX
Denny C Dement III
1429 Mona Loop
Hilo HI 96720

Call Sign: WH6CCZ
James S Otani
1704 Mona Loop
Hilo HI 96720

Call Sign: KH7EP
Paul J Matsumoto
334 Ohukea St
Hilo HI 96720

Call Sign: NH7SW
Josh M Stueber
16 Olena St
Hilo HI 96720

Call Sign: NH7GG
Franklin Valdez
1518 Mona Lp
Hilo HI 96720

Call Sign: NH7LJ
Lynda K Aina
121 Ohuohu St
Hilo HI 96720

Call Sign: NH7SX
Elisa V Stueber
16 Olena St
Hilo HI 96720

Call Sign: NH7HY
Lynette L Valdez
1518 Mona Lp
Hilo HI 96720

Call Sign: NH7GJ
Simon S Fong
145 Ohuohu St
Hilo HI 96720

Call Sign: NH7VA
Dianne E Peterson
16 Olena St
Hilo HI 96720

Call Sign: AH6GO
Myles M Masuhara
1191 N Kumuwaina Pl
Hilo HI 96720-2795

Call Sign: NH7GK
Lawrence Y Fong
145 Ohuohu St
Hilo HI 96720

Call Sign: KH6WT
Hawaii Chapter Qcwa
22 Olena St
Hilo HI 96720-1864

Call Sign: NH6AT
Earl K Kunimoto
208 Naniakea St
Hilo HI 96720

Call Sign: NH7JD
Joyce Fong
145 Ohuohu St
Hilo HI 96720

Call Sign: NH7D
Benjamin P Blatt
22 Olena St
Hilo HI 96720-1864

Call Sign: WH6LN
Jonathan M Koshi
270 Naniakea St
Hilo HI 96720

Call Sign: NH7JE
Mona Lee Fong
145 Ohuohu St
Hilo HI 96720

Call Sign: AH6JA
Harvey S Motomura
1026 Olioli Way
Hilo HI 96720

Call Sign: NH7QJ
Bryce H Hamamoto
282B Nohea St
Hilo HI 96720

Call Sign: KH6LW
Loren J Wolff
1202 Oihana St
Hilo HI 96720

Call Sign: WH6YB
Nancy Kishi
197 Olu St
Hilo HI 96720

Call Sign: NH7HR
Tjaye A Forsythe
1659 Nohoana Pl
Hilo HI 96720

Call Sign: NH6VM
Darlene M Wolff
1202 Oihana St
Hilo HI 96720

Call Sign: WH6VX
Matthew T Geballe
1645 Oneand Pl
Hilo HI 96720

Call Sign: KH6GPC
John T Jensen
545 Ocean View Dr
Hilo HI 96720

Call Sign: NH7SA
Sean Stueber
16 Olena St
Hilo HI 96720

Call Sign: WH6CSM
Daniel K Aina Sr
15 Paipai St
Hilo HI 96720

Call Sign: WH7QG
Kunio H Sewell
40 Palua Loop
Hilo HI 96720

Call Sign: KH6AK
Masaaki Masuda
264 Palua Loop
Hilo HI 96720-5546

Call Sign: KH6KL
Patrick K T Chu
25-191 Papali St
Hilo HI 96720

Call Sign: WH6CTD
Jonathan T Doi
2326 Piihonua Rd
Hilo HI 96720

Call Sign: AH6IK
Glenn S Hara
18 Pikake Pl
Hilo HI 96720

Call Sign: WH6BW
Janet W Hara
18 Pikake Pl
Hilo HI 96720

Call Sign: NH6OG
Ralph Dunphy Jr
81 Pilialoha St
Hilo HI 96720

Call Sign: AH6NS
Adam P Keliipio
66 Pilipaa St
Hilo HI 96720

Call Sign: KH6JIC
Adam P Keliipio
66 Pilipaa St
Hilo HI 96720

Call Sign: WH6CI
Leslie N Kaholoaa
85 Pilipaa St
Hilo HI 96720

Call Sign: WH6DP
Jason K Kaholoaa
85 Pilipaa St
Hilo HI 96720

Call Sign: WH7IJ
Heather K Keamo
150 Pilipaa St
Hilo HI 96720

Call Sign: WH6CWN
Shayne L K Pea
15 Pohai St
Hilo HI 96720

Call Sign: KH7NR
Baron P Ahulau
16 Pohai St
Hilo HI 96720-5225

Call Sign: KH6AU
Haruwo Yamamoto
21 Pohakulani St
Hilo HI 96720

Call Sign: AH6NK
William K Crowl
63 Pohakulani St
Hilo HI 96720-3115

Call Sign: NH6UK
Ruben A Casile Sr
120 Pohakulani St
Hilo HI 96720

Call Sign: KH6AQE
Seijin Hokama
488 Pohakulani St
Hilo HI 96720

Call Sign: KH7SN
Lucio Ramos Jr
135A Pohakulani St
Hilo HI 96720

Call Sign: NH7U
Palmyra Island Amateur
Radio Club
45 Pokahu St
Hilo HI 96720

Call Sign: NH7MH
Lawrence Nerveza
17 Poni Moi Pl
Hilo HI 96720

Call Sign: WH6CDI
Daniel C Iwamoto
18 Poni Moi Pl
Hilo HI 96720

Call Sign: NH7JV
Jean E Bezilla
222 Pua Ave
Hilo HI 96720

Call Sign: KA6SVW
Howard E Jones
15 Puamelia Pl
Hilo HI 96720

Call Sign: KB6SWL
Diana J Jones
15 Puamelia Pl
Hilo HI 96720

Call Sign: KH7BT
Stephan M Kitagawa
1270 A Puhau St
Hilo HI 96720

Call Sign: WH7FP
Lance T Mento
102 Puhili Pl
Hilo HI 96720

Call Sign: WH6CVA
Alan K Iwasaki
1504 Pukana Pl
Hilo HI 96720

Call Sign: WH6BOH
Douglas L K Bumatay
940 RailRd Ave
Hilo HI 96720

Call Sign: NH7II
Kapaea M Bongolan
331 Todd Ave
Hilo HI 96720

Call Sign: KH7VY
David L Skaife
84 Pukihae St 1401
Hilo HI 96720

Call Sign: WH6DSY
Douglas K Awai Jr
967 RailRd Ave
Hilo HI 96720

Call Sign: NH7IM
Natalynn A Mahi
331 Todd Ave
Hilo HI 96720

Call Sign: WH7FZ
Moses Y Kealamakia Jr
1059 Puku St
Hilo HI 96720

Call Sign: NH7JW
Amaroal N Borges
1002 RailRd Ave
Hilo HI 96720

Call Sign: WH6DAX
Darnell K Mahi
331 Todd Ave
Hilo HI 96720

Call Sign: NH7LU
Skylane K Ishibashi
2901 Pulima Dr
Hilo HI 96720

Call Sign: NH7HD
Stanley K Kelekolio
1155 RailRd Ave
Hilo HI 96720

Call Sign: WH6DXH
Darnell K Mahi
331 Todd Ave
Hilo HI 96720

Call Sign: NH7NN
Tina K Ishibashi
2901 Pulima Dr
Hilo HI 96720

Call Sign: WH7JL
Muncie L Pea
1953 RailRd Ave
Hilo HI 96720

Call Sign: WH6DLN
Jamie L Cookson
25-133 Ua Nahele St
Hilo HI 96720

Call Sign: WH6CMC
Bernard A Klingshirn
2939A Pulima Dr
Hilo HI 96720

Call Sign: WH6CQP
Matsu Uehara Jr
Rfd Kaiwiki Rd Wainaku
Hilo HI 96720

Call Sign: NH7QX
Barry E Bolln
10 Ualehua
Hilo HI 96720

Call Sign: WH6IA
Christian K Alameda
561 Puloku St
Hilo HI 96720

Call Sign: WH6BT
Ponciano Robia
22 Santos Ln
Hilo HI 96720

Call Sign: NH7TX
Jay A Yokoyama
807 Uilani Pl
Hilo HI 96720

Call Sign: KH7WC
Joseph Eruntina
120 Puueo St Apt B308
Hilo HI 96720

Call Sign: WH7II
Randall R Jose-Brannam
149 Todd Ave
Hilo HI 96720

Call Sign: NH7LT
Kody K Agbayani
407 Ulu Mau Pl
Hilo HI 96720

Call Sign: WH7IL
Howard K Pe'A
600 RailRd
Hilo HI 96720

Call Sign: WH6DSZ
Aaron K Auna
213 Todd Ave
Hilo HI 96720

Call Sign: WH6DEL
Adelbert H Winn Jr
925 Ululani St Apt C
Hilo HI 96720

Call Sign: WH6DTL
Adelbert H Winn Jr
925 Ululani St Apt C
Hilo HI 96720

Call Sign: WH6PR
Brandon P Noguchi
514 W Kawailani St
Hilo HI 96720

Call Sign: AH6SS
Yoshiharu Takeda
430 W Kawili St 25C
Hilo HI 96720

Call Sign: KH6BAR
Ellsworth H Takata Jr
445 Waianuenue Ave
Hilo HI 96720

Call Sign: NH7GO
Shannon K Lyons
1726 Wailuku Dr
Hilo HI 96720

Call Sign: NH7HA
Phillip J Quintal
1726 Wailuku Dr
Hilo HI 96720

Call Sign: WH6DXG
Aukai E Sewell
668 B Wainaku
Hilo HI 96720

Call Sign: WH6PJ
Ryan S Nagata
348 Walelia Pl
Hilo HI 96720

Call Sign: WH7WS
Tyron Y Hamamoto
133 West Kawailani St
Hilo HI 96720

Call Sign: KH7ML
Lance T Amano
133B West Kawailani St
Hilo HI 96720

Call Sign: WH6CZX
Robert F Anstedt
1141A West Kawailani St
Hilo HI 96720

Call Sign: WH6DLK
Rodney H Clark Jr
338 West Puainako St
Hilo HI 96720

Call Sign: AD6YJ
Richard E Frazier
Hilo HI 96720

Call Sign: AH6SC
Charles E Epperson
Hilo HI 96720

Call Sign: KH6DX
Donald W Stribling
Hilo HI 96720

Call Sign: KH6KM
Kelvin L Mc Grew
Hilo HI 96720

Call Sign: KH7LH
Ronald D Sewell
Hilo HI 96720

Call Sign: NH6CV
Alfred A V Vea Sr
Hilo HI 96720

Call Sign: NH6DE
Carol R Ioane
Hilo HI 96720

Call Sign: NH6DF

Kelii W Ioane Jr
Hilo HI 96720

Call Sign: NH6EX
James E Iopa
Hilo HI 96720

Call Sign: NH6FB
Barbara L Paculba
Hilo HI 96720

Call Sign: NH6FD
Alberta J Vea
Hilo HI 96720

Call Sign: NH6FG
Daniel L Vea
Hilo HI 96720

Call Sign: NH6FH
Roberta A Vea
Hilo HI 96720

Call Sign: NH6FI
Francis K Laimana Jr
Hilo HI 96720

Call Sign: NH6FN
George T Gibo
Hilo HI 96720

Call Sign: NH6FQ
Moke K Angay
Hilo HI 96720

Call Sign: NH6FR
Ainaaloha W Ioane
Hilo HI 96720

Call Sign: NH6FS
Lawton K Kipapa
Hilo HI 96720

Call Sign: NH6FU
Christopher H Meyermoss

Hilo HI 96720

Call Sign: NH6FW
Hana Viritua Sr
Hilo HI 96720

Call Sign: NH6FY
Tehchu Anthony
Hilo HI 96720

Call Sign: NH6OH
Glen S Fujinaga
Hilo HI 96720

Call Sign: NH6QB
Johanna P Greenleaf
Hilo HI 96720

Call Sign: NH7BA
Alfred A V Vea Sr
Hilo HI 96720

Call Sign: NH7BD
Carol R Ioane
Hilo HI 96720

Call Sign: NH7BE
Kelii W Ioane Jr
Hilo HI 96720

Call Sign: NH7BN
James E Iopa
Hilo HI 96720

Call Sign: NH7BO
Barbara L Paculba
Hilo HI 96720

Call Sign: NH7BP
Alberta J Vea
Hilo HI 96720

Call Sign: NH7BQ
Daniel L Vea
Hilo HI 96720

Call Sign: NH7BR
Roberta A Vea
Hilo HI 96720

Call Sign: NH7BS
Francis K Laimana Jr
Hilo HI 96720

Call Sign: NH7BU
Moke K Angay
Hilo HI 96720

Call Sign: NH7BV
Ainaaloha W Ioane
Hilo HI 96720

Call Sign: NH7BW
Lawton K Kipapa
Hilo HI 96720

Call Sign: NH7BX
Christopher H Meyermoss
Hilo HI 96720

Call Sign: NH7BY
Hana Viritua Sr
Hilo HI 96720

Call Sign: NH7BZ
Tehchu Anthony
Hilo HI 96720

Call Sign: NH7DO
Kapena L Ioane
Hilo HI 96720

Call Sign: NH7DP
Wayson K Ioane
Hilo HI 96720

Call Sign: NH7GI
Lovette E Crowley
Hilo HI 96720

Call Sign: NH7HC
Terrance L Crowley
Hilo HI 96720

Call Sign: NH7IB
Stephanie Lewi
Hilo HI 96720

Call Sign: NH7IC
Joseph H Lewi Sr
Hilo HI 96720

Call Sign: NH7JA
Dana W Mahiai
Hilo HI 96720

Call Sign: NH7LC
Frank H Kawaauhau Jr
Hilo HI 96720

Call Sign: NH7MR
Edward A Grantz
Hilo HI 96720

Call Sign: NH7NY
Caroline N Hao
Hilo HI 96720

Call Sign: NH7SY
Francis L Benevides Jr
Hilo HI 96720

Call Sign: NH7UG
Richard G Salinas
Hilo HI 96720

Call Sign: NH7XG
Adan W Rodrigues
Hilo HI 96720

Call Sign: WH6CNW
James L Nevins
Hilo HI 96720

Call Sign: WH6CNX

Carole M Nevins
Hilo HI 96720

Call Sign: WH6DPN
Ernest K Kelii
Hilo HI 96720

Call Sign: WH6DPR
Betty C Suetomi
Hilo HI 96720

Call Sign: WH6DPS
Jeffrey T Steele
Hilo HI 96720

Call Sign: WH6DVA
Joseph S Frazer
Hilo HI 96720

Call Sign: WH6DVD
Corey J Connell
Hilo HI 96720

Call Sign: K3QHP
Richard D Fetchen
Hilo HI 96721

Call Sign: K6FK
Mary J Brown
Hilo HI 96721

Call Sign: K6MIO
James R Kennedy
Hilo HI 96721

Call Sign: KB7KQA
Edna L Buchan Ms
Hilo HI 96721

Call Sign: KC7KJT
Raymond C Nyberg
Hilo HI 96721

Call Sign: KC8YOR
Garrett L Jenks

Hilo HI 96721

Call Sign: KH6BGE
Florence L Kumukahi
Hilo HI 96721

Call Sign: KH6DLK
John D Bush
Hilo HI 96721

Call Sign: KH6EJ
Big Island Amateur Radio
Club
Hilo HI 96721

Call Sign: KH6NE
Charles F Wakely
Hilo HI 96721

Call Sign: KH6WE
Richard D Fetchen
Hilo HI 96721

Call Sign: KH7ZH
Louis K Pelekane Jr
Hilo HI 96721

Call Sign: KH7ZO
Laurie L Pelekane
Hilo HI 96721

Call Sign: KH7ZX
Delson K Maikui
Hilo HI 96721

Call Sign: NH6KB
Kaumana Wireless Society
Hilo HI 96721

Call Sign: NH7IJ
Rose K Hatori
Hilo HI 96721

Call Sign: NH7LP
Joseph H Day

Hilo HI 96721

Call Sign: NH7NZ
Joshua Arron I Hatori Jr
Hilo HI 96721

Call Sign: NH7O
Ahahui Uweaole Kaumana
Hilo HI 96721

Call Sign: NH7OA
Jonah Nicholas K Retutal
Hilo HI 96721

Call Sign: NH7OD
Sidney E Sellers
Hilo HI 96721

Call Sign: NH7OH
Shirley N Golden
Hilo HI 96721

Call Sign: NH7PC
Gilbert P Barba
Hilo HI 96721

Call Sign: WA6AOG
Philip M Saetveit
Hilo HI 96721

Call Sign: WH6DGN
Ahahui Uweaole Kaumana
Hilo HI 96721

Call Sign: WH6VJ
Michele D Estebon
Hilo HI 96721

Call Sign: WH6VK
Timothy O Bryan
Hilo HI 96721

Call Sign: WH6XM
Robert K Newcomb Jr
Hilo HI 96721

Call Sign: WH7JR
Michael Evans
Hilo HI 96721

Call Sign: WH7UM
Bruce C Mccullough
Hilo HI 96721

Call Sign: KH6HME
Paul D Lieb
Hilo HI 96720-0146

Call Sign: WH6DFT
Crossed Field Antenna
Society
Hilo HI 96720-0146

Call Sign: AH6D
Harrison J Klein
Hilo HI 96720-0934

Call Sign: KH6HAO
Joseph K Hao
Hilo HI 96720-6762

Call Sign: WH6PL
Marvin Cabatic
Hilo HI 96721-5525

Call Sign: KH6AFS
Samuel K Kumukahi
Hilo HI 96720

Call Sign: NH6PI
Carl D Halstead
Hilo HI 96720

Call Sign: WH6AF
Edmund O Breatchel
Hilo HI 96720

Call Sign: WH6BS
Leslie B Ito
Hilo HI 96720

Call Sign: WH6BWO
Kurt A Minges
Hilo HI 96720

Call Sign: WH6BXA
Lynn H Behrens
Hilo HI 96720

Call Sign: KH6ORS
Volcano Amateur Radio
Society
Hilo HI 96721

Call Sign: N6KB
Kenneth D Brown
Hilo HI 96721

Call Sign: WH6CFM
Nancy A Oppenheim
Hilo HI 96721

Call Sign: WH6DO
Susan D Carey
Hilo HI 96721

Call Sign: WH6EV
Wanda I Rivera
Hilo HI 96721

FCC Amateur Radio License in Holualoa

Call Sign: AH6I
Lewis H Strauss
Box 452
Holualoa HI 96725

Call Sign: WH6DWM
Philip H Fernandez
75-796 Hiona St
Holualoa HI 96725

Call Sign: N7SWA
Lutz F Hoffmann

76-5859 Mamalahoa Hwy
Holualoa HI 96725

Call Sign: NH7PY
Joshua Jenkins
75-5259 Mamalahoa Hwy
Apt D
Holualoa HI 96725

Call Sign: WH6WK
Robin C Barrett
75-5326 Mamalahoa Hwy
E
Holualoa HI 96725

Call Sign: AH6GT
Robert L Stoffer
Holualoa HI 96725

Call Sign: KH6BFT
Philip S Matsuyama
Holualoa HI 96725

Call Sign: KH7FU
Shirley J Stoffer
Holualoa HI 96725

Call Sign: N1ZQP
Noah B Salzman
Holualoa HI 96725

Call Sign: NH7CX
Julius L Gunn
Holualoa HI 96725

Call Sign: NH7PU
Kelly W Tatz
Holualoa HI 96725

Call Sign: NH7PV
Richard D Tatz
Holualoa HI 96725

Call Sign: WH6DRM
Craig C Stevenson

Holualoa HI 96725

FCC Amateur Radio License in Honaunau

Call Sign: AH6QH
James H Hall Jr
Honaunau HI 96726

Call Sign: NH6BJ
Linda A Hall
Honaunau HI 96726

Call Sign: NH6QW
Emilio E Dinson Sr
Honaunau HI 96726

Call Sign: WH6WN
David M Medeiros
Honaunau HI 96726

Call Sign: WH6YP
John M Butler
Honaunau HI 96726

Call Sign: KH7VR
Ahreum Kang
6236 Keokea Pl
Honlolulu HI 96825

FCC Amateur Radio License in Honokaa

Call Sign: WB6VBM
Richard V Abbott
44-2019 Kaapahu Rd
Honokaa HI 96727

Call Sign: NH7YE
Roy A Young
44-2719 Kalopa Mauka Rd
Honokaa HI 96727

Call Sign: KF7KAD
Barry J Brick

45-3478 Koa St F
Honokaa HI 96727

Call Sign: NH7QY
Harlan K Seo
45-3312 Ohai St
Honokaa HI 96727

Call Sign: WH6CZJ
Harlan K Seo
45-3312 Ohai St
Honokaa HI 96727

Call Sign: WH6CVW
Gay L Mathews
1 Olapua Pl
Honokaa HI 96727

Call Sign: WB5NVV
Peter J Handleson
Honokaa HI 96727

Call Sign: WH6DLL
Thomas C Avila
Honokaa HI 96727

Call Sign: WH6TE
Sundie Aribal
Honokaa HI 96727

FCC Amateur Radio License in Honolulu

Call Sign: KH7DE
Clifford T Kakuda
2759 1 Booth Rd
Honolulu HI 96813

Call Sign: KH6FGN
Urban H Young
623 10Th Ave
Honolulu HI 96816

Call Sign: KH7CHI
Crissy T Kawamoto

2022 10Th Ave
Honolulu HI 96816-2930

Call Sign: KH7YW
Crissy E Terawaki
2022 10Th Ave
Honolulu HI 96816-2930

Call Sign: WH6CRM
Hiroko Koga
2028 10Th Ave
Honolulu HI 96816

Call Sign: KH7IB
Rodney H Kahalepuna
1436 A 10Th Ave
Honolulu HI 96816

Call Sign: AH6JD
Ryan N Ueoka
1859A 10Th Ave
Honolulu HI 96816

Call Sign: NH6ZO
Sherry F Vann
1941B 10Th Ave
Honolulu HI 96816

Call Sign: KH7PY
Jim V Thurstan
2442 D 10Th Ave
Honolulu HI 96816

Call Sign: WH7JY
Rodney Nishimoto
2378 10Th Ave Pl
Honolulu HI 96816

Call Sign: KH6SO
Kenji Arakaki
536 11Th Ave
Honolulu HI 96816

Call Sign: AH6KP
Melvin Y Ohara

544 11Th Ave
Honolulu HI 96816

Call Sign: NH7IE
Constance J Mc Curdy
740 11Th Ave
Honolulu HI 96816

Call Sign: NH7OL
Thomas A Mccurdy
740 11Th Ave
Honolulu HI 96816

Call Sign: WH6BVC
Karl T Suenishi
949 11Th Ave
Honolulu HI 96816

Call Sign: KE6DPC
Douglas F Quinn
210 11Th St
Honolulu HI 96818-4749

Call Sign: NH6YZ
Takashi Hirose
1142 12Th Ave Radio
Koho
Honolulu HI 96816

Call Sign: KH6AW
David L Lau
925 14Th Ave
Honolulu HI 96816

Call Sign: WH6YI
Terry G M Kwok
1056 14Th Ave
Honolulu HI 96816

Call Sign: WH6CVK
Caroline S Goupil
819 16Th Ave
Honolulu HI 96816

Call Sign: KH6KH

Francis T Blatt
836 17Th Ave
Honolulu HI 96816

Call Sign: KH7JW
Ernest K Lee
856 17Th Ave
Honolulu HI 96816-4104

Call Sign: KH7QQ
Nora H Lee
856 17Th Ave
Honolulu HI 96816-4104

Call Sign: NI1J
Masaru Hirano
C/O Isumi Soma 1041
18Th Ave
Honolulu HI 96816

Call Sign: ND1A
Yoshito Yagi
C/O Isumi Soma 1041
18Th Ave
Honolulu HI 96828

Call Sign: WH7JN
Yoshito Yagi
C/O Isumi Soma 1041
18Th Ave
Honolulu HI 96828

Call Sign: WH7QL
Masaru Hirano
Co Isumi Soma 1041 18Th
Ave
Honolulu HI 96816

Call Sign: NH7QU
Donna M Fullerton
850 19Th Ave
Honolulu HI 96816

Call Sign: KH7RG
Heidi L Jones

204 A 19Th St
Honolulu HI 96818

Call Sign: KH7QH
Donald W Wolfe Jr
204D 19Th St
Honolulu HI 96818

Call Sign: KH6CW
Yau Fai Lum
717 20Th Ave
Honolulu HI 96816

Call Sign: W6RGR
Charles R Holdaway
748 21St Ave
Honolulu HI 96816-4516

Call Sign: NH6DY
Reynold I Watanabe
1109 21St Ave
Honolulu HI 96816

Call Sign: KH7OM
Ryan T Hironaka
912 22Nd Ave
Honolulu HI 96816

Call Sign: WH6CUV
Sarah J Schindele
205 4Th St
Honolulu HI 96818-4937

Call Sign: KH6BLI
Ray K Stone
1003 5Th Ave
Honolulu HI 96816-1607

Call Sign: WH6CAO
Herbert R Loebl
1108 5Th Ave
Honolulu HI 96816

Call Sign: KH7AF
Vernon K Haahanui Jr

1312 7Th Ave
Honolulu HI 96816

Call Sign: KH6AWG
Samuel B Y Lum
1337C 7Th Ave
Honolulu HI 96816

Call Sign: KH7CK
Christopher D Smith
226 8 St
Honolulu HI 96818

Call Sign: NH7UX
Daniel W Sadler
832 8Th Ave
Honolulu HI 96816

Call Sign: WH6CTK
Traci K Ing
1235 8Th Ave
Honolulu HI 96816

Call Sign: KH6FIY
Ronald C Fukuhara
1312 8Th Ave
Honolulu HI 96816-2605

Call Sign: KH6NJ
Dennis F Morisada
1326 8Th Ave
Honolulu HI 96816

Call Sign: KH6API
Clyde A Phillips
839 9Th Ave
Honolulu HI 96816

Call Sign: KH7JX
Bryan L Thompson
839 9Th Ave
Honolulu HI 96816

Call Sign: KH6ERD
Walter T Furuyama

1801 9Th Ave
Honolulu HI 96816-2903

Call Sign: WH6CNJ
Brenden K M Lum
1219A 9Th Ave
Honolulu HI 96816

Call Sign: WH6CNK
Dwight D W Lum
1219A 9Th Ave
Honolulu HI 96816

Call Sign: WH6CNI
Brennan S Hanaoka
1220A 9Th Ave
Honolulu HI 96816

Call Sign: KH7EC
Jeffrey K Spencer
925 9Th Ave Unit A
Honolulu HI 96816

Call Sign: NH6CL
Darren M Oshiro
2139 A 10Th Ave
Honolulu HI 96816

Call Sign: NH7AY
Darren M Oshiro
2139 A 10Th Ave
Honolulu HI 96816

Call Sign: KE6HNZ
Gary Sullivan
643 A 12Th Ave
Honolulu HI 96816

Call Sign: NH7QA
Phillip S Janssen
1003 A 3Rd Ave
Honolulu HI 96816

Call Sign: WH7UN
Kazuo Saito

Co Wakida 2123 A Booth
Rd
Honolulu HI 96813

Call Sign: WH7UO
Mitsuo Noto
Co Wakida 2123 A Booth
Rd
Honolulu HI 96813

Call Sign: KH6ZX
Alfred M Viernes
3159 A Lincoln Ave
Honolulu HI 96816

Call Sign: WH6DQY
Alfred M Viernes
3159 A Lincoln Ave
Honolulu HI 96816

Call Sign: KH7AL
Sittiron Vannarith
3134 A Waialae Ave 204
Honolulu HI 96816

Call Sign: WH6DAF
Robert Korn
F Mariko Slobodben 1702
A Wil Rise
Honolulu HI 96816

Call Sign: NH6NK
Scott W Young
3402 A1A Hinalo Pl
Honolulu HI 96818

Call Sign: WH6BYB
Teddy Lii
1317 Aala St
Honolulu HI 96817

Call Sign: WH7X
Anthony S Akamine
1450 Aala St 404
Honolulu HI 96817

Call Sign: WH6CMO
Linda A Foster
1450 Aala St 705
Honolulu HI 96817

Call Sign: WH6BYD
Stanley K Palama
1342 Aala St Apt 103
Honolulu HI 96817

Call Sign: WH6BYE
Francine M P Palama
1342 Aala St Apt 103
Honolulu HI 96817

Call Sign: WH6RC
Robert K Merce
2467 Aha Aina Pl
Honolulu HI 96821

Call Sign: WH6ZG
Chau P Chrones
910 Ahana St 1002
Honolulu HI 96814

Call Sign: KH6LY
William C Schoneweis
910 Ahana St 408
Honolulu HI 96814

Call Sign: WH7SB
Anthony P Kato
910 Ahana St Apt 1207
Honolulu HI 96814

Call Sign: NH7IV
Kerwin J Stenstrom
2105-A Ahapii Pl
Honolulu HI 96821

Call Sign: WH6CUD
Deanne S Kawamura
3207 Ahinahina Pl
Honolulu HI 96816

Call Sign: KH7YL
Laurel W Soon
5269 Aholehole St
Honolulu HI 96821

Call Sign: NH6CP
Scott C Moura
1920 Ahuahu Pl
Honolulu HI 96819

Call Sign: WH7XG
Trenton Fong
773 Ahukini St
Honolulu HI 96825

Call Sign: NH6ZZ
Keith Johnson
2996 Aia Napuaa Pl 302
Honolulu HI 96818

Call Sign: WH6QL
Bob L Awana
327 Ainahou St
Honolulu HI 96825

Call Sign: NH6DV
Michael K Isobe
7418 Ainanani Pl
Honolulu HI 96825

Call Sign: KH6BYO
Brian T Watanabe
7251 Aipo Pl
Honolulu HI 96825

Call Sign: KH7UO
Brian T Watanabe
7251 Aipo Pl
Honolulu HI 96825

Call Sign: KH7D
Edward M Watanabe
7251 Aipo Pl
Honolulu HI 96825

Call Sign: WH6DWA
Ross T Mukai
3512 Akaka Pl
Honolulu HI 96822

Call Sign: AH6BX
David R Lynn
27 Akilolo St
Honolulu HI 96821

Call Sign: KH6JAO
Howard T Lynn
27 Akilolo St
Honolulu HI 96821-1501

Call Sign: WH6SM
Clement K Chang
1350 Ala Amoamo St
Honolulu HI 96819

Call Sign: WH6BWX
Danny R Mc Williams
1412 Ala Amoamo St
Honolulu HI 96819

Call Sign: WH6CEZ
Wilma R Pinensky
1412 Ala Amoamo St
Honolulu HI 96819

Call Sign: KH6KE
Kathryn Engle
1545 Ala Amoamo St
Honolulu HI 96819

Call Sign: WH6DVQ
Kathryn Engle
1545 Ala Amoamo St
Honolulu HI 96819

Call Sign: WH7BN
John R Maurais
1360 Ala Aolani St
Honolulu HI 96819

Call Sign: WH7QR
Curtis H Nishihara
1231 Ala Aupaka Pl
Honolulu HI 96818

Call Sign: NH6TH
Bryan A Kubo
3448 Ala Haukulu St
Honolulu HI 96818

Call Sign: WH6CXJ
Vittal K Saggare
3477 Ala Haukulu St
Honolulu HI 96818

Call Sign: KH6IB
Randolph H C Young
3402 Ala Hinalo Pl
Honolulu HI 96818

Call Sign: WH6BUJ
Angelita B Young
3402 Ala Hinalo Pl
Honolulu HI 96818

Call Sign: WH6CYZ
Mae K Uehara
3402 Ala Hinalo Pl
Honolulu HI 96818

Call Sign: WH6CZA
Nikki A Young
3402 Ala Hinalo Pl
Honolulu HI 96818

Call Sign: WH6DAW
Lynn N Uehara
3402 Ala Hinalo Pl
Honolulu HI 96818

Call Sign: WH6BTS
Melvin T Kai Jr
1335 Ala Hoku Pl
Honolulu HI 96819

Call Sign: KH6GNX
Clemente Castro
1342 Ala Hoku Pl
Honolulu HI 96819

Call Sign: WH6XP
Ryan K Kamae
1343 Ala Hoku Pl
Honolulu HI 96819

Call Sign: KB0DPH
Michael T Kimball
3230 Ala Ilima 503
Honolulu HI 96818

Call Sign: KH7MU
Dennis N Egge
2920 Ala Ilima Apt 703
Honolulu HI 96818

Call Sign: KH6JO
James J Higa
3458 Ala Ilima St
Honolulu HI 96818

Call Sign: NH6RL
Charleen M Hammond
3161 Ala Ilima St 105
Honolulu HI 96818

Call Sign: NH6RN
Kimberly P Caporoz
3161 Ala Ilima St 105
Honolulu HI 96818

Call Sign: NE7SO
Nelson Toda
3161 Ala Ilima St 815
Honolulu HI 96818

Call Sign: WH6DKV
Nelson M Toda
3161 Ala Ilima St 815
Honolulu HI 96818

Call Sign: WH6DJT
Michael A Tenney
3030 Ala Ilima St 905
Honolulu HI 96818

Call Sign: KA7AZA
Nancy K Wilimek
2976 Ala Ilima St Apt 103
Honolulu HI 96818

Call Sign: WH6BNS
Jennifer L Bartolome
3121 Ala Ilima St Apt 211
Honolulu HI 96818

Call Sign: AH6EK
Alan C Q Jay
2888 Ala Ilima St Apt
2912
Honolulu HI 96818

Call Sign: KH7HK
Terance K Morimoto
2888 Ala Ilima St Apt 901
Honolulu HI 96818

Call Sign: KH7JB
Trina O Diorec
3215 Ala Ilima St Bph4
Honolulu HI 96818

Call Sign: KH7JC
Margery M Macadangdang
3215 Ala Ilima St Bph4
Honolulu HI 96818

Call Sign: WH6QR
Robin J Ono
1001 Ala Kapua St
Honolulu HI 96818

Call Sign: KB7ZSI
Lisa C Oshiro
1332 Ala Kapuna St 406

Honolulu HI 96819

Honolulu HI 96818-2311

Honolulu HI 96815

Call Sign: NH6CR
William M Wong
3227 Ala Laulani St
Honolulu HI 96818

Call Sign: NH7EJ
Thomas R Thornton
1005 Ala Lilikoi St
Honolulu HI 96818

Call Sign: WH6CPU
Vickie D Bucher
1784 Ala Moana 54
Honolulu HI 96815

Call Sign: NH7AZ
William M Wong
3227 Ala Laulani St
Honolulu HI 96818

Call Sign: NH7YY
Gail A Higashi
1064 Ala Lilikoi St
Honolulu HI 96818

Call Sign: WH6CPV
Kenneth E Bucher
1784 Ala Moana 54
Honolulu HI 96815

Call Sign: WH6ZT
Stephen L Wong
3227 Ala Laulani St
Honolulu HI 96818

Call Sign: AH6IG
Alfred Coelho
1405 Ala Mahamoe
Honolulu HI 96819

Call Sign: KD7FWF
Mark J Meyer
1741 Ala Moana Bl 118
Honolulu HI 96815

Call Sign: AH6QG
Francis K H Fong
3322 Ala Lehua Pl
Honolulu HI 96818

Call Sign: WH6CMH
Kevin J Lieders
1405 Ala Mahamoe Apt A
Honolulu HI 96819

Call Sign: KD7CBK
Gayle K Hughes
1777 Ala Moana Blv Ste
107 Box 77
Honolulu HI 96815

Call Sign: AH7FF
Francis K H Fong
3322 Ala Lehua Pl
Honolulu HI 96818

Call Sign: WH6UG
Melvin F Inouye
1575 Ala Mahamoe B
Honolulu HI 96819

Call Sign: KH6CE
Frank L Fullaway
1600 Ala Moana Blvd
Honolulu HI 96815

Call Sign: KH7VF
Velma K H Fong
3322 Ala Lehua Pl
Honolulu HI 96818

Call Sign: AH6EH
Raymond M Kitashiro
1373 Ala Mahamoe St
Honolulu HI 96819-1762

Call Sign: KK7JW
Bill T Andrews
1651 Ala Moana Blvd
Honolulu HI 96815

Call Sign: WH6F
Francis K H Fong
3322 Ala Lehua Pl
Honolulu HI 96818

Call Sign: WH6TP
Robin M Inouye
1575 Ala Mahamoe St
Honolulu HI 96819

Call Sign: WH6CKN
Peter W Marshall
1651 Ala Moana Blvd
Honolulu HI 96815

Call Sign: KH6BWT
Wallace K Izuo
960 Ala Lehua St
Honolulu HI 96818-2302

Call Sign: KH7FT
William K P Fong
2012 Ala Mahamoe St
Honolulu HI 96819

Call Sign: KH7GR
Jeffery V Barrett
1741 Ala Moana Blvd
Honolulu HI 96815

Call Sign: KH7AK
Antonio R Bacungan Jr
1066 Ala Lilikoi

Call Sign: KH6UM
Michael E Simpson
1778 Ala Moana 3005

Call Sign: KH7GS
Aaron M Barrett

1741 Ala Moana Blvd
Honolulu HI 96815

Call Sign: KH7GT
Jeffery D Barrett
1741 Ala Moana Blvd
Honolulu HI 96815

Call Sign: KH7GU
Constance D Barrett
1741 Ala Moana Blvd
Honolulu HI 96815

Call Sign: WH6CKM
Ethel C Marshall
1851 Ala Moana Blvd
Honolulu HI 96815

Call Sign: NH7AE
Robert W Hinman
1739 C Ala Moana Blvd
Honolulu HI 96815

Call Sign: KH7GG
Gail D Ashburn
1739 C Ala Moana Blvd
Honolulu HI 96815

Call Sign: NH6AM
Robert W Hinman
1739 C Ala Moana Blvd
Honolulu HI 96815

Call Sign: WH6CKD
Richard A Witte
1739 C Ala Moana Blvd
Honolulu HI 96815

Call Sign: KH6GGD
Keith W Kibler
1739 C Ala Moana Blvd
Honolulu HI 96815

Call Sign: NH6BZ
Douglas C Vann

1739 C Ala Moana Blvd
Honolulu HI 96815

Call Sign: WH6CKS
William B Paulk
1739 C Ala Moana Blvd
Honolulu HI 96815

Call Sign: KE6ZVT
James S Donaldson
1739 C Ala Moana Blvd
Honolulu HI 96815-1492

Call Sign: NH6MB
Roger C Florent
Harbour Master 1651 Ala
Moana Blvd
Honolulu HI 96815

Call Sign: NH6BL
Maryann D Barnett
1676 Ala Moana Blvd
1004
Honolulu HI 96815

Call Sign: NH7AP
Maryann D Barnett
1676 Ala Moana Blvd
1004
Honolulu HI 96815

Call Sign: KH7VX
Tracy Wang
1676 Ala Moana Blvd
1202
Honolulu HI 96815

Call Sign: WH6NR
James W Dolan
1720 Ala Moana Blvd
1206A
Honolulu HI 96815

Call Sign: WH6V
Wayne R Huffman

1946 Ala Moana Blvd 121
Honolulu HI 96815-1898

Call Sign: KH7CQ
Lawrence M Hoover
1741 Ala Moana Blvd 14
Honolulu HI 96815

Call Sign: AH6HM
Neal T Pinckney
1650 Ala Moana Blvd
1601
Honolulu HI 96815-1411

Call Sign: KH6QX
William E Orenstein
1778 Ala Moana Blvd
1619
Honolulu HI 96815

Call Sign: WH7PU
Alexander G Stengel
1778 Ala Moana Blvd
1619
Honolulu HI 96815

Call Sign: WY5C
James R Cypert
1650 Ala Moana Blvd
1709
Honolulu HI 96815

Call Sign: W3GEJ
Paul S Bear
1720 Ala Moana Blvd
208B
Honolulu HI 96815

Call Sign: WH7MW
Jimmy L Lagunero
1350 Ala Moana Blvd
2607
Honolulu HI 96814

Call Sign: WH6QZ

Michael L Wagner
1741 Ala Moana Blvd 28
Honolulu HI 96815

Call Sign: WH6DVR
Charles N Yoon
1350 Ala Moana Blvd
2903
Honolulu HI 96814

Call Sign: WH6DTM
Jeffrey A Naus
1330 Ala Moana Blvd
3304
Honolulu HI 96814

Call Sign: KH7GO
Carol L Freebairn
1741 Ala Moana Blvd 54
Honolulu HI 96815

Call Sign: WA6VMS
Olaf Seyler
1741 Ala Moana Blvd 65
Honolulu HI 96815

Call Sign: WH6FO
Richard G Messier
1741 Ala Moana Blvd 67
Honolulu HI 96815

Call Sign: AH6OE
Linda M Darby
1741 Ala Moana Blvd 7
Honolulu HI 96815

Call Sign: NH7SH
Shawn I Needham
1920 Ala Moana Blvd 702
Honolulu HI 96815

Call Sign: AH6SP
Lawrence G Sue
1676 Ala Moana Blvd 705
Honolulu HI 96815-1441

Call Sign: KC7NZ
Lawrence G Sue
1676 Ala Moana Blvd 705
Honolulu HI 96815-1441

Call Sign: KH7IY
Charity A Palmatier
1741 Ala Moana Blvd 76
Honolulu HI 96815

Call Sign: N7LRW
Lester K Parsons
1741 Ala Moana Blvd 82
Honolulu HI 96815

Call Sign: WH6CKE
Iwo P Zembal
1651 Ala Moana Blvd Ala
Wai Boat Hb
Honolulu HI 96815

Call Sign: KE6GRG
Ricardo M Bautista Jr
1720 Ala Moana Blvd Apt
1204B
Honolulu HI 96815

Call Sign: WH6DVX
Sarah Beth Delgado
1777 Ala Moana Blvd Apt
1423
Honolulu HI 96815

Call Sign: KO6KW
Rafael Martinez
1684 Ala Moana Blvd Apt
152
Honolulu HI 96815

Call Sign: WH7TS
Ramona R Fillman
1350 Ala Moana Blvd Apt
2908
Honolulu HI 96814

Call Sign: N8LIV
Charles D Henley Sr
1765 Ala Moana Blvd Apt
384
Honolulu HI 96815

Call Sign: KA2CEH
Victor Hilf
1720 Ala Moana Blvd Apt
B804
Honolulu HI 96815

Call Sign: KH7JK
Charles R Erickson
1741 Ala Moana Blvd Box
72
Honolulu HI 96815

Call Sign: KC0END
Peter D Leary
300 Ala Moana Blvd Rm 5
231
Honolulu HI 96850

Call Sign: AA7WI
Kieran J O Connor
1777 Ala Moana Blvd Ste
107148
Honolulu HI 96815

Call Sign: KH7QP
Carol R Nord
1741 Ala Moana Blvd Unit
7
Honolulu HI 96815

Call Sign: KH7WI
Janice Du Bois
1741 Ala Moana Blvd Unit
7
Honolulu HI 96815

Call Sign: KH7ZB
Charles L Snyder

1741 Ala Moana Blvd Unit 7
Honolulu HI 96815

Call Sign: NH6EA
Charles L Snyder
1741 Ala Moana Blvd Unit 7
Honolulu HI 96815

Call Sign: WH6CRE
Debra C Baker
1651 Ala Moana Fuel Dock
Honolulu HI 96815

Call Sign: KH7IX
Thomas M Palmatier
1471 Ala Moona Blvd 76
Honolulu HI 96815

Call Sign: WH6BNG
Brenty A Vaughan
990 Ala Nanala St 10A
Honolulu HI 96818

Call Sign: WH7XY
Bryce Tano
909 Ala Nanala St 1602
Honolulu HI 96818

Call Sign: WH7US
Josephine M K Huddy
990 Ala Nanala St 2 B
Honolulu HI 96818

Call Sign: AH6BC
Eric K P Chang
990 Ala Nanala St Apt 7A
Honolulu HI 96818

Call Sign: WH7ZS
Gregory C Lichy
3045 Ala Napuaa Pl 1003
Honolulu HI 96818

Call Sign: KC7SJC
Stefan N Bishay
3045 Ala Napuaa Pl 1408
Honolulu HI 96818

Call Sign: KH7SC
Mei Li Greenleaf
3020 Ala Napuaa Pl 202
Honolulu HI 96818

Call Sign: NH6PQ
Wayne O Greenleaf
3020 Ala Napuaa Pl 202
Honolulu HI 96818

Call Sign: WH6DIG
Hawaii Private Repeater Network
3020 Ala Napuaa Pl 202
Honolulu HI 96818

Call Sign: WH6DJS
Chad Morimoto
3033 Ala Napuaa Pl 205
Honolulu HI 96818

Call Sign: NH6KC
Jack A Cotner
1160 Ala Napunani 1404
Honolulu HI 96818

Call Sign: WH6CEM
Curtis E Lum
1601 Ala Napunani St
Honolulu HI 96818

Call Sign: KH7LW
Fiafia S Sataraka
1015 Ala Napunani St 302
Honolulu HI 96818

Call Sign: NH6PN
Evan H Miyaki
1015 Ala Napunani St 702

Honolulu HI 96818

Call Sign: WH6DJQ
Robert K Fujii
1099 Ala Napunani St 802
Honolulu HI 96818

Call Sign: WH6QF
Pankaj Bhanot
1080 Ala Napunani St Apt 406
Honolulu HI 96818-1787

Call Sign: NH6TC
Arlene M Lacad
1121 Ala Napunani St Ph 1
Honolulu HI 96818

Call Sign: KH7DP
Lynn T Nakamura
1241 Ala Pili Lp
Honolulu HI 96818

Call Sign: KH6BH
Brent M Hirata
3075 Ala Poha 1909
Honolulu HI 96818

Call Sign: NH7F
Arthur R Von Ploennies
3054 Ala Poha Pl 1904
Honolulu HI 96818

Call Sign: WH6DJH
Clifford Kaahanui
3075 Ala Poha Pl 204
Honolulu HI 96818

Call Sign: WH6DMB
Ikaika T Kaahanu
3075 Ala Poha Pl 204
Honolulu HI 96818

Call Sign: KH7QB
Justine B Mattos

2972 Ala Punene Pl
Honolulu HI 96818

Call Sign: NH6TJ
Michael C Steward
2609 Ala Wai Blvd 1004
Honolulu HI 96815

Call Sign: NH6VF
Alvin F Neal
2211 Ala Wai Blvd 1110
Honolulu HI 96815

Call Sign: WH6DRH
Ophemia Perez-Hoffman
2085 Ala Wai Blvd 122
Honolulu HI 96815

Call Sign: NH6XT
Bob W Brown Sr
2533 Ala Wai Blvd 204
Honolulu HI 96815

Call Sign: WH7WN
Kimberly M Yamahara
1717 Ala Wai Blvd 2405
Honolulu HI 96815

Call Sign: KH6AQZ
Gail D Chamberlain
2611 Ala Wai Blvd 708
Honolulu HI 96815

Call Sign: KH6CB
William W Chamberlain
2611 Ala Wai Blvd 708
Honolulu HI 96815

Call Sign: KD7VZG
Eric R Ruuhela
2121 Ala Wai Blvd Apt
1806
Honolulu HI 96815

Call Sign: KH6DAR

Kenneth K Higa
2115 Ala Wai Blvd Apt
203
Honolulu HI 96815-2202

Call Sign: WH6AY
Laura L P Mc Intyre
1645 Ala Wai Blvd Apt
Ph4
Honolulu HI 96815

Call Sign: WH6AD
Andrew J Mc Intyre
1645 Ala Wai Blvd Ph4
Honolulu HI 96815

Call Sign: KH6XR
Michael H C Chun
2076 Alaeloa St
Honolulu HI 96821

Call Sign: KH6XL
Alwynne Rose
1860 Alamoana Blvd 1509
Honolulu HI 96815

Call Sign: WH6DS
Ron C Du Bois
1741 Alamoana Blvd 7
Honolulu HI 96815

Call Sign: KH7OH
Keka R Ichinose
866 Alamuku St
Honolulu HI 96821-1712

Call Sign: KH6ETG
Gordon W S Loui
3263 Alani Dr
Honolulu HI 96822

Call Sign: KH6GL
Gordon W S Loui
3263 Alani Dr
Honolulu HI 96822

Call Sign: KH7LU
Chris K Green
3323 Alani Dr
Honolulu HI 96822

Call Sign: W6UZC
Noah M Jung
3523 Alani Dr
Honolulu HI 96822

Call Sign: WH6DNZ
Noah M Jung
3523 Alani Dr
Honolulu HI 96822

Call Sign: WH6DOA
Rocxanne M Jung
3523 Alani Dr
Honolulu HI 96822

Call Sign: KH7CV
Dale A Gardner
1326 Alapai St 403
Honolulu HI 96813

Call Sign: KH7RH
Robert K Johnston
3054 Alapoha Pl Apt 205
Honolulu HI 96818

Call Sign: NH7TU
Richard S Yee
2532 Alaula Way
Honolulu HI 96822

Call Sign: KH7TX
Terrence K Teruya
1849 Alaweo St
Honolulu HI 96821

Call Sign: N6LQQ
Michael C Parsons
1893 Alaweo St
Honolulu HI 96821

Call Sign: WH6DOD
Monica M Umeda
3026 Alencastre Pl
Honolulu HI 96816

Call Sign: WH6CSC
Naiad Wong
1487 Alencastre St
Honolulu HI 96816

Call Sign: WH6CTZ
Kelly A Yuen
1728 Alencastre St
Honolulu HI 96816

Call Sign: KH6KC
Richard K Takemoto
1829 Alewa Dr
Honolulu HI 96817

Call Sign: WH6CYV
Gaylin M Yee
1446 Alewa Dr Apt D
Honolulu HI 96817-1265

Call Sign: NH6AP
Sally S Vergara Clement
1521 Alexander St 501
Honolulu HI 96822

Call Sign: AH6HI
Roy K Nakata Mr
1505 Alexander St 902
Honolulu HI 96822

Call Sign: AH7HI
Aloha Dx Club
1505 Alexander St 902
Honolulu HI 96822

Call Sign: KH6HKL
Roy K Nakata
1505 Alexander St 902
Honolulu HI 96822

Call Sign: WH6DNG
Ryan K Nakata
1505 Alexander St 902
Honolulu HI 96822

Call Sign: WH6ZQ
Gail N Nakata
1505 Alexander St 902
Honolulu HI 96822

Call Sign: KH6BX
Frank J Bishop
2121 Algaroba St Apt
1205
Honolulu HI 96826

Call Sign: WH6JZ
Joel U Mc Farland
2092 Aliali Pl
Honolulu HI 96821

Call Sign: KH7LA
Edward P Funtanilla
3448 Aliamanu St
Honolulu HI 96818

Call Sign: WH6DJU
Brian C Wong
4521 Aliikoa St
Honolulu HI 96821

Call Sign: WH6DQE
Esther F Lau
3162 Alika Ave
Honolulu HI 96817

Call Sign: NH6ZG
Ronald L Fox
7305A Aloalo St
Honolulu HI 96818

Call Sign: WH7ND
Tracy K Young
3455 Alohea Ave

Honolulu HI 96816

Call Sign: WH6CQC
Diane J Canada
3671 Alohea Ave
Honolulu HI 96816

Call Sign: KH6IPE
Kenneth R Burd
1651 Alu Moanu Blvd Box
122
Honolulu HI 96810-0122

Call Sign: KH6AEK
William Amoroso
1809 Alu Pl
Honolulu HI 96819-3602

Call Sign: AH6RZ
Shoji Takeda
747 Amana St 1217
Honolulu HI 96814

Call Sign: KH7MI
Violeta D Labuguen
1529 Amelia St
Honolulu HI 96819

Call Sign: WH7IE
Scott Seu
4752 Analii St
Honolulu HI 96821

Call Sign: KH6WG
Frank A Fung Jr
189 Anapalau St
Honolulu HI 96825

Call Sign: WH6CQV
Sora Lee
1638 Anapuni St J
Honolulu HI 96822

Call Sign: WH7AL

Yesid Elaine Y Romero
Romero
1718 Anapuni St203
Honolulu HI 96822

Call Sign: KH7UI
Colin A Ybarra
787 Anderson Cir
Honolulu HI 96818

Call Sign: KH7UG
Zac Coe
806 Anderson Cir
Honolulu HI 96818

Call Sign: NH7ZM
Jerry M Neumann Jr
2105 Anianiku St
Honolulu HI 96813

Call Sign: AK0P
Adam B Kanis
3357 Anoai Pl
Honolulu HI 96822

Call Sign: WH6M
Adam B Kanis
3357 Anoai Pl
Honolulu HI 96822

Call Sign: KH7MH
Louise B Piper
455 Anolani St
Honolulu HI 96821

Call Sign: KH6Z
Norman S Murakami
3746 Anuhea St
Honolulu HI 96816-3802

Call Sign: WH6DLB
Johnnuel D Alves
2660 Anuu Pl
Honolulu HI 96819

Call Sign: NH7NF
Charles O Bellman Jr
57 Arizona Memorial Dr
105
Honolulu HI 96818

Call Sign: KH7OW
Kimberly L Bean
57 Arizona Memorial Dr
114
Honolulu HI 96818

Call Sign: KH7OT
Mackey A Scott
57 Arizona Memorial Dr
123
Honolulu HI 96818

Call Sign: NH7NE
William B Gentle
57 Arizona Memorial Dr
133
Honolulu HI 96818

Call Sign: KH6CKJ
Leonard Withington Jr
2107 Atheaton Rd
Honolulu HI 96822-2138

Call Sign: KH6ION
Stanley N De Rieux
419 Atkinson Dr 1406
Honolulu HI 96814-4710

Call Sign: KH6HEP
James W Welch
419A Atkinson Dr Apt
1001
Honolulu HI 96814

Call Sign: WH6DAB
Feliciano A Vea
419A Atkinson Dr Ste 404
Honolulu HI 96814

Call Sign: WH6DDS
Kure Dx Society
1142 Auahi St 3500
Honolulu HI 96814

Call Sign: N6LBW
Judy A Knutson
1142 Auahi St Ste 3013
Honolulu HI 96814

Call Sign: WH6VQ
John N Spadaro
4734 Aukai Ave
Honolulu HI 96816

Call Sign: WH6UP
James T Zukemura
1516 Auld Ln
Honolulu HI 96817

Call Sign: NH7VD
Sydney N Hutson
81 Aupaka St
Honolulu HI 96818

Call Sign: NH6NI
Fred K Adams
2204 Aupuni St
Honolulu HI 96817

Call Sign: NH6PA
Linda R Balazs
992A Awaawaanoa Pl
Honolulu HI 96825

Call Sign: WH6BLP
George C Balazs
992A Awaawaanoa Pl
Honolulu HI 96825

Call Sign: WH6BLQ
George H Balazs
992A Awaawaanoa Pl
Honolulu HI 96825

Call Sign: WH6CAG
Herman Y M Leong
1417 B1 Alexander St
Honolulu HI 96822

Call Sign: WH7IM
Tasker I Tanaka
329 Bates St
Honolulu HI 96817-2339

Call Sign: KH7BI
Steven M Asaumi
409 Bates St
Honolulu HI 96817

Call Sign: KG4HZF
Sonny K Makalena
266 Bauhina Pl 101
Honolulu HI 96818-6610

Call Sign: AH6GV
Glenn K Sakimura
1834 Bertram St
Honolulu HI 96816

Call Sign: NH6EM
Jean N Sakimura
1834 Bertram St
Honolulu HI 96816

Call Sign: KH6KY
Clarence K B Fong
1934 Bertram St
Honolulu HI 96816

Call Sign: NH6DH
Herbert Kaanehe
3619A Bethshan Rd
Honolulu HI 96816

Call Sign: WH6CPE
Reginald P Fong
2047 Bingham St
Honolulu HI 96826

Call Sign: WH6DBA
George W Lecompte
1164 Bishop St 124
Honolulu HI 96813

Call Sign: KC7PLG
Randy B Collier
1050 Bishop St 269
Honolulu HI 96813

Call Sign: KH7UV
Caryn K Young
1001 Bishop St 370
Honolulu HI 96813

Call Sign: AH6QK
Richard Hacker
1188 Bishop St Apt 1311
Honolulu HI 96813

Call Sign: KH7QR
Larry L Gilbert
1001 Bishop St Pauahi
2300
Honolulu HI 96813

Call Sign: WH7LS
Aaron C Savage
1050 Bishop St Pmb 102
Honolulu HI 96813

Call Sign: WH6CMU
Jay A Shinn
1164 Bishop St Ste 124
Honolulu HI 96813

Call Sign: KL7USI
U S Islands Last Frontier
Arc
1132 Bishop St Ste 2101
Honolulu HI 96813

Call Sign: KH7JU
George S Michalski
1188 Bishop St Ste 2804

Honolulu HI 96813-3311

Call Sign: KH7TZ
Terence Q Young
1003 Bishop St Ste 370
Honolulu HI 96813

Call Sign: NH7YA
Marie P Luke
4033 Black Point Rd
Honolulu HI 96816

Call Sign: WH6VZ
Linda A Holt
4106 Black Point Rd
Honolulu HI 96816

Call Sign: WH6WC
Larry K Holt
4106 Black Point Rd
Honolulu HI 96816

Call Sign: WH6DC
Michael G Clark
2173 Booth Rd
Honolulu HI 96813

Call Sign: WH6CEN
Jonathan P Briones
2730 Booth Rd
Honolulu HI 96813

Call Sign: WH6DVZ
Edward J Minor
2453 Booth Rd Unit A
Honolulu HI 96813

Call Sign: WH7ZV
Emily L Sumbad
4725 Bougainville Dr 297
Honolulu HI 96818

Call Sign: WH6DID
Aloha Amateur Radio
Club

Box 22471
Honolulu HI 96823

C/O Mr Soma
Honolulu HI 96828

Call Sign: WH7ZA
Kazuhiro Umemura
2234 Citon St L
Honolulu HI 96826

Call Sign: AH6KC
Robert D Osterland
Box 22812
Honolulu HI 96823

Call Sign: W8AYD
Masatoshi Shishido
C/O Soma
Honolulu HI 96828

Call Sign: AH6TT
Yoichi Hasegawa
C/O Etsuko Addison 2234
Citon St L
Honolulu HI 96826

Call Sign: WA4CJX
Earl B Gordon
Box 26132
Honolulu HI 96825-6132

Call Sign: WH6DLE
Masatoshi Shishido
C/O Soma
Honolulu HI 96828

Call Sign: WH6DWZ
Tsuneo Kan
C/O Etsuko Addison 2234
Citon St L
Honolulu HI 96826

Call Sign: KH6IPC
Paul D Connors
Box 8933
Honolulu HI 96830

Call Sign: WH6CTL
Linh T Tran
3240 Castle St
Honolulu HI 96815

Call Sign: WH7XL
Yoichi Hasegawa
C/O Etsuko Addison 2234
Citon St L
Honolulu HI 96826

Call Sign: WH7OT
Iameli I Kaio
129A Boyd Ln
Honolulu HI 96813

Call Sign: NH6PL
Jerry J Funakura
3134 Catherine St
Honolulu HI 96815

Call Sign: NH7XW
Jake N Lee
1425 Brigham St
Honolulu HI 96817

Call Sign: NH6UO
Jonalynn L Sing
3134 Catherine St
Honolulu HI 96815

Call Sign: WH6BXU
Collin G L Sin
1729B Citron St
Honolulu HI 96826

Call Sign: WH6DOB
Toy Lim
3126 Brokaw St Apt A
Honolulu HI 96815

Call Sign: AH6TV
Masahiro Kaneko
C/O Etsuko Addison 2234
Citon St Apt L
Honolulu HI 96826

Call Sign: KE7MW
John D Cummings
2222 Citron St Apt 1003
Honolulu HI 96826

Call Sign: WH6CTF
Ka Man Cheung
1290 C D Maunakea St
Honolulu HI 96817

Call Sign: WH6DVT
Masahiro Kaneko
C/O Etsuko Addison 2234
Citon St Apt L
Honolulu HI 96826

Call Sign: NH7SJ
Thomas J Mizuno
1617 Clark St 802
Honolulu HI 96822

Call Sign: AH6CQ
Elmer M F Liu
2168 C Maha Pl
Honolulu HI 96819

Call Sign: WH7C
Kazuhiro Umemura
2234 Citon St L
Honolulu HI 96826

Call Sign: KF6YTS
Michael W Foy
2423 Cleghorn St 101
Honolulu HI 96815

Call Sign: AH6SE
Hideki Yabe

Call Sign: AH6FP
David J Chamberlin III

2432 Cleghorn St Apt 302
Honolulu HI 96815

Call Sign: AC5AZ
Donald W Eubank
119 Cocos Pl 101
Honolulu HI 96818

Call Sign: WH6XI
Blaine Southward
A1902 -575 Cooke St
Honolulu HI 96813

Call Sign: WH6DST
Barbara K Shirland
575 Cooke St Pmb 1615
Honolulu HI 96813

Call Sign: WH6DKW
Charles Noyes
575 Cooke St Ste A 1510
Honolulu HI 96813

Call Sign: WH6DKC
Julie B Noyes
575 Cooke St Ste A 1510
Honolulu HI 96813

Call Sign: KH7UK
Todd N Kawamoto
575 Cooke St Ste A Pmb
2215
Honolulu HI 96813-5274

Call Sign: WH6BUC
Sherilyn C Yim
826 Coolidge Ct 1
Honolulu HI 96826

Call Sign: WH7IH
Raymond M Tanabe
2525 Correa Rd Ste 250
Honolulu HI 96822

Call Sign: AH6T

Harvey J Rhinelander
21 Craigside Pl 6C
Honolulu HI 96817

Call Sign: KH6HNU
Samuel P J Chiang
928 Crater Pl
Honolulu HI 96816

Call Sign: KH6XL
Darrell R Omuro
876 Curtis St 1509
Honolulu HI 96813

Call Sign: WH6DUF
Taylor K Omuro
876 Curtis St 1509
Honolulu HI 96813

Call Sign: WH7NA
Christen M Omuro
876 Curtis St 1509
Honolulu HI 96813

Call Sign: WH7NB
Darrell R Omuro
876 Curtis St 1509
Honolulu HI 96813

Call Sign: WH7RB
Trenton K Omuro
876 Curtis St 1509
Honolulu HI 96813

Call Sign: WH7OS
Tony V Giles
876 Curtis St Apt 3203
Honolulu HI 96813

Call Sign: KH7UQ
Teodorico S Candaliza III
1994 D Kilmer Lp
Honolulu HI 96818

Call Sign: KH7UR

Teodorico S Candaliza Jr
1994 D Kilmer Lp
Honolulu HI 96818

Call Sign: KH7US
Mary Jean M Mabaquiao
1994 D Kilmer Lp
Honolulu HI 96818

Call Sign: AH6PM
Joeriza M Nasis
2047 D Kukui Pl
Honolulu HI 96818

Call Sign: KH7OD
Jamie Riza M Nasis
2047 D Kukui Pl
Honolulu HI 96818

Call Sign: KH7OE
Jimmy M Nasis
2047 D Kukui Pl
Honolulu HI 96818

Call Sign: KH7OF
Jonathan M Nasis
2047 D Kukui Pl
Honolulu HI 96818

Call Sign: KH7SF
Darryl C Nasis
2047 D Kukui Pl
Honolulu HI 96818

Call Sign: AH6LT
Raymond A Moody
2440 Date Apt 402
Honolulu HI 96826

Call Sign: KH7GL
John C Calhoun
2924 Date St
Honolulu HI 96816-1120

Call Sign: WH6TO

Dorothy T Wheeler
Apt 3005 2525 Date St
Honolulu HI 96826

Call Sign: NH7OM
Robert W Marshman
2542 Date St 1002
Honolulu HI 96826

Call Sign: NH7RM
Norihito Ueki
2522 Date St 1205
Honolulu HI 96826

Call Sign: NH7ZD
Stephen G Hall
2563 Date St 128
Honolulu HI 96826-5446

Call Sign: WH6SY
Mary Jo Noonan
2100 Date St 2201
Honolulu HI 96826

Call Sign: NH7FR
Richard M Robertson
2916 Date St 25K
Honolulu HI 96816

Call Sign: WH6OD
David Y Tasaka
2525 Date St 3005
Honolulu HI 96826

Call Sign: NH6PY
Ralph H Toyama
2440 Date St 306
Honolulu HI 96826

Call Sign: NH7SR
Michael J Hebert
2450 Date St 4
Honolulu HI 96826

Call Sign: NH6QH

Manuel E Punzal Jr
2620 Date St 5
Honolulu HI 96826

Call Sign: WH7BL
Gloria L Hall
2563 Date St Apt 128
Honolulu HI 96826

Call Sign: WH7BTE
Gloria L Hall
2563 Date St Apt 128
Honolulu HI 96826

Call Sign: KH6FR
Francis S Rellesiva
1816 Democrat St Apt 6
Honolulu HI 96819

Call Sign: NH2HU
Francis S Rellesiva
1816 Democrat St Apt 6
Honolulu HI 96819

Call Sign: N6ZAB
Christopher E Mullin Sr
3715 Diamond Head Cir
Honolulu HI 96815-4424

Call Sign: KH6BKB
George Torres Sr
3040 Diamond Head Rd
Honolulu HI 96815

Call Sign: WH6ARC
Aloha Amateur Radio
Club
4155 Diamond Head Rd
Honolulu HI 96816

Call Sign: NH7ZY
Julie H Greenly
3949 Diamond Head Rd
Civil Defense Division
Honolulu HI 96816

Call Sign: WH6EH
Edwin M Alcoran
1470 Dillingham Apt 311B
Honolulu HI 96817-4821

Call Sign: AH6IA
Jack E Hargraves
989 Dillingham Blvd
Honolulu HI 96817

Call Sign: KH6BBH
Blood Bank Of Hawaii
2043 Dillingham Blvd
Honolulu HI 96819

Call Sign: KH7JD
Cayton Alcoran
1470 Dillingham Blvd
311B
Honolulu HI 96817

Call Sign: KH7JG
Daisy S Alcoran
1470 Dillingham Blvd
311B
Honolulu HI 96817

Call Sign: KH7IQ
Gilbert C Mabuti
1514 Dillingham Blvd 316
Honolulu HI 96817

Call Sign: KH7OB
Bethie Ann K Alcoran
1470 Dillingham Blvd Apt
311B
Honolulu HI 96817

Call Sign: WX0H
Hideki Takayasu
1735 Dole St 203
Honolulu HI 96822

Call Sign: WH6BUB

Theodore J Fabella
1727 Dole St 3
Honolulu HI 96822

Call Sign: NH6QZ
Michael S Takahashi
1624 Dole St 701
Honolulu HI 96822

Call Sign: KH6IMJ
David Dengler
1645 Dole St Apt 403
Honolulu HI 96822-4854

Call Sign: KH7DD
David Dengler
1645 Dole St Apt 403
Honolulu HI 96822-4854

Call Sign: W6POI
David Dengler
1645 Dole St Apt 403
Honolulu HI 96822-4854

Call Sign: NS5O
Jason P Halbert
2583 Dole St Apt 884B
Honolulu HI 96822-2381

Call Sign: AH7I
Robert M Duckworth
2640 Dole St C131
Honolulu HI 96822

Call Sign: WH6TJ
Caroline V Riedl
1438A Dominis St
Honolulu HI 96822

Call Sign: KH6JNX
Charles I Agena
1438C Dominis St
Honolulu HI 96822

Call Sign: WH6DLW

Lara E Payne
2828 Dow St
Honolulu HI 96817

Call Sign: WH6ZN
Amod A Sarnaik
72 Dowsett Ave
Honolulu HI 96817

Call Sign: WH6ZO
Catherine J Walters
72 Dowsett Ave
Honolulu HI 96817

Call Sign: KB9QFE
Casey W Brown
2353 E Gemini Ave
Honolulu HI 96818

Call Sign: WH6CED
Thomas R Chesney
3145 E Kalihi
Honolulu HI 96819

Call Sign: KH7EG
Sidney M Veal
1963 E Koelsch Cir
Honolulu HI 96818

Call Sign: KH7GI
Laurence E Leonard
2440 E Manoa Rd
Honolulu HI 96822

Call Sign: KH7MF
Kenneth H Abe
2611 E Manoa Rd
Honolulu HI 96822

Call Sign: KH6ALF
Rikio Nishioka
2693 E Manoa Rd
Honolulu HI 96822

Call Sign: WH6RP

Steve M Sakamoto
3082 E Manoa Rd
Honolulu HI 96822

Call Sign: KH7ND
Jolene J Ditucci
3360 A E Manoa Rd
Honolulu HI 96822

Call Sign: KH7GK
Adrian Ditucci
3360A E Manoa Rd
Honolulu HI 96822

Call Sign: WH6XC
Thanit Pewnim
1777 E West Rd 1745
Honolulu HI 96848

Call Sign: WH6XB
Maneewan Pewnim
1777 E West Rd Box 1745
Honolulu HI 96848

Call Sign: NH7XV
Dixson Lau
3044 East Manoa Rd
Honolulu HI 96822

Call Sign: WH7GT
Jarod W Ring
1711 East West Rd
Honolulu HI 96848

Call Sign: WH6JB
Nopadon Sahachaisaeree
Enc Box 1070 1777 East
West Rd
Honolulu HI 96848

Call Sign: WH6NP
Suwanna Chotisukan
1777 East West Rd Apt
1025
Honolulu HI 96848

Call Sign: NH6ZR
Gerrit B Osborne
1430 Ehupua St
Honolulu HI 96821

Call Sign: KH6ALB
Ernest T Shima
1234 Ekaha Ave
Honolulu HI 96816-4202

Call Sign: WH6GB
Gary F Kuwasaki
720 Ekekela Pl
Honolulu HI 96817

Call Sign: KH7IK
Douglas F Vaioleti
417 B Elena St
Honolulu HI 96817

Call Sign: WH7YX
Greg B Tully
728 Elepaio St
Honolulu HI 96816

Call Sign: KH6EDR
Herbert W H Dang
758 Elepaio St
Honolulu HI 96816

Call Sign: KH7LB
Marivic R Laguda
1810 Eluwene St
Honolulu HI 96819

Call Sign: NH7AC
Rose M Thater
1814 Eluwene St
Honolulu HI 96819

Call Sign: KH6RAM
Anselmo M Ramirez
1804 Eluwene St
Honolulu HI 96819

Call Sign: KH6SCT
Salvador C Templa
1804 Eluwene St
Honolulu HI 96819

Call Sign: NH2IC
Anselmo M Ramirez
1804 Eluwene St
Honolulu HI 96819

Call Sign: NH2IF
Salvador C Templa
1804 Eluwene St
Honolulu HI 96819

Call Sign: KH7NZ
Virginia T Knickerbocker
1910 Eluwene St
Honolulu HI 96819

Call Sign: WB9DWL
Henry A Kaul
1614 Emerson St 12
Honolulu HI 96813

Call Sign: KH6HAK
Henry A Kaul
1615 Emerson St 2
Honolulu HI 96813

Call Sign: KC7PVQ
John D O Neill
425 Ena Rd
Honolulu HI 96815-1712

Call Sign: KH6GOG
Frank W Adams
425 Ena Rd 305C
Honolulu HI 96815

Call Sign: WH6IJ
Thomas P Mc Carthy
478A Ena Rd 41
Honolulu HI 96815

Call Sign: WH6CCI
Leslie G Olson
478A Ena Rd 45
Honolulu HI 96815

Call Sign: WH6CCS
Creig A Olson
478A Ena Rd 45
Honolulu HI 96815

Call Sign: WA3ZEM
Burton B Barr
469 Ena Rd Apt 3010
Honolulu HI 96815

Call Sign: WH6CLO
Joanne V Weldon
1443 F Emerson St
Honolulu HI 96813

Call Sign: KB8SKX
Joshua W Buckwalter
7241 F Pakalana Pl
Honolulu HI 96818

Call Sign: NH7UN
Jennifer R Buckwalter
7241 F Pakalana Pl
Honolulu HI 96818

Call Sign: KH6AAA
Thomas A Seale
84 265 Farrington Hwy
Unit 114
Honolulu HI 96792

Call Sign: NH6VP
Vance M Apolo
2007 Fern St 206
Honolulu HI 96826

Call Sign: NH6XP
Thomas C Simon
2030 Fern St Unit C

Honolulu HI 96826

Honolulu HI 96818

Honolulu HI 96825

Call Sign: WH7JH
Frederick K Watson
1718 Fernandez St
Honolulu HI 96819

Call Sign: KB3IOC
Stuart S Stone
2352 Gemini Ave Apt B
Honolulu HI 96818

Call Sign: W9AW
Motoaki Uotome
501 Hahaione St 14K
Honolulu HI 96825

Call Sign: N3VDM
Jason D Gaboury
142 Flame Pl Unit 104
Honolulu HI 96818

Call Sign: KH7GJ
Ramon M Olis
1042 Green St Apt 3
Honolulu HI 96822

Call Sign: W9BO
Motoaki Uotome
501 Hahaione St 14K
Honolulu HI 96825

Call Sign: NH7YK
Jason D Gaboury
142 Flame Pl Unit 104
Honolulu HI 96818

Call Sign: WH6UI
Swain K Ah Yuen
1239 Gulick Ave
Honolulu HI 96819

Call Sign: WH7AA
Aloha Dx Contest Team
501 Hahaione St 14K
Honolulu HI 96825

Call Sign: KH7ES
Joseph S Y Hu
900 Fort St Mall Ste 910
Honolulu HI 96813

Call Sign: WB8NGS
Robert L Hoyt
531 Hahaione 2D
Honolulu HI 96825

Call Sign: WH7J
A1 Op Club
501 Hahaione St 14K
Honolulu HI 96825

Call Sign: WH2AEG
John J Goold
3507 Forward Ave
Honolulu HI 96819

Call Sign: NH7QB
Ernest V Murphy
531 Hahaione St 14B
Honolulu HI 96825

Call Sign: WH6TA
Eddie K Lee
501 Hahaione St 5K
Honolulu HI 96825

Call Sign: WH6DLQ
Christopher A Smith
1929 Fox Blvd
Honolulu HI 96818

Call Sign: WH7EM
Ernest V Murphy
531 Hahaione St 14B
Honolulu HI 96825

Call Sign: WH2U
John N Van Der Pyl
531 Hahaione St 9A
Honolulu HI 96825

Call Sign: WH6M
Anthony P Skinner
1397 Frank St
Honolulu HI 96816

Call Sign: KH7WW
Hawaii Dx Gang
501 Hahaione St 14K
Honolulu HI 96825

Call Sign: KH7LZ
Todd J Condon
95 246 Haike Pl
Honolulu HI 96789

Call Sign: WH6CIK
Jerry J Hiyakumoto
1618 Frog Ln D3
Honolulu HI 96817

Call Sign: KH8J
Samoa Dx Contest Team
501 Hahaione St 14K
Honolulu HI 96825

Call Sign: NH6YX
Michael J Heilman
2643B Haili Rd
Honolulu HI 96813

Call Sign: N5FGZ
Walter R Townsend
2368D Gemini Ave

Call Sign: NH7AA
Aloha Dx Contest Team
501 Hahaione St 14K

Call Sign: KH6AYC
Edwin L Young
650 Hakaka Pl

Honolulu HI 96816

Call Sign: AH6IH
William E Rhoden
1313 Hala Dr
Honolulu HI 96817

Call Sign: AH6II
Sharon P Rhoden
1313 Hala Dr
Honolulu HI 96817

Call Sign: WH6DSX
Peyton L Andrews
2185 Halakau St
Honolulu HI 96821

Call Sign: WH6BTY
William D Kaneko
363 Halaki St
Honolulu HI 96821

Call Sign: WH6DGC
Gloria Dalton
5274 Halapepe St
Honolulu HI 96821

Call Sign: KI4FHG
James E Shelton
418 Halawa View Loop
Unit 101
Honolulu HI 96818

Call Sign: KH6ILU
Maurice Sapienza
2394 Halehaka St
Honolulu HI 96821

Call Sign: KN5G
Joseph M Barr
1496 Halekoa
Honolulu HI 96821

Call Sign: NH7YB
Alan A Mukakami

1435 Halekoa Dr
Honolulu HI 96821

Call Sign: KH6GT
Scott M Cooley
1749 Halekoa Dr
Honolulu HI 96821-1026

Call Sign: WH6CXW
Scott M Cooley
1749 Halekoa Dr
Honolulu HI 96821-1026

Call Sign: KH6DUE
Beauclerc G Hunt
1892 Halekoa Dr
Honolulu HI 96821

Call Sign: NH6WM
Jacob W Gerritsen
2043 Halekoa Dr
Honolulu HI 96821

Call Sign: KB5C
Michael R Albright
2344 Halekoa Dr
Honolulu HI 96821

Call Sign: KH6FGA
William H Crawley
2386 Halekoa Dr
Honolulu HI 98621

Call Sign: NH6ZT
William A Arnemann
2477 Halekoa Dr
Honolulu HI 96821

Call Sign: WH7OV
David R Langdon
1532 A Halekoa Dr
Honolulu HI 96821

Call Sign: WH6DCM
Abraham J Grogan

2464 Halelaau Pl
Honolulu HI 96816

Call Sign: WH6CVT
Pearl City High School
Amateur Radio Club
2464 Halelaau Pl
Honolulu HI 96782-1498

Call Sign: WH6CVB
James E Humble III
3319 Halelani Dr
Honolulu HI 96822

Call Sign: KH7AI
Nelson H Case III
435 Haleloa Pl B
Honolulu HI 96821

Call Sign: AH6LO
Edward Michelman
381 Halemaumau Pl
Honolulu HI 96821

Call Sign: NH6AA
Gaylen J Endo
5901 Haleola St
Honolulu HI 96821

Call Sign: NH6QN
Christopher J Combs
1461 Haloa Dr
Honolulu HI 96818

Call Sign: WH6BZK
Songkyu M Combs
1461 Haloa Dr
Honolulu HI 96818

Call Sign: KA1LAX
Eaton M Kempshall
4259 Halupa St
Honolulu HI 96818-1818

Call Sign: KH7RL

Timmy T Niuelua
1720 Hamoana Apt 104
Honolulu HI 96715

Call Sign: KH7UD
Chase E Mahaffey
3117 Hampton Cir
Honolulu HI 96818

Call Sign: KB7AKH
Jeremy C Mcdermond
229 Hanakapiai St
Honolulu HI 96825

Call Sign: KH7MB
Jarrett K Hew
317 Hanakoa St
Honolulu HI 96826

Call Sign: KH6DS
Bert N Yoshida
2007 Hanalima Pl
Honolulu HI 96817

Call Sign: KH7OY
Dawn A Robinson
116 Hanupaoa Pl
Honolulu HI 96822

Call Sign: KH7YM
Isaac T Imoto
3758 Harding Ave
Honolulu HI 96816

Call Sign: WH6CHE
Joan A Wall
1214C Hase Dr
Honolulu HI 96819

Call Sign: WH7VX
Jason De Jesus
1120 Hassinger St 101
Honolulu HI 96822

Call Sign: KH6EV

Richard T Maruyama
1637 Hauiki St
Honolulu HI 96819

Call Sign: KH7LX
Gabriel L Moniz
737 Hauoli St
Honolulu HI 96826

Call Sign: KH7HU
Paolo T Torres
807 Hausten St 8
Honolulu HI 96826

Call Sign: NH7PS
John M Guris
713 Hausten St Apt A
Honolulu HI 96826

Call Sign: KL0GO
Michael R Watkins
6710 Hawaii Kai Dr
Honolulu HI 96825

Call Sign: WH6DLR
Jeffrey T Kang
6871 Hawaii Kai Dr
Honolulu III 96825

Call Sign: KH6CWT
Lawrence A Julian Jr
6710 Hawaii Kai Dr 202
Honolulu HI 96825

Call Sign: WH6BGK
William K Darrow
6370 Hawaii Kai Dr 25
Honolulu HI 96825

Call Sign: WH7XK
Walter L Harvey III
7088 Hawaii Kai Dr 67
Honolulu HI 96825

Call Sign: WB0RUA

Bill D Strayer
7007 Hawaii Kai Dr A26
Honolulu HI 96825

Call Sign: NH7VE
Robin R Grant
6710 Hawaii Kai Dr Apt
1500
Honolulu HI 96825

Call Sign: K2PCC
Charles W Haas Jr
6710 Hawaii Kai Dr Apt
1800
Honolulu HI 96825

Call Sign: KH6EG
John S Silva Sr
3222 Hayden St
Honolulu HI 96815

Call Sign: KH7UH
Craig Anderson
832 Hays Cir
Honolulu HI 96818

Call Sign: KH7FD
Bradley Y Choy
2617 Henry St
Honolulu HI 96817

Call Sign: KH7HL
Kiyomu Koyanagi
2617 Henry St
Honolulu HI 96817

Call Sign: KH7MP
Denise H Choy
2617 Henry St
Honolulu HI 96817

Call Sign: KH7PF
Bradley K Choy
2617 Henry St
Honolulu HI 96817

Call Sign: KH6AFM
Raymond C Mikami
3209 Herbert St
Honolulu HI 96815-3834

Call Sign: NH6JD
Ryan N Ueoka
3258 Herbert St Unit A
Honolulu HI 96815

Call Sign: KH7XY
Jan E Lenkeit
1310 Heulu St 1902
Honolulu HI 96822

Call Sign: KH6IM
Edward Y Kawano
1315 Heulu St 303B
Honolulu HI 96822

Call Sign: KH6CUQ
Edward J Chong Jr
1333 Heulu St 704
Honolulu HI 96822

Call Sign: KH6AUX
Jonathan I Levy
1422 Heulu St A203
Honolulu HI 96822

Call Sign: WH7UT
Jonathan I Levy
1422 Heulu St A203
Honolulu HI 96822

Call Sign: AH7O
Sadao Tsuchiya
2444 Hihiwai St Apt 2406
Honolulu HI 96826-5114

Call Sign: KH6ACY
Nobuhiro Iseri
1459 Hiikala Pl
Honolulu HI 96816

Call Sign: KH6BZ
Wilfred M Komine
1477 Hiikala Pl
Honolulu HI 96816

Call Sign: NH6VD
Chizuho Mizuno
2626 Hillside Ave
Honolulu HI 96822

Call Sign: WH6CFZ
Mikio Nagaoka
2626 Hillside Ave
Honolulu HI 96822

Call Sign: WH6CGA
Yasuhisa Nakamura
2626 Hillside Ave
Honolulu HI 96822

Call Sign: KH7IJ
Marvis S Tauala
3517 Hinahina St
Honolulu HI 96816

Call Sign: KH7IT
Jason M Uehara
3017 Hinano St
Honolulu HI 96815-4208

Call Sign: KH6AY
Manuel D Pires
721 Hind Dr
Honolulu HI 96821

Call Sign: KD6DSY
Amos C Hathway
2707 Hipawai Pl
Honolulu HI 96822

Call Sign: WH6DQG
Junbae Kong
2707 Hipawai Pl
Honolulu HI 96822

Call Sign: NH6SE
Armando M Aguada
2248 Hiu St
Honolulu HI 96819

Call Sign: WH6DV
Jacob H Verhoeff
1539 Hoaaina Str
Honolulu HI 96821

Call Sign: WH6DKB
Linda Okamoto
3278 Hoanoho Pl
Honolulu HI 96816

Call Sign: WH6CEJ
Ta Ting Lo
1106-2 Hoawa Ln
Honolulu HI 96826

Call Sign: AH6TO
Keith Radford
411 Hobron Apt 2912
Honolulu HI 96815

Call Sign: KH6ZU
Keith Radford
411 Hobron Apt 2912
Honolulu HI 96815

Call Sign: KG6IER
Issei Hamamoto
400 Hobron Ln 1714
Honolulu HI 96815

Call Sign: N8AOJ
Donald R Farmer
400 Hobron Ln 3104
Honolulu HI 96815

Call Sign: NH6BM
John David Kerley
411 Hobron Ln 3113
Honolulu HI 96815

Call Sign: AH6TC
Robert A Holmes
400 Hobron Ln Apt 2511
Honolulu HI 96815

Call Sign: KE8FV
Robert A Holmes
400 Hobron Ln Apt 2511
Honolulu HI 96815

Call Sign: KH6OO
William N Kendall
411 Hobron Ln Apt 2912
Honolulu HI 96815

Call Sign: N0CO
William N Kendall
411 Hobron Ln Apt 2912
Honolulu HI 96815

Call Sign: KH6CO
Waikiki Amateur Radio
Club
411 Hobron Ln Apt 2912
Honolulu HI 96815

Call Sign: N0COU
Baxter Amateur Radio
Club
411 Hobron Ln Apt 2912
Honolulu HI 96815

Call Sign: WH6DIM
Waikiki Amateur Radio
Club
411 Hobron Ln Apt 2912
Honolulu HI 96815

Call Sign: WH6DLF
Baxter Amateur Radio
Club
411 Hobron Ln Apt 2912
Honolulu HI 96815

Call Sign: WH7ET
Dorothy H Hazlett
904 Hokulani St
Honolulu HI 96825

Call Sign: WH7EU
Mark A Hazlett
904 Hokulani St
Honolulu HI 96825

Call Sign: KC2FIY
Akira Takano
Don Kim 899 Hokulani St
Honolulu HI 96825

Call Sign: KI4MGS
Brad V Burnham
845 Hokulani St Unit A
Honolulu HI 96825

Call Sign: WH6CQ
Takeshi Hayashi
801 Holiday Manor 1650
Kanunu St
Honolulu HI 96814

Call Sign: WA6VAA
Anthony R Cara
361 Holokai Pl
Honolulu HI 96825-2887

Call Sign: KF7ANI
Luis D Vergara
3040 Holua Pl
Honolulu HI 96819

Call Sign: WH7FM
Wilfredo P Santos
3040 Holua Pl
Honolulu HI 96819

Call Sign: WH6CCW
Yasuko Kadowaki
C/O H Nakano 1914
Homerule St

Honolulu HI 96819

Call Sign: AH6JS
Shinichi Kadowaki
C/O H Nakano 1914
Homerule St
Honolulu HI 96819

Call Sign: WH6BCF
Donald E Fanell
1177 Honokahua St
Honolulu HI 96825

Call Sign: WH6SR
Eric S Mak
1186 Honokahua St
Honolulu HI 96825

Call Sign: WH6CON
Stephen S Mc Call
3249 Hoolulu St
Honolulu HI 96815

Call Sign: AH6HD
Kevin L Q Watson
1035 Hoomaikai St
Honolulu HI 96817

Call Sign: WH6CEQ
Chris S Kuzmanoff
2237 Hoonanca St
Honolulu HI 96822

Call Sign: WH6RK
Michael F Ching
2317 Hoonanea St
Honolulu HI 96822

Call Sign: KH6MS
Jon P Lewis
2228A Hoonanea St
Honolulu HI 96822

Call Sign: WH6ES
John Paul R Fryckman

3302C Hooper Pl
Honolulu HI 96818

Call Sign: WH6CIB
William G Hardey
1626 Houghtailing St
Honolulu HI 96817

Call Sign: WH6CID
Lyle A Hardey
1630 Houghtailing St
Honolulu HI 96817

Call Sign: KH7HF
Barbara M Young
1843 Houghtailing St
Honolulu HI 96817

Call Sign: KH7VN
Robert Y Lee
2005 Huake Pl
Honolulu HI 96817

Call Sign: NH6UA
Antoinette A Lee
2005 Huake Pl
Honolulu HI 96817

Call Sign: NH6UD
Robert Y Lee
2005 Huake Pl
Honolulu HI 96817

Call Sign: KH6IJ
Frances A Mckenney
4207 Huanui St
Honolulu HI 96816

Call Sign: AH6CK
Frank A Buffalano
3145 Huelani Dr
Honolulu HI 96822

Call Sign: KH7CT
Henriette M Taylor

2411 Huene St
Honolulu HI 96817

Call Sign: NH7VC
Charles M Koike
3090 Hulu Pl
Honolulu HI 96882-1528

Call Sign: AH6RY
Eugene R Uemura
1754 Huma St
Honolulu HI 96817

Call Sign: WH6COP
Ray A Brown
1720 Huna St 407
Honolulu HI 96817

Call Sign: WH7LV
Robert S Stubbs
1720 Huna Str 10
Honolulu HI 96817

Call Sign: WH7OW
James L Moikeha
515 Iavkea St
Honolulu HI 96813

Call Sign: KF6ZVS
Kinzo Hashimoto
Bernadette Tsukada 1660
Ihiloa Loop
Honolulu HI 96821-1320

Call Sign: KG9KI
Jacques H Le Roy
110 Ikena Pl
Honolulu HI 96821

Call Sign: WH7I
Jacques H Le Roy
110 Ikena Pl
Honolulu HI 96821

Call Sign: KH6ESH

Edwin S Ho
1043-B Ilima Dr
Honolulu HI 96817

Call Sign: WH7AX
Edwin S Ho
1043-B Ilima Dr
Honolulu HI 96817

Call Sign: NH6WU
Shirley J Fake
605 Inuwai Pl
Honolulu HI 96825

Call Sign: NH6OR
Thomas E Fake
605 Inuwai Pl
Honolulu HI 96825-2926

Call Sign: WH6JA
Kin Ho Tung
512 Iolani Ave Apt 303
Honolulu HI 96813

Call Sign: WH6DLA
Darren A Cantrill
246 Jack Ln Apt B
Honolulu HI 96817

Call Sign: KG4FJB
Ernand V Pedriquez
3320 Jaluit Ln
Honolulu HI 96818

Call Sign: KH6DSH
Stanley Martin Jr
2360 Jasmine St
Honolulu HI 96816

Call Sign: WH7VE
Daniel M Ford
2257 Jennie St
Honolulu HI 96819

Call Sign: KA6ULU

Clifford K H Lau
1964 Judd Hillside
Honolulu HI 96822

Call Sign: WA6NTF
Adrienne W Lau
1964 Judd Hillside
Honolulu HI 96822

Call Sign: WH6US
Robert T Bonham
55 Judd St
Honolulu HI 96817

Call Sign: WH6HN
Kirk K L Chuang
2752 Ka Aha St 104
Honolulu HI 96826

Call Sign: NH6TQ
George T Sumida
2752 Kaaha St 206
Honolulu HI 96826

Call Sign: NH6YQ
Arnold W Siemsen Jr
2752 Kaaha St 408
Honolulu HI 96826

Call Sign: KH7DJ
Elaine W Akau
2752 Kaaha St 409
Honolulu HI 96826

Call Sign: WH7MS
Natasha N Gobeil
2733 Kaaha St Apt A8
Honolulu HI 96826

Call Sign: KH7YI
Russell A Won
94 778 Kaaholo St
Honolulu HI 96797

Call Sign: KH6AKK

Reginald N S Nikaido
2911 Kaamalio Dr
Honolulu HI 96822

Call Sign: WH6BUN
Bartt T Tsuruda
3464 Kaau St
Honolulu HI 96816

Call Sign: AH6QM
Elizabeth F Peralta
1221 Kaauwai Pl
Honolulu HI 96817

Call Sign: KH7XA
Scott J Foster
1350 Kaeleku St
Honolulu HI 96825

Call Sign: KD7KL
James A Chaney
C/O Commercial Roofing;
2002 Kahai St
Honolulu HI 96819

Call Sign: WH7ZU
Margaret Rains
1848 Kahakai Dr 2308
Honolulu HI 96814

Call Sign: WH6DG
Bruce M Middleton
1848 Kahakai Dr 903
Honolulu HI 96814

Call Sign: KH6K
Thomas J Larrabee
1848 Kahakai Dr Apt 1208
Honolulu HI 96814

Call Sign: NH6DI
Sumi Larrabee
1848 Kahakai Dr Apt 1208
Honolulu HI 96814

Call Sign: KA6IWP
George T Pray
4382 Kahala Ave
Honolulu HI 96816

Call Sign: NH7TI
Debra A O Brien
4999 Kahala Ave 162
Honolulu HI 96816

Call Sign: AH6NG
Leo A Fitzek
2790 Kahaloa Dr Apt 501
Honolulu HI 96822

Call Sign: WH6DVK
Celso S Jose
1917 Kahana St
Honolulu HI 96819

Call Sign: KH7AD
Leslie Ann Y Palmer
930 Kaheka St 1705
Honolulu HI 96814-2457

Call Sign: NH6TP
Senarath K Gunatilaka
923 Kahena
Honolulu HI 96825

Call Sign: NH7PO
Jacqueline M Bogan
6606 Kahena Pl
Honolulu HI 96825

Call Sign: AH6QO
Kevin C Bogan
6606 Kahena Pl
Honolulu HI 96825-1016

Call Sign: WH6ML
Kevin C Bogan
6606 Kahena Pl
Honolulu HI 96825-1016

Call Sign: KH6FT
Wayne A Alexander
3412 Kahikolu Way
Honolulu HI 96818

Call Sign: NH7QN
Rae A Kurashige
455 Kahinu St
Honolulu HI 96821

Call Sign: NH7QO
Lauren E Kurashige
455 Kahinu St
Honolulu HI 96821

Call Sign: WH6AJ
Randall H Kurashige
455 Kahinu St
Honolulu HI 96821-2216

Call Sign: AH6Q
Randall H Kurashige
455 Kahinu St
Honolulu HI 96821

Call Sign: WH7IO
David P Luis
2752 Kahoaloha Ln Apt
303
Honolulu HI 96826

Call Sign: W1PTJ
Stanley H Zisk
1224 Kahului St
Honolulu HI 96825

Call Sign: NH7CZ
Claude F Mc Carley
1024 Kaili St
Honolulu HI 96819

Call Sign: KH6OS
Thomas S Hori
3168 Kaimuki Ave
Honolulu HI 96816

Call Sign: AH6CM
Mervin H Chang
4146 Kaimuki Ave
Honolulu HI 96816

Call Sign: KH6NN
Karen J Chang
4146 Kaimuki Ave
Honolulu HI 96816

Call Sign: KH7LY
Lyman P Zablan Jr
2914 Kaimuki Ave 6
Honolulu HI 96816

Call Sign: WH6CD
Walter W L Loo
245 Kaiolohia Pl
Honolulu HI 96825

Call Sign: KH6RK
Richard D Johnston
445 Kaiolu St 204
Honolulu HI 96815

Call Sign: WH6CXC
Jerald K Dolak
218 Kaiulani 4
Honolulu HI 96815-3040

Call Sign: KH6APS
Augustine J Perry
1563 Kalaepaa Dr
Honolulu HI 96819

Call Sign: KH7GN
Hans T Kashiwabara
1525 Kalaepohaku Pl
Honolulu HI 96816

Call Sign: KH6MR
Peter B Woollett
111 Kalaiopua Pl
Honolulu HI 96822

Call Sign: WH7RA
Chi U Mok
2552 Kalakaua Ave
Honolulu HI 96815

Call Sign: KH7JJ
Edward K Conklin
2969 Kalakaua Ave 1004
Honolulu HI 96815-4625

Call Sign: NH7PJ
Kazuo Saito
C/O Atsuko Sonoda 1670
Kalakaua Ave 1004
Honolulu HI 96826

Call Sign: KD7TZ
Clayton J Deaver
2877 Kalakaua Ave 103
Honolulu HI 98615

Call Sign: KH7AN
James F Treichel
1750 Kalakaua Ave 1204
Honolulu HI 96826

Call Sign: WH7EW
William E Berg
1925 Kalakaua Ave 1902
Honolulu HI 96815

Call Sign: WH6RB
Frank E Francisco
2500 Kalakaua Ave 1902
Honolulu HI 96815

Call Sign: KH7GH
Makanani P Marcusson
1545 Kalakaua Ave 909
Honolulu HI 96826-2457

Call Sign: WH6CZM
Teh Hsiung Chen

2957 Kalakaua Ave Apt
506
Honolulu HI 96815

Call Sign: NH6TS
Manuel L Nunes Jr
1551 Kalakaua Ave E101
Honolulu HI 96826

Call Sign: KF6PNA
Eugene L Seybold
1750 Kalakaua Ave Ste
103 3166
Honolulu HI 96826-3795

Call Sign: KH6ATL
Jack G Kummer
1750 Kalakaua Ave Ste 3
765
Honolulu HI 96826-3754

Call Sign: NH6NH
Beverly J Reeve
1750 Kalakaua Ave Ste
3170
Honolulu HI 96826

Call Sign: KH7MM
Natale Borghetti
C/O Layne 1833 Kalakaua
Ave Ste 908
Honolulu HI 96815

Call Sign: WH7AH
Natale Borghetti
C/O Layne 1833 Kalakaua
Ave Ste 908
Honolulu HI 96815

Call Sign: WH7RM
Donna M Sambueno
2552 Kalakaua Ave
Waikiki Beach Marriott
Honolulu HI 96815

Call Sign: WH6CKR
Richard C Page
144 Kalalau St
Honolulu HI 96825-2014

Call Sign: WH6BF
Albert D Dakujaku
795 Kalalea St
Honolulu HI 96825

Call Sign: WH6CQM
Matthew K Acosta
1924 Kalani
Honolulu HI 96819

Call Sign: WH6DU
George E Oakes
5076 Kalanianaole Hwy
Honolulu HI 96821

Call Sign: AH6ED
Jeffrey S Piper
5827 Kalanianaole Hwy
Honolulu HI 96821

Call Sign: KH6DEH
Henry M Cremer
7072 Kalanianaole Hwy
Honolulu HI 96825-2008

Call Sign: KH7ER
Dickson W F Chow
7371 Kalanianaole Hwy
Honolulu HI 96825

Call Sign: AH6H
William R Brown
1520 Kalaniiki St
Honolulu HI 96821

Call Sign: KH6NW
Roger M White
1520 Kalaniiki St
Honolulu HI 96821

Call Sign: KH7RY
Mark R Largosa
839 Kalanipuu St
Honolulu HI 96825-2501

Call Sign: K7PJV
Wallace V Parcels
988 Kalapaki St
Honolulu HI 96825

Call Sign: KH7AH
Daniel H De Fries
2920 Kalei Rd
Honolulu HI 96826

Call Sign: WH6CDB
Sonny L Ah Kui
2206C Kalena Dr
Honolulu HI 96819

Call Sign: WA6VWK
Barney A Kukolsky
2161 Kalia Rd 1310
Honolulu HI 96815

Call Sign: WH6K
Barney A Cagle
293 Kalihi St
Honolulu HI 96819

Call Sign: KH6TLH
Fred Y Terya
2885 Kalihi St
Honolulu HI 96819

Call Sign: KH7YR
Leland M Cadoy
2947 Kalihi St
Honolulu HI 96819

Call Sign: WH6NF
William E Heinrich
3148 Kalihi St
Honolulu HI 96819

Call Sign: NH6TF
John R Aguiar Jr
2007C Kalihi St
Honolulu HI 96819

Call Sign: WH6CBK
George Ahia
2007C Kalihi St
Honolulu HI 96819

Call Sign: WH6OF
Maughn Matsuoka
1005 Kalikimaka St
Honolulu HI 96817

Call Sign: AH6DK
Richard W K Lum
1025 Kalikimaka St
Honolulu HI 96817

Call Sign: WH6DCK
Kevin C J Wong
3461 Kalua Rd
Honolulu HI 96816

Call Sign: WH6XW
Maile Nicholas
844 Kaluanui Rd
Honolulu HI 96825-1354

Call Sign: N4ABC
Joseph A Moyer
795 Kaluanui Way
Honolulu HI 96825

Call Sign: WH6RA
Fred A Kobashikawa
1261 Kaluawaa St
Honolulu HI 96816

Call Sign: WH6DGD
First Hawaiian Bank
Amateur Radio Club
2339 Kam Hwy
Honolulu HI 96819

Call Sign: KH7AP
Jerry K Tasoe
1065 Kamakee Vista 1906
Honolulu HI 96814

Call Sign: NH6UZ
Donna J Hamber
1619 Kamamalu Ave 306
Honolulu HI 96813

Call Sign: NH6UT
Stephen H Hamber
1619 Kamamalu Ave 306
Honolulu HI 96813

Call Sign: NH7XL
Charles E Hanebuth
1290 Kamehame Dr
Honolulu HI 96825-3505

Call Sign: K4AJQ
Walter J Atkins Jr
1305 Kamehame Dr
Honolulu HI 96825

Call Sign: NH7AX
Donald B Marks
2199 Kamehameha Hwy
Honolulu HI 96819

Call Sign: KA3YIK
Jamie L Snellings
5170 Kamehameha Loop
Honolulu HI 96818

Call Sign: WH6CXB
Ross S Imada
7130 Kamilo St
Honolulu HI 96825

Call Sign: K1GUC
Leslie R Babb
596 Kamoku St
Honolulu HI 96826

Call Sign: KH6OT
Louis J Polskin
583 Kamoku St Apt 3903
Honolulu HI 96826

Call Sign: WH6CPK
Ralph E Macey Sr
529 Kamoku St C5
Honolulu HI 96821

Call Sign: KH6FMS
Robin A Chung
1636 Kanalui St
Honolulu HI 96816

Call Sign: WH7OR
Robin A Chung
1636 Kanalui St
Honolulu HI 96816

Call Sign: KH7RA
Tali P Kulihaapai
2118 Kanealii Ave
Honolulu HI 96813

Call Sign: WH6CLU
Nesanet S Mitiku
1295 Kanewai St
Honolulu HI 96816

Call Sign: N9GAE
Donald W May
7274 Kanoenoe St
Honolulu HI 96825

Call Sign: KH6MF
Harry W C Goo
1560 Kanunu St 1606
Honolulu HI 96814

Call Sign: NH6IS
Sarah H Noda
1610 Kanunu St 508
Honolulu HI 96814

Call Sign: KH6EXM
Gary Y Noda
1610 Kanunu St 508
Honolulu HI 96814-2704

Call Sign: KH6CS
Charles C Schenck
1650 Kanunu St Apt 1312
Honolulu HI 96814

Call Sign: KB6GWW
Ronald J Hendrickson
1560 Kanunu St Apt 414
Honolulu HI 96814

Call Sign: WH6CAC
Frederick C Franke
3151 Kaohinani Dr
Honolulu HI 96817

Call Sign: AH6RP
Ira K Byerly
2826 Kaonawai Pl Apt 3B
Honolulu HI 96822

Call Sign: WH6CKT
Peter B Richards
98-1092 Kaonohi St
Honolulu HI 96701

Call Sign: NH6LC
Jack K Watts
98-288 Kaonohi St 3502
Honolulu HI 96701

Call Sign: WH7JB
Robin L Rogers
1071 Kaoopulu Pl
Honolulu HI 96825

Call Sign: W7EQU
Edward C Ferrel
918 Kapaakea Ln 5
Honolulu HI 96826-3116

Call Sign: WH6CLA
Rudolph Gerlach
124 Kapahulu 301
Honolulu HI 96819

Call Sign: WH7CK
Martin Hafner
758 Kapahulu 355
Honolulu HI 96816

Call Sign: WH6DBQ
Blythe N Goya
747 Kapahulu Ave
Honolulu HI 96816

Call Sign: AH7X
Scott K Nishimoto
411-F Kapahulu Ave
Honolulu HI 96815

Call Sign: NH7FN
Scott K Nishimoto
411-F Kapahulu Ave
Honolulu HI 96815

Call Sign: K6GCN
Robert J Cunningham
758 Kapahulu Ave 136
Honolulu HI 96816

Call Sign: KG4JKJ
William T Hogan
758 Kapahulu Ave 301
Honolulu HI 96816

Call Sign: KB4NGN
Dale E Fajardo
758 Kapahulu Ave 343
Honolulu HI 96816

Call Sign: WH7LI
Robert Ludovisi
758 Kapahulu Ave 540
Honolulu HI 96816

Call Sign: AH6FW
Gene T Yu
922 Kapahulu Ave Apt
101
Honolulu HI 96816-1444

Call Sign: NH7WE
Ronald Verderame
465 Kapahulu Ave Apt 3G
Honolulu HI 96815

Call Sign: NH6EZ
Davin C Wong
546 Kapaia St
Honolulu HI 96825

Call Sign: WH7OQ
Donald W Baldwin Jr
229 Kapale St
Honolulu HI 96813

Call Sign: NH6PC
Derrick K H Wong
190 Kapalu St
Honolulu HI 96813

Call Sign: KB1CKW
Dawn M Nekorchuk
2210-2 Kapiolani Blvd
Honolulu HI 96826

Call Sign: AA6MS
Mark S Schnitzer
1288 Kapiolani Blvd
Honolulu HI 96814

Call Sign: K1HZM
Stephen T Hazam
1288 Kapiolani Blvd 1104
Honolulu HI 96814-2867

Call Sign: KH6AC
Emi Chang
725 Kapiolani Blvd 1016

Honolulu HI 96813

Call Sign: KH7BE
Emi Chang
725 Kapiolani Blvd 1016
Honolulu HI 96813

Call Sign: KH6IFZ
Jensen Y Kino
2333 Kapiolani Blvd 1605
Honolulu HI 96826

Call Sign: WH6YL
Richard W Voeltzke
2499 Kapiolani Blvd 2501
Honolulu HI 96826

Call Sign: W4TP
Timothy J Petersen
2333 Kapiolani Blvd 3007
Honolulu HI 96826

Call Sign: W6UG
Timothy J Petersen
2333 Kapiolani Blvd 3007
Honolulu HI 96826

Call Sign: KH7GQ
Andrew F Viers
2333 Kapiolani Blvd 3516
Honolulu HI 96826

Call Sign: AH0A
Joseph P Speroni
2781 Kapiolani Blvd 502
Honolulu HI 96826

Call Sign: K1PPI
Kippi L Speroni
2781 Kapiolani Blvd 502
Honolulu HI 96826

Call Sign: KR1STA
Krista L Speroni
2781 Kapiolani Blvd 502

Honolulu HI 96826

Call Sign: NH6CT
Michael H K Loo
1867 Kapiolani Blvd 6
Honolulu HI 96826

Call Sign: KH7F
Alexander C S Chang
725 Kapiolani Blvd 617
Honolulu HI 96813

Call Sign: KE4YBM
Amanda D Matteson
2333 Kapiolani Blvd Apt
1908
Honolulu HI 96826

Call Sign: AH6NQ
Koichi Aoki
2333 Kapiolani Blvd Apt
2813
Honolulu HI 96826

Call Sign: WH6SE
Guy P Archer
2499 Kapiolani Blvd Apt
3405
Honolulu HI 96826

Call Sign: KI6QDQ
Alexander J Beecroft
1296 Kapiolani Blvd Apt
4503
Honolulu HI 96814

Call Sign: WH6DQD
Lucille S James
725 Kapiolani Blvd Apt
705
Honolulu HI 96813

Call Sign: KH7II
David B Kurata
2132 Kapiolani Blvd Apt 8

Honolulu HI 96826

Call Sign: NH6TK
Maggie M Kibota
777 Kapiolani Blvd Ste
2714
Honolulu HI 96813

Call Sign: KH7WV
Lyndon D Fong
1441 Kapiolani Blvd Ste
616
Honolulu HI 96814

Call Sign: WH6DWS
Reinaldo Del Rios
1357 Kapiolani Blvd Ste
920
Honolulu HI 96814

Call Sign: NH7OO
Stephen C Kohn
757 Kapulena Loop
Honolulu HI 96825

Call Sign: NH7SF
Andrew R Yukitomo
761 Kapulena Lp
Honolulu HI 96825

Call Sign: KH6JBS
Peter W Yuen
7312 Kauhako St
Honolulu HI 96825

Call Sign: AH6NX
Lance B Koyama
253 Kaumakani St
Honolulu HI 96825

Call Sign: WH7QX
Douglas P Dang
456 Kaumakani St
Honolulu HI 96825

Call Sign: N3VHF
James C Weyman
1111 Kaumoku St
Honolulu HI 96825

Call Sign: NH6WN
Melinda P Andres
1441 Kaumualii St 139
Honolulu HI 96817

Call Sign: NH7ZP
Stephen E Levy
1045 Kaupaku Pl
Honolulu HI 96825

Call Sign: WA2QLE
Robert D Sebring
1044 A Kaupaku Pl
Honolulu HI 96825-1302

Call Sign: KH7HE
Camille A Oribio
1065 Kawaiahao St 2209
Honolulu HI 96814

Call Sign: WH6RH
Gaelyn R Penberthy
939 Kawaiki Pl
Honolulu HI 96825

Call Sign: WH6DKM
Edward L Howard
105-E Kawananakoa Pl
Honolulu HI 96817

Call Sign: NH7CN
Hiroshi Ueda
Kawato 3406 ~Keahi St
Honolulu HI 96822-1208

Call Sign: KH7JY
Ernest G Magaoay
4219 Keaka Dr
Honolulu HI 96818

Call Sign: KH7EQ
Justin Mark J U Young
529 Kealahou St
Honolulu HI 96825

Call Sign: KG6MLA
Richard V Wang
2819 Keama Pl
Honolulu HI 96822

Call Sign: WH6CNN
Seamus T Puette
3363A Keanu St
Honolulu HI 96816

Call Sign: KH6FV
Carter W Davis
3736A Keanu St
Honolulu HI 96816

Call Sign: WH7CW
Martin D Guiles
1628 Keeaumoka 902
Honolulu HI 96822

Call Sign: KH7OL
Dale C Ho
1925 Keeaumoku St
Honolulu HI 96822

Call Sign: WH6CPW
Vixay Sysouthavongsa
1931 Keeaumoku St
Honolulu HI 96822

Call Sign: WH7MU
Kory K Kamauoha
1717 Keeaumoku St 208
Honolulu HI 96822

Call Sign: WH6DSM
Dean T Uchimura
1648 Keeaumoku St 2A
Honolulu HI 96822

Call Sign: WH6EJ
Margo N Ooka
1620 Keeaumoku St Apt
504
Honolulu HI 96822-4324

Call Sign: NH7SL
William E Ingram
1508 Keeaumoku St Apt
B403
Honolulu HI 96822

Call Sign: NH7ZT
Danny S Tengan
5361 Keikilani Circle
Honolulu HI 96821

Call Sign: WH6CGU
William A Grant Jr
7545 Kekaa
Honolulu HI 96825

Call Sign: NH6QV
Yvette K Ito
2472 Kekuanoni St
Honolulu HI 96813

Call Sign: WH7WF
C Candy M Iha
469 Kekupua St
Honolulu HI 96825

Call Sign: NH6PJ
Jeffrey D Kim
533 Kekupua St
Honolulu HI 96825

Call Sign: KH7VS
Dawoon Kang
6236 Keokea Pl
Honolulu HI 96825

Call Sign: W4QBW
Lawrence V Price
6202 Keokea Pl

Honolulu HI 96825-1200

Honolulu HI 96816

Honolulu HI 96813

Call Sign: WH6BZE
Cheung T Wong
1907 Keonaona St
Honolulu HI 96817

Call Sign: NH7WN
Robert A Smith
5123 Kilauea Ave
Honolulu HI 96816

Call Sign: KH6DDP
Yukio Higa
824 Kinau St 1101
Honolulu HI 96813

Call Sign: KH6EKD
Melvyn S Uchida
3511 Kepuhi St
Honolulu HI 96815

Call Sign: KH6MP
Mitchell H Pinkerton
3732A Kilauea Ave
Honolulu HI 96816

Call Sign: KH6DDP
Yukio Higa
824 Kinau St 1101
Honolulu HI 96813

Call Sign: WH6CSD
Deborah R Kula
718 Kii St
Honolulu HI 96825-1007

Call Sign: NH6YM
Mitchell H Pinkerton
3732A Kilauea Ave
Honolulu HI 96816

Call Sign: WH7UR
Yukio Higa
824 Kinau St 1101
Honolulu HI 96813

Call Sign: WH7PN
Bode A Uale
729 Kii St
Honolulu HI 96825

Call Sign: KH7VV
Sandy C Liang
4846 3 Kilauea Ave
Honolulu HI 96816-5766

Call Sign: WH6UM
Cristobal S Inos
1073 Kinau St 402
Honolulu HI 96814

Call Sign: KH6BER
Herbert K Okita
1008 Kiionioni Loop
Honolulu HI 96816-4246

Call Sign: AH6SU
James M Baker
775 Kinalau Pl Apt 2202
Honolulu HI 96813

Call Sign: WH7QZ
John M Holtzclaw
824 Kinau St Apt 1008
Honolulu HI 96813

Call Sign: AH6TU
Kevin M Connor
758 Kikanai Loop
Honolulu HI 96818

Call Sign: WH7RQ
James M Baker
775 Kinalau Pl Apt 2202
Honolulu HI 96813

Call Sign: AH6MU
Robert W Sinton
1040 Kinau St Apt 1105
Honolulu HI 96814

Call Sign: NH6TY
Eric K Ty
3379 Kilauea Ave
Honolulu HI 96816

Call Sign: WH7AY
Eric Y Lee
1050 Kinan St 1001
Honolulu HI 96814

Call Sign: NH7LL
John B Gwaltney
824 Kinau St Apt 1211
Honolulu HI 96813

Call Sign: WH7JE
Eric K Ty
3379 Kilauea Ave
Honolulu HI 96816

Call Sign: KA7FVR
Hope V Talen
814 Kinau 301
Honolulu HI 96813

Call Sign: WH7PL
Akira P Sakamoto
1409 Kinau St Apt 3
Honolulu HI 96814

Call Sign: WH7JF
Lori S K Ty
3379 Kilauea Ave

Call Sign: WH6CVY
Michael W Cashman
709A Kinau St

Call Sign: WH6CEL
Grant K Kailikea
1232 Kinau St Apt 7

Honolulu HI 96814   Honolulu HI 96818-4169   Honolulu HI 96817

Call Sign: WH6CMZ
Minh L Tran
1032 Kinau St Ph 2
Honolulu HI 96814

Call Sign: KE6OHF
Dyland M Ramos
1424 Kohou St
Honolulu HI 96817

Call Sign: NH6MH
Michael J Ahn
1529 Kokea St
Honolulu HI 96817

Call Sign: WH6DJW
Kevin Shaw
1112 Kinaw St 203
Honolulu HI 96814

Call Sign: KE6OHG
Vigilia B Ramos
1424 Kohou St
Honolulu HI 96817

Call Sign: KH6FD
Gregory K C Ching
1534 Kokea St
Honolulu HI 96817

Call Sign: WH6NM
Mark N Sakihara
1728 Kino St
Honolulu HI 96819

Call Sign: KF6LQF
Magic B Ramos
1424 Kohou St
Honolulu HI 96817

Call Sign: KH7EX
Roseline F Salazar
1109 Kokea St I 202
Honolulu HI 96817

Call Sign: NH7RW
Ronald A Holmberg
1673A Kino St
Honolulu HI 96819

Call Sign: KH2YB
Emilio A Baldonado Jr
1424 Kohou St
Honolulu HI 96817

Call Sign: WH7EX
Roseline F Salazar
1109 Kokea St I 202
Honolulu HI 96817

Call Sign: NH7TV
Matthew G Siko
5466 Kirkwood Pl
Honolulu HI 96821

Call Sign: KH6INC
Scan-I Hawaii Chapter
1424 Kohou St
Honolulu HI 96817

Call Sign: NH7ZU
Marc S Nonaka
4065 Koko Dr
Honolulu HI 96816

Call Sign: KH6HFN
Donald L Cook
2450 Koa Av 106A
Honolulu HI 96815

Call Sign: WH6DHF
Scan-I Hawaii Chapter
1424 Kohou St
Honolulu HI 96817

Call Sign: NH7YD
Linda Soma
4193 Koko Dr
Honolulu HI 96816

Call Sign: WH6DQF
Tyler F Wong
936 Koae St
Honolulu HI 96816

Call Sign: WH6SJ
Lyle M Nagahiro
1440 Kohou St
Honolulu HI 96817-2742

Call Sign: WH7IY
Ross M Halsted
603 Koko Isle Cr
Honolulu HI 96825

Call Sign: KD5YBF
Suzette Smith
4537 Kobashigawa St
Honolulu HI 96818-4169

Call Sign: KH7HD
Ladden L Panis
650 Kohou St Ste A
Honolulu HI 96817

Call Sign: WH6BAQ
Roberta A Sprague
2874 Komaia Pl
Honolulu HI 96822

Call Sign: KE4LWT
Jack R Smith
4537 Kobashigawa St

Call Sign: KH6AGE
Patrick G Tom
1512 Kokea St

Call Sign: KH6GPI
Arthur Y Sprague
2874 Komaia Pl

Honolulu HI 96822-1745

Honolulu HI 96825

Honolulu HI 96826

Call Sign: N7WAP
Joseph Mac Naughton
2242 Komo Mai Dr
Honolulu HI 96782-1220

Call Sign: NH7SM
Carlton P Champagne
2092 Kuhio 1505
Honolulu HI 96815

Call Sign: KH7EU
Raymond M Yee
2648 Kuilei St Apt C34
Honolulu HI 96826

Call Sign: WH6BWB
Earl F Kaopuiki Jr
538 Krauss St
Honolulu HI 96813

Call Sign: WH6NG
Thomas A Wyatt
2240 Kuhio Apt 1011
Honolulu HI 96815

Call Sign: KH7HW
Wallace W Weatherwax
7171 Kukii St
Honolulu HI 96825

Call Sign: NH6UL
Shelly K F P Kaniho
546 Krauss St
Honolulu HI 96813

Call Sign: KH6KX
Thomas M Boyles
2426 Kuhio Ave 1205
Honolulu HI 96815

Call Sign: K7ALH
Dwayne L Teal
1134 Kukila St
Honolulu HI 96818-1954

Call Sign: WH6DMM
Michael F Yamamoto
347 A Krukowski Rd
Honolulu HI 96819

Call Sign: KD5ZHE
Nicholas F Bludworth
2140 Kuhio Ave 704
Honolulu HI 96815

Call Sign: AH6BG
Clifford H Horikawa
554 Kukuiula Lp
Honolulu HI 96825

Call Sign: N7NVI
Kent Hunter
858 Ku Ikahi St Apt 6
Honolulu HI 96826

Call Sign: WL7ER
Jerry A Gilley
2575 Kuhio Ave Apt 1503
Honolulu HI 96815

Call Sign: KH6HIQ
Terrance K Nimori
2455 Kula Kolea Dr
Honolulu HI 96819

Call Sign: NH6BS
James G Shaner
7200 Kuaehu Pl
Honolulu HI 96825

Call Sign: WH6DUH
William G Hall
2118 Kuhio Ave Apt 304
Honolulu HI 96815

Call Sign: NH7FE
Ryan M Yamashiro
2459 Kula Kolea Dr
Honolulu HI 96819

Call Sign: NH6EI
Jean E Shaner
7200 Kuaehu Pl
Honolulu HI 96825

Call Sign: KH6EPA
Eddie P Agno
1808 Kuikele St
Honolulu HI 96819

Call Sign: NH6NN
Darene N Lau
2111 Kula St
Honolulu HI 96817

Call Sign: WH6RG
Scott B Kawahara
2348 Kuahea St
Honolulu HI 96816

Call Sign: NH2ID
Eddie P Agno
1808 Kuikele St
Honolulu HI 96819

Call Sign: NH7PR
Mark D Lindsay
4051 Kulamanu St
Honolulu HI 96816

Call Sign: KI4ASQ
Kent A Bankhead
356 Kuanalu Pl

Call Sign: WH7MR
Daniel Eum
2740 Kuilei St 2105

Call Sign: WH6CGK
Holly A Chung
4051 Kulamanu St

Honolulu HI 96816

Honolulu HI 96822

Honolulu HI 96817

Call Sign: WH6CGX
Frederick C Martin
4072 Kulamanu St
Honolulu HI 96816

Call Sign: KH6PX
Robert K Yoshimura
3662 Kumu St
Honolulu HI 96822-1104

Call Sign: KH6AKR
Edward Y Nikaido
2445 Lakoloa Pl
Honolulu HI 96819

Call Sign: WH6DAC
John W Thorpe Jr
1130 Kulauala Way
Honolulu HI 96825

Call Sign: AH6FQ
Myron P Hoefer
3636 Kumu St
Honolulu HI 96822

Call Sign: WH6DTH
Sarah C Ewing
205 Lamahai Pl
Honolulu HI 96825

Call Sign: KE7DFK
Christina L Neiss
45-329 Kulauli St
Honolulu HI 96744

Call Sign: WH6LA
Craig T Hishinuma
647 Kunawci Ln 115
Honolulu HI 96817

Call Sign: WH7RV
Willa C Donnelly
1700 Lanakila Ave Rm
201
Honolulu HI 96817

Call Sign: K6UCC
Alexander E Benton
692 Kuliouou Rd
Honolulu HI 96821

Call Sign: N7NYY
Bert Y Matsuoka
435 Kupaua Pl
Honolulu HI 96821

Call Sign: WH7SC
Melissa Quinn
1700 Lanakila Ave Rm
201
Honolulu HI 96817

Call Sign: KH6SW
Skywarn
3597 Kuma St
Honolulu HI 96822

Call Sign: NH7ZV
Bert Y Matsuoka
435 Kupaua Pl
Honolulu HI 96821

Call Sign: NH7YX
Wilfred Y Higashi
3070 Lanikaula St
Honolulu HI 96822

Call Sign: NH6UB
Alan S Chun
786 Kumu Kahi Pl
Honolulu HI 96825

Call Sign: WH6BUZ
Evan Chong
4433 Laakea St
Honolulu HI 96818

Call Sign: KH6CAQ
William J Hayduk
3077 Lanikaula St
Honolulu HI 96822

Call Sign: KH6GUN
Nathan D Ichiriu
3447 Kumu St
Honolulu HI 96822

Call Sign: N7IPC
Donald Y Shinmoto
2950 Laelae Way
Honolulu HI 96819

Call Sign: NH6WI
Edward W L Dung
558 Lauiki St
Honolulu HI 96826

Call Sign: WH6DVY
Nathan D Ichiriu
3447 Kumu St
Honolulu HI 96822

Call Sign: WH7GJ
Ralph E Knight
824 Laila Way Apt 4
Honolulu HI 96814

Call Sign: KH6JK
Fred H Hosokawa
1988 Laukahi St
Honolulu HI 96821

Call Sign: KH6DQ
Jackson M Tsujimura
3597 Kumu St

Call Sign: KH6AGG
James M Nunokawa
962 Laki Rd

Call Sign: KH6KM

Robert M Reeve
2938 Laukoa Pl
Honolulu HI 96813

Call Sign: AH6F
Paul S Honda
2970 Laukoa Pl
Honolulu HI 96813

Call Sign: NH2HS
Lyndon M Godoy
1559 Laumaile St
Honolulu HI 96819

Call Sign: NH6LG
Lyndon M Godoy
1559 Laumaile St
Honolulu HI 96819

Call Sign: W6AUS
Robert C Lile
5270 Lawelawe Pl
Honolulu HI 96821

Call Sign: KH6JX
David S Sugimoto
845 Lawelawe St
Honolulu HI 96821

Call Sign: WA7KDU
Byron L Mc Cann
719-A Lawelawe St
Honolulu HI 96821

Call Sign: WH6RL
William L Mc Garry
1421 Lehia St
Honolulu HI 96818

Call Sign: KH6CAB
Charles A Clark
1619 Lehia St
Honolulu HI 96818

Call Sign: WH6DAN

Charles A Clark
1619 Lehia St
Honolulu HI 96818

Call Sign: KH7AY
Maylene L Hao
2734 Leialoha Ave
Honolulu HI 96816

Call Sign: KH6YU
Julius M Vetter
333 Lewers St
Honolulu HI 96815

Call Sign: KD7ZAI
Douglas J Rothenburger
421 Lewers St Apt E
Honolulu HI 96815

Call Sign: WH7IN
Lucas E Moxey
1503 Liho Liho St Apt 404
Honolulu HI 96822

Call Sign: KH7MG
Robert K Lum
1616 Liholiho St 1202
Honolulu HI 96822

Call Sign: KH7IF
Tiloi H Lolotai Jr
1631 Liholiho St 205
Honolulu HI 96822

Call Sign: AH6MS
Lloyd H Yamase
1610 Liholiho St 301
Honolulu HI 96822-2904

Call Sign: WH6DBG
Jane R Choe
1452 Liholiho St 504
Honolulu HI 96822

Call Sign: KH6JQN

James L Ripley
1630 Liholiho St Apt 2202
Honolulu HI 96822

Call Sign: WH7LG
Jeremy K Chan
5090 Likin St 1103
Honolulu HI 96818

Call Sign: AH6QV
Randolph R Folk
4207 Likini St
Honolulu HI 96818

Call Sign: KB5FCV
Randolph R Folk
4207 Likini St
Honolulu HI 96818

Call Sign: K6YNY
Roger F Vore
4711 Likini St
Honolulu HI 96818

Call Sign: WH6BUU
Ichizo Suzuki
5080 Likini St 1215
Honolulu HI 96818

Call Sign: WH6MZ
Richard V Richards
5090 Likini St 203
Honolulu HI 96818

Call Sign: NH6D
Wilton P Myerson
5090 Likini St 204
Honolulu HI 96818

Call Sign: WH7QK
Michael Miranda
5122 Likini St 206
Honolulu HI 96818

Call Sign: KH6DXB

Harvey L Beagle
5080 Likini St 214
Honolulu HI 96818

Call Sign: WH6VS
Jonathan J Voje
5122 Likini St 602
Honolulu HI 96818

Call Sign: WH6CPA
Bruce R Johns
5210 Likini St Apt 506
Honolulu HI 96818

Call Sign: KH2IZ
Ferdinand B Guinto
5180 Likini St Apt 703
Honolulu HI 96818-3033

Call Sign: WH6ACK
Jitsunin Kawanishi
1710 Liliha St
Honolulu HI 96817

Call Sign: KH6BRV
George K Yamamoto
2214 Liliha St
Honolulu HI 96817

Call Sign: WH6DJ
Allen P Y Tyau
2293A Liliha St
Honolulu HI 96817

Call Sign: NH6XH
Shin Yee Lau
1107 Liliha St 104
Honolulu HI 96817

Call Sign: WH6CLY
Ching Wan Marr
1001 Liliha St Apt 101
Honolulu HI 96817

Call Sign: WH6ANJ

Wendell K Chong
1101 Liliha St Apt 106
Honolulu HI 96817

Call Sign: WH6BDV
Po Chun Tsui
1203 Liliha St Apt 201
Honolulu HI 96817

Call Sign: WH6CMK
Scott T Asai
1541A Lilikoi Way
Honolulu HI 96818

Call Sign: AA6KY
David A Dutcher
3668 Lilinoe Pl
Honolulu HI 96816

Call Sign: WH6TU
Henry E Nowicki
307 Liliuokalani
Honolulu HI 96815

Call Sign: WH6CRG
Yoshitaka Ishimura
320 Liliuokalani Ave 1702
Honolulu HI 96815

Call Sign: WH7TP
Karen M Poggi
303 Liliuokalani Ave 603
Honolulu HI 96815

Call Sign: KH6BLA
Thomas Geier
303 Liliuokalani Ave 901
Honolulu HI 96815

Call Sign: WH6DJF
Thomas Geier
303 Liliuokalani Ave 901
Honolulu HI 96815

Call Sign: KB1PCX

David L Cantrell Jr
303 Liliuokalani Ave Apt
603
Honolulu HI 96815

Call Sign: WH6VT
Gregory C Tupper
2116 Lime St 204
Honolulu HI 96826

Call Sign: NH7RU
D Bart Aronoff
2015 Lime St 402
Honolulu HI 96826

Call Sign: NH6W
Richard H Abel Jr
2116 Lime St Apt 202
Honolulu HI 96826

Call Sign: NH7XY
Dwayne Cramer
1824 Lime St Apt 3
Honolulu HI 96826

Call Sign: NH7XZ
Russell G Ventenilla
2224 Lime St Apt 3A
Honolulu HI 96822

Call Sign: NH6AO
Seikichi Uehara
1314 Liona St Apt 1
Honolulu HI 96814

Call Sign: WH6DBT
Seikichi Uehara
1314 Liona St Apt 1
Honolulu HI 96814

Call Sign: NH7YV
Sarah J Marston
2543 Liuha St
Honolulu HI 98617

Call Sign: KH7AB
Leighton M Ige
3290 Loke Pl
Honolulu HI 96816

Call Sign: KH7AC
Jordan T Ige
3290 Loke Pl
Honolulu HI 96816

Call Sign: KH6AMY
Amy M Akina
935B Lolena St
Honolulu HI 96817

Call Sign: WH6DUN
Amy M Akina
935B Lolena St
Honolulu HI 96817

Call Sign: WH6NN
Arnold Y Ikeda
95-333 Lonomea St
Honolulu HI 96789

Call Sign: KH7J
Tadao Yamamoto
2917 Loomis St
Honolulu HI 96821

Call Sign: NH7X
Youth For Dx Contest
2917 Loomis St
Honolulu HI 96821

Call Sign: NH6GY
Anthony M Campbell
3554 Loulu St
Honolulu HI 96822

Call Sign: KH6GEZ
Arthur W Park
2750A Lowrey Ave
Honolulu HI 96822-1636

Call Sign: K2KGH
John M J Madey
3030 Lowrey Ave 114
Honolulu HI 96822

Call Sign: KH7NF
Kevin T Jim
3029 Lowrey Ave I 3110
Honolulu HI 96822

Call Sign: KH7NG
Katherine S Heinzen
3029 Lowrey Ave M2213
Honolulu HI 96822

Call Sign: NH6JY
Francis Button
724 Luakaha St
Honolulu HI 96816

Call Sign: NH7FD
Glenn E Arai
1204 Luawai St
Honolulu HI 96816

Call Sign: WH6BE
Mark T Kawahigashi
7227 Luhi Pl
Honolulu HI 96825

Call Sign: KH7LV
Gilbert K Lagrimas
847 Lukepane Ave
Honolulu HI 96826

Call Sign: WH6DTG
James M Ewing
205 Lumahai Pl
Honolulu HI 96825

Call Sign: WH6DWD
Bryan J Buck
5 Lumahai St
Honolulu HI 96825

Call Sign: WH7DX
Bryan J Buck Mr.
5 Lumahai St
Honolulu HI 96825

Call Sign: WH7CH
Edward K Tomasu Jr
353 Lunalilo Home Rd
Honolulu HI 96825

Call Sign: KH7MD
Lea R Anspach
708 Lunalilo Home Rd
Honolulu HI 96825

Call Sign: WH6CLT
Paula F Nishida
1070 Lunalilo Home Rd
Honolulu HI 96825

Call Sign: KH6JGD
Douglas P Lynn
1252 Lunalilo Home Rd
Honolulu HI 96825

Call Sign: NH6NU
William E Templeman
500 Lunalilo Home Rd
24L
Honolulu HI 96825

Call Sign: KH7AX
Charlotte K Herzog
444 Lunalilo Home Rd 407
Honolulu HI 96825

Call Sign: KD4YFV
Gerald R Quimby
444 Lunalilo Home Rd 605
Honolulu HI 96825

Call Sign: NH7RL
Gerald R Quimby
444 Lunalilo Home Rd 605
Honolulu HI 96825

Call Sign: KH6L
Craig R Knedler
520 Lunalilo Home Rd
Unit 6119
Honolulu HI 96825

Call Sign: WH6DUQ
Marc W Nuzzo
520 Lunalilo Home Rd
Unit 8311
Honolulu HI 96825

Call Sign: WH6SKY
Marc W Nuzzo
520 Lunalilo Home Rd
Unit 8311
Honolulu HI 96825

Call Sign: WH6DUK
Brian C Faxvog
710 Lunalilo St 703
Honolulu HI 96813

Call Sign: WH6CNL
Paul R Kuromoto
710 Lunalilo St Apt 101
Honolulu HI 96813

Call Sign: WH6DIS
David A Rezachek
710 Lunalilo St Apt 1107
Honolulu HI 96813

Call Sign: NH6CC
Edward J Haade
3802 Lurline Dr
Honolulu HI 96816

Call Sign: NH6CD
Julia M Haade
3802 Lurline Dr
Honolulu HI 96816

Call Sign: KH6TC

Guerrero F Reyes
1823 Lusitana St
Honolulu HI 96813

Call Sign: WH7OX
Guerrero F Reyes
1823 Lusitana St
Honolulu HI 96813

Call Sign: NH6RM
Patricia A Domen
1846 Lusitana St
Honolulu HI 96813

Call Sign: WH7WD
Bryan E Hirano
1442 Lusitana St 201
Honolulu HI 96813

Call Sign: WH7BG
Jeremy S Markle
1650 Lusitana St Apt 6
Honolulu HI 96813

Call Sign: WH7BB
Elsie Y Watanabe
1582 Machado St
Honolulu HI 96813

Call Sign: KH6ARM
Peter Machado
1603 Machado St
Honolulu HI 96819

Call Sign: WH6BUP
Susan E Schultz
3310A Mack Pl
Honolulu HI 96818

Call Sign: WH6BMB
Arnold S Takemoto
1534 Magazine St A2
Honolulu HI 96822

Call Sign: WH6DIQ

Paul R Flebbe
1509 Magazine St Apt B
Honolulu HI 96822

Call Sign: KH7MW
Crichton C Roberts
410 Magellan Ave Apt
1003
Honolulu HI 96813-1857

Call Sign: WH6CQD
Heinz G Pink
410 Magellan Ave Ph1002
Honolulu HI 96813

Call Sign: WH6HK
Darrell Y C Chun
2106A Maha Pl
Honolulu HI 96819

Call Sign: KH7H
Dennis K Carvalho
1847 Mahana St
Honolulu HI 96816

Call Sign: NH7MX
Jim E Hayden
1836A Mahana St
Honolulu HI 96816

Call Sign: WH6AAY
James A Mc Guire
1544 Mahie Pl
Honolulu HI 96818

Call Sign: WH6BJK
Derek Y Yonemura
5785 Mahimahi St
Honolulu HI 96821

Call Sign: WH7UQ
Raymond K Fujii
1552 Mahiole St
Honolulu HI 96819

Call Sign: WH6RR
Donald K Young
3049 Maigret St
Honolulu HI 96816

Call Sign: KB6BZN
Sharon L Robinette
124 Main St
Honolulu HI 96818

Call Sign: WH6LT
George K Ohara
7117 Maka A St
Honolulu HI 96825

Call Sign: WH6XZ
Ken Ohara
7117 Maka A St
Honolulu HI 96825

Call Sign: WH6BXZ
Ithaw Aw
7413 Maka A St Hawaii
Kai
Honolulu HI 96825

Call Sign: WH6CBZ
Dennis S Ryusaki
919 Makahiki Way Apt G
Honolulu HI 96826

Call Sign: WH6DBE
Jennifer S Y Ma
730 Makaleka Ave 505
Honolulu HI 96816

Call Sign: NH7SS
Christopher Y Langdon
2047 Makanani Dr
Honolulu HI 96817

Call Sign: WH6CUB
Sahnybel V Tan
204 Makee Rd Apt 204
Honolulu HI 96815

Call Sign: KB7WLV
Phillip S Janssen
1710 Makiki St 503
Honolulu HI 99682

Call Sign: WH6DAZ
Grace R Takeuchi
1517 Makiki St 904
Honolulu HI 96822

Call Sign: WH7RC
Kerri-Ann K Oshiro
1717 Makiki St Apt 203
Honolulu HI 96822

Call Sign: W9PQN
Roy E Waite
92 966 Makikilo Dr 50 Co
Gutzeit
Honolulu HI 96707

Call Sign: KH6AGH
Abraham L H Char
308 Mamaki St
Honolulu HI 96821-2124

Call Sign: WH6DKS
Barbara A Coles
364 Mamaki St
Honolulu HI 96821

Call Sign: KH6JCY
Thomas A Seale
480 R Mananai Pl
Honolulu HI 96818

Call Sign: KH6RX
Saint Louis High School
Arc
5328 Manauwea St
Honolulu HI 96821

Call Sign: KH6GG
Frederick M K Lam

2512 Manoa Rd
Honolulu HI 96822

Call Sign: WH6NI
Gerald F Toyomura
2602 Manoa Rd
Honolulu HI 96822

Call Sign: AH6CR
Richard O Buchanan Jr
3511 Manoa Rd
Honolulu HI 96822

Call Sign: WH7IC
Harry C Miller Jr
3041 A Manoa Rd
Honolulu HI 96822

Call Sign: KH6DP
Vernon R South
6088 Manukapu Pl
Honolulu HI 96821

Call Sign: WH6BZW
Jocelyna R Melgar
1192 Manuwa Dr
Honolulu HI 96818

Call Sign: WH6JU
Douglas K Tom
123 Maono Pl
Honolulu HI 96821

Call Sign: WH6LS
Edmund F Desmond
1724A Marques St
Honolulu HI 96822

Call Sign: NH7XT
David J Imada
3212 Martha St
Honolulu HI 96815

Call Sign: WH6AMU
Ryan H Namaka

3248 Martha St
Honolulu HI 96815

Call Sign: NH7YT
Gwendolyn M Wong
4836 Matsonia Dr
Honolulu HI 96816

Call Sign: WH6BYN
Oscar R Libed
1035C Matzie Ln
Honolulu HI 96817

Call Sign: WH6CCU
Frank H Okimoto
640 Maui St
Honolulu HI 96817

Call Sign: KH6DSY
Hing H Chun
2143 Mauna Pl
Honolulu HI 96822

Call Sign: NH6YN
Bruce R Nakamura
2142A Mauna Pl
Honolulu HI 96822

Call Sign: WH6DBI
Russell V Houlton
1025 Maunaihi Pl 202
Honolulu HI 96822-3404

Call Sign: WH7O
Russell V Houlton
1025 Maunaihi Pl 202
Honolulu HI 96822-3404

Call Sign: KH6QK
Robert H Naganuma
3456 Maunalei Ave
Honolulu HI 96816

Call Sign: KH6QD
Lewis S Trusty

117A Maunalua Ave
Honolulu HI 96821

Call Sign: WH6DKE
Sean R Mina
2618 Maunawai Pl 52
Honolulu HI 96826

Call Sign: AH6BZ
George R Masunari
620 Mc Cully St 706
Honolulu HI 96826

Call Sign: NH7NH
Matthew S Langley
57 Memorial Dr 110
Honolulu HI 96818

Call Sign: WH7JA
Cynthia Kaimimoku
728 Menehune Ln
Honolulu HI 96827

Call Sign: WH7JC
Lawrence A Sayurin
728 Menehune Ln
Honolulu HI 96826

Call Sign: WH7NC
Jane V Schramko
1645 Merkle St
Honolulu HI 96819

Call Sign: KH7SK
Sharon A Kelly
2141 Metcalf St
Honolulu HI 96822

Call Sign: WH6CQZ
Ricky Iosia
1589 Meyers St
Honolulu HI 96819

Call Sign: KH6ABU
James M Horikoshi

1718 Mikahala Way
Honolulu HI 96816

Call Sign: KH6AYB
Wesley G Holland
44-317 Mikiola Dr
Honolulu HI 96744

Call Sign: KH7AL
Allen C Levie
1003 Mills Blvd
Honolulu HI 96818

Call Sign: KL3FN
Allen C Levie
1003 Mills Blvd
Honolulu HI 96818

Call Sign: WH6EA
Jacob H Verhoeff
6247 Milolii Pl
Honolulu HI 96825

Call Sign: WH6DET
Kaiser Foundation
Hospital Hawaii
3288 Moanalua Rd
Honolulu HI 96819

Call Sign: WH7JZ
Robert G Verner
1350 Moanalualani Pl Apt
D
Honolulu HI 96819

Call Sign: WH7RGV
Robert G Verner
1350 Moanalualani Pl Apt
D
Honolulu HI 96819

Call Sign: WH7Z
Hickam Contest Group
1309 D Moanalualani Way
Honolulu HI 96819

Call Sign: KH6JFJ
Daryl S Fukunaga
1329 Moanalualani Way
Apt E
Honolulu HI 96819

Call Sign: KH6DWW
Allen K Okamura
1330 Moelola Pl
Honolulu HI 96819

Call Sign: WH7GL
Mark S Want
1171 Mokuhano St E102
Honolulu HI 96825

Call Sign: KB8TNA
Michael R Heisler
1173 Mokuhano St F205
Honolulu HI 96825

Call Sign: KH6A
James R Bedient
1464 Molehu Dr
Honolulu HI 96818

Call Sign: WH6EF
James R Bedient
1464 Molehu Dr
Honolulu HI 96818

Call Sign: WH7F
James R Bedient
1464 Molehu Dr
Honolulu HI 96818

Call Sign: KA6KAB
Harry R Rothschild
17 Moloaa St
Honolulu HI 96825

Call Sign: KH6EN
Harvey A Sunada
1157 Mona St

Honolulu HI 96821

Call Sign: NH7JH
Jason K Redulla
3324 Monsarrat Ave
Honolulu HI 96815

Call Sign: WH6DMA
Brett S Molale
1572 Monte St
Honolulu HI 96819

Call Sign: NH6YW
Chester T Koga
1583 Monte St
Honolulu HI 96819

Call Sign: WH6IE
James T Rigsby
3957 Monterey Pl
Honolulu HI 96816

Call Sign: KH7GP
James D Reay
304 Monthan St
Honolulu HI 96818

Call Sign: NH6OX
Edward Choi
1337 Mookaula St
Honolulu HI 96817

Call Sign: KH7YN
David W Barnett
298 Moomuku Pl
Honolulu HI 96821

Call Sign: AH7V
Akira Yamada
Mr S Minamoto - 201Ohua
Ave., #501-1
Honolulu HI 96815

Call Sign: KG6PQQ
John Mersberg Jr

870 Murray Dr
Honolulu HI 96818

Call Sign: KH6IKF
Victor M Abbatiello
7121 Naakea St
Honolulu HI 96825

Call Sign: AH6SX
Ronald A Amrhein Sr
431 Nahua St 1203
Honolulu HI 96815

Call Sign: K2IO
Ronald A Amrhein Sr
431 Nahua St 1203
Honolulu HI 96815

Call Sign: WH6BKR
Lynley K Mc Arthur
1806 Naio St
Honolulu HI 96817

Call Sign: AH6PI
Reynaldo R Torres
630 Nalanui St D
Honolulu HI 96817

Call Sign: WH6AZL
Ann K H Fernandez
432 Namahana St Apt 404
Honolulu HI 96815

Call Sign: KH6CVA
Lawrence A Julian Sr
1161 Namahealani Pl
Honolulu HI 96825-2874

Call Sign: WH6CNG
Devin Q U Leong
1704 Nanea St
Honolulu HI 96826

Call Sign: AH6MA
Kenneth J Gibes

7505D Nanu St
Honolulu HI 96818

1047 Nettle Dr
Honolulu HI 96818

7041 Niumalu Loop
Honolulu HI 96825

Call Sign: WH7IQ
Zachary K Lee Ho
7238 Naohe St
Honolulu HI 96825

Call Sign: KA6QOD
Clyde T Miyaki
2333 Nihi St
Honolulu HI 96819

Call Sign: WA6FB
Mitsuhiro Yashiro
7041 Niumalu Loop
Honolulu HI 96825

Call Sign: KH7EV
Harold F Griffith
83 Nawiliwili St
Honolulu HI 96825

Call Sign: AH6DO
Albert J Mariani
3630 Nihipali Pl
Honolulu HI 96816

Call Sign: NH6P
Lee R Dawson
2257 Noah St
Honolulu HI 96816

Call Sign: KH6IIQ
Ralph E Cook
153 Nawiliwili St
Honolulu HI 96825

Call Sign: KH6MD
Albert J Mariani
3630 Nihipali Pl
Honolulu HI 96816

Call Sign: KH7VW
Elna M Oshiro
2264 Noah St
Honolulu HI 96816

Call Sign: KH6UW
Robert D Spears II
7601E Nehe St
Honolulu HI 96818

Call Sign: KH6CD
Wah How Lee
3849 Nikolo St
Honolulu HI 96815-4508

Call Sign: KH7YA
Garrett A Teves
1591 Nobrega St
Honolulu HI 96819

Call Sign: NL7UW
Robert D Spears II II
7601E Nehe St
Honolulu HI 96818

Call Sign: WH7TN
Michael Amor Aguinaldo
1748 Nilani St
Honolulu HI 96819

Call Sign: KC4AIS
Tareq I Hoque
3207 Noela Dr
Honolulu HI 96815

Call Sign: KH6NZ
Hiroichi T Muramoto
1356 Nehoa St
Honolulu HI 96822

Call Sign: NH7VY
Shoji Takeda
444 Niu St 2105
Honolulu HI 96815

Call Sign: AH6W
Bryson L T Nishimura
94 1126 Noheaiki Way
Honolulu HI 96797

Call Sign: NH7ZA
Susan A Lee
207 Nenue St
Honolulu HI 96821

Call Sign: WH6PN
Nancy E Rocheleau
6871 Niumalu Loop
Honolulu HI 96825

Call Sign: AH6SQ
Leonard M Pheobus
7247 Nohili St
Honolulu HI 96825

Call Sign: KH6ICX
Vincent H S Lee
207 Nenue St
Honolulu HI 96821-1811

Call Sign: AH6CE
Herman J Davey
6901 Niumalu Loop
Honolulu HI 96825

Call Sign: N3LP
Leonard M Pheobus
7247 Nohili St
Honolulu HI 96825

Call Sign: WH6BVA
Charles K Fellows

Call Sign: KD7FBB
Kunihiro Shinji

Call Sign: WH7F
Leonard M Pheobus

7247 Nohili St
Honolulu HI 96825

Call Sign: KH6CF
Carol A Ferreira
111 North Beretania 905
Honolulu HI 96817

Call Sign: WH6CTN
Carol A Ferreira
111 North Beretania 905
Honolulu HI 96817

Call Sign: WH6HS
Claire Chun
60 North Beretania St 2310
Honolulu HI 96817

Call Sign: WH7UC
Jason C Thoel
60 North Beretania St Apt 3210
Honolulu HI 96817

Call Sign: NH7ON
Edmund K Lee
425 North Judd St
Honolulu HI 96817

Call Sign: KH7ZP
Isaia Robins
117Th North Judd St
Honolulu HI 96815

Call Sign: KH7QN
Barney Peterson
2024 North King St 201A
Honolulu HI 96819

Call Sign: ND2Y
Tomio Yamazaki
C/O Sara Johansson 215 North King St Apt 1903
Honolulu HI 96817

Call Sign: WH6BNA
Joseph Evans
607 North King St Apt 254A
Honolulu HI 96817

Call Sign: KH6KMC
Kuakini Medical Center
347 North Kuakini St
Honolulu HI 96817

Call Sign: WH6BXF
Warren S Yagi
611 North Kuakini St 201
Honolulu HI 96817

Call Sign: KH7SV
Jason A Jaboneta
629 North Kuakini St 301
Honolulu HI 96817

Call Sign: KH7SW
James A Jaboneta
629 North Kuakini St 301
Honolulu HI 96817

Call Sign: KH6XW
Leonard L Polinar
35 North Kukui St Apt 1006
Honolulu HI 96817

Call Sign: WH6BVR
Sup S Um
53 North Kukui St Apt 704
Honolulu HI 96817

Call Sign: KH7VU
Peggy M Lau
35 North Kukuist 2801
Honolulu HI 96817

Call Sign: KD4CPU
Robert E Stone
3085 North Nimitz

Honolulu HI 96819

Call Sign: K6FBK
Salem Communications
Radio Club
560 North Nimitz
Highway Ste 114B
Honolulu HI 96817

Call Sign: KH6FM
Salem Communications
Radio Club
560 North Nimitz
Highway Ste 114B
Honolulu HI 96817

Call Sign: NH7JJ
Joan E Jacob
167 North Pauahi St 607
Honolulu HI 96817

Call Sign: WH6CWA
Cesar S Libed
1801 North School St
Honolulu HI 96819

Call Sign: WH7VH
Marlireen P Aquino
2470 North School St Apt B
Honolulu HI 96819

Call Sign: KH6IOL
Jefferson D Childs III
1015 North School St Apt B606
Honolulu HI 96817-2940

Call Sign: KH7LO
Austin T Faletufuga
404 North Vineyard Blvd
Honolulu HI 96817

Call Sign: NH7SK
William Mar

301 North Vineyard Blvd
214
Honolulu HI 96817

Call Sign: N2MVH
Kevin S Roberts
1519 Nuuanu Ave
Honolulu HI 96817-3755

Call Sign: NH6UU
Frederick T Hoppe
2040 Nuuanu Ave
Honolulu HI 96817

Call Sign: KH7CX
Alexander G Stengel
2313 Nuuanu Ave
Honolulu HI 96817

Call Sign: NH6UR
Lori A Hoppe
2040 Nuuanu Ave 1401
Honolulu HI 96817

Call Sign: NH7YU
Yolanda M Valiente
2029 Nuuanu Ave 1504
Honolulu HI 96817

Call Sign: WH6CG
Sibyl L Sur
2029 Nuuanu Ave 1707
Honolulu HI 96817

Call Sign: NH7OB
Sarah S Lee
1170 Nuuanu Ave 2004
Honolulu HI 96817

Call Sign: AH6NF
Beverley A Yuen
2047 Nuuanu Ave 2202
Honolulu HI 96817-2522

Call Sign: WH6GS

James Yuen
2047 Nuuanu Ave 2202
Honolulu HI 96817-2522

Call Sign: N6GGG
John A Thorne
2033 Nuuanu Ave 27C
Honolulu HI 96817

Call Sign: WH6BU
Michael J Carey
1634 Nuuanu Ave Apt 215
Honolulu HI 96817

Call Sign: WH7PT
Jason T Akagi
2101 Nuuanu Ave Apt 906
Honolulu HI 96817

Call Sign: KH6FHB
Irvin C Young
1515 Nuuanu Ave Q82
Honolulu HI 96817

Call Sign: KH6ZZ
Robert H Tanimoto
1515 Nuuanu Ave Qt103
Honolulu HI 96817-3761

Call Sign: WH6OE
Jonah H N Thompson
7245 Nuulolo St
Honolulu HI 96825

Call Sign: WH6CGH
Dorin J Matney
757 Nye Cir
Honolulu HI 96818

Call Sign: KH7FE
Kevin M Sullivan
768 Nye Cir
Honolulu HI 96818

Call Sign: KH6JQQ

Maryknoll Schools
Amateur Radio Club
2106 Oahu Ave
Honolulu HI 96822

Call Sign: KH6HCU
Clinton J Clausen
2106 Oahu Ave
Honolulu HI 96822-2207

Call Sign: KH6PF
Kinji Kanazawa
2316 Oahu Ave
Honolulu HI 96822

Call Sign: KH6IBM
Clifford K Mirikitani
2336 Oahu Ave
Honolulu HI 96822

Call Sign: KH6HRY
Wesley K Inouye
3174 Oahu Ave
Honolulu HI 96822

Call Sign: WH7YW
David K Marchant
3185 Oahu Ave
Honolulu HI 96822

Call Sign: WH6PT
James H Osborne
3209 Oahu Ave
Honolulu HI 96822

Call Sign: KH7JH
Thomas M Vines
2323 Oanu Ave
Honolulu HI 96822-1966

Call Sign: KH6AS
John Keawe Jr
714 Ocean View Dr
Honolulu HI 96816

Call Sign: WH6DKJ
Glynis Lewis
914 Ocean View Dr
Honolulu HI 96816

Call Sign: WH6BZB
Merlin A Petersen
827 Oceanview Dr
Honolulu HI 96816

Call Sign: KC5RDQ
Miguel A Robles
887 Ohana Nui Cir
Honolulu HI 96818

Call Sign: NH6ZU
Robert M Finan
1525 Ohialoke St
Honolulu HI 96821

Call Sign: WH6CPY
Amy S Caragay
250 Ohua Ave 10G
Honolulu HI 96815

Call Sign: KH6KT
John C Sanders
1070 Oilipuu Pl
Honolulu HI 96825

Call Sign: AH6HU
Walter A Simmons
2278 Okoa St
Honolulu HI 96821

Call Sign: KH6GD
Gale A Dowdy
4327 Olaloa St
Honolulu HI 96818-1970

Call Sign: KH6EBA
Wah C Ching
3742B Old Pali Rd
Honolulu HI 96817

Call Sign: WH6HT
Daniel L Leatherman
7541 Olili Pl
Honolulu HI 96825

Call Sign: WB4STN
John S Ross
502A Olive Pl
Honolulu HI 96818

Call Sign: WH6CXK
Thomas W S Hee
3173 Olu St
Honolulu HI 96816

Call Sign: KH7AJ
Richard W Caldwell
One Keahole Pl 2111
Honolulu HI 96825

Call Sign: WH6DEK
Msys Packet Amateur
Radio Club
3041 One St
Honolulu HI 96822

Call Sign: KH6GFZ
Robert C Causton
493 Opihikao Pl
Honolulu HI 96825

Call Sign: WH6CRD
Donna M Wendt
170 Opihikao Way
Honolulu HI 96825

Call Sign: KH6WK
Walter M Shiraishi
214 Opihikao Way
Honolulu HI 96825

Call Sign: WH6AYQ
Daniel D Okada
2018 Oswald St
Honolulu HI 96816

Call Sign: KH6RT
Eric K Ty
2358 Owene Ln
Honolulu HI 96819

Call Sign: KH6UH
Jerry P Wine
P.O. Box 1424
Honolulu HI 96701-1424

Call Sign: KH7OP
Aaron K Keliikoa
P.O. Box 30551
Honolulu HI 96820

Call Sign: AH7GK
George M Kaneshige
807 Paahana St
Honolulu HI 96816

Call Sign: KH6EDH
William Y K Young
3465 Paalea St
Honolulu HI 96816-2832

Call Sign: KH6IQT
David H F Tong
767 Paani St
Honolulu HI 96826

Call Sign: WA6JMB
Theodore Y H Mau
772 Paani St 1603
Honolulu HI 96826

Call Sign: AH6RX
William E Ridgway Jr
3230 Pacific Heights Rd
Honolulu HI 96813

Call Sign: AH6TW
William E Ridgway Jr
3230 Pacific Heights Rd
Honolulu HI 96813

Call Sign: NH7TH
William E Ridgway Jr
3230 Pacific Heights Rd
Honolulu HI 96813

Call Sign: N2LTL
Paul J Weissman
3260 Pacific Heights Rd
Honolulu HI 96813

Call Sign: AH6AV
Leonard K H Lau
3334 Pahoa Ave
Honolulu HI 96816

Call Sign: KH6FG
Marjorie C Lau
3334 Pahoa Ave
Honolulu HI 96816

Call Sign: KH7SI
Victor D C Choy
3915 Pahoa Ave
Honolulu HI 96816

Call Sign: KH6EC
Edward Y J Choy
3915 Pahoa Ave
Honolulu HI 96816

Call Sign: KH7FI
Carolann K Pilimai
3915 Pahoa Ave
Honolulu HI 96816

Call Sign: KH7MQ
Arthur Y M Choy
3915 Pahoa Ave
Honolulu HI 96816

Call Sign: KH7SJ
Lynn K K Choy
3915 Pahoa Ave
Honolulu HI 96816

Call Sign: KH7SL
Christina K Choy
3915 Pahoa Ave
Honolulu HI 96816

Call Sign: KH7SM
Cassandra K Choy
3915 Pahoa Ave
Honolulu HI 96816

Call Sign: WH6DWE
Akira Kawagoe
4340 Pahoa Ave 7C
Honolulu HI 96816

Call Sign: NH6RQ
Agnes A Abrigo
1577 Pahulu St
Honolulu HI 96819

Call Sign: KH6GLP
Richard H P Sia
656 Paikau St
Honolulu HI 96816

Call Sign: AH6GL
Gary H Ting
4001 Pakahi Pl
Honolulu HI 96816

Call Sign: NH7YG
Gary H Ting
4001 Pakahi Pl
Honolulu HI 96816

Call Sign: KH6BSA
Hawaii Scouts
4001 Pakahi Pl
Honolulu HI 96816

Call Sign: WH6DHY
Hawaii Scouts
4001 Pakahi Pl
Honolulu HI 96816

Call Sign: KH6GBC
David T Motooka
3812 Paki Ave
Honolulu HI 96815

Call Sign: KH6DGS
Heine I Kamai
3433 Pakui St
Honolulu HI 96816

Call Sign: KH6BN
Joseph K Ting Sr
3514 Pakui St
Honolulu HI 96816

Call Sign: KH6JC
Arnold A Ting
3514 Pakui St
Honolulu HI 96816

Call Sign: KH6NF
Mc Kinley High School
Arc
2752 H Pali Hwy
Honolulu HI 96817

Call Sign: WH6CB
Mary Ann M Kadooka
2752H Pali Hwy
Honolulu HI 96817

Call Sign: NH7QW
Elizabeth A Knuth
2825-B Pali Hwy
Honolulu HI 96817

Call Sign: KH7UN
Trevor P Johannsen
15 Palmyra Dr
Honolulu HI 96818

Call Sign: WH6HO
Daniel J Peters
1707A Palolo Ave

Honolulu HI 96816 Honolulu HI 96816 Honolulu HI 96815

Call Sign: NH6GO
Richard K Shimabukurd
2265B Palolo Ave
Honolulu HI 96816

Call Sign: AH7W
Toivo Hallikivi
4231 Papu Cir
Honolulu HI 96816

Call Sign: WH6JN
Carmel L Davis
1715 Paula Dr
Honolulu HI 96816

Call Sign: WH7PK
Windell H Jones
1760 Palolo Ave Apt H
Honolulu HI 96816

Call Sign: KH6BKE
Eddie W S Lum
2817 Park St
Honolulu HI 96817

Call Sign: AH6SM
Nathan S Ching
2161 Pauoa Rd
Honolulu HI 96813

Call Sign: NH7OY
Aaron T Ohta
3255-A Palolo Terr Pl
Honolulu HI 96816

Call Sign: WH6DJE
Mark Ellis
2950 Park St
Honolulu HI 96817

Call Sign: WH7QP
Roger S Kort
2668 Pawoa Rd
Honolulu HI 96813

Call Sign: NH6LS
Patrick S Yamada
4006 Palua Pl
Honolulu HI 96816

Call Sign: AG4FH
William R Frost
1331 Parks Pl
Honolulu HI 96819

Call Sign: WH6CUT
Kotaro Koizumi
1515C Pele St
Honolulu HI 96813

Call Sign: N6AGZ
Bernard F Cassidy
2727 Pamoa Rd
Honolulu HI 96822

Call Sign: N6DXW
Maria C Brown
1373 Parks Rd
Honolulu HI 96819

Call Sign: WH7AR
David H Kikau
1454 Pele St 301
Honolulu HI 96813

Call Sign: KH6BPE
Wayne T Takemoto
5256 Papai St
Honolulu HI 96821

Call Sign: AC7LR
Francisco J Escalera
150 Patch Pl
Honolulu HI 96819-4823

Call Sign: KH6KOI
Kotaro Koizumi
1515 Pele St Apt C
Honolulu HI 96813

Call Sign: WH6DMR
Wendell J Naumu
2925 Papali St
Honolulu HI 96819

Call Sign: KH7CR
Alfred J Fortin
3303 Paty Dr
Honolulu HI 96822

Call Sign: WH7LT
Kotaro Koizumi
1515 Pele St Apt C
Honolulu HI 96813

Call Sign: KH6BYZ
Ronald Q Tam
4160 Papu Cir
Honolulu HI 96816

Call Sign: WH6GR
Betty P L Yee
3303 Paty Dr
Honolulu HI 96822-1441

Call Sign: KH7UJ
Clifford F Mc Donald
628 Peltier Ave
Honolulu HI 96818

Call Sign: KH6EM
George Tam
4160 Papu Cir

Call Sign: KH7AV
Mitchell C Johnson
444 Pau St Apt E

Call Sign: WH6OH
Brett W Collars
724 Peltier Ave

Honolulu HI 96818

Honolulu HI 96816

Honolulu HI 96819

Call Sign: WH6IG
Long N Phan Jr
739 Pensacola St
Honolulu HI 96814

Call Sign: WH6AO
Joseph E Flory
1201 Pihana St
Honolulu HI 96825

Call Sign: KH6SE
Mark S Noda
3541 Pinocula Pl
Honolulu HI 96822

Call Sign: WH7MP
Darryl Cunningham
1524 Pensacola St 318
Honolulu HI 96822

Call Sign: WH6BID
Judith G Jones
1656 Piikea St
Honolulu HI 96818-1843

Call Sign: AH6HY
David A Flack
Po Box 29761
Honolulu HI 96820-2161

Call Sign: KH7YY
Yvette S Lee
1561 Pensacola St 606
Honolulu HI 96822

Call Sign: NH7IX
Maude C Williams
1556 Piikoi St 1803
Honolulu HI 96822

Call Sign: KH6CDO
Franklin S H Young
2816 Poelua
Honolulu HI 96822

Call Sign: AH6DP
Alice May Drury
1561 Pensacola St 801
Honolulu HI 96822

Call Sign: KE7AVG
Tsuyoshi Nagano
725 Piikoi St 203
Honolulu HI 96814

Call Sign: KH6ZS
Lawrence F H Zane
2831 Poelua St
Honolulu HI 96822-1311

Call Sign: NH6OD
Lawrence H K Baptista
515 Pepeekeo Pl
Honolulu HI 96825

Call Sign: WH6FA
Matthew R Walker
1556 Piikoi St Apt 1502
Honolulu HI 96822

Call Sign: KH6IAU
William K C Wong
2832 Poelua St
Honolulu HI 96822

Call Sign: WH7QS
Richard N Kiyabu
519 Pepeekeo Pl
Honolulu HI 96825

Call Sign: WH6CMF
Scott A Shultis
404 Piikoi St Box C16
Honolulu HI 96814

Call Sign: KH6AZG
Edwin Naito
2920 Poelua St
Honolulu HI 96822-1312

Call Sign: WH6DBS
Burr C Fee
521 6 Pepeekeo St
Honolulu HI 96825

Call Sign: WH6AXR
Stephen M Tonaki
2749 Piliwai St
Honolulu HI 96819-2841

Call Sign: KH7BB
Stacey J Agcaoili
1510 Pohaku St
Honolulu HI 96817

Call Sign: WH6BIO
Brian T Apo
1415 Peter Buck St
Honolulu HI 96817

Call Sign: NH6PZ
John G Popovich Sr
1149 Pinkham St
Honolulu HI 96819

Call Sign: KH7YK
Marya L Baker
1707 Poki St
Honolulu HI 96822

Call Sign: WH6HY
Gordon Y Piianaia
2822 Peter St

Call Sign: WH6CAR
Johnathan F L Favinger
1149 Pinkham St

Call Sign: WH6NW
Gail T Iwamoto
3020 Polohilani Pl

Honolulu HI 96817

Call Sign: WH6FD
Neil Y Iwamoto
3020 Polohilani Pl
Honolulu HI 96817

Call Sign: NH7YW
Maria A Lutz
109 Poloke Pl
Honolulu HI 96822

Call Sign: KB8JLV
Stanley E Lewis Jr
710 Pool St
Honolulu HI 96818

Call Sign: KH7UE
Jacob Hill
725 Pool St
Honolulu HI 96818

Call Sign: WH7ZN
Terence M Bryan
5496 Poola St
Honolulu HI 96821

Call Sign: NH7JL
David A Newman
394 Portlock Rd
Honolulu HI 96825

Call Sign: NH6CM
William Snyder
550 Portlock Rd
Honolulu HI 96825

Call Sign: KH6CQR
William K L Chow
101 Prospect St
Honolulu HI 96813

Call Sign: KH6EU
William P Sullivan
927 Prospect St 1401

Honolulu HI 96822

Call Sign: NH7XU
Dean T Kawamoto
303 Prospect St 4
Honolulu HI 96813

Call Sign: WH7WC
Jason Y Hiramoto
1011 Prospect St 410
Honolulu HI 96822

Call Sign: AH6RH
Ronald I Hashiro
1013 Prospect St 618
Honolulu HI 96822-3447

Call Sign: NH6PF
Dwight T Martin
1013 Prospect St Apt 1212
Honolulu HI 96822

Call Sign: NH7CV
Steven C K Young
666 Prospect St Apt 709
Honolulu HI 96813

Call Sign: WH6DOY
Tsung Ping Ma
217 Prospect St Apt F6
Honolulu HI 96813

Call Sign: WH7PW
Ta-Wei Kao
217 Prospect St Apt F6
Honolulu HI 96813

Call Sign: KH6AKB
Frederic K T Chun
802 Prospect St Penthouse
Honolulu HI 96813

Call Sign: WH6GX
Ravi K Gupta
1120 Pua Ln 103

Honolulu HI 98614

Call Sign: WH6CEI
Mike C K Chan
1118 Pua Ln 308
Honolulu HI 96817

Call Sign: KH6IRT
Peter R Brown
5332 Puahia Pl
Honolulu HI 96821

Call Sign: KH6TK
Edward H Carus Jr
2600 Pualani Way 2201
Honolulu HI 96815

Call Sign: KH7QW
Richard G Rolston
3061 305 Pualei Cir
Honolulu HI 96815

Call Sign: NH6TA
Jack Knapp
3111 Pualei Cir 106
Honolulu HI 96815

Call Sign: NH6UP
Donna M Giarraputo
Knapp
3111 Pualei Cir 106
Honolulu HI 96815

Call Sign: WH6HX
Emil W Klimpl
1480 Puanakau St
Honolulu HI 96818

Call Sign: KH6IFO
Jeffrey C Kam
1034 Pueo St
Honolulu HI 96816

Call Sign: WH7OZ
Robert M Wai Jr

3071A Puhala Rise
Honolulu HI 96822

Call Sign: KH6SHC
Shriners Hospital
1310 Punahou St
Honolulu HI 96826

Call Sign: KH6KWC
Kapi Olani Med Cntr For
Women & Children Arg
1319 Punahou St
Honolulu HI 96826

Call Sign: WH6CBF
Linda Q Green
Castle Hall 1601 Punahou
St
Honolulu HI 96822

Call Sign: WH7NI
Koi Hallonquist
1521 Punahou St 1002
Honolulu HI 96822

Call Sign: KH7MY
Frances A Hallonquist
1521 Punahou St Apt 1002
Honolulu HI 96822

Call Sign: KH7MZ
Normand A Hallonquist
1521 Punahou St Apt 1002
Honolulu HI 96822

Call Sign: WH6COL
Willis F Kemp
1434 Punahou St Apt 1200
Honolulu HI 96822-4748

Call Sign: WH7QY
Ongor E Dengokl
1425 Punahou St Apt 203
Honolulu HI 96822

Call Sign: KH6AFG
Leonard Withington
1434 Punahou St Apt 504
505
Honolulu HI 96822

Call Sign: KH6QMC
Queens Medical Center
Amateur Radio Club
1301 Punchbowl St
Honolulu HI 96813

Call Sign: N1AQR
Joseph A Sileo
1848 Puowaina Dr
Honolulu HI 96813-1706

Call Sign: WH7MF
Noah Hafner
1931 Puowaina Dr
Honolulu HI 96813

Call Sign: WH7LW
Wansuree Massagram
1931 Puowaina Dr
Honolulu HI 96813

Call Sign: KH6VF
Wayne D Walker
1983 Puowaina Dr
Honolulu HI 96813

Call Sign: WH6FK
Mark T Tomita
2155B Puowaina Dr
Honolulu HI 96813

Call Sign: WH6COO
Brian F Benevedes
4409A Puu Panini Ave
Honolulu HI 96816

Call Sign: NH6UI
Mary C Kamalii
348 Puuhale Rd 304

Honolulu HI 96819

Call Sign: KH7TN
Rosemarie Lum
2802 Puuhonua St
Honolulu HI 96822

Call Sign: AH6RW
Dion K Li
344 Puuhue Pl Apt 1
Honolulu HI 96817

Call Sign: AH7I
Jeffrey A Brennan
865 Puuikema Dr
Honolulu HI 96821-2564

Call Sign: KH7PA
Jon K Matsuo
690 Puuikena Dr
Honolulu HI 96821-2509

Call Sign: NH7ZO
David A Rae
2020 Puukapu St
Honolulu HI 96819

Call Sign: KH6JF
Joseph F Fenn
3612 Puuku Makai Dr
Honolulu HI 96818

Call Sign: WH6CAT
Samuel M Mc Cline
3636A Puuku Makai Dr
Honolulu HI 96818

Call Sign: WH6DKP
Robert M Galino
3548 Puuku Mauka Dr
Honolulu HI 96818

Call Sign: KH7MAC
Milton C Q Lau Mr.
2737 Puunui Ave

Honolulu HI 96817

Honolulu HI 96818

Honolulu HI 96822

Call Sign: WH6JM
Mark R Van Der Pyl
902 Puuomao Pl
Honolulu HI 96825

Call Sign: WH7BM
Robert I Pickering
365-A Reno Rd
Honolulu HI 96819

Call Sign: KH7GE
Roger R Leonard
4146 Round Top Dr
Honolulu HI 96822-5020

Call Sign: WH6COS
Ken W Fass
4409A Puupanini Ave
Honolulu HI 96816

Call Sign: KH7FC
William V Kelly
700 Richards St 2108
Honolulu HI 96813

Call Sign: AH6GI
Cory K Hamasaki
2014 Round Top Ter
Honolulu HI 96822

Call Sign: K9GOR
Ernest D Winchester
1177 Queen St 2601
Honolulu HI 96814

Call Sign: WH7F
William V Kelly
700 Richards St 2108
Honolulu HI 96813

Call Sign: KH6CXK
Philip Y T Kam
1552 Saint Louis Dr
Honolulu HI 96816-1921

Call Sign: WH6AWC
Harris M Gitlin
1646 Quincy Pl
Honolulu HI 96816

Call Sign: KH7PU
John M Swatek
1055 River St Apt 310
Honolulu HI 96817

Call Sign: KH6PW
Patrick W Wong
2471 Saint Louis Dr
Honolulu HI 96816

Call Sign: KH7LF
Nicholas J Hensz
572 R Mananai Pl
Honolulu HI 96818

Call Sign: AH6G
Katsushi Ono
2728 Rooke Ave
Honolulu HI 96817

Call Sign: KB6CIE
Soo N Han
3616 Salt Lake Blvd
Honolulu HI 96818

Call Sign: WH7IT
Glen Badua
572 R Mananai Pl
Honolulu HI 96818

Call Sign: KD7NBA
Katsushi Ono
2728 Rooke Ave
Honolulu HI 96817

Call Sign: NH7ZK
S Frank Nacino
3752 Salt Lake Blvd
Honolulu HI 96818

Call Sign: NH2IO
Danilo Lumatas
1010 Rawlins Ln Apt R
Honolulu HI 96817

Call Sign: KH7U
Kimo C Chun
2728 Rooke Ave
Honolulu HI 96817

Call Sign: WH6CLD
Don J Johnson
4510 Salt Lake Blvd
Honolulu HI 96818

Call Sign: KH6DIL
Danilo Lumantas
1010 Rawlins Ln Apt R
Honolulu HI 96817

Call Sign: K3LNE
Siegbert D Busch
2346 Round Top Dr
Honolulu HI 96822

Call Sign: WH6CKX
Craig Cournoyer
24 Sand Is Rd 27
Honolulu HI 96819

Call Sign: KH7UL
Edmond J Pechaty
379 F Reasoner Rd

Call Sign: KG6SI
Siegbert D Busch
2346 Round Top Dr

Call Sign: WH6RQ
Graham J Darby

50E Sand Island Access
Rd
Honolulu HI 96819

Call Sign: WH6SO
Else J Jakubenko
50E Sand Island Dr
Honolulu HI 96819

Call Sign: WH6RS
Gregory A Jakubenko
50E Sand Island Rd
Honolulu HI 96819

Call Sign: WH6CMV
David L Lyman
4 Sand Island Rd 1
Honolulu HI 96819

Call Sign: KB6TMQ
David A J Wright
24 Sand Island Rd 27
Honolulu HI 96819

Call Sign: WH6CQO
Melissa A Gionet
24 Sand Island Rd 27
Honolulu HI 96819

Call Sign: WH6WV
Ira D Hawver
24 Sand Island Rd 27
Honolulu HI 96819

Call Sign: WH6LK
Chris A Dacus Mr.
440 Seaside Ave 303
Honolulu HI 96815

Call Sign: WH6TZ
Randolph J Glass
620 Sheridan St Apt 407
Honolulu HI 96814

Call Sign: KH7UZ

Tim L Cagadas
735 Sibley St
Honolulu HI 96818

Call Sign: WH6NH
Carl J Lenander Iv
4024 Sierra Dr
Honolulu HI 96816

Call Sign: NH7SZ
Satoshi Yamashita
4483 Sierra Dr
Honolulu HI 96816

Call Sign: WH6CXL
Jonathan A K Kekipi
4483 Sierra Dr
Honolulu HI 96816

Call Sign: WH6CXZ
Thomas J Kekipi
4483 Sierra Dr
Honolulu HI 96816

Call Sign: NH7TA
Osamu Nakamura
Ryan Miyashiro 4483
Sierra Dr
Honolulu HI 96816

Call Sign: NH7TB
Saori Kawahara
Ryan Miyashiro 4483
Sierra Dr
Honolulu HI 96816

Call Sign: NH7TC
Keisuke Tsukiashi
Ryan Miyashiro 4483
Sierra Dr
Honolulu HI 96816

Call Sign: NH7TE
Haruka Kugita

Ryan Miyashiro 4483
Sierra Dr
Honolulu HI 96816

Call Sign: NH7TF
Motoaki Umeno
Ryan Miyashiro 4483
Sierra Dr
Honolulu HI 96816

Call Sign: NH7TD
Yuki Kondo
Ryan Miyashiro 4483
Sierra Dr
Honolulu HI 98616

Call Sign: NH7EH
Bruce K Chu
931 Simon Rd
Honolulu HI 96817

Call Sign: KH6OO
Thomas P Lange
129 Singleton Court
Honolulu HI 96818

Call Sign: W4MDL
Thomas P Lange
129 Singleton Court
Honolulu HI 96818

Call Sign: KH6JQL
David B Oishi
1702 Skyline Dr
Honolulu HI 96817

Call Sign: KB1LZL
Walter W Hayward
1162 Smith St Apt E
Honolulu HI 96817

Call Sign: WH7WP
Walter W Hayward
1162 Smith St Apt E
Honolulu HI 96817

Call Sign: WH7UP
Jeremy G Figueroa
3206 Snyder Ct
Honolulu HI 96818

Call Sign: KH6EDD
William W L Dang
181 So Kukui St
Honolulu HI 96813

Call Sign: WH6DHM
N. V. C. G.
Soma
Honolulu HI 96828

Call Sign: NH7WF
Karl Chang
2449 Sonoma St
Honolulu HI 96822

Call Sign: WH2Y
Hiromichi Ishio
1088 South Beretania St
Honolulu HI 96814

Call Sign: WH6ZY
Donald J Gau Jr
1406 South Beretania St
Honolulu HI 96814

Call Sign: KH6OH
Norris A Michelson
1617 South Beretania St
1201
Honolulu HI 96826

Call Sign: WH6CLE
Seizo Ito
1760 South Beretania St
12B
Honolulu HI 96826

Call Sign: WH6RE
Marilyn G Marco

2357 South Beretania St
135
Honolulu HI 96826

Call Sign: KH6BY
Edward V Rubie
1617 South Beretania St
505
Honolulu HI 96826-1109

Call Sign: WH7PM
Byron L Wolfe
55 South Judd St 1808
Honolulu HI 96817

Call Sign: NH7SE
Dung P Nguyen
2920 South King Apt 801
Honolulu HI 96826

Call Sign: WC6ABE
Oahu Civil Defense
Agency
650 South King St
Honolulu HI 96813

Call Sign: KA6ESQ
Corrine H White
1540 South King St
Honolulu HI 96826-1919

Call Sign: N6CBR
Reginald A White
1540 South King St
Honolulu HI 96826-1919

Call Sign: WB2LVF
Joseph J Tubito
1640 South King St
Honolulu HI 96826

Call Sign: NH6NJ
Lawrence M Koga
2469 South King St
Honolulu HI 96826

Call Sign: WH6BOF
Duane A Jennings
2469 South King St
Honolulu HI 96826

Call Sign: WH6AA
Ralph E Knight
2717 South King St Apt
303
Honolulu HI 96826

Call Sign: AH7R
Michael W Burger
2825 South King St Apt
602
Honolulu HI 96826

Call Sign: KH6OCD
Civil Defense Amateur
Radio Club
650 South King St Bsmt
Honolulu HI 96813

Call Sign: WH6CSZ
Jun Kojima
1314 South King St
Executive Office 625
Honolulu HI 96814

Call Sign: KH6STB
Straub Clinic And Hospital
Amateur Radio Club
888 South King St Palma 4
Honolulu HI 96813

Call Sign: WH6DHP
Straub Clinic And Hospital
Amateur Radio Club
888 South King St Palma 4
Honolulu HI 96813

Call Sign: N3MG
Mark S Gerber
888 South King St Palma 4

Honolulu HI 96813

Call Sign: WH7W
Mark S Gerber
888 South King St Palma 4
Honolulu HI 96813

Call Sign: AH6RN
James C Steele
801 South King St Ph07
Honolulu HI 96813

Call Sign: KH6YI
James W Miller
55 South Kukui St 1908
Honolulu HI 98613

Call Sign: WH6DRI
Elba Reyes
55 South Kukui St 2305
Honolulu HI 96813

Call Sign: WH6DQV
Carolyn L Hall
55 South Kukui St 301
Honolulu HI 96813

Call Sign: WH7SD
David A Leonoras
55 South Kukui St Apt 313
Honolulu HI 96813

Call Sign: WH6PK
Grant S Shiroma
112 South School St 209
Honolulu HI 96813

Call Sign: WH6CVI
Gabriel G Keress
60 South School St Apt 42
Honolulu HI 96813

Call Sign: KH6FKA
Michael K M Au
415 South St 4201

Honolulu HI 96813

Call Sign: WH7T
Thomas F Overman
415 South St Apt 3303
Honolulu HI 96813

Call Sign: KH7VT
Anna C Ho
201 South Vineyard St
Honolulu HI 96813

Call Sign: NH6QA
Patrick G S Chow
905 Spencer St 801
Honolulu HI 96822

Call Sign: AH6MQ
Thomas E Johnson
1948 St Louis Dr
Honolulu HI 96816

Call Sign: NH6SA
Philomena Q Preece
2049 St Louis Dr
Honolulu HI 96816

Call Sign: KH6DZ
David R Addington
2134 St Louis Dr
Honolulu HI 96816

Call Sign: WH6DNY
David R Addington
2134 St Louis Dr
Honolulu HI 96816

Call Sign: KH6YK
Henry K K Wong
2471 St Louis Dr
Honolulu HI 96816

Call Sign: KH6TZ
Wayne Y Carvalho
2481 St Louis Dr

Honolulu HI 96816

Call Sign: WH6BGJ
Cynthia A Wiig
2481 St Louis Dr
Honolulu HI 96816

Call Sign: KH2KX
John M Cummings III
2204 Star Rd
Honolulu HI 96813

Call Sign: KH6AOQ
David H Ching
2215 Star Rd
Honolulu HI 96813

Call Sign: WH6BVB
Jerry I Wilson
Ste 1450 220 S King St
Honolulu HI 96813

Call Sign: WH6ASQ
John J Rapp
Ste 2121 841 Bishop St
Honolulu HI 96813

Call Sign: WH6LX
Steven R Graeff
907 Stowell Cir
Honolulu HI 96818

Call Sign: WH6KE
Norman S Ulmer III
925 Stowell Cir
Honolulu HI 96818

Call Sign: WH6DLV
Warren N Hoopii
6134 Summer St
Honolulu HI 96821

Call Sign: KC3BW
Allen L Gilbert
350 Sumner St

Honolulu HI 96817

Call Sign: KH6PS
John J F Yee
797 Sunset Ave
Honolulu HI 96816

Call Sign: KH6SY
Roxanne S Yee
797 Sunset Ave
Honolulu HI 96816

Call Sign: KB1IVD
Vada P M Turner
1567 Tampa Dr
Honolulu HI 96819

Call Sign: W7HJ
Harley J Huntemann
1088 Taney Cir
Honolulu HI 96818

Call Sign: WH6DHH
Red Hill Amateur Radio
Club
1088 Taney Cir
Honolulu HI 96818

Call Sign: WH7OU
Roland A Koki
2128 Tantalus Dr
Honolulu HI 96813

Call Sign: NH6RP
Joseph K Kealohapauole
2165 Tantalus Dr
Honolulu HI 96813

Call Sign: WH6BVE
Darren K Chow
2165 Tantalus Dr
Honolulu HI 96813

Call Sign: WH6BYC
Jerry S Tanaka

2165 Tantalus Dr
Honolulu HI 96813

Call Sign: NH6RO
William C Mutch Jr
2321 Tantalus Dr
Honolulu HI 96813

Call Sign: WH6AGW
Garton E Wall
2667 Tantalus Dr
Honolulu HI 96813-1204

Call Sign: KH6TT
Lynn L Oakley
3310 Tantalus Dr
Honolulu HI 96822

Call Sign: KH7UC
Andrew Bilodeau
718 Tapp St
Honolulu HI 96818

Call Sign: AH6SI
Bryan M Brown Jr
3460 Taylor St
Honolulu HI 96818

Call Sign: NH7XR
Bryan M Brown Jr
3460 Taylor St
Honolulu HI 96818

Call Sign: W1BMB
Bryan M Brown Jr
3460 Taylor St
Honolulu HI 96818

Call Sign: AH6JP
Guy K Sueoka
2097 Tenth Ave
Honolulu HI 96816

Call Sign: NH6JA
Takahiro Sato

2635 Terrace Dr
Honolulu HI 96822

Call Sign: NH6VG
Takahiro Sato
2635 Terrace Dr
Honolulu HI 96822

Call Sign: WH6UW
Gabriela A Gomez
1471 Thurston Ave 402
Honolulu HI 96822

Call Sign: AH6RJ
Derek J Low
1523 Thurston Ave Apt A
Honolulu HI 96822

Call Sign: K7LS
Lawrence Shipley
2421 Tusitala St
Honolulu HI 96815

Call Sign: NH6TN
Michael W Stoychoff
2421 Tusitala St 2202
Honolulu HI 96815

Call Sign: W9JVE
Richard E Weimer
2452 Tusitala St Apt 2010
Honolulu HI 96815

Call Sign: NH7FM
Brian Gross
1619 Ua Dr
Honolulu HI 96816

Call Sign: KH6TE
Sandwich Islands
Shortwave Club
3049 Ualena St Ste 1005
Honolulu HI 96819

Call Sign: WH6DIO

Sandwich Islands
Shortwave Club
3049 Ualena St Ste 1005
Honolulu HI 96819

Call Sign: WH6R
Eran Agmon
3049 Ualena St Ste 1005
Honolulu HI 96819

Call Sign: NH7WH
Edoardo S Biagioni
Uh / Ics 168 East-West Rd
Honolulu HI 96822

Call Sign: KH6AI
Frank I Yamamoto
418 Uhini Pl
Honolulu HI 96813

Call Sign: KH6CF
Archie W Chatterley
1372 Uila St
Honolulu HI 96818

Call Sign: KH6OJ
Ilan Sirley
1418 Uila St
Honolulu HI 96818

Call Sign: KH6LT
Carl E Fischer
1418 Uila St
Honolulu HI 96818-1940

Call Sign: KH6GOQ
Francis K Aona Jr
726 Ulili St
Honolulu HI 96816

Call Sign: KH7EN
Felecissimo M Alcoran
719 Umi St Apt D
Honolulu HI 96819

Call Sign: KH7NC
Florida D Alcoran
719 Umi St Apt D
Honolulu HI 96819

Call Sign: WH7BO
Eric K Grossman
1040 Unit C Simpson Lp
Honolulu HI 96819

Call Sign: KH6AIJ
Edwin T Kawamura
810-205 University Ave
Honolulu HI 96826

Call Sign: WH7IA
Robert A Ballard
500 University Ave 1403
Honolulu HI 96826

Call Sign: WH6DMQ
Kevin Y Oshiro
500 University Ave 927
Honolulu HI 96826

Call Sign: KH7YE
Michael J Kawamoto
3457 Upper St
Honolulu HI 96815-4365

Call Sign: WH7ZR
Regina L Lambert
423 103 Valley View Loop
Honolulu HI 96818

Call Sign: WH6BUS
Sean R O Kelley
614C Valley View Loop
Honolulu HI 96818

Call Sign: WH7IB
Liliana E Bonilla
185 Valley View Lp 102
Honolulu HI 96818

Call Sign: W9AGH
Steven R H Scott
466 Valley View Lp Apt
105
Honolulu HI 96818

Call Sign: KH7DZ
Charles J Malefyt
1821 Vancouver Pl
Honolulu HI 96822

Call Sign: KH7FH
Steven Y Isagawa
2908 Varsity Cir Apt 1
Honolulu HI 96826

Call Sign: WH6DLP
Michael R Hadmack
1441 Victoria St 1605
Honolulu HI 96822

Call Sign: WH6CRC
Robert E Fortier
1415 Victoria St 614
Honolulu HI 96822

Call Sign: WH7TF
Kenneth L Jackson
1415 Victoria St Apt 1001
Honolulu HI 96822

Call Sign: KH6JJJ
Dale A Wyatt
1704 Violet St
Honolulu HI 96819-3865

Call Sign: KC5CWA
John R Carriveau III
808 W Teaff Ct
Honolulu HI 96818

Call Sign: WH6CNM
Eunice T Kuromoto
3521 Waakaua St
Honolulu HI 96822

Call Sign: AH6PE
Harold S Gouveia Sr
2717 Waialae Ave
Honolulu HI 96826

Call Sign: WH7HC
Shelton P Yamashiro
3954 Waialae Ave
Honolulu HI 96816

Call Sign: KH6IGT
Renato C Equila
4049 Waialae Ave
Honolulu HI 96816

Call Sign: WH6BUT
Elena C Equila
4049 Waialae Ave
Honolulu HI 96816

Call Sign: WH6LQ
Roberto Santilla
3125 Waialae Ave 101
Honolulu HI 96816

Call Sign: W2KXA
Fotios J Photiadis
3138 Waialae Ave 625
Honolulu HI 96816

Call Sign: N6ZBI
Richard R Hardy
4300 Waialae Ave A 804
Honolulu HI 96816

Call Sign: WH7ZB
Richard R Hardy
4300 Waialae Ave A 804
Honolulu HI 96816

Call Sign: WH6CZO
Clarence H Moke Puha
2845 Waialae Ave Apt 212
Honolulu HI 96826-1814

Call Sign: WH6CMG
Jay Calvin Uyemura Reyes
3138 Waialae Ave
Regency Pk 603
Honolulu HI 96816

Call Sign: KD5FGA
James W Thompson
4224 Waialae Ave Ste 5
Pmb 551
Honolulu HI 96816

Call Sign: KG6AA
Robert G Adams
3138 Waialae Ave Unit
726
Honolulu HI 96816-1549

Call Sign: K3DJ
Kiyoshi L Nakamura
4224 Waialae Ste 5
Honolulu HI 96816

Call Sign: KH6DJ
Kiyoshi L Nakamura
4224 Waialae Ste 5
Honolulu HI 96816

Call Sign: AD2R
Kiyoshi L Nakamura
4224 Waialae Ste5 392
Honolulu HI 96816

Call Sign: WH7S
Kiyoshi L Nakamura
4224 Waialae Ste5392
Honolulu HI 96816

Call Sign: KH6VH
Willard Y Miyahira
926 Waiiki St
Honolulu HI 96821

Call Sign: KC2SRW

Eric Hafner
1240 Waimanu St Unit D
Honolulu HI 96814

Call Sign: KH6AAN
Solomon K F Kam
1653 Waiola St
Honolulu HI 96826

Call Sign: KH6IGQ
Philip K Y Kam
1653A Waiola St
Honolulu HI 96826

Call Sign: WH6BXV
Haruyoshi Ikawa
936 Waioli St
Honolulu HI 96825

Call Sign: WH6CGL
Janet Bender
2323 Walu Way
Honolulu HI 96822

Call Sign: WH7YA
Henry Poulei
1254 Wanaka St
Honolulu HI 96818

Call Sign: KH6HS
Helen H Sanpei
2517 Waolani Ave
Honolulu HI 96817

Call Sign: KH6KAZ
Charles K Sanpei
2517 Waolani Ave
Honolulu HI 96817

Call Sign: WH6DUS
Helen H Sanpei
2517 Waolani Ave
Honolulu HI 96817

Call Sign: WH6DWG

Charles K Sanpei
2517 Waolani Ave
Honolulu HI 96817

Call Sign: WH7GU
Melvin W Won
2604 Waolani Ave
Honolulu HI 96817

Call Sign: KH6LN
Gary T Isono
2512A Waolani Ave
Honolulu HI 96817

Call Sign: WH7ZP
Dena M Fernandez
2651 Waozani Ave
Honolulu HI 96817

Call Sign: NH7ID
Neva Keres
610 Ward Ave
Honolulu HI 96814

Call Sign: KH7XV
Nita Ferreira
350 Ward Ave 106287
Honolulu HI 96814-4004

Call Sign: KH7SE
Warner Sutton
350 Ward Ave 106
Honolulu HI 96814

Call Sign: AH6EN
Nicholas Ratiani
350 Ward Ave 106
Honolulu HI 96814

Call Sign: KH6JP
Joyce E Miller
350 Ward Ave 106259
Honolulu HI 96814

Call Sign: KB1EUJ

J Scott Ferguson
350 Ward Ave 106259
Honolulu HI 96814

Call Sign: KH7XR
Louis P Bliemeister
350 Ward Ave 106287
Honolulu HI 96814

Call Sign: NH7SG
Marek N Rajesh
1516 Ward Ave 207
Honolulu HI 96822

Call Sign: KH6FDG
Carl W Boyer Jr
920 Ward Ave Apt 17Dd
Honolulu HI 96814

Call Sign: WH7IV
David W Barlow
1515 Ward Ave Apt 501
Honolulu HI 96822

Call Sign: WH6DTP
Patricio C Sugue
2010 Waterhouse St Apt
1A
Honolulu HI 96819

Call Sign: WH6AA
D Bart Aronoff
1015 Wilder Ave
Honolulu HI 96822-2640

Call Sign: KH6HC
Health Comm
1015 Wilder Ave 305
Honolulu HI 96822

Call Sign: WH6DKD
Lester M Nishi
1114 Wilder Ave 407
Honolulu HI 96822

Call Sign: KH7GM
Lois A Oliver
1201 Wilder Ave 603
Honolulu HI 96822-3154

Call Sign: KH6GAN
Daniel H Pang
1001 Wilder Ave 704
Honolulu HI 96822

Call Sign: KH6IBI
Kailua Intermediate Sch
Ar Clb
1001 Wilder Ave 704
Honolulu HI 96822

Call Sign: WH7RX
Kayla C Rosenfeld
1001 Wilder Ave 704
Honolulu HI 96822

Call Sign: AH6PS
Michael A Bacon
1155 Wilder Ave 708
Honolulu HI 96822

Call Sign: KH6VV
Peggy Priest
1201 Wilder Ave 803
Honolulu HI 96822

Call Sign: WH6BVP
Bill G Schallenberg
1025 Wilder Ave 8B
Honolulu HI 96822

Call Sign: WH6CTH
Annie Yu
1201 Wilder Ave 904
Honolulu HI 96822

Call Sign: NH7WB
Joseph P Mcguffey
1001 Wilder Ave Apt 1002
Honolulu HI 96822

Call Sign: KE7LRE
Steven T Vander Giessen
1238 Wilder Ave Apt A
Honolulu HI 96822

Call Sign: WH7UE
Sharring F Niusulu
1550 Wilder Ave Apt
A410
Honolulu HI 96817

Call Sign: WH7YS
Joseph K Doggett
2212 Wilder Ave Apt C
Honolulu HI 96822

Call Sign: W6HTH
William A Boykin
1201 Wilder Ave Ph1
Honolulu HI 96822

Call Sign: AH6QR
Maryann D Barnett
1915 Wilhelmina Rise
Honolulu HI 96816

Call Sign: NH7SV
Thomas Webb
1915 Wilhelmina Rise
Honolulu HI 96816

Call Sign: WH6CFR
Barry W Moeller
1079 Wiliki Dr
Honolulu HI 96818

Call Sign: NH6IP
Martine J Bell
837 Wiliwili St
Honolulu HI 96826

Call Sign: WH6DH
Newton Y T Lin
2225 Wilson St

Honolulu HI 96819

Call Sign: NH6IT
Ronald T Uchino
2277 Wilson St
Honolulu HI 96819

Call Sign: NH7VI
Gordon W Lee
3457 Winam Ave
Honolulu HI 96815

Call Sign: WH6CEV
David A Carreiro
1046 Wong Ln 6
Honolulu HI 96814

Call Sign: WH6CEX
Pearl M Konanui
1046 Wong Ln 6
Honolulu HI 96814

Call Sign: NH7NL
Richard J Wainscoat
2680 Woodlawn Dr
Honolulu HI 96822

Call Sign: NH6FE
Robert J Higa
2840 Woodlawn Dr
Honolulu HI 96822

Call Sign: KH7IZ
Ann M Baginski
3422 Woodlawn Dr
Honolulu HI 96822

Call Sign: KH6GAU
Joseph H Seung
3542 Woodlawn Dr
Honolulu HI 96822

Call Sign: KH7ZA
Clyde T Miyaki
3683 B Woodlawn Dr

Honolulu HI 96822

Call Sign: NH6TO
Stacie K Nakagawa
3011 Woolsey Pl
Honolulu HI 96822

Call Sign: KB0UNL
Steven L Becker
9 Worchester Dr
Honolulu HI 96818

Call Sign: NH6HC
Donald J Donnarumma Sr
636 Wyllie St
Honolulu HI 96817

Call Sign: KH6OI
Bradley Y Soo
701 Wyllie St
Honolulu HI 96817

Call Sign: WH7PR
Calvin W Cheung
1259 Young St
Honolulu HI 96814

Call Sign: KH6HQN
Nelson P O Tan
1718 Young St
Honolulu HI 96826

Call Sign: AH6NM
Richard S Flagg
1721-I Young St
Honolulu HI 96826

Call Sign: WH6DGI
Sacred Hearts Academy
Radio Club
1721-I Young St
Honolulu HI 96826

Call Sign: WH6Y
Kenneth T Sakamoto

1448 Young St Apt 1603
Honolulu HI 96814-1862

Call Sign: WH7CI
Jan Hafner
2051 Young St 32
Honolulu HI 96826

Call Sign: WH7MX
Wesley D Maxwell III
1125 Young St 907
Honolulu HI 96814

Call Sign: KB6MOO
Kenneth K Obayashi
1448 Young St Apt 207
Honolulu HI 96814-1849

Call Sign: WH6BRR
Jimen Ching
1450 Young St Apt 2107
Honolulu HI 96814

Call Sign: KH6JJR
Howard R Green
Honolulu HI 96801

Call Sign: WH6HR
Tracy A Hino
Honolulu HI 96802

Call Sign: WH6CKL
Diane C Marques
Honolulu HI 96806

Call Sign: KH6AR
Pacific Communications
Club
Honolulu HI 96812

Call Sign: KH6ASC
Thida Denpruektham
Honolulu HI 96812

Call Sign: WH6DHI

Pacific Communications
Club
Honolulu HI 96812

Call Sign: WH6DQR
Thida Denpruektham
Honolulu HI 96812

Call Sign: WH6DQS
Peeranat Wisawapalanont
Honolulu HI 96812

Call Sign: WH6EU
Brec Brown Gen
Honolulu HI 96812

Call Sign: WH6HL
Kim M Brown
Honolulu HI 96812

Call Sign: WH6SX
Lon Polk
Honolulu HI 96812

Call Sign: KH6QJ
Kenneth D Taylor
Honolulu HI 96813

Call Sign: AH6QQ
Elaine C Kam
Honolulu HI 96816

Call Sign: AL7FV
James H Mulligan III
Honolulu HI 96816

Call Sign: KD5BSK
Anthony A Phonpituck
Honolulu HI 96816

Call Sign: KH6HPZ
Hawaii State Races Assn
Honolulu HI 96816

Call Sign: KH7DH

Karen K Lattanzi
Honolulu HI 96816

Call Sign: KH7PN
Toshinari Hirooka
Honolulu HI 96816

Call Sign: KH7YQ
Elaine C Kam
Honolulu HI 96816

Call Sign: WH6AAS
Nora S Meijide
Honolulu HI 96816

Call Sign: WH7MN
Sarah M Ching
Honolulu HI 96816

Call Sign: KH7XH
William T Lu
Honolulu HI 96817

Call Sign: NH7VJ
Robert Libed
Honolulu HI 96817

Call Sign: NH7ZW
Jeffrey K Marabellas
Honolulu HI 96817

Call Sign: WH6DKQ
Gordon J Erece
Honolulu HI 96817

Call Sign: WH6LP
Michael S Vincent
Honolulu HI 96817

Call Sign: WH6MV
Michael S Vincent
Honolulu HI 96817

Call Sign: WH7TM
Raynell K Anes

Honolulu HI 96817

Call Sign: KH6CE
Emergency Amateur Radio
Club
Honolulu HI 96820

Call Sign: KH6IDP
Timothy P Flournoy
Honolulu HI 96820

Call Sign: KH6LJB
Laurie J Bechler
Honolulu HI 96820

Call Sign: KH6MEI
Wayne O Greenleaf
Honolulu HI 96820

Call Sign: KH6MG
Mei Li Greenleaf
Honolulu HI 96820

Call Sign: KH7OK
Andrew K Keliikoa
Honolulu HI 96820

Call Sign: KH7RM
Wendi O Torricer
Honolulu HI 96820

Call Sign: KH7RN
Liang Han Yu
Honolulu HI 96820

Call Sign: KH7SB
Christopher P Lavoie
Honolulu HI 96820

Call Sign: KH8PPG
Tutuila Iota Club
Honolulu HI 96820

Call Sign: NH6AR
John B Wills

Honolulu HI 96820

Call Sign: NH6VB
Hans P Scheller
Honolulu HI 96820

Call Sign: NH7JK
Jared K Redulla
Honolulu HI 96820

Call Sign: NH7ST
Sue Ann Saunders
Honolulu HI 96820

Call Sign: NH7SU
Allan L Saunders
Honolulu HI 96820

Call Sign: NH7TP
Laurie J Bechler
Honolulu HI 96820

Call Sign: WH6DIJ
Hawaii Medical Center
East
Honolulu HI 96820

Call Sign: WH6DLG
Emergency Amateur Radio
Club
Honolulu HI 96820

Call Sign: WH6DLO
Emergency Amateur Radio
Club
Honolulu HI 96820

Call Sign: WH7BY
Michelle S Otake
Honolulu HI 96820

Call Sign: WH7CZ
William A Macdonald
Honolulu HI 96820

Call Sign: WH7MO
Michelle S Otake
Honolulu HI 96820

Call Sign: WH7VG
Bret C Desmond
Honolulu HI 96820

Call Sign: WH6CWU
Peter E Wood
Honolulu HI 96822

Call Sign: KH7AW
Robert L Hunter
Honolulu HI 96823

Call Sign: NH7SN
Miguel A Abdala
Honolulu HI 96823

Call Sign: WH6DIN
Bsa Troop 49
Honolulu HI 96823

Call Sign: WH6DKI
John W Malingdan
Honolulu HI 96823

Call Sign: WH6DMT
Peter T Hughes
Honolulu HI 96823

Call Sign: WH6DRD
Joey K Shibata Garcza
Honolulu HI 96823

Call Sign: WH7HZ
Richard E Ando Jr
Honolulu HI 96823

Call Sign: WH7RH
Ryan E Ando
Honolulu HI 96823

Call Sign: WH7UF

Richard Y Ambo
Honolulu HI 96823

Call Sign: WH7XF
Lynn K Ando
Honolulu HI 96823

Call Sign: AH6IX
Jeffrey Y Sue
Honolulu HI 96825

Call Sign: AH7M
Masao Tokura
Honolulu HI 96825

Call Sign: KH7EZ
Amy M Sue
Honolulu HI 96825

Call Sign: KH7FA
Alan J Sue
Honolulu HI 96825

Call Sign: KH7RV
David A Phears
Honolulu HI 96825

Call Sign: NH6OU
Nancy S Sue
Honolulu HI 96825

Call Sign: W9LIA
John H Sayles
Honolulu HI 96825

Call Sign: WH7RS
Scott M Tsutsumi
Honolulu HI 96825

Call Sign: KH7CW
Ricky W Fong
Honolulu HI 96827

Call Sign: AC6IF
Mark S Wood

Honolulu HI 96828

Call Sign: AH6SB
Mark S Wood
Honolulu HI 96828

Call Sign: AH7U
Yutaka Tanaka
Honolulu HI 96828

Call Sign: KE2CX
Yoshikazu Katoh
Honolulu HI 96828

Call Sign: KH6ASA
Robert N Asakura
Honolulu HI 96828

Call Sign: KH6HK
Shinji Kamata
Honolulu HI 96828

Call Sign: KH6JA
Izumi Soma
Honolulu HI 96828

Call Sign: KR6JA
Honolulu International
Japanese Amateur Radio
Club
Honolulu HI 96828

Call Sign: WH6DEM
Aac Memorial Station
Honolulu HI 96828

Call Sign: WH6DHB
Honolulu International
Japanese Amateur Radio
Club
Honolulu HI 96828

Call Sign: WH6DLY
Jerrold M Hancock
Honolulu HI 96828

Call Sign: WH6DPC
Robert N Asakura
Honolulu HI 96828

Call Sign: WH6DUI
Raj K Bose
Honolulu HI 96828

Call Sign: WH7ID
Alan T Nakayama
Honolulu HI 96828

Call Sign: KA6LPT
Brian K Caldwell
Honolulu HI 96830

Call Sign: KA6LPU
Janet D Caldwell
Honolulu HI 96830

Call Sign: KH6AX
Earle D Schmitz
Honolulu HI 96830

Call Sign: KH6EAK
Bennett W Mark
Honolulu HI 96830

Call Sign: N6GOZ
Michael J Scott
Honolulu HI 96830

Call Sign: NH7OW
Faye A Chambers
Honolulu HI 96830

Call Sign: WD9HVH
Larry M Cosby
Honolulu HI 96830

Call Sign: WH6DDN
Pacific Isle Dx Society
Honolulu HI 96830

Call Sign: WH6DDO
Kamaaina Kilowatt Club
Honolulu HI 96830

Call Sign: WH6DDQ
Manana Island Iota Group
Honolulu HI 96830

Call Sign: WH6DMC
Jimmy C Higham
Honolulu HI 96830

Call Sign: WH6DWF
Todd Wilson
Honolulu HI 96830

Call Sign: WH6RO
Yoshiko Kamatsuka
Honolulu HI 96830

Call Sign: WH6SQ
Masaaki Kamatsuka
Honolulu HI 96830

Call Sign: KH7QY
Sean Mc Keever
Honolulu HI 96836

Call Sign: N6QQT
Nancy L Gills
Honolulu HI 96836

Call Sign: NH7DD
Susan T Ray
Honolulu HI 96836

Call Sign: WH6DMZ
Steven H Yamase
Honolulu HI 96836

Call Sign: KC4ZTF
Richard L Yount
Honolulu HI 96837

Call Sign: KH7WS

Jean O Young
Honolulu HI 96837

Call Sign: KH7XN
Hubert D Biete
Honolulu HI 96839

Call Sign: WH6BKG
Carol A Bourgois
Honolulu HI 96839

Call Sign: WH7YU
Beatrix L Hu
Honolulu HI 96839

Call Sign: WH6AIT
Ernesto P Mostoles
Honolulu HI 96803-2684

Call Sign: KH6GRS
Jon H Pegg
Honolulu HI 96807-1384

Call Sign: KH6HFD
Honolulu Fire Department
Amateur Radio Club
Honolulu HI 96816-0421

Call Sign: WH6DHG
Honolulu Fire Department
Amateur Radio Club
Honolulu HI 96816-0421

Call Sign: AH6QN
David J Cabatu
Honolulu HI 96816-0923

Call Sign: AH7E
David J Cabatu
Honolulu HI 96816-0923

Call Sign: NH6BP
David J Cabatu
Honolulu HI 96816-0923

Call Sign: WH6DGT
Ofu Island Arc
Honolulu HI 96818-0005

Call Sign: KH7SX
Emmanuel C Carpio
Honolulu HI 96818-0159

Call Sign: WH6DIL
Hawaii Medical Center
West
Honolulu HI 96820-0100

Call Sign: WH6CZB
Emergency Amateur Radio
Club Inc
Honolulu HI 96820-0315

Call Sign: KH6XX
Randall F Sobol
Honolulu HI 96820-0909

Call Sign: WH6BGI
Iris E Sobol
Honolulu HI 96820-0909

Call Sign: KH7X
Oahu Contest Club
Honolulu HI 96820-1193

Call Sign: KD6UQB
William P Starkgraf Jr
Honolulu HI 96820-1322

Call Sign: KH6DXR
Glyn O Jones
Honolulu HI 96820-2161

Call Sign: KH8OFU
Ofu Island Iota Club
Honolulu HI 96820-2161

Call Sign: WH6BAR
Gerhard J Jaeger
Honolulu HI 96820-2161

Call Sign: WH7BF
Glyn O Jones
Honolulu HI 96820-2161

Call Sign: KH7PC
Anne K Holt Iona
Honolulu HI 96823-2201

Call Sign: AH6WA
Michael M Zanoni
Honolulu HI 96823-2471

Call Sign: NG7A
Michael M Zanoni
Honolulu HI 96823-2471

Call Sign: KH7RF
Wesley Y Seto
Honolulu HI 96823-2479

Call Sign: WH6CZP
Hawaii Emergency
Amateur Radio Team
Honolulu HI 96823-2479

Call Sign: NH7FP
Patrick I Donegan
Honolulu HI 96823-2801

Call Sign: AH6OK
Delwyn W M Ching
Honolulu HI 96823-3029

Call Sign: KH6DC
Delwyn W Ching
Honolulu HI 96823-3029

Call Sign: WH6BGG
William L Hill
Honolulu HI 96823-3317

Call Sign: WH7CQ
William L Hill
Honolulu HI 96823-3317

Call Sign: KH6EN
Paul A Sunada
Honolulu HI 96824-0272

Call Sign: KH6LD
Paul A Sunada
Honolulu HI 96824-0272

Call Sign: WH6AVM
Sharon L Sunada
Honolulu HI 96824-0272

Call Sign: KC6WOB
Kathleen M Gregory
Honolulu HI 96824-0693

Call Sign: KH7EE
Reginald K Yee
Honolulu HI 96825-0191

Call Sign: KA1YJ
Stanley R Schwartz
Honolulu HI 96825-0756

Call Sign: KH6CG
Stanley R Schwartz
Honolulu HI 96825-0756

Call Sign: WH6DTK
James F Stack
Honolulu HI 96825-0941

Call Sign: KC6WNW
Delbert S Gregory
Honolulu HI 96825-2911

Call Sign: NH7ZI
Martin W Grant
Honolulu HI 96828-0311

Call Sign: WH7HF
Andres A Mariano Jr
Honolulu HI 96828-0375

Call Sign: WH7BA
Penelope Tukimaka
Honolulu HI 96828-3147

Call Sign: KH0XX
Saipan Contest Team
Honolulu HI 96830-5008

Call Sign: KH2XX
The A Team
Honolulu HI 96830-5008

Call Sign: KH6WW
World Wide Dx Contest
Club
Honolulu HI 96830-5008

Call Sign: AH6DS
James F Atkinson
Honolulu HI 96830-8089

Call Sign: WH6BJQ
Clyde M Furushima
Honolulu HI 96804

Call Sign: WH6CKW
E G Kris Brenno
Honolulu HI 96809

Call Sign: WH6ARK
Clinton R Ashford
Honolulu HI 96810

Call Sign: KH6FOA
Elliott Kawahara
Honolulu HI 96812

Call Sign: WH6BQW
Linda M Watson
Honolulu HI 96815

Call Sign: AH6CP
Robin M Liu
Honolulu HI 96816

Call Sign: AH6MG
Aimee S Ching
Honolulu HI 96816

Call Sign: KH7O
Rickerd K Ching
Honolulu HI 96816

Call Sign: WH6CPF
Gavin P Tomlinson
Honolulu HI 96816

Call Sign: KH6ND
Michael J Gibson
Honolulu HI 96820

Call Sign: NH6WB
Jack R Poole
Honolulu HI 96820

Call Sign: W1DDV
David B Perrier
Honolulu HI 96820

Call Sign: WH6AC
Marianne P S Rudnitski
Honolulu HI 96820

Call Sign: WH6BZI
Kevin J Hood
Honolulu HI 96820

Call Sign: WH6CKF
Mike P Rossman
Honolulu HI 96820

Call Sign: WH6FN
Michael E Randall
Honolulu HI 96820

Call Sign: KH6JPK
Karl H Bathen
Honolulu HI 96821

Call Sign: KH6BON

Ralph H Moltzau Jr
Honolulu HI 96822

Call Sign: WH6APH
Lee S Winnagle
Honolulu HI 96822

Call Sign: WH6CIN
Carla T Robinson
Honolulu HI 96822

Call Sign: NH6YV
Harlan R White
Honolulu HI 96823

Call Sign: WH6AZR
Robert B Trombly
Honolulu HI 96823

Call Sign: KD6FCT
Janet A Crawford
Honolulu HI 96825

Call Sign: KH6AL
Alva K Nakamura
Honolulu HI 96825

Call Sign: NH6SW
Glen C Showalter
Honolulu HI 96827

Call Sign: WH6HM
Dennis D Y Chiu
Honolulu HI 96827

Call Sign: NH6VN
Victor M Mori
Honolulu HI 96828

Call Sign: AH6NC
John H Coleman
Honolulu HI 96830

Call Sign: WB2HHO
Joseph M Tripoli

Honolulu HI 96830

Call Sign: KH6SFW
Saint Francis West
Honolulu HI 96820-0100

Call Sign: KH6EAR
Hawaiian Empire Amateur
Radio Society
Honolulu HI 96820-0226

Call Sign: WH6GJV
Hawaiian Empire Amateur
Radio Society
Honolulu HI 96820-0226

Call Sign: KH7Q
Oahu Cq Contesting Club
Honolulu HI 96823-3509

Call Sign: KH6SFL
Saint Francis Medical
Center Liliha
Honolulu HI 96824-0197

Call Sign: AH7AA
Honolulu Contest Team
Honolulu HI 96830-5008

Call Sign: KH6FOC
Foc
Honolulu HI 96830-5008

Call Sign: KH6VHF
The A Team
Honolulu HI 96830-5008

Call Sign: KH7MM
Sakurada Contest Team
Honolulu HI 96830-5008

**FCC Amateur Radio
License in Honomu**

Call Sign: W3DL

Harold D Lung
28-253 Kalani Lp
Honomu HI 96728-0033

Call Sign: AH6DL
Harold D Lung
28-716 Kokoke Kai Pl
Honomu HI 96728-0033

Call Sign: KH7ZK
John F Gallipeau
Honomu HI 96728

Call Sign: NH6CA
Stacey T Nagareda
Honomu HI 96728

Call Sign: NH7AV
Stacey T Nagareda
Honomu HI 96728

Call Sign: NH7EB
Linda M Wagner
Honomu HI 96728

Call Sign: NH7EC
Walter L Wagner
Honomu HI 96728

Call Sign: NH7GC
Aaron T Ishigo
Honomu HI 96728

Call Sign: NH7IK
Keith A Hughes
Honomu HI 96728

Call Sign: WH6AW
Arman E Wiggins
Honomu HI 96728

Call Sign: WH6BVZ
Arman E Wiggins
Honomu HI 96728

Call Sign: WH7AG
Linus A E Wiggins
Honomu HI 96728

FCC Amateur Radio License in Hoolehua

Call Sign: KH6DOC
William J Martin
Hoolehua HI 96729

Call Sign: WG0V
George E Huizinga
Hoolehua HI 96729

Call Sign: NH7VF
Philip Zenn III
Hoolehua HI 96761

Call Sign: N9UDI
William J Martin
Hoolehua HI 96729

Call Sign: WH6IU
Dan C Marcellino
Hoolehua HI 96729

FCC Amateur Radio License in Kaaawa

Call Sign: NH7WC
William L Greene III
51-055 Huamalani
Kaaawa HI 96730

Call Sign: WH6DRA
Jayme R Cooper
51-636 Kamehameha Hwy
Apt 415
Kaaawa HI 96730

Call Sign: WH6CYL
James Woolsey
Kaaawa HI 96730

Call Sign: WH6DMO
Joel D Walker
Kaaawa HI 96730

Call Sign: WH6WW
Kaehu J Shapiro
Kaaawa HI 96730

Call Sign: WH6XQ
Norman B Shapiro
Kaaawa HI 96730

FCC Amateur Radio License in Kahala Beach

Call Sign: KA6WVO
Edward E Watts
4340 Pahoa Ave
Kahala Beach HI 96816

FCC Amateur Radio License in Kahalauu

Call Sign: KH7TV
George A Phocas
47 313 Lulani St
Kahaluu HI 96744

Call Sign: AH2CN
George A Phocas
47-313 Lulani St
Kahaluu HI 96744

FCC Amateur Radio License in Kahuku

Call Sign: KC6MRK
Lee Ann L Akina
57-101 Kuilima Dr 56 W
Kahuku HI 96731

Call Sign: KH7XQ
Joseph H Kugler
56 340 Olauniu Pl
Kahuku HI 96731

Call Sign: WH6DQB
Michael Gary
Kahuku HI 96731

Call Sign: WH6DSS
Norvana A Miranda
Kahuku HI 96731

Call Sign: WH6DSW
Francisco Tejada Jr
Kahuku HI 96731

Call Sign: KA3HRU
Thomas A Reyburn
Kahuku HI 96731-0220

Call Sign: KH7TC
Naomi M Nihipali
Kahuku HI 96731-0275

Call Sign: KH7TD
Peggy Nihipali
Kahuku HI 96731-0275

**FCC Amateur Radio
License in Kahului**

Call Sign: WH6BXH
Chris S Tobita
81 Aiai St
Kahului HI 96732

Call Sign: KH6RS
Maui Amateur Radio Club
Box 1791
Kahului HI 96732

Call Sign: KH6HW
Noboru Nakao
356 Hilu Pl
Kahului HI 96732

Call Sign: NH6LP
Richard J Camara Jr

7 Hoomoku Loop
Kahului HI 96732

Call Sign: WH6VA
Wayne C Tamanaha
422 Kahiki St
Kahului HI 96732

Call Sign: KH6EXK
Michael J Tamanaha
422 Kahiki St
Kahului HI 96732

Call Sign: WH6BCP
Kazuyoshi B Tokuoka
692 Kalili Way
Kahului HI 96732

Call Sign: KH6EXJ
Roy S Okada
181 Kane St
Kahului HI 96732

Call Sign: KH6US
Milton M Onaga
434 Kaulana St
Kahului HI 96732-2050

Call Sign: KH6JWB
Donald S Higa
170 Kaulawahine St
Kahului HI 96732

Call Sign: WH7UJ
Jason S Takayama
58 Kealohilani St
Kahului HI 96732

Call Sign: WH6CZD
Itsuo Yano
80 Lehua St
Kahului HI 96732

Call Sign: KH6HOO
Donald Y Suzuki

102 Lehua St
Kahului HI 96732

Call Sign: KH6IDT
Norman M Sato
214 Lono Ave
Kahului HI 96732

Call Sign: KH6BXG
Harry T Ito
351 Lono Ave
Kahului HI 96732

Call Sign: KH6ABM
Wallace J Arakawa
382 Maalo St
Kahului HI 96732

Call Sign: KH6EXR
Charles P Aki
109 Molokai Akau
Kahului HI 96732

Call Sign: KH6CFA
Kiyoto Murakami
110 Molokai Akau St
Kahului HI 96732

Call Sign: WH6OV
Kris Y Shibano
730 Molokai Akau St
Kahului HI 96732

Call Sign: KH6BCT
Kenneth E Mc Corkle
132 MolokaiAkau St
Kahului HI 96732

Call Sign: KH6BXH
Yoshiteru Nagata
428 Oahu St
Kahului HI 96732

Call Sign: NH6MF
Nelson N Kina

550 Onehee Ave
Kahului HI 96732

Call Sign: KD4KSE
Martha C Hooper
29 Pahe'E Pl
Kahului HI 96732

Call Sign: KH6ILA
Manuel J Silva
713 Pala Cir
Kahului HI 96732-1310

Call Sign: WH7UK
Kevin K Segundo
738 Pala Circle
Kahului HI 96732

Call Sign: NH6RJ
Robert T Nishimoto
288 Palama Dr
Kahului HI 96732-1450

Call Sign: K4RAC
Robert A Collesano
269 Papa Pl 101
Kahului HI 96732

Call Sign: WH6BQJ
Gerald M Matsunaga
426 S Palama Dr
Kahului HI 96732

Call Sign: KH6COM
Maui County Emergency
Amateur Radio Club
153 W Kane St
Kahului HI 96732

Call Sign: WH6BXK
Jayson T Kohama
153 W Kane St
Kahului HI 96732

Call Sign: WH6DUY

Maui County Emergency
Amateur Radio Club
153 W Kane St
Kahului HI 96732

Call Sign: KH6OB
David E Culnan
268A W Lanai St
Kahului HI 96732

Call Sign: KH6WA
Margaret J Culnan
268A W Lanai St
Kahului HI 96732

Call Sign: KH6CIO
Mathew M Saito
170 West Lanai St
Kahului HI 96732

Call Sign: NH6UF
Gary K KamalII
78 West Waikea Ave
Kahului HI 96732

Call Sign: NH6VU
Earl Takabayashi
Kahului HI 96732

Call Sign: WH6CRT
Larry D Enfeild
Kahului HI 96732

Call Sign: AH6TS
Lineka N Haley
Kahului HI 96733

Call Sign: KF5EAP
Lineka N Haley
Kahului HI 96733

Call Sign: NH7NC
Terence B Bicoy
Kahului HI 96733

Call Sign: WH6CDT
Reid A Matsui
Kahului HI 96733

Call Sign: WH6CRR
Eva G Panta
Kahului HI 96733

Call Sign: WH6DSE
Lena E Staton
Kahului HI 96733

Call Sign: WH7UI
Leomer T Domingo
Kahului HI 96733

Call Sign: WH6CWF
Richelle H Tavares
Kahului HI 96733-0904

Call Sign: WH6VE
Alvin G Battad
Kahului HI 96733-6622

Call Sign: NH6QF
Carl M Koike
Kahului HI 96732

Call Sign: WH6KX
Eli L Ku Jr
Kahului HI 96733-0904

**FCC Amateur Radio
License in Kailua**

Call Sign: KH7SA
Nathan I Lui
603 A Halela St
Kailua HI 96734

Call Sign: KH6NF
Koa Contest Club
1011 A1 Maunawili Rd
Kailua HI 96734-4625

Call Sign: NH7QC
Richard W Grant
60 Aalapapa Pl
Kailua HI 96734

Call Sign: WH6YJ
Jason A Souza
1403 Akiikii Pl
Kailua HI 96734

Call Sign: NH7ZZ
Anson M Kimura
1239 Aloha Oe Dr
Kailua HI 96734

Call Sign: AH6DM
Asaharu T Nakamura
1788 Akaakaawa St
Kailua HI 96734

Call Sign: KH6EEF
Winfred T Inouye
1440 Akiikii Pl
Kailua HI 96734

Call Sign: WH6JS
Richard H Hakanson
1030 Aoloa Pl 108B
Kailua HI 96734

Call Sign: WH6DKT
Jonathan T Boxold
1359 Akamai St
Kailua HI 96734

Call Sign: NH7RC
Dane H Minami
1276 Akipohe St
Kailua HI 96734

Call Sign: AH6S
Tiffany Lawyer
1030 Aoloa Pl 311B
Kailua HI 96734

Call Sign: KH6ASW
Gene H Guild
1410 Akamai St
Kailua HI 96734-4130

Call Sign: KH7HX
Peter A Inafuku
1148 Akipola St
Kailua HI 96734

Call Sign: KB2LCQ
Kristina V Lawyer
1030 Aoloa Pl 311B
Kailua HI 96734

Call Sign: NH7OP
David R Yokoi
1448 Akeke Pl
Kailua HI 96734

Call Sign: WH6DAH
Susan D Holmes
1446 Akuleana Pl
Kailua HI 96734

Call Sign: W2TL
Tiffany Lawyer
1030 Aoloa Pl 311B
Kailua HI 96734

Call Sign: KH7BA
Josh T Anderson
1490 Akeke Pl
Kailua HI 96734

Call Sign: NH6EY
George F Murray
829 Akumu St
Kailua HI 96734

Call Sign: AH6MW
Kenneth J Shultis Jr
333 Aoloa St
Kailua HI 96734

Call Sign: NH6MA
Jeffrey M Ideta
1250 Akiahala St
Kailua HI 96734

Call Sign: WH7MG
Dale M Glenn
208 Alala Rd
Kailua HI 96734

Call Sign: NH6JZ
James Salmond IV
333 Aoloa St 240
Kailua HI 96734

Call Sign: NH6L
Robert K Kaneko III
1384 Akiahala St
Kailua HI 96734

Call Sign: KH7XB
Karen Y Miyahara
579 Alihi Pl
Kailua HI 96734

Call Sign: N2DCQ
Philip W Wehrman
322 Aoloa St 901
Kailua HI 96734-3011

Call Sign: KH7HO
Clement H Jung
1443 Akialoa Pl
Kailua HI 96734

Call Sign: KH6AEI
Masato B Harada
1205 Aloha Oe Dr
Kailua HI 96734

Call Sign: KH7AZ
Carol L Brittingham
355 Aoloa St H 102
Kailua HI 96734

Call Sign: KH7YG
Michael I Brede Jr
980 Apokula St
Kailua HI 96734

Call Sign: KH6AUO
Francis K Tomita
1133 Aukele St
Kailua HI 96734-3617

Call Sign: AH6NU
Leslie K Nunes
1291 Aulepe St
Kailua HI 96734

Call Sign: WH7RW
Henry E Gibson
1003 Auloa Rd
Kailua HI 96734

Call Sign: AH6BR
Scott Allen
1457 Aunauna St
Kailua HI 96734

Call Sign: WH7ME
Kathleen M Hikida
1464 Aunauna St
Kailua HI 96734

Call Sign: WH7MM
Wayne T Hikida
1464 Aunauna St
Kailua HI 96734

Call Sign: WH6DQC
James E Hallstrom Jr
1456 Aunauna St Apt B
Kailua HI 96734

Call Sign: KH6KKH
Kathleen K Hallstrom
1456 Aunauna St B
Kailua HI 96734

Call Sign: WH6DNI
Kathleen K Hallstrom
1456 Aunauna St B
Kailua HI 96734

Call Sign: KH6DGH
Eugene W Carvalho
1256 Aupapa Ohe St
Kailua HI 96734

Call Sign: WH6DXI
Thomas B Abbott
1284 Aupapaohe St
Kailua HI 96734

Call Sign: WH6GU
Michael R O Hara
1340 Aupupu St
Kailua HI 96734

Call Sign: AH6LV
Robert A Epstein
1293 Auwaiku St
Kailua HI 96734

Call Sign: KH7HB
Myles S Sakaguchi
1313 Auwaiku St
Kailua HI 96734

Call Sign: NH7DU
Bernard P Knoblich
648 Auwina
Kailua HI 96734

Call Sign: KH7BM
Alfred A Rivera
324 Auwinala Rd
Kailua HI 96734

Call Sign: KH7BV
Jane W Kienutske
324 Auwinala Rd
Kailua HI 96734

Call Sign: WH6BIU
John W Murley
Box 1025
Kailua HI 96734

Call Sign: KB9ERX
Eric C Brown
6230B Castaneda St
Kailua HI 96734

Call Sign: WD4KWF
Alfred W Baumann Jr
2661 B Connor Lp
Kailua HI 96734

Call Sign: NH6VK
Scott A Jefferys
2421B Dodson St
Kailua HI 96734

Call Sign: KH6FHA
Robert O Dame
400 Dune Cir
Kailua HI 96734

Call Sign: WH7AV
Lawrence A Grayson
647 Halela St
Kailua HI 96734

Call Sign: KH7HN
Timothy M Wiktor
150 Hamakua Dr 421
Kailua HI 96734

Call Sign: WH7YP
Cherub W Akin
150 Hamakua Dr 816
Kailua HI 96734-0816

Call Sign: AH6DX
Hawaiian Islands Amateur
Radio Club
150 Hamakua Dr 816
Kailua HI 96734-0816

Call Sign: AH6PT
Albert L Kaopuiki
1358 Hele St
Kailua HI 96734

Call Sign: NH6UH
Garilyn M Pearson
1463 Humuwili Pl
Kailua HI 96734

Call Sign: AH6GK
Richard C Muelheim
508 Ilimano St
Kailua HI 96734

Call Sign: KH7TY
Eddie M Boswell Jr
1358 Hele St
Kailua HI 96734

Call Sign: N7KZO
Don D Faust
548 Iliaina St
Kailua HI 96734

Call Sign: NH7ZX
Augustina Manuzak
428 Iliwahi Loop
Kailua HI 96734

Call Sign: WH7MV
Naomi Kusayanagi
447 Hinano Way
Kailua HI 96734

Call Sign: WH6DSL
David T Hafner Jr
626 Ilikai St
Kailua HI 96734

Call Sign: WH6DE
Robert F Manuzak
428 Iliwahi Loop
Kailua HI 96734

Call Sign: KD7ZIW
Robert M Jackson
515A Hooulu St
Kailua HI 96734

Call Sign: KH6JDE
Christopher W Beuret
649 Ilikai St
Kailua HI 96734

Call Sign: WH6DRK
Susan A Scott
356A Kaelepulu Dr
Kailua HI 96734

Call Sign: WH6CWB
Keanini M Morse
241-C Hualani St
Kailua HI 96734

Call Sign: KH6KIT
Christopher W Beuret
649 Ilikai St
Kailua HI 96734

Call Sign: WH6DRN
Craig S Thomas
356 Kaelepulu Dr Apt A
Kailua HI 96734

Call Sign: KA3AFT
Casey A Cummings
411 D Hualani St
Kailua HI 96734

Call Sign: WH6CLV
Melissa K Ledgerwood
317 Ilimalia Loop
Kailua HI 96734

Call Sign: KH7AO
Jac I Thomas
504 Kaha St
Kailua HI 96734

Call Sign: KH7AS
John N Limahai Jr
1434 Humuula St
Kailua HI 96734

Call Sign: NH6PS
Patricia J Muelheim
508 Ilimano
Kailua HI 96734

Call Sign: NH7QT
Carmen L Craig
543 Kaha St
Kailua HI 96734

Call Sign: WH6CWY
Patricia L Onogi
1453 Humuula St
Kailua HI 96734

Call Sign: AH6PQ
Carter J Thompson
326 Ilimano St
Kailua HI 96734

Call Sign: WH6DVS
Tyler M Marting
282 Kahako St
Kailua HI 96734

Call Sign: KH6EDG
Thomas T Yamamoto
1468 Humuula St
Kailua HI 96734-3708

Call Sign: KH6FIK
John Del Rosario
430 Ilimano St
Kailua HI 96734

Call Sign: KH7MA
Davie A Felipe
122 A Kahako St
Kailua HI 96734

Call Sign: WH7GG
Keith K Higa
1016 Kahili St
Kailua HI 96734

Call Sign: WH6CKK
James Krentler
40B Kai One Pl
Kailua HI 96734

Call Sign: WH6CTJ
Sarah Ann N Gilman
12A Kailua Rd
Kailua HI 96734

Call Sign: N5IPS
Conrad R Laughinghouse
386 Kailua Rd 308
Kailua HI 96734-2901

Call Sign: KH6EBE
Frank J Failla
596 Kaimalino
Kailua HI 96734

Call Sign: WH7AZ
Leslie K Nunes
613 Kaimalino Pl
Kailua HI 96734

Call Sign: WH7MC
Michael F Holland
1128 Kainalu Dr
Kailua HI 96734

Call Sign: WH6BJL
Chozen Kanetake
18 Kainehe St
Kailua HI 96734

Call Sign: WH7AJ
William F Warren
1131 Kainui Dr
Kailua HI 96734

Call Sign: WH7AP
Larry C Coffin
1549 Kanapuu Dr
Kailua HI 96934

Call Sign: WH6DKO
Jan L Henry
116 Kanapuu Pl
Kailua HI 96734

Call Sign: AH6HV
Munehisa Arashiro
137 Kapaa St
Kailua HI 96734

Call Sign: WH6AGR
Robert E Begley Jr
138A Kapaa St
Kailua HI 96734-2146

Call Sign: WA0BVV
David L Shores
521E Kawailoa Rd
Kailua HI 96734-3306

Call Sign: WH7FA
Gordon P Ching
327-C Keaniani St
Kailua HI 96734

Call Sign: KI6SVS
Brandon N
Sundheimermeyer
6561A Kekahuna Pl
Kailua HI 96734

Call Sign: WH7OD
Henry Tripp
1224 Keolu Dr
Kailua HI 96734-3851

Call Sign: KG4MGL
Brittain M Caldwell
559C Keolu Dr
Kailua HI 96734

Call Sign: WH6DTF
Brittain M Caldwell
559C Keolu Dr
Kailua HI 96734

Call Sign: WH6H
Stuart P Browne
583 B Keolu Dr
Kailua HI 96734

Call Sign: NL7YZ
Jeffrey A Soots
535 Keolu Dr Apt C
Kailua HI 96734

Call Sign: WH7TA
Toaalii S Tauga
720 Kihapai Pl A1
Kailua HI 96734

Call Sign: NH6MJ
George Costa Jr
150B Kihapai St
Kailua HI 96734

Call Sign: WH6CWZ
David F De Lima
252A Kihapai St
Kailua HI 96734

Call Sign: NH6WK
Clifford R Robinson
1482 Kina St
Kailua HI 96734-3729

Call Sign: NH6ZC
Irwin H Ukishima
1536 Kina St
Kailua HI 96734

Call Sign: KH6OM
Richard M Kimitsuka
1377 Kina St

Kailua HI 96734   Kailua HI 96734-3652   Kailua HI 96734

Call Sign: KH6CLV   Call Sign: KH6U   Call Sign: KH6NFN
George Y H Do   John D Morgan   Leonard H L Young
527 Kipuka Pl   1576 Kupau St   1297 Maleko St
Kailua HI 96734   Kailua HI 96734   Kailua HI 96734

Call Sign: AH6SR   Call Sign: KH6D   Call Sign: WH6BH
Curtis H Ho   Melvin S Vittum   Derek K Y Young
1364 Kuloaa Pl   218 Kuuhoa Pl   1297 Maleko St
Kailua HI 96734   Kailua HI 96734   Kailua HI 96734

Call Sign: NH6YL   Call Sign: KH6RR   Call Sign: KH6W
Curtis H Ho   Lanikai Dx Assn   Ann E Miller
1364 Kuloaa Pl   333 Lapa Pl   339 Manae St
Kailua HI 96734   Kailua HI 96734   Kailua HI 96734

Call Sign: KH7XX   Call Sign: WH7W   Call Sign: NH7QS
Hawaii Dx Society   Lanikai Dx Assn   Ann E Miller
1056 Kupau St   333 Lapa Pl   339 Manae St
Kailua HI 96734   Kailua HI 96734   Kailua HI 96734

Call Sign: WH6T   Call Sign: WH6CBX   Call Sign: WH7F
Richard D La Chance   Joseph D Coco Jr   Ann E Miller
1056 Kupau St   1765A Lawrence Rd   339 Manae St
Kailua HI 96734   Kailua HI 96734   Kailua HI 96734

Call Sign: WH7ZX   Call Sign: WH6TS   Call Sign: NH6HJ
Evelyn Zangl-Milbrard   Joseph G Thomas   Ann Lopes
1214 Kupau St   1206 Loho St   318B Manono St
Kailua HI 96734   Kailua HI 96734   Kailua HI 96734

Call Sign: WH6CAN   Call Sign: WH6BIZ   Call Sign: KH7TK
Judy P Yee   Jack D Peters   Herbert T Kaneshige
1459 Kupau St   1057 Lunaai St   401 B Manono St
Kailua HI 96734   Kailua HI 96734-4633   Kailua HI 96734

Call Sign: AH6QF   Call Sign: WH6DY   Call Sign: KH6AVG
Benjamin S B Yee   Gary A Fuller   Thomas M Sanders
1459 Kupau St   1131 Lunaai St   1243 Manu Mele St
Kailua HI 96734-3652   Kailua HI 96734   Kailua HI 96734

Call Sign: NH6US   Call Sign: W6MQB   Call Sign: AH6AS
Benjamin S B Yee   Verne G Moldt   Carl C Campbell
1459 Kupau St   1263 Maleko St   1111 Manulani St

Kailua HI 96734

Call Sign: KH6SH
John M Hillyer
1011A Maunawili Rd
Kailua HI 96734-4625

Call Sign: KC8IEL
Kyle J Tolla
2605 Maxam Pl Apt A
Kailua HI 96734

Call Sign: KH6GQL
Hugh B Erminger Jr
739 Mokapu Rd
Kailua HI 96734

Call Sign: NH6UE
Richard T Hollinger
798 Mokapu Rd
Kailua HI 96734

Call Sign: KH6CO
Odia E Howe
1527 Mokulua Dr
Kailua HI 96734

Call Sign: N5IE
Bruce G Hosmer
127 Mokumanu Dr
Kailua HI 96734

Call Sign: NH7TQ
Akira Yamada
Mr S Minamoto - 1202
~~Lunaai St
Kailua HI 96734

Call Sign: KH6CI
William K Doi Jr
105A N Kainalu Dr
Kailua HI 96734

Call Sign: KH6BBY
Porfirio J Garcia

271A N Kainalu Dr
Kailua HI 96734

Call Sign: AH6HG
Kenneth M Rappolt
783 N Kalaheo Ave
Kailua HI 96734

Call Sign: KH7YZ
Janet L Mitchell
156B N Kalaheo Ave
Kailua HI 96734-2345

Call Sign: WH6CVU
Bradley V Pearson
82 Namala Pl
Kailua HI 96734

Call Sign: WH6DUV
Robert A Gilman
1259 Nanawale Way
Kailua HI 96734

Call Sign: KH6IX
Fred J Titcomb
1018 Nanialii St
Kailua HI 96734-3813

Call Sign: NH6GT
Sebastian Salomon Jr
1125 Nanialii St
Kailua HI 96734

Call Sign: WH6BZG
Sam V Idian
1326 Nanialii St
Kailua HI 96734

Call Sign: WH6DKN
Michael J Hopper
1374 Nanialii St
Kailua HI 96734

Call Sign: WH6GD
Eugene Dashiell

728 Nunu St
Kailua HI 96734

Call Sign: WH7IS
Eugene Dashiell
728 Nunu St
Kailua HI 96734

Call Sign: AH6PR
Mark L Pascal
161 2 Oko St
Kailua HI 96734

Call Sign: WH6CWI
Kailua Amateur Radio
Assn
161-2 Oko St
Kailua HI 96734-1723

Call Sign: WH6BWP
Gerald G Vincent
433 A Olamana St
Kailua HI 96734

Call Sign: WH7MI
Jerry Bangerter
710 Old Mokapu Rd
Kailua HI 96734

Call Sign: AH6BW
Antonio A Querubin Jr
411-C Olomana St
Kailua HI 96734

Call Sign: AH6E
Norman Thompson
712 Oneawa
Kailua HI 96734-2052

Call Sign: KH6JKS
Tom K Nishikawa
454 Oneawa St
Kailua HI 96734

Call Sign: NH6MC

Jimmy M Parker
840 Oneawa St
Kailua HI 96734

Call Sign: KH7FS
Douglas A Hoffman
915 Oneawa St
Kailua HI 96734

Call Sign: N2RWX
David B Jacobs
555 Paakiki Pl
Kailua HI 96734

Call Sign: WH6AI
Melvyn Y C Chow
117 Palapu St
Kailua HI 96734

Call Sign: NH6VS
Cornell B Bostwick
576 Paokano Pl
Kailua HI 96734

Call Sign: NH6BT
Albert S Chung
576 Papalani St
Kailua HI 96734

Call Sign: KH7HP
Wayne K Ogino
1608 Paukiki St
Kailua HI 96734-4176

Call Sign: KH6AQ
Warren O Smith
525 Pauku St
Kailua HI 96734

Call Sign: WH6DRO
Richard J Tibbetts Jr
525 Pauku St
Kailua HI 96734

Call Sign: KH7UM

Mark C Waldvogel
534 Paulele St
Kailua HI 96734

Call Sign: KH7XE
Burma K Barnes
532 Paumakua Pl
Kailua HI 96734

Call Sign: WH7QM
Sidney D Sanders Jr
19A Pilipu Pl
Kailua HI 96734-2120

Call Sign: AH6CI
Herbert W Hodge
20 Pilpu Pl
Kailua HI 96734

Call Sign: KH7OA
Vincent F Goo
1169 Punua Pl
Kailua HI 96734

Call Sign: NH6IN
Leslie M Murakami
1220 Punua Pl
Kailua HI 96734

Call Sign: WH6TH
Chad K Taniguchi
538 Uluhaku St
Kailua HI 96734

Call Sign: WH6DGE
Cmc Amateur Radio Club
640 Ulukahiki St
Kailua HI 96734-4498

Call Sign: WH6DUO
Castle Medical Center
Amateur Radio Club
640 Ulukahiki St
Kailua HI 96734

Call Sign: KH7XG
Denis J Gilbert
665 Ulukahiki St
Kailua HI 96734

Call Sign: KH6BCN
Alexander M Takaki
509 Ululani St
Kailua HI 96734

Call Sign: WH6CND
Grant K K Chock
694 Ululani St
Kailua HI 96734

Call Sign: WH7MB
Robert J Hoopii Jr
703 Ululani St
Kailua HI 96734

Call Sign: NH6BX
Daniel E Schwarz
661 Ulumalu St
Kailua HI 96734

Call Sign: WH7MH
Edmund L Char
540 Ulumawao St
Kailua HI 96734

Call Sign: WH6DBF
Gloria F Saguto
517 Ulumu St
Kailua HI 96734

Call Sign: NH6IG
Shepard C Williams
531 Ulumu St
Kailua HI 96734

Call Sign: KH7USA
Hawaii Pacific Pavones
Surfers Arc
1265 Ulunahele St
Kailua HI 96734

Call Sign: N0SBC
Thomas Chlebecek
420 Uluniu St
Kailua HI 96734

Call Sign: WA2YZD
Robert L Rodin
315 Uluniu St 201A
Kailua HI 96734

Call Sign: KH6JV
Kenneth L Vaughan
619 Uluoa
Kailua HI 96734

Call Sign: W6CNB
John R Willey
545 Uluoa St
Kailua HI 96734-4343

Call Sign: KH7YT
Ronald E Chow
548 Uluoa St
Kailua HI 96734

Call Sign: KH6DIC
Kenneth S Kamei
1252 Ulupalakua St
Kailua HI 96734

Call Sign: KH6BI
Frederick B H Maertens
1254 Ulupii St
Kailua HI 96734

Call Sign: WH6BZU
Cary A Stevens
1260 Ulupii St
Kailua HI 96734

Call Sign: AH6HH
Sylvester Sneidar
1328 Ulupuni St
Kailua HI 96734

Call Sign: KH7YP
Lawrence M Sugai
1510 Ulupuni St
Kailua HI 96734

Call Sign: NH7NK
Toshiaki Matsuura
725 Wanaao Rd
Kailua HI 96734

Call Sign: AH6DG
Merle H Arnold Jr
768 Wanaao Rd
Kailua HI 96734

Call Sign: KH6AYP
Thomas T Midomaru
812 Wanaao Rd
Kailua HI 96734

Call Sign: WH7ML
Irene P Ahlo
740 Wanaas Rd
Kailua HI 96734

Call Sign: WH6FT
Alois M Palenchar
70 Wilikoki Pl
Kailua HI 96734

Call Sign: KH6GO
Thomas A Celentano
Kailua HI 96734

Call Sign: KH7IA
David K Nagayama
Kailua HI 96734

Call Sign: NH7DW
Diane L Scot
Kailua HI 96734

Call Sign: WH6DSQ
Leslie D Huddleston

Kailua HI 96734

Call Sign: WH7AM
David D Randles
Kailua HI 96734

Call Sign: WH7CY
Christine A Kerner
Kailua HI 96734

Call Sign: WH7GI
Cynthia L Keolanoi
Kailua HI 96734

Call Sign: WH7Y
J. Mitchell
Kailua HI 96734

Call Sign: NH7MZ
Rodney L Williams
Kailua HI 96734-1338

Call Sign: KH6IMQ
Gerald K J Chang
Kailua HI 96734

Call Sign: WH6COR
John J Chadwick
Kailua HI 96734

**FCC Amateur Radio
License in Kailua Kona**

Call Sign: NH6KE
Patrick H Callahan
76 979 Aeo St
Kailua Kona HI 96740

Call Sign: KH6JTD
Mike A Mc Coy
73 109 Ahikawa St
Kailua Kona HI 96740

Call Sign: AH6KW
Thomas H Daniel

73-1036 Ahikawa St
Kailua Kona HI 96740

Call Sign: WH6CBW
William K Spence
75-5916 Alii Dr
Kailua Kona HI 96740

Call Sign: WH6BJ
John G Helms
75-6002 Alii Dr
Kailua Kona HI 96740

Call Sign: KH6CW
Kona Contest Club
77-6409 Alii Dr
Kailua Kona HI 96740

Call Sign: NH6OQ
Frank M Mead
77-6489 Alii Dr
Kailua Kona HI 96740

Call Sign: W0XC
Clinton C Allen
78-6689A Alii Dr
Kailua Kona HI 96740

Call Sign: AH6SN
Peter Golitzen
77 6469 Alii Dr 212
Kailua Kona HI 96740

Call Sign: KF6BS
Peter Golitzen
77 6469 Alii Dr 212
Kailua Kona HI 96740

Call Sign: KA0VHP
Allen L Hart
76-6246 Alii Dr 231
Kailua Kona HI 96740

Call Sign: AH6OG
Clement S Simon

75-6016 Alii Dr 241
Kailua Kona HI 96740

Call Sign: WA6RWM
Richard L Gray
76-6268 Alii Dr 301
Kailua Kona HI 96740

Call Sign: WH6DBV
Kenny C Park
78 7070 Alii Dr A302
Kailua Kona HI 96740

Call Sign: KB2RUZ
Paul W Rollman Jr
75-6081 Alii Dr Alii Lani
Mm101
Kailua Kona HI 96740-
2374

Call Sign: AH6PV
Scott J Thompson
78 6665 Alii Dr Apt 203
Kailua Kona HI 96740

Call Sign: WB6LNX
David B Mescon
75-6081 Alii Dr K202
Kailua Kona HI 96740

Call Sign: K6ERG
Richard P Stauduhar
73 4914 Anini St
Kailua Kona HI 96740

Call Sign: ND6O
Steven L Benson
78 7022 Aumoe St
Kailua Kona HI 96740

Call Sign: AH6RO
Russell E Boutell
73-1315 Awakea St
Kailua Kona HI 96740

Call Sign: WD0FTF
Russell E Boutell
73-1315 Awakea St
Kailua Kona HI 96740

Call Sign: AH6PL
Howard Shermer
76 6298 Haku Pl
Kailua Kona HI 96740

Call Sign: W6HS
Howard Shermer
76 6298 Haku Pl
Kailua Kona HI 96740

Call Sign: KF6DJ
James B Dusel
73 1414 Hamiha St
Kailua Kona HI 96740

Call Sign: AH6JB
Douglas B Green
75 5706 Hanama Pl 201A
Kailua Kona HI 96740

Call Sign: KE6CJ
Nancy L Ferguson
77-5591 Hienaloli Rd
Kailua Kona HI 96740

Call Sign: KH6QR
Douglas Cataraha
74 5158 Himeni Pl
Kailua Kona HI 96740

Call Sign: WH6WI
Douglas Cataraha
74 5158 Himeni Pl
Kailua Kona HI 96740

Call Sign: WH7C
Mitsuya Tamaki
Himoto 76 ~4306 ~Leilani
St
Kailua Kona HI 96740

Call Sign: WH6CSX
Sandra L Graham
73-4730 Hina Lani
Kailua Kona HI 96740

Call Sign: KV6J
William G Graham
73-4730 Hina Lani St
Kailua Kona HI 96740

Call Sign: WH7WI
Jamie D Mallardi
78-135 Holua Rd
Kailua Kona HI 96740

Call Sign: KH6GKR
Harley E Mc Nichols
73-4343 Ilemano Pl
Kailua Kona HI 96740

Call Sign: KC7ULO
Ralph V Johnson Jr
75-6114 Ka Ane E Pl
Kailua Kona HI 96740

Call Sign: KH6AG
Ralph V Johnson Jr
75-6114 Ka Ane E Pl
Kailua Kona HI 96740

Call Sign: WH6DRZ
Ralph V Johnson Jr
75-6114 Ka Ane E Pl
Kailua Kona HI 96740

Call Sign: AH6LC
Clark M Richardson
76-6310 Kaheiau St
Kailua Kona HI 96740

Call Sign: K7BT
Ronald D Mayer
73-1145 Kahuna A O Rd
Kailua Kona HI 96740

Call Sign: WH6BB
Susan J Santangelo
73-2175 Kaloko Dr
Kailua Kona HI 96740

Call Sign: AH6MV
Robert E Manfredi
76 126 Kamehamalu St
Kailua Kona HI 96740

Call Sign: KH6LS
Lawrence A Scadden
76-177 Kamehamalu St
Kailua Kona HI 96740

Call Sign: K6HWT
Lawrence A Scadden
76-177 Kamehamalu St
Kailua Kona HI 96740

Call Sign: KD6KSF
Dan J Walker
75-110 Kamilo St
Kailua Kona HI 96740

Call Sign: KD6KSH
Shannon M Walker
75-110 Kamilo St
Kailua Kona HI 96740

Call Sign: N0LZT
Heather A Sangster Halsey
73-4840 Kanalani St Pmb
295
Kailua Kona HI 96740

Call Sign: N6OEY
Steve J Halsey
73-4840 Kanalani St Pmb
295
Kailua Kona HI 96740

Call Sign: NH6XA
Virginia Gerlach

74-425 Kealakehe Pky 16
Kailua Kona HI 96740

Call Sign: WH6CPR
Joshua R Andrews
74-5101 Kealapua Pl
Kailua Kona HI 96740

Call Sign: KD6HYW
Robert D Mc Carthy
76-4312 Kinau St
Kailua Kona HI 96740

Call Sign: NH7IT
Van R Malan
73-1370 Kinoulu Pl
Kailua Kona HI 96740-
8665

Call Sign: WH7WO
Peter W Ogilvie
73-4519 Kohanaiki Rd
Box 13
Kailua Kona HI 96740

Call Sign: KH6GF
Kauai Vhf/Uhf Arc
75-664 Koiula Pl
Kailua Kona HI 96740

Call Sign: KH6IT
Campbell Hawaii Arc
75-664 Koiula Pl
Kailua Kona HI 96740

Call Sign: WH6NT
Abraham H Lee
75-5851 Kuakini Hwy
Kailua Kona HI 96740

Call Sign: WH6CWO
William A Mayse
75 5722 Kuakini Hwy 213
Kailua Kona HI 96740

Call Sign: KH7DM
Daniel A Monck
80 77-6425 Kuakini Hwy
C2
Kailua Kona HI 96740

Call Sign: WB2AHM
Daniel A Monck
80 77-6425 Kuakini Hwy
C2
Kailua Kona HI 96740

Call Sign: NH6NR
Richard H Mc Kowen
78-6827 Kuhinanui St
Kailua Kona HI 96740

Call Sign: WB9IME
Jack E Murphy
76 6260 Kupuna St
Kailua Kona HI 96740

Call Sign: N6EJY
Raymond F Stewart
77 6380 Kupuna St
Kailua Kona HI 96740

Call Sign: WH6DAE
Vaughn M Stewart
77 6380 Kupuna St
Kailua Kona HI 96740

Call Sign: AH6JR
Stanley A Tomyl
73-4103 Lapa Au Pl
Kailua Kona HI 96740

Call Sign: KH6BFD
Frank H Roff
76-6196 Lehua Rd
Kailua Kona HI 96745

Call Sign: AB6AP
George P Ingraham
76-4385 Leilani St

Kailua Kona HI 96740-
7925

Call Sign: AH6SA
George P Ingraham
76-4385 Leilani St
Kailua Kona HI 96740-
7925

Call Sign: NO7DB
George P Ingraham
76-4385 Leilani St
Kailua Kona HI 96740-
7925

Call Sign: WH6CRX
Charles F De Wolf
76 6287 Leone St
Kailua Kona HI 96740

Call Sign: WH6DOZ
William A Foulk
75-156 Lunapule Rd Apt D
Kailua Kona HI 96740

Call Sign: N6MHA
Merle D Stewart
75-5818 Lupa Pl
Kailua Kona HI 96740

Call Sign: KH7WA
Randy E Rice
73-1091 Mahilani Dr
Kailua Kona HI 96740-
8410

Call Sign: WH6BZD
Dien Short
73-1219 Mahilani Dr
Kailua Kona HI 96740

Call Sign: NH6QU
David Magallanes Sr
75-347 Makamae Pl
Kailua Kona HI 96740

Call Sign: WH6ZM
Beverly A Vanderbeek
73 4355 Malalo Pl
Kailua Kona HI 96740

Call Sign: KH7HG
Harold P Stene
73 4181 Malino Pl
Kailua Kona HI 96740

Call Sign: KD6LRA
Van R Malan
73-4425 Mamalahoa Hwy
Kailua Kona HI 96740-
9188

Call Sign: WH7BH
Cheyne B Laver
74-991 Manawalea St
B206
Kailua Kona HI 96740

Call Sign: NH7XJ
Brandon J Boyl
73-4878 Manu Mela St
Kailua Kona HI 96740

Call Sign: WH6CM
Joe P Catanzaro
78-270 Manukai St
Kailua Kona HI 96740

Call Sign: KH6GMP
Gary E Belcher
75 5772 Milena Pl
Kailua Kona HI 96740

Call Sign: KH6HGP
Red Hill Amateur Radio
Club
75 5772 Milena Pl
Kailua Kona HI 96740

Call Sign: WH6DGS

Kona Hawaii Dx Club
75 5772 Milena Pl
Kailua Kona HI 96740

Call Sign: NH7T
Rico Schurig
Belcher 75 5772 Milena Pl
Kailua Kona HI 96740

Call Sign: WH7B
Reinhard Fendler
Belcher 75 5772 Milena Pl
Kailua Kona HI 96740

Call Sign: KH7NY
Melvin H Shapiro
Msc 115 ~75 ~1027
~Henry St 111A
Kailua Kona HI 96740

Call Sign: KH7NX
Rebecca G Shapiro
Msc 155 ~75 ~1027
~Henry St 111A
Kailua Kona HI 96740

Call Sign: KH7AR
Lester P Zaviski
75-626 N Mea Lanakila Pl
Kailua Kona HI 96740

Call Sign: WA7HEO
Lester P Zaviski
75-626 N Mea Lanakila Pl
Kailua Kona HI 96740

Call Sign: KH2TE
Jannie Van Tuyl
75-252 Nani Kailua Dr 10
Kailua Kona HI 96740

Call Sign: N7SUG
Larry E Fredrickson
75 234 Nani Kailua Dr 68
Kailua Kona HI 96740

Call Sign: AB6WI
James A Gustin
75-252 Nani Kailua Dr
Unit 10
Kailua Kona HI 96740-
2073

Call Sign: KM6WZ
Janice I Gustin
75-252 Nani Kailua Unit
10
Kailua Kona HI 96740

Call Sign: KH2TD
Jacco Van Tuyl
75-252 Nani Lailua Dr 10
Kailua Kona HI 96740

Call Sign: KH7GW
Gary R Miltimore
75-5784 Nele Pl
Kailua Kona HI 96740

Call Sign: KB1UAG
Ryan Cohen
77-357 Nohealani St
Kailua Kona HI 96740

Call Sign: KB1UBP
Daniel R Cohen
77-357 Nohealani St
Kailua Kona HI 96740

Call Sign: AH6RU
Arlene Mckinnon
73-4176 Oluolu Pl
Kailua Kona HI 96740

Call Sign: N0NWC
Setsuo T Takai
73 1344 One One Pl
Kailua Kona HI 96740

Call Sign: NH7TO

Dianna N Lally
73-1341 One One Pl
Kailua Kona HI 96740

Call Sign: KC6UMR
Michael M Kamegawa
73-4315 One One St
Kailua Kona HI 96740

Call Sign: KH2KW
Lonnie T King II
77-6455 Ono Rd
Kailua Kona HI 96740

Call Sign: KH2GJ
Jean M Thompson
77-6458 Ono Rd
Kailua Kona HI 96740

Call Sign: WH7GB
Elizabeth Star
73-1436 Punihaole Pl
Kailua Kona HI 96740

Call Sign: WH6CSA
William H Bottrell
72 1085 Puukala Rd
Kailua Kona HI 96740

Call Sign: WH7CG
Jay E Hanson
78-7230 Puupele Rd
Kailua Kona HI 96740

Call Sign: WH7WQ
Nicholas G Fisher
76-206 Royal Poinciana Dr
Kailua Kona HI 96740

Call Sign: KD7GWM
Frank H Roff
77 6455 Sea View Circle
Kailua Kona HI 96740

Call Sign: NH7PM

Brent L Weyer
73-1544 Uanani Pl
Kailua Kona HI 96740

Call Sign: WB6FOX
Charles W Conklin
75-5782 Waiola Pl
Kailua Kona HI 96740

Call Sign: WH6FOX
Charles W Conklin
75-5782 Waiola Pl
Kailua Kona HI 96740

Call Sign: K6RMM
Sheldon M Kurtzman
77 6479 Walua Rd
Kailua Kona HI 96740

Call Sign: KH6HH
Sheldon M Kurtzman
77 6479 Walua Rd
Kailua Kona HI 96740

Call Sign: KH6HWK
Elijah Hawk
75-5873 Walua Rd Apt
C209
Kailua Kona HI 96740

Call Sign: KH7HWK
Beverly A Hawk
75-5873 Walua Rd Apt
C209
Kailua Kona HI 96740

Call Sign: KH7DX
Stuart E Johnston
Kailua Kona HI 96745

Call Sign: AH6RR
Roland M Spoon
Kailua Kona HI 96745

Call Sign: KH6BCK

Ben F Matsuoka
Kailua Kona HI 96745

Call Sign: KH6DFW
Takeo Kuwada
Kailua Kona HI 96745

Call Sign: KH6DHG
Peter K Park
Kailua Kona HI 96745

Call Sign: KH6DXC
Kona Hawaii Dx Club
Kailua Kona HI 96745

Call Sign: KH6WW
Big Island Contest Club
Kailua Kona HI 96745

Call Sign: KH7B
Kona Contest Club
Kailua Kona HI 96745

Call Sign: KH7MS
Blake F Stene
Kailua Kona HI 96745

Call Sign: N5JKJ
Roland M Spoon
Kailua Kona HI 96745

Call Sign: NH6DR
Stuart E Johnston
Kailua Kona HI 96745

Call Sign: NH6LR
Victor M Limacher
Kailua Kona HI 96745

Call Sign: NH6M
Dewey D Proietti
Kailua Kona HI 96745

Call Sign: NH7DM
Tonya D Deroche

Kailua Kona HI 96745

Call Sign: W6OKJ
Russell P Journigan
Kailua Kona HI 96745

Call Sign: WD8OBO
Wayne Bassani
Kailua Kona HI 96745

Call Sign: WH6DEW
Kona Amateur Radio
Society
Kailua Kona HI 96745

Call Sign: WH6DGW
Big Island Contest Club
Kailua Kona HI 96745

Call Sign: WH6DRS
Sharlene G Naidas
Kailua Kona HI 96745

Call Sign: WH6DRT
Eric M Mitsnyoshi
Kailua Kona HI 96745

Call Sign: WH6DRV
Alice R St Onge
Kailua Kona HI 96745

Call Sign: WH6WJ
Kevin E Bowsher
Kailua Kona HI 96745

Call Sign: WH6WP
Michael J Lauro
Kailua Kona HI 96745

Call Sign: WH6WQ
Jinny L M Park
Kailua Kona HI 96745

Call Sign: WH6XG
Diane Stone

Kailua Kona HI 96745

Call Sign: WH6YO
Sandra L Miranda
Kailua Kona HI 96745

Call Sign: WH7HN
Thomas W Hohler
Kailua Kona HI 96745

Call Sign: KC7MRF
Ron B Anger
Kailua Kona HI 96745

Call Sign: KC7TPO
John M Bertsch
Kailua Kona HI 96745

Call Sign: KH6JIM
James A Metcalf
Kailua Kona HI 96745

Call Sign: NH7OJ
Corey M Johnson
Kailua Kona HI 96745

Call Sign: WH6CPD
Raymond B Henderson
Kailua Kona HI 96745

Call Sign: WH6DGZ
Kona Amateur Radio
Society
Kailua Kona HI 96745

Call Sign: WH6JP
James A Metcalf
Kailua Kona HI 96745

Call Sign: WH6DGX
Hawaii West Amateur
Radio Society/Kona
Amateur Radio Society
Kailua Kona HI 96745

Call Sign: KA5CDS
Doris J Millard
Kailua Kona HI 96745-
0745

Call Sign: WD5FFZ
Maydwell H Millard
Kailua Kona HI 96745-
0745

Call Sign: WH6WG
Irene B Horvath
Kailua Kona HI 96745-
1213

Call Sign: KH7ZY
Charles D Kaminski
Kailua Kona HI 96745-
3114

Call Sign: WH6DGU
Kona Contest Club
Kailua Kona HI 96745-
5076

Call Sign: KB0FBQ
Lori D Johnson
Kailua Kona HI 96745-
5278

Call Sign: NO0H
Michael P Johnson
Kailua Kona HI 96745-
5278

Call Sign: WH6CL
Charlie J Porter
Kailua Kona HI 96739

Call Sign: K6HI
Theodore N Leaf
Kailua Kona HI 96745

Call Sign: NH6CH
Samuel A Moore

Kailua Kona HI 96745

Call Sign: NH6GM
Robert S Mc Clean
Kailua Kona HI 96745

Call Sign: NH6TW
Dameon D Welch
Kailua Kona HI 96745

Call Sign: WH6AN
Joseph C Tyler III
Kailua Kona HI 96745

Call Sign: WH6BA
James B Russell
Kailua Kona HI 96745

Call Sign: WH6CFB
Jonathan D Murai
Kailua Kona HI 96745

Call Sign: WH6CPQ
Leland T Chong Jr
Kailua Kona HI 96745

Call Sign: WH6FM
Leland A Chong Sr
Kailua Kona HI 96745

Call Sign: WH6JK
Randee C Chong
Kailua Kona HI 96745

Call Sign: WH6NS
Rex D Horton
Kailua Kona HI 96745

Call Sign: KB6VJZ
Robert L Brown
Kailua Kona HI 96745

Call Sign: N6UXN
Leonard J Mascari
Kailua Kona HI 96745

Call Sign: KF6VDT
Genora L Travis
Kailua Kona HI 96745

FCC Amateur Radio License in Kaiula

Call Sign: KH7YC
Jennifer H Rodriguez
324-A Manono St
Kaiula HI 96734

FCC Amateur Radio License in Kalaheo

Call Sign: NH6GP
Robin D Rosendaal
4388 Ahopueo Dr
Kalaheo HI 96741

Call Sign: NH7CH
Robin D Rosendaal
4388 Ahopueo Dr
Kalaheo HI 96741

Call Sign: KH6FGS
Roger M Caires
Box 777
Kalaheo HI 96741

Call Sign: KH6PN
Donald W Traller
3639 Ilima Pl
Kalaheo HI 96741

Call Sign: NH7TM
Gayle K Hughes
4370 Kalaheo Dr Unit 8
Kalaheo HI 96741

Call Sign: KH6PP
Papapaholahola Dx Group
5171 Kikala Rd
Kalaheo HI 96741

Call Sign: KH6S
William D Baisley
Memorial Repeater Asso
5171 Kikala Rd
Kalaheo HI 96741

Call Sign: NH6HI
James R Pilgram
5171 Kikala Rd
Kalaheo HI 96741

Call Sign: WH6DGK
South Kauai Digital
Association
5171 Kikala Rd
Kalaheo HI 96741

Call Sign: WH6DGL
Papapaholahola Dx Group
5171 Kikala Rd
Kalaheo HI 96741

Call Sign: WH6DGR
William D Baisley
Memorial Repeater Asso
5171 Kikala Rd
Kalaheo HI 96741

Call Sign: WH6FG
South Kauai Digital
Association
5171 Kikala Rd
Kalaheo HI 96741

Call Sign: WH6FG
James R Pilgram
5171 Kikala Rd
Kalaheo HI 96741

Call Sign: WA0TFB
Gary A Appel
3714 Kikee Rd
Kalaheo HI 96741-9710

Call Sign: KH6FBQ
Norman S Nitta
3794 Kikee Rd
Kalaheo HI 96741

Call Sign: KH6FCH
Stephen W Haynes
3818 Kikee Rd
Kalaheo HI 96741

Call Sign: KH6LM
Noel C Patricio
4555 Kuilei St
Kalaheo HI 96741-9139

Call Sign: KH7WY
William F Georgi
4568 Kuli Rd
Kalaheo HI 96741

Call Sign: KB7LFB
Minde M Hine
3565 Lilikoi Pl
Kalaheo HI 96741

Call Sign: KB7LFC
Larry E Hine
3565 Lilikoi Pl
Kalaheo HI 96741

Call Sign: KH6BBM
Itsuo Sakata
4295 Maka Rd
Kalaheo HI 96741

Call Sign: NH7DK
Jo D Farris
3794 Nanakai Rd
Kalaheo HI 96741

Call Sign: NH7UR
Barbara L Fontana
4069 Oni Pl
Kalaheo HI 96741

Call Sign: WH6CZG
Val D Tsuchiya
3897 Ulu Alii St
Kalaheo HI 96741

Call Sign: NH7CP
Millicent M Robison-
Crown
3980 Waha Rd
Kalaheo HI 96741

Call Sign: KH6JI
Ron D Crown
3980 Waha Rd
Kalaheo HI 96741

Call Sign: AH6JC
Richard H Nagoshi
Kalaheo HI 96741

Call Sign: KH6AJ
Joseph A Soares
Kalaheo HI 96741

Call Sign: KH6EA
Stephen L Spears
Kalaheo HI 96741

Call Sign: KH6IPK
George M Taguma
Kalaheo HI 96741

Call Sign: KH6JJC
Juan P Lorenzo Jr
Kalaheo HI 96741

Call Sign: NH6GH
Jonathan J Cummings
Kalaheo HI 96741

Call Sign: NH6GK
Paul N Kamai
Kalaheo HI 96741

Call Sign: NH6QD

Albert C Edwards
Kalaheo HI 96741

Call Sign: NH7CE
Jonathan J Cummings
Kalaheo HI 96741

Call Sign: NH7CF
Paul N Kamai
Kalaheo HI 96741

Call Sign: NH7EF
John P Rapozo
Kalaheo HI 96741

Call Sign: NH7LS
Cory R Halpin
Kalaheo HI 96741

Call Sign: NH7NI
Samantha L Cummings
Kalaheo HI 96741

Call Sign: WH6CSK
Jean Paul R Guillemot
Kalaheo HI 96741

Call Sign: WH6DGB
Collin C Dana
Kalaheo HI 96741

Call Sign: WH6DTY
Patrick Y Nakagawa Jr
Kalaheo HI 96741

Call Sign: WJ8A
Stephen L Spears
Kalaheo HI 96741

Call Sign: KH7TV
Ed F De Deo
Kalaheo HI 96756

Call Sign: KH7JS
Chris B Berg

Kalaheo HI 96741-0788

Call Sign: K6AUA
Frederick O Gulliver
Kalaheo HI 96741

Call Sign: KH6CH
Yutaka Arakaki
Kalaheo HI 96741

Call Sign: KH6JEF
Robert A Dzina
Kalaheo HI 96741

Call Sign: NH6XS
Stefan P Schweitzer
Kalaheo HI 96741

Call Sign: WH6ASY
Robert Romero
Kalaheo HI 96741

Call Sign: WH6BWF
Matthew A Taba
Kalaheo HI 96741

Call Sign: WH6BXE
Kawika J Fujita
Kalaheo HI 96741

Call Sign: WH6CGR
Lawrence K Gonsalves
Kalaheo HI 96741

Call Sign: WH6CGS
Kevin M Takekuma
Kalaheo HI 96741

Call Sign: WH6CHH
Toshi Hirabayashi
Kalaheo HI 96741

Call Sign: WH6EC
William G Mustard
Kalaheo HI 96741

Call Sign: WH6LI
Daniel S Momohara
Kalaheo HI 96741

Call Sign: WH6MP
Gary J Hall
Kalaheo HI 96741

Call Sign: WH6JH
Michelle M Momohara
Kalaheo HI 96741

Call Sign: KH6BWG
William O Kupele
Memorial Club Station
Attn. Steve Prokop
Wh6Dts
Kalaupapa HI 96742

Call Sign: WH6DTS
Stephen B Prokop
172 Baldwin St
Kalaupapa HI 96742

Call Sign: AH6IS
William O Kupele
Memorial Club Station
Kalaupapa HI 96742

Call Sign: WH6DTZ
Lionel W Kaawaloa
Kalaupapa HI 96742

Call Sign: WH6DUP
Rafael Torres
Kalaupapa HI 96742

Call Sign: NH7RY

Michelle K F T Medeiros
65-1285 C Kawaihae Rd
Kamuela HI 96743

Call Sign: W7RI
Richard Rowe
Hcr 1 Kv-45
Kamuela HI 96743

Call Sign: WH6YU
Jeri L Douglas
5230 Kihei Rd
Kamuela HI 96743

Call Sign: WH6DJO
Lauren K Woodhams
64-951 Mamalahoa Hwy
Kamuela HI 96743

Call Sign: WH6BHG
Rodolfo M Aurello Sr
64-5321 Nani Waimea St
Kamuela HI 96743

Call Sign: KH6HHH
Jupiter Research
Foundation Amateur Radio
Club
46 Puako Beach Dr
Kamuela HI 96743

Call Sign: WH6DHS
Jupiter Research
Foundation Amateur Radio
Club
46 Puako Beach Dr
Kamuela HI 96743

Call Sign: WH6CGY
David R Schmeltz
107 Puako Beach Dr
Kamuela HI 96743

Call Sign: WH7HB
Sara L Fuller

69-1647 Puako Beach Dr
301
Kamuela HI 96743

Call Sign: WH6WR
Patrick R Nance
83 Puaro Beach Rd
Kamuela HI 96743

Call Sign: KE6HLS
John K Harrison
62 1217 Walemi Pl
Kamuela HI 96743

Call Sign: NI7Y
Forest C Yelverton
67-5015 Yutaka Pen Pl
Kamuela HI 96743-8379

Call Sign: AH7AA
Timothy J Petersen
Kamuela HI 96743

Call Sign: W2FF
Timothy J Petersen
Kamuela HI 96743

Call Sign: AH6DD
Hamakua Coast Contest
Club
Kamuela HI 96743

Call Sign: K7CMK
Forrest R Mcfall
Kamuela HI 96743

Call Sign: KA6NJV
Gerry Reilly
Kamuela HI 96743

Call Sign: KA6NJW
Doris Reilly
Kamuela HI 96743

Call Sign: KD7RMG

Sean M Adkins
Kamuela HI 96743

Call Sign: KH6IHG
Curtis D Shoemaker
Kamuela HI 96743

Call Sign: KH6IPI
Samuel P Gingrich
Kamuela HI 96743

Call Sign: KH6KCC
Kohala Hamakua Radio
Club
Kamuela HI 96743

Call Sign: KH6PI
Mary A Lake
Kamuela HI 96743

Call Sign: KH6WT
Carlton M Cherrigan
Kamuela HI 96743

Call Sign: KH7RMG
Sean M Adkins
Kamuela HI 96743

Call Sign: KH7VM
Anita L Gerhard
Kamuela HI 96743

Call Sign: KH7ZQ
Thomas N Seabury
Kamuela HI 96743

Call Sign: N6XIV
William C Jakubowski
Kamuela HI 96743

Call Sign: NH7PX
Benjamin A Martin
Kamuela HI 96743

Call Sign: NH7UK

Christian Boado
Kamuela HI 96743

Call Sign: NH7UY
Forrest R Mcfall
Kamuela HI 96743

Call Sign: NH7YI
Victor I Gouge
Kamuela HI 96743

Call Sign: W7QKS
Judy Ann Williams
Kamuela HI 96743

Call Sign: WH6CSR
Karl J Toubman
Kamuela HI 96743

Call Sign: WH6DHQ
Kohala Hamakua Radio
Club
Kamuela HI 96743

Call Sign: WH6DIB
Hama Kua Coast Contest
Club
Kamuela HI 96743

Call Sign: WH6DPV
Shane A Bowman
Kamuela HI 96743

Call Sign: WH6DVC
James S Hodgins Jr
Kamuela HI 96743

Call Sign: WH6DWL
Thomas N Benedict
Kamuela HI 96743

Call Sign: WH7BI
Ponoi G Lake
Kamuela HI 96743

Call Sign: WH7BJ
Christopher L Langan
Kamuela HI 96743

Call Sign: WH7BK
Judy Ann Williams
Kamuela HI 96743

Call Sign: WH7BZ
Colin P O Connor
Kamuela HI 96743

Call Sign: WH7CA
M Maloney
Kamuela HI 96743

Call Sign: WH7TV
Joseph D Richardson
Kamuela HI 96743

Call Sign: WH7TW
Stephen C Doyle
Kamuela HI 96743

Call Sign: WH7WU
Morgan G Hanneken
Kamuela HI 96743

Call Sign: WH7WV
Suzanne E Hanneken
Kamuela HI 96743

Call Sign: WH7WY
Mikki L Hastings
Kamuela HI 96743

Call Sign: WH7HA
Michael A Kapchinske
Kamuela HI 96743

Call Sign: KH7T
John R Buck
Kamuela HI 96743-0489

Call Sign: NH7HI

Hawaii West Amateur
Radio Society
Kamuela HI 96743-0489

Call Sign: WH6DGF
Hawaii West Amateur
Radio Society
Kamuela HI 96743-0489

Call Sign: NH7UA
Norman R Cohler
Kamuela HI 96743-4598

Call Sign: KH6CQ
Eric J Grabowski
Kamuela HI 96743-6127

Call Sign: NH7ZF
Mary K Grabowski
Kamuela HI 96743-6127

Call Sign: WA8HEB
Eric J Grabowski
Kamuela HI 96743-6127

Call Sign: WD8LIB
Mary K Grabowski
Kamuela HI 96743-6127

Call Sign: K1KK
World Wide Dx Contest
Club
Kamuela HI 96743-6333

Call Sign: K1RJ
Atsushi Tatomi
Kamuela HI 96743-6333

Call Sign: KH0AA
The A Team
Kamuela HI 96743-6333

Call Sign: KH0B
Yuji Isawa
Kamuela HI 96743-6333

Call Sign: KH0DQ
Seiichiro Morikawa
Kamuela HI 96743-6333

Call Sign: KH7A
Akito Nagi
Kamuela HI 96743-6333

Call Sign: KH7AA
The A Team
Kamuela HI 96743-6333

Call Sign: NH6J
Satoshi Nakamura
Kamuela HI 96743-6333

Call Sign: W7YL
Rie Nagi
Kamuela HI 96743-6333

Call Sign: AH6RV
Steven M Milner
Kamuela HI 96743-6573

Call Sign: WB1HAL
Steven M Milner
Kamuela HI 96743-6573

Call Sign: WH6N
Steven M Milner
Kamuela HI 96743-6573

Call Sign: KH6CCL
Ernest J Kurlansky
Kamuela HI 96743

Call Sign: WH6AZ
Marie C K Lindsey
Kamuela HI 96743

Call Sign: WH6BGU
Ivy N Alcoran
Kamuela HI 96743

Call Sign: KH7TA
Pekka J Holstila
Kamuela HI 96743-6333

FCC Amateur Radio License in Kanagawa Japan

Call Sign: NH7FZ
Matsuyoshi Nakajima
2/23/1933 Shukugawara
TamaKu Kawasaki
Kanagawa,Japan HI 96744

FCC Amateur Radio License in Kaneohe

Call Sign: WH7LF
Matthew D Corry
45-544 A Loihi Pl
Kaneohe HI 96744

Call Sign: KH7QV
Darrell K Travis
46 165 Aeloa St
Kaneohe HI 96744

Call Sign: KH6IDU
Earl B Dedell
46 212 Aeloa St
Kaneohe HI 96744

Call Sign: N5XIG
John C Mc Cain
47-389 Ahaolelo Rd
Kaneohe HI 96744

Call Sign: KH6ASP
Kazumi Takeuchi
47-516 Ahuimanu Rd
Kaneohe HI 96744

Call Sign: KH6J
Koolau Amateur Radio
Club

47-726 Akakoa Pl B
Kaneohe HI 96744-5001

Call Sign: KH6VQ
Ronald M Taniguchi
46-189 Alaloa St
Kaneohe HI 96744

Call Sign: AH6MD
Edgar P Clark III
45 860A Anoi Rd
Kaneohe HI 96744

Call Sign: KH6EUM
Gerald K Chong
45-715 Anoi Rd
Kaneohe HI 96744

Call Sign: NH7ND
Miki K Morris
45-501 Apapane St
Kaneohe HI 96744

Call Sign: AH6RK
Randy Morris
45-501 Apapane St
Kaneohe HI 96744-1913

Call Sign: N7WLR
Joseph C Roessler
45-480A Apiki St
Kaneohe HI 96744

Call Sign: NH7OU
Louis H Ickler
44-465 Aumoana Way
Kaneohe HI 96744

Call Sign: NH7OV
Kim W Ickler
44-465 Aumoana Way
Kaneohe HI 96744

Call Sign: NH7VR
Thomas M Reppuhn

46-32 Auna St
Kaneohe HI 96744

Call Sign: WH6AH
Michael G Bowles
47-157 B Okana Rd
Kaneohe HI 96744

Call Sign: KH7OU
Cindy A Hucko
45 211 C Wm Henry Rd
Kaneohe HI 96744

Call Sign: KH7PG
Richard Hucko
45 211 C Wm Henry Rd
Kaneohe HI 96744

Call Sign: WH6TQ
Joseph M Morello
Ceo H & Hs Co Mars
Kaneohe HI 96863

Call Sign: KH7TT
Reynante R Bautista
Cssg 3 Lsc Eng Plt
Kaneohe HI 96863

Call Sign: KH7SG
Sandra T Jessmon
45 202 Ct Lilipuna Rd
Kaneohe HI 96744

Call Sign: KH7SH
Sharayah E K Jessmon
45 202 Ct Lilipuna Rd
Kaneohe HI 96744

Call Sign: KH7LN
Manuel A Hernandez
47 573 Dua Doo Pl
Kaneohe HI 96744

Call Sign: WH7RP
Dean M Matsukawa

45-573 Duncan Dr
Kaneohe HI 96744

Call Sign: WH6JV
Keith K Kabasawa
45-860 E Anoi Rd
Kaneohe HI 96744

Call Sign: KB3DMT
Albert G Burnelis Jr
46-078 Emepela Pl Apt
G200
Kaneohe HI 96744

Call Sign: K4REG
Richard E Gaucher
46-078 Emepela Pl B206
Kaneohe HI 96744-3964

Call Sign: NH7RB
George L Thornton Jr
46-078 Emepela Pl K101
Kaneohe HI 96744

Call Sign: WH7HK
William K Waters
46-063 Emepela Pl Q202
Kaneohe HI 96744

Call Sign: KH6TM
Michael H Takashita
46-1061 Emepela Way 5U
Kaneohe HI 96744

Call Sign: KW6DX
Richard Z Miyashiro
45-455 Haiku Plantation
Dr
Kaneohe HI 96744

Call Sign: WH6LD
Dave A Cundiff
46-318 Haiku Rd 10
Kaneohe HI 96744

Call Sign: AH6EL
Clayton F Caughill
46-318 Haiku Rd 60
Kaneohe HI 96744

Call Sign: WH6CLN
John D Himmelmann
46-369 Haiku Rd E11
Kaneohe HI 96744

Call Sign: KH6IJM
Henry Kanada
45-1130 Haleloke Pl
Kaneohe HI 96744-3101

Call Sign: WH7LC
Terence Miyahana
47-699 Halemanu St
Kaneohe HI 96744

Call Sign: NH6DP
Joel R Ching
47 121 Heno Pl
Kaneohe HI 96744

Call Sign: NH7BH
Joel R Ching
47 121 Heno Pl
Kaneohe HI 96744

Call Sign: WH6ZS
Evan K Ching
47 121 Heno Pl
Kaneohe HI 96744

Call Sign: WH7MQ
Reuben Danao
45-458 Hiipoi St
Kaneohe HI 96744

Call Sign: KH7IN
Gregory K Umiamaka
45-635 Hinamoe Pl
Kaneohe HI 96744

Call Sign: WH6DNR
Mervyn K Rickard
46-109 Hinapu St
Kaneohe HI 96744

Call Sign: WD2Y
Tony D Insalaco
Hmm 165 ~Mag 24 ~1St
Meb Kaneohe Mcas
Kaneohe HI 96863

Call Sign: KH7GD
Kent A Reinker
46 407 Holoanai Way
Kaneohe HI 96744

Call Sign: NH7RG
Kori M Wenman
47-112 Honekoa St
Kaneohe HI 96744

Call Sign: WH7MA
George H Kaluhiokalani
47-223 Hui Aeko St
Kaneohe HI 96744-4570

Call Sign: AH6JO
Tatsuro Suzuki
47-229 Hui Aeko St
Kaneohe HI 96744

Call Sign: KH6BS
Daniel T Ferguson
47-706 Hui Alala St
Kaneohe HI 96744

Call Sign: WH6BQT
Jennifer L Ferguson-Cole
47-706 Hui Alala St
Kaneohe HI 96744

Call Sign: KH6HF
Sidney W Kent
47-432 Hui Io St
Kaneohe HI 96744

Call Sign: KA9VGO
Duane E Wenzel
47 394 1 Hui Iwa St
Kaneohe HI 96744

Call Sign: NH7RH
Crescentia P Morris
47-358 Hui Iwa St
Kaneohe HI 96744

Call Sign: KH6HIH
Harvey A Hartenstein
47-548 Hui Iwa St
Kaneohe HI 96744

Call Sign: KH6HII
Rohna G Hartenstein
47-548 Hui Iwa St
Kaneohe HI 96744

Call Sign: KH7AU
Naeole T Kapele
47 420 Hui Iwa St A202
Kaneohe HI 96744

Call Sign: KH7AQ
Dean C Tamayoshi
47 503 Hui Kelu St
Kaneohe HI 96744

Call Sign: KH6EII
Robert T Leau
47 722 2 Hui Kelu St
Kaneohe HI 96744-4558

Call Sign: KH6RQ
Eugene V Souza
47-585 Hui Kelu St
Kaneohe HI 96744

Call Sign: WH6ZE
Keith E Webster
47-748 Hui Kelu St 5
Kaneohe HI 96744

Call Sign: NH6EG
Bryant W Schultz
47-728 Hui Kelu St 9
Kaneohe HI 96744

Call Sign: AH6OZ
Walter P Niemczura
47-757 Hui Kelu St Apt 5
Kaneohe HI 96744-4588

Call Sign: KH7EB
Marjorie D Niemczura
47-757 Hui Kelu St Apt 5
Kaneohe HI 96744-4588

Call Sign: WH6BHN
Merrill K Gerard
47-355 Hui Koloa Pl
Kaneohe HI 96744

Call Sign: WH6CTM
Brigitta A Tanzer
47 149 Hui Oo Pl
Kaneohe HI 96744

Call Sign: KH6VE
Robert A Seo
47-694 Hui Ulili St
Kaneohe HI 96744

Call Sign: WH7QT
Brent Naluai
47-785 Hui Ulili St
Kaneohe HI 96744

Call Sign: KH6XO
George E Zustak
47 661 Huikelu St 3
Kaneohe HI 96744

Call Sign: WH6SH
Constance B Smales
46-422 Hulupala Pl
Kaneohe HI 96744

Call Sign: NH6SD
Jeffery A Naus
46-301 Ikiiki St
Kaneohe HI 96744

Call Sign: WH6ME
Fred W Brunson Jr
47-160 Iuiu St
Kaneohe HI 96744-4707

Call Sign: NH6YO
Dorrel A Whinery
45-145 Kahanahou
Kaneohe HI 96744

Call Sign: NH7RV
Jess A Williams
45-336 Kahiko St
Kaneohe HI 96744

Call Sign: KE4G
Daniel C Brookins
46-270 Kahuhipa St A310
Kaneohe HI 96744

Call Sign: WH7RO
Michael J Gonzalez
46-232 Kahuhipa St Apt
A204
Kaneohe HI 96744

Call Sign: NH6OM
Neil T Kamikawa
46 306 Kalali St
Kaneohe HI 96744-4129

Call Sign: NH7RJ
Michael P Donahue
47-240 Kam Hwy
Kaneohe HI 96744

Call Sign: KH6CRQ
Takeo Sato
47 801 Kamakoi Pl

Kaneohe HI 96744

Call Sign: AH6JK
Wilfred T Sato
47-801 Kamakoi Pl
Kaneohe HI 96744

Call Sign: AH6F
Theodore Diehl
47-849 Kamehameha
Highway
Kaneohe HI 96744

Call Sign: AH6TP
Theodore Diehl
47-849 Kamehameha
Highway
Kaneohe HI 96744

Call Sign: WH6BHR
Michael E Chaffin
46-276 Kamehameha Hwy
Kaneohe HI 96744

Call Sign: K4UHL
Peter J Long Jr
47-194 Kamehameha Hwy
Kaneohe HI 96744

Call Sign: WH6XV
Samuel M Thayer
48 449 Kamehameha Hwy
Kaneohe HI 96744

Call Sign: KH7XF
Angele M Armstrong
49-041 A Kamehameha
Hwy
Kaneohe HI 96744

Call Sign: KH7OQ
Marsha Colotario
45-664 Kamehameha Hwy
Kaneohe HI 96744

Call Sign: WH6JY
Shawn Colotario
45-664 Kamehameha Hwy
Kaneohe HI 96744

Call Sign: WH6DBP
Kelsey A Mihara
45 500 Kamooalii St
Kaneohe HI 96744

Call Sign: WH6CLS
Katie A Mihara
45-500 Kamooalii St
Kaneohe HI 96744

Call Sign: WH7GS
Kurt M Nagano
45-589 Kanaka Pl
Kaneohe HI 96744

Call Sign: KH6IGC
Seiichi Yagi
45-444 Kanaka St
Kaneohe HI 96744

Call Sign: W6RWW
Wendell C Johnson
44 515 Kaneohe Bay Dr
Kaneohe HI 96744

Call Sign: KH7PW
David G Nottage Jr
44 653 C Kaneohe Bay Dr
Kaneohe HI 96744

Call Sign: WH7ZL
Maureen L Bates
44 368 Kaneohe Bay Dr
Kaneohe HI 96744

Call Sign: KH6HMJ
Robert E Hiller
44-404 Kaneohe Bay Dr
Kaneohe HI 96744

Call Sign: N9GFL
Douglas A White
44-653C Kaneohe Bay Dr
Kaneohe HI 96744

Call Sign: WH7E
Douglas A White
44-653C Kaneohe Bay Dr
Kaneohe HI 96744

Call Sign: AH6JF
Shido Takahashi
44-668 Kaneohe Bay Dr
Kaneohe HI 96744

Call Sign: KH7C
Oahu Contest Club
44-668 Kaneohe Bay Dr
Kaneohe HI 96744

Call Sign: WH6CQF
Yuichi Takahashi
44-668 Kaneohe Bay Dr
Kaneohe HI 96744

Call Sign: WH6BQQ
Eric R Brienzo
44-757 Kaneohe Bay Dr
Kaneohe HI 96744

Call Sign: WH6DGY
Castle High School Knight
Talkers
45-386 Kaneohe Bay Dr
Kaneohe HI 96744

Call Sign: WH7GF
Mary I Basilio
45-455 Kapalai Rd
Kaneohe HI 96744

Call Sign: NH7UZ
Michael Y Takamori
45-516 Kapalai Rd
Kaneohe HI 96744

Call Sign: WH6SN
William Hanohano Jr
45-577 Keaahala Rd
Kaneohe HI 96744

Call Sign: WH6UE
Randal T Grainger
44-116 Keaalau Pl
Kaneohe HI 96744

Call Sign: KH6VV
Pacific Mobile Maritime
Amateur Radio Club
46 158 Keoe Pl
Kaneohe HI 96744

Call Sign: KG6DV
Ronald D Ellis
46-158 Keoe Pl
Kaneohe HI 96744

Call Sign: KH6DV
Ronald D Ellis
46-158 Keoe Pl
Kaneohe HI 96744

Call Sign: NH6PR
Caroline J B Ellis
46-158 Keoe Pl
Kaneohe HI 96744

Call Sign: WH6DGO
Pacific Mobile Maritime
Amateur Radio Club
46-158 Keoe Pl
Kaneohe HI 96744

Call Sign: KH6JL
Lawrence Lockett
45 178 Kokokahi Pl
Kaneohe HI 96744

Call Sign: NH7XS
Lawrence Lockett

45 178 Kokokahi Pl
Kaneohe HI 96744

45-530 Kuuipo Pl
Kaneohe HI 96744

45 161 Lilipuna Rd
Kaneohe HI 96744

Call Sign: WH6CQ
Lawrence Lockett
45 178 Kokokahi Pl
Kaneohe HI 96744

Call Sign: KH8AE
Jill A Mc Cready
47-016 Laenani Dr
Kaneohe HI 96744

Call Sign: KH7AG
Michael H Harai
45 315B Lilipuna Rd
Kaneohe HI 96744

Call Sign: KH7CS
Edward R Howland
45-154 Kokokahi Pl
Kaneohe HI 96744

Call Sign: KB6VEU
Rick D Hamill
44-121 Laha St 3
Kaneohe HI 96744

Call Sign: WH6AGT
H Ray Millard
46 041 Lilipuna Rd
Kaneohe HI 96744

Call Sign: KH6IQ
Kevin R Azama
45-541 Koolau View Dr
Kaneohe HI 96744

Call Sign: WH6BIE
Kyle O Ebisutani
47 578 Laniwela Way
Kaneohe HI 96744

Call Sign: KH6CDM
Roy J Yee
46-117 Lilipuna Rd
Kaneohe HI 96744

Call Sign: KH6DZ
Walter S Dang
45-531 Koolau Vw Dr
Kaneohe HI 96744

Call Sign: KH6BFF
Christopher K Smith
45 306 Lehuuila St
Kaneohe HI 96744

Call Sign: W0PPQ
Albert F Regler
45-487 Lipalu St
Kaneohe HI 96744

Call Sign: KH7TF
Lisa A Hashimura
45 684 Kuahulu Pl
Kaneohe HI 96744-3501

Call Sign: WH7LY
Carl K Kawakami
45-106 Leleua Pl
Kaneohe HI 96744

Call Sign: KH7RE
Gary K Loo
45 622 Liula St
Kaneohe HI 96744

Call Sign: KC6RUJ
Matsuyoshi Nakajima
45 682 Kulu Keoe St
Kaneohe HI 96744

Call Sign: KU4OY
C Dennis Ferguson
47-005 Lihikai Dr
Kaneohe HI 96744

Call Sign: KH7PX
William G Enos
45 513 Lokea Pl
Kaneohe HI 96744

Call Sign: WY3B
Richard M Tuggle
46-469 Kuneki St
Kaneohe HI 96744-3536

Call Sign: WH6P
Henry S Mc Coy Jr
45 030 Lilipuna Rd
Kaneohe HI 96744-3018

Call Sign: NH7YJ
Takahiro Tamura
45 601 E Luluku Rd
Kane Ohe HI 96744-1855

Call Sign: KH7AM
Tevita M Tuifua
45 544 Kuuipo Pl
Kaneohe HI 96744

Call Sign: KH7OI
Regina M Lelenoa
45 161 Lilipuna Rd
Kaneohe HI 96744

Call Sign: KH6OR
North Shore Dx Club
45-601 F Luluku Rd
Kane Ohe HI 96744-1858

Call Sign: NH6MN
Randall S Miyagawa

Call Sign: KH7TE
Brunston G Punahele

Call Sign: WH6DIE
North Shore Dx Club

45-601 F Luluku Rd
Kane Ohe HI 96744-1859

Call Sign: KH6JFV
Douglas A Embrey
45-667 Luluka Rd
Kaneohe HI 96744

Call Sign: KH6FO
Hawaii Five Oh Arc
45 601 Luluku Rd
Kaneohe HI 96744-1856

Call Sign: WH6DTQ
Hawaii Five Oh Arc
45 601 Luluku Rd
Kaneohe HI 96744-1857

Call Sign: KH6PAN
Hey Bruddah Dx Club
45 601 G Luluku Rd
Kaneohe HI 96744-1854

Call Sign: WH6DII
Hey Bruddah Dx Club
45 601 G Luluku Rd
Kaneohe HI 96744-1854

Call Sign: WH6CZC
Tadayuki Tominaga
45-601 Luluku Rd
Kaneohe HI 96744-1854

Call Sign: KH6IS
Iolani School Amateur
Radio Club
45-601 Luluku Rd
Kaneohe HI 96744-1854

Call Sign: KH6BZF
Lee R Wical
45-601 Luluku Rd
Kaneohe HI 96744-1860

Call Sign: NH6JO

Kiyoshi Mizoguchi
45-601-C Luluku Rd
Kaneohe HI 96744-1854

Call Sign: NH7TL
Atsuhiro Ikeda
45-601-D Luluku Rd
Kaneohe HI 96744-1854

Call Sign: NH6JL
Tomonobu Tanaka
C/O Lee Wical 45-601A
Luluku Rd
Kaneohe HI 96744-1854

Call Sign: KH6JHM
Pacific Radio Ama
Transmitting Soc
45-601 Luluku Rd Yagi
Acres
Kaneohe HI 96744-1854

Call Sign: KH6RAT
Oceanic Radio Amateur
Transmitting Society
45-601 Luluku Rd Yagi
Acres
Kaneohe HI 96744-1854

Call Sign: WH6CER
Michael A Auld
45-424 Lupo St
Kaneohe HI 96744

Call Sign: KD6VTU
James C Steele
45 - 180 Mahalani Pl 14
Kaneohe HI 96744

Call Sign: KH6RV
Henry L Smith
45-327 Mahalani St
Kaneohe HI 96744

Call Sign: KH6HHM

Emil D Bruner
45626 Mahinui Rd
Kaneohe HI 96744

Call Sign: NH6MK
George T Miyake
45-1112 Maka Pl
Kaneohe HI 96744

Call Sign: NH7QP
John P Brack
44-207 Malae Pl
Kaneohe HI 96744

Call Sign: NH7QQ
Carol Y Brack
44-207 Malae Pl
Kaneohe HI 96744

Call Sign: WH7PC
Daniel Brizuela
44-006 Malukai Pl
Kaneohe HI 96744

Call Sign: WH6BMZ
Arthur E Deimel
45-020 Malulani St
Kaneohe HI 96744

Call Sign: KH7XZ
Ronalene White
47-765 Malumalu Pl
Kaneohe HI 96744

Call Sign: KH7YS
Gerald L White
47-765 Malumalu Pl
Kaneohe HI 96744

Call Sign: KH7WT
Roanne E Muronaga
45 120 Mauli Pl
Kaneohe HI 96744

Call Sign: WH6CLF

Lowell I Terada
45-112 Mikihilina St
Kaneohe HI 96744

Gail C Okamura
45-415 Mokulele Dr10
Kaneohe HI 96744

Bert I Oshiro
45-332 Nakuluai St
Kaneohe HI 96744

Call Sign: N1VWB
Jeffrey S Lefebure
45-142 Mikihilina St
Kaneohe HI 96744

Call Sign: WH6RD
Jerel D Fonseca
46-318 Nahewai St
Kaneohe HI 96744

Call Sign: KH6BFZ
Joseph K Keola Jr
45-529 Nakuluai St
Kaneohe HI 96744

Call Sign: NH6QI
Patricia H Mulherin
45-145 Mikihilina St
Kaneohe HI 96744

Call Sign: WH6RN
Jeffrey D Fadness
46-378 Nahewai St
Kaneohe HI 96744

Call Sign: AH6CS
Charles C Le Grand
46-011 Nana Pl
Kaneohe HI 96744

Call Sign: WH6BKQ
Gerald P Mulherin
45-145 Mikihilina St
Kaneohe HI 96744

Call Sign: WH6CIY
John M Aki Jr
46-382 Nahewai St
Kaneohe HI 96744

Call Sign: WH6KZ
Paul A Le Grand
46-011 Nana Pl
Kaneohe HI 96744

Call Sign: WH6DWB
William H Sager
44211 Mikiola Dr
Kaneohe HI 96744

Call Sign: NH7XO
Lance E Mathes
46-135 Nahewal Pl
Kaneohe HI 96744

Call Sign: AH6LJ
Janine M Le Grand
46-011 Nana Pl
Kaneohe HI 96744

Call Sign: NH7VQ
Malcom Medrano
47-237 Miomio Loop
Kaneohe HI 96744

Call Sign: NH7XP
Ernest E Mathes
46 135 Nahewal Pl
Kaneohe HI 96844

Call Sign: KH6MWG
Mark W Goodin
44 141 Nanamoana St
Kaneohe HI 96744

Call Sign: WH6DBZ
Kristyn M Ho
45 522 Mokulele Dr
Kaneohe HI 96744-1745

Call Sign: KH6BB
Bola C Lowe
46-139 Nahiku Pl
Kaneohe HI 96744

Call Sign: WH6DMU
Mark W Goodin
44-141 Nanamoana St
Kaneohe HI 96744

Call Sign: KD5UG
Ann E Lemke
45-125 Mokulele Dr
Kaneohe HI 96744

Call Sign: WH6LF
Howard R Williams
46-164 Nahiku Pl
Kaneohe HI 96744

Call Sign: WH6BVD
Leona A Minami
45-758 Nanihoku Way
Kaneohe HI 96744

Call Sign: NH7PA
Wayne A Shiroma
45-241 Mokulele Dr
Kaneohe HI 96744

Call Sign: KH7EF
Eric K Miyata
45 210 Nakuluai St
Kaneohe HI 96744

Call Sign: WH7LX
Steve F Laulu
45-807 Nanihoku Way
Kaneohe HI 96744-3162

Call Sign: WH7AN

Call Sign: WH7RL

Call Sign: NH7RI

Justin M Joaquin
45-798 Nanilani Way
Kaneohe HI 96744

Call Sign: WH6DF
John Barry B Yee
45-661 Nawahine Pl
Kaneohe HI 96744

Call Sign: WH6DWW
David R Tumilowicz
45-167 Neepu Pl
Kaneohe HI 96744

Call Sign: WH7IG
Marsha N Tamura
45-517 Ohala Pl
Kanedhe HI 96744

Call Sign: KE6OO
John R Mc Creedy
45-423 Ohaha St
Kaneohe HI 96744

Call Sign: WH6CC
Anthony M Yee
46-137 Ohala St
Kaneohe HI 96744

Call Sign: WH6BDS
Gary W Brookins
44-354 Olina St 4
Kaneohe HI 96744-2659

Call Sign: WH6BKY
Erminie C Gartley
45-311 Paliiki Pl
Kaneohe HI 96744

Call Sign: WH6ADI
Dan S Tamashiro
45-716 Pilina Pl
Kaneohe HI 96744

Call Sign: KH6PY

Martin H Y Wong
45-239 Popoki Pl
Kaneohe HI 96744

Call Sign: WH6AEB
Robert W T Yuen
45-240 Popoki Pl
Kaneohe HI 96744

Call Sign: WH6CTI
Taliesa A Chojnacki
45 406 Puahuula Pl
Kaneohe HI 96744

Call Sign: KF6PJ
David G Reeves
46-064 Puulena St 1011
Kaneohe HI 96744

Call Sign: W6WMC
Howard M Zeidler
46-054 Puulena St No 922
Kaneohe HI 96744

Call Sign: NH7OS
Philiip M Magalios
1St Radio Bn A Co
Kaneohe HI 96863

Call Sign: AH6LG
Patricia H Cramer
45-060 Springer Pl
Kaneohe HI 96744

Call Sign: WH7QU
Godfrey K Kaonohi
47-641 Uakea Pl
Kaneohe HI 96744

Call Sign: KH6GHE
Philip S T Dang
45-653 Uhilehua Pl
Kaneohe HI 96744

Call Sign: NH7EI

Gerald T Iseri Jr
45-113 Waikalua Rd
Kaneohe HI 96744

Call Sign: WH6DRP
Morgan A Torris-Hedlund
45-117 Waikalua Rd Apt
D
Kaneohe HI 96744

Call Sign: KH7UY
Michael C Choy
45 035 Waikalualoko
Loop
Kaneohe HI 96744

Call Sign: WH6CLZ
Howard R Andrus
47 670 Wailehua Pl
Kaneohe HI 96744

Call Sign: WH6DAA
Alice Andrus
47 670 Wailehua Pl
Kaneohe HI 96744

Call Sign: WH6JD
Milton M Yokota
47 690 Wailehua Pl
Kaneohe HI 96744

Call Sign: WH6KI
Brandon T Yokota
47-690 Wailehua Pl
Kaneohe HI 96744

Call Sign: WH6BBP
Dorothea U A Uchima
45-1013 Wailele Rd
Kaneohe HI 96744

Call Sign: WH6UJ
Robert J Rupnow
45-995 Wailele Rd 23
Kaneohe HI 96744

Call Sign: KB6HVQ
Brian J Malecek
45-995 Wailele Rd 5
Kaneohe HI 96744

Call Sign: KB6HVR
Cheryl Malecek
45-995 Wailele Rd 5
Kaneohe HI 96744

Call Sign: NH7VZ
Paul C Pollitt
45 995 Wailele Rd 51
Kaneohe HI 96744

Call Sign: NH7LN
Ronald T Thompson
45-995 Wailele Rd 58
Kaneohe HI 96744

Call Sign: KH6LP
Geoffrey S Curran
45-995 Wailele Rd 80
Kaneohe HI 96744

Call Sign: WH7EN
Albert K Basilio
47 699 Waiohia St
Kaneohe HI 96744

Call Sign: KH7NA
John Y Ching Jr
47 518 Waipua Pl
Kaneohe HI 96744

Call Sign: KH7NB
Jonathan F Ching
47 518 Waipua Pl
Kaneohe HI 96744

Call Sign: WH6BC
Mark S Hucko
45 211C William Henry
Rd

Kaneohe HI 96744

Call Sign: WH6NV
Clinton K Kauahi
45-265 Wm Henry Rd J1
Kaneohe HI 96744

Call Sign: KH6XO
Joyce R Hlivak
Kaneohe HI 96744

Call Sign: KH7EH
Randall B Scott
Kaneohe HI 96744

Call Sign: WH6BVV
Robert J Lee
Kaneohe HI 96744

Call Sign: WH6DMN
William L Richter
Kaneohe HI 96744

Call Sign: WH7LU
Allan F Teruya
Kaneohe HI 96744

Call Sign: WH7QO
Willard A Gilbert III
Kaneohe HI 96744

Call Sign: WH7WL
Randall W Mikulik
Kaneohe HI 96744

Call Sign: KH7HS
Ayres K Taylor
Kaneohe HI 96744-0899

Call Sign: KH7NQ
Guy F Adams
Kaneohe HI 96744-8311

Call Sign: NH7I
Randall B Scott

Kaneohe HI 96744-8643

Call Sign: KH6CPW
Elliott R Chang
Kaneohe HI 96744-8716

Call Sign: NH6XO
Robert J Hlivak
Kaneohe HI 96744

Call Sign: NH6YI
Joyce R Hlivak
Kaneohe HI 96744

Call Sign: WH6MX
John R Ryan
Kaneohe HI 96744

Call Sign: WH6TM
Rothwell K Ahulau
Kaneohe HI 96744

FCC Amateur Radio License in Kapaa

Call Sign: AC4TA
Edward J Resor
239 Aina Lani Pl
Kapaa HI 96746

Call Sign: KG6JJH
Kenneth M Da Vico
315 Aina Mahi Pl
Kapaa HI 96746

Call Sign: KH6E
Kauai Amateur Radio Club
6605 Alahele St
Kapaa HI 96746

Call Sign: KH6RA
Rodney T Takahashi
91 Aleo St
Kapaa HI 96746

Call Sign: KH6TV
Glen I Takahashi
91 Aleo St
Kapaa HI 96746

Call Sign: KH6TW
Alice S Takahashi
91 Aleo St
Kapaa HI 96746

Call Sign: WH6QU
Sherwin K Y Stevens
1781 Awa A Pl
Kapaa HI 96746

Call Sign: KH6ZT
Albert S Morgan
4916 Haleilio
Kapaa HI 96746

Call Sign: KH6PB
Ernest W Duarte
4773 Hauaala Rd
Kapaa HI 96746

Call Sign: NH6EO
Judy Y Sokei
5128 Hauaala Rd
Kapaa HI 96746

Call Sign: KH6JMM
John M Montalbano
298 Hie St
Kapaa HI 96746

Call Sign: KB3QEL
John M Montalbano
298 Hie St
Kapaa HI 96746

Call Sign: KH7RAM
Ruth A Montalbano
298 Hie St
Kapaa HI 96746

Call Sign: WH6DSD
Ruth A Montalbano
298 Hie St
Kapaa HI 96746

Call Sign: AH6BT
Carl R Cremer
1957 Hulali Loop
Kapaa HI 96746

Call Sign: WH7TY
Thomas K Liu
1753 Kaehulua Pl
Kapaa HI 96746

Call Sign: WH6Z
Semon Francisco
7060 Kaholalele Pl
Kapaa HI 96746

Call Sign: KH6DO
Richard N Olsen
411 Kaholalele Rd
Kapaa HI 96746

Call Sign: KC1QF
Peter P Vekinis
411 Kaholalele Rd
Kapaa HI 96746

Call Sign: KH6VP
Peter P Vekinis
411 Kaholalele Rd
Kapaa HI 96746

Call Sign: NH6RH
Rita Habermann
411 Kaholalele Rd
Kapaa HI 96746

Call Sign: WH6DQL
Rita Habermann
411 Kaholalele Rd
Kapaa HI 96746

Call Sign: N7JIM
James A Tamme
6510 Kahuna
Kapaa HI 96746

Call Sign: WH7HQ
Annette L Anderson
6447 Kahuna Rd
Kapaa HI 96746

Call Sign: KE6TFR
Robert B Anderson
6447 Kahuna Rd
Kapaa HI 96746-9129

Call Sign: KH6AS
Robert B Anderson
6447 Kahuna Rd
Kapaa HI 96746-9129

Call Sign: WH7CC
Paul L Daniels
7084 Kahuna Rd
Kapaa HI 96746

Call Sign: WH7CE
Noreen R Ohai Daniels
7084 Kahuna Rd
Kapaa HI 96746

Call Sign: AH6RL
Edward J Neil
373 Kaima Pl
Kapaa HI 96746

Call Sign: NH7MB
Edward J Neil
373 Kaima Pl
Kapaa HI 96746

Call Sign: WH7J
Edward J Neil
373 Kaima Pl
Kapaa HI 96746

Call Sign: KH6KWS
Wailua Amateur Radio
Assn
6421 Kalama Rd
Kapaa HI 96746

Call Sign: W7KWS
Robert M Fuller
6421 Kalama Rd
Kapaa HI 96746

Call Sign: KH6JPT
Ronald L Victorino
262 Kamalu Rd
Kapaa HI 96746

Call Sign: NH6O
Kenneth L Dorland
4461 Kamoa Rd No Mail
Delivery
Kapaa HI 96746

Call Sign: KH6ILL
Robert G J Rivard Sr
346 Kamokila Rd
Kapaa HI 96746

Call Sign: KA1ICJ
Albert W Smith
1418 Kanepoonui Rd
Kapaa HI 96746

Call Sign: WH6AIR
Ernest C Punzal
6007 Kapahi Rd
Kapaa HI 96746

Call Sign: WH6CDY
Michael W Kiyabu
5994 Kawaihau Rd
Kapaa HI 96746

Call Sign: WH6DON
Patty L Kaliher
5680 Keapana Rd

Kapaa HI 96746

Call Sign: WH6DOP
John R Kirby
5680 Keapana Rd
Kapaa HI 96746

Call Sign: WH6DOK
Duana L Deblake
5660 Kei Pl
Kapaa HI 96746

Call Sign: NH6HF
Clifford Ikeda
342 Kihapai St
Kapaa HI 96746

Call Sign: WH6YW
Frederick T Morreall
5230 Kihei Rd
Kapaa HI 96746

Call Sign: WH7XE
Johnathan F Wortley
5949 Kini Pl
Kapaa HI 96746

Call Sign: KA7OAB
Ronald L Farrar
1330 Kiowai Pl
Kapaa HI 96746-9711

Call Sign: KH6ESO
Albert M Hashimoto
218 Koili Ln
Kapaa HI 96746

Call Sign: WH6DOT
Travis F Medina
6633 Kuhaho St
Kapaa HI 96746

Call Sign: KD6ULY
Susan P Wolcott

4-1191 Kuhio Highway
130
Kapaa HI 96746

Call Sign: KD6ULZ
Peter M Wolcott
4-1191 Kuhio Highway
130
Kapaa HI 96746

Call Sign: K2GT
Gustave L Treewater
4-1191 Kuhio Hwy
Kapaa HI 96746-1674

Call Sign: KH6AV
Gustave L Treewater
4-1191 Kuhio Hwy
Kapaa HI 96746-1674

Call Sign: KH6EXU
James S Fernandes
4-649 Kuhio Hwy
Kapaa HI 96746

Call Sign: NII7NJ
Allan M Branco
5640 Kula Mauu St
Kapaa HI 96746

Call Sign: WH6GK
Kevin C Devitt
371 Laaukea Pl
Kapaa HI 96746

Call Sign: AH6QC
Jonathan A K Kekipi
273 A Lanakila Rd
Kapaa HI 96746

Call Sign: WH6ZL
Philip G Harrison
4471 Lanikai St
Kapaa HI 96746

Call Sign: WH7SX
Ellen T Vitt
5736 Lokelani Rd
Kapaa HI 96746

Call Sign: WH6DOI
Christina M Bieber
5015 Malie Rd
Kapaa HI 96746

Call Sign: WB2JDN
David D Schlesselman
6227B Opaekaa Rd
Kapaa HI 96746

Call Sign: WH6DOS
Rita G Mcdonald
71 Loloa St
Kapaa HI 96746

Call Sign: WH6CTX
Tito Castillo
393 Miulana Pl
Kapaa HI 96746

Call Sign: WH6DOW
Karen J Rupp
6420 Opaekaa Rd A
Kapaa HI 96746

Call Sign: WH6CFE
David R Sears
190 Lulo Rd
Kapaa HI 96746

Call Sign: AH7L
Edward J Coan
1311 Nahele Pl
Kapaa HI 96746

Call Sign: KH6DLW
Club Aloha
1670 Papau St
Kapaa HI 96746

Call Sign: NH6JC
Mitchell I Oishi
206 Lulo Rd
Kapaa HI 96746

Call Sign: WH6QH
Kiyoko S Coan
1311 Nahele Pl
Kapaa HI 96746

Call Sign: WH7CS
Jess M Jensen
5974 Pilikua Pl
Kapaa HI 96746

Call Sign: NH7ZS
Caroline C Miura
4477 Makaha Rd
Kapaa HI 96746

Call Sign: WH6DTW
Dominic A Guidici
341 Nana Pl
Kapaa HI 96746

Call Sign: WH6FB
Kimo M Keawe
6675 Puu Pilo Pl
Kapaa HI 96746

Call Sign: WH6TF
Nicholas P Lo Cicero
5489 Makaloa St
Kapaa HI 96746

Call Sign: WH7CF
Walter M Kiilau
4891 Nonou Rd
Kapaa HI 96746

Call Sign: NH7UT
Gerald D Shinn
636 Puuopae Rd
Kapaa HI 96746

Call Sign: K4XV
Thomas C Ellis
6485 Makana Rd
Kapaa HI 96746

Call Sign: NH6HD
Charlene K Ono
6785 C Olohena Rd
Kapaa HI 96746

Call Sign: WH6DUW
Allen W Kapali
1313 Puuopae Rd
Kapaa HI 96746

Call Sign: W7OQV
Roger P Beer
302 Makani Rd
Kapaa HI 96746

Call Sign: NH7CL
Charlene K Ono
6785 C Olohena Rd
Kapaa HI 96746

Call Sign: WH6DXB
Allen W Kapali
1313 Puuopae Rd
Kapaa HI 96746

Call Sign: WH6DOJ
Rolf H Bieber
5015 Malie Rd
Kapaa HI 96746

Call Sign: K7DXT
Scott Mc Intire
6486 Opaekaa Rd
Kapaa HI 96746

Call Sign: NH7XB
Kamuela M Mokuahi
6613 Waiakea Rd
Kapaa HI 96746

Call Sign: AH6MR
Clayton K Boyer
420 Wailua Kai St
Kapaa HI 96746

Call Sign: WH6LG
Lisa G Boyer
420 Wailua Kai St
Kapaa HI 96746

Call Sign: WH7CT
Greg L Allen
161 Wailua Rd
Kapaa HI 96746

Call Sign: WH6DOR
Shirley A Machado
6119 Waipouli Rd
Kapaa HI 96746

Call Sign: WH6CVR
Mark R Brewer
1481 Wanaao Rd
Kapaa HI 96747

Call Sign: KH6DLZ
Harry I Wakayama
Kapaa HI 96746

Call Sign: KH7HM
Marilyn A Mackinnon
Kapaa HI 96746

Call Sign: KH7WO
Kelvin K S Sett
Kapaa HI 96746

Call Sign: N3WHX
Mark W Coccimiglio
Kapaa HI 96746

Call Sign: NH6WZ
Kurt T Momohara
Kapaa HI 96746

Call Sign: WH6DOQ
Terrie A Lazarus
Kapaa HI 96746

Call Sign: WH7EO
Kahele J Keawe
Kapaa HI 96746

Call Sign: WH7JV
Harriet L Juarez
Kapaa HI 96746

Call Sign: WH7ST
Catherine L Stovall
Kapaa HI 96746

Call Sign: WH7XA
Michelle M Blake
Kapaa HI 96746

Call Sign: WH7XD
Michelle J Panoke
Kapaa HI 96746

Call Sign: WH7ZI
Randall C Blake
Kapaa HI 96746

**FCC Amateur Radio
License in Kapaa Kauai**

Call Sign: K2RUP
Edward F Koell
5604 Ohelo Rd
Kapaa Kauai HI 96746

Call Sign: WH6JF
Matthew C Lopes
1979 Puu Kaa St
Kapaa Kauai HI 96746

**FCC Amateur Radio
License in Kapaau**

Call Sign: KC6YKD

Craig D Combes
General Delivery
Kapaau HI 96755

Call Sign: KD4ML
Howard J Olsen
Kapaau HI 96755

Call Sign: KH6GQM
Henry Ah Sam
Kapaau HI 96755

Call Sign: KH6ZRT
Garrith E Stewart
Kapaau HI 96755

Call Sign: KH7LZ
Roger D Cox
Kapaau HI 96755

Call Sign: NH7SB
George S Emeliano
Kapaau HI 96755

Call Sign: NH7XH
Kirk R Kiriu
Kapaau HI 96755

Call Sign: W6KZL
Roger D Cox
Kapaau HI 96755

Call Sign: WH6DLM
Micah K Hood
Kapaau HI 96755

Call Sign: WH6DPZ
Garrith E Stewart
Kapaau HI 96755

Call Sign: WH7PH
Joel Levey
Kapaau HI 96755

Call Sign: WH7PJ

Michelle Levey
Kapaau HI 96755

Call Sign: WH7RD
Karin E Cooke
Kapaau HI 96755

Call Sign: WH7RE
John D Winter
Kapaau HI 96755

Call Sign: WH7VB
Roger D Cox
Kapaau HI 96755

Call Sign: WH7WW
Michael B Sumja
Kapaau HI 96755

Call Sign: WH7PI
William Kaye
Kapaau HI 96755-0850

Call Sign: WH7WK
William Kaye
Kapaau HI 96755-0850

Call Sign: WH6CDC
Eileen P Durkin
Kapaau HI 96755

Call Sign: KH6HQA
Joseph M Maeda
Kapaau HI 96755

Call Sign: WH6JL
Judith C Ah Sam
Kapaau HI 96755

**FCC Amateur Radio
License in Kapolei**

Call Sign: WH7OF
Elizabeth T Yates
92 691 Aahualii St

Kapolei HI 96707

Call Sign: WH7RN
James R Yates Jr
92-691 Aahualii St
Kapolei HI 96707

Call Sign: WH7NN
Chauna Mae K Faumuina
92 634 Adloko St
Kapolei HI 96707

Call Sign: KH6XP
Jose Padilla
92-509 Aka Ula St
Kapolei HI 96707

Call Sign: KH6JMA
Mark C Propios
92 520 Akaawa St
Kapolei HI 96707

Call Sign: KH7QF
Kathy M Yanik
92 1531 Aliinui Dr
Kapolei HI 96707

Call Sign: KH6JDV
Robert R Roberts
92 1545 Aliinui Dr Apt C
Kapolei HI 96707-2226

Call Sign: NH6JM
Richard S Mc Dowell
92-626 Anipeahi St
Kapolei HI 96707

Call Sign: NH6XR
Frank A Nelson
92-731 Aoloko Pl
Kapolei HI 96707

Call Sign: KU6A
Thomas A Akin
92 627 Aoloko St

Kapolei HI 96707

Call Sign: WH6DHA
Hawaiian Islands Amateur
Radio Club
92 627 Aoloko St
Kapolei HI 96707-1120

Call Sign: WH6DJG
Tommy J Jessop
92-556 Awawa St
Kapolei HI 96707

Call Sign: N2KJU
Mark D Silliman
91-1010 C Kalehuna St
Kapolei HI 96707

Call Sign: WH6DNB
David M Bolender
92-7049 Elele St 40
Kapolei HI 96707

Call Sign: N3FZR
James M Stamm
92 7049 Elele St Unit 60
Kapolei HI 96707

Call Sign: WH7HG
Michael W Tauson
590 Farrington Hwy 210
Pmb 117
Kapolei HI 96707

Call Sign: WH7NZ
Voi R Taeoalii
91 215 Hoanaulu Pl
Kapolei HI 96707

Call Sign: KJ7EH
Donald M Kyle
94 1004 Hokuwe Kiu St
Kapolei HI 96707

Call Sign: WH6BG

John S Lee
91 1031 Holi St
Kapolei HI 96707

Call Sign: NH6YP
Yutaka Kisaka
91-1025 Holoimua St
Kapolei HI 96707-1959

Call Sign: KH7ZE
Steven C Cabuslay
92 347 Hookili Pl
Kapolei HI 96707

Call Sign: AH6ZZ
Thomas R Thornton
92-1364 Hunekai St
Kapolei HI 96707

Call Sign: KH6HI
Albert E Ingalls
92-1364 Hunekai St
Kapolei HI 96707

Call Sign: KH7IL
Gordon A Rezentes
92 783 Kaaoao Pl
Kapolei HI 96707

Call Sign: KH7IO
Jason K Rezentes
92 783 Kaaoao Pl
Kapolei HI 96707

Call Sign: WH6DXJ
Roxanne Abdul
92-435 Kaiaulu St
Kapolei HI 96707

Call Sign: WH6DXK
William D Abdul
92-435 Kaiaulu St
Kapolei HI 96707

Call Sign: KH6OWL

Darren S Holbrook
91-1000 Kanihaalilo St
Kapolei HI 96707

Call Sign: WH7LH
Darren S Holbrook
91-1000 Kanihaalilo St
Kapolei HI 96707

Call Sign: NH6LO
Carlos W S Pang
91 1033 Keokolo St C
Kapolei HI 96707

Call Sign: KB6HQS
Richard A Balser
92-1284 Kikaha St 66
Kapolei HI 96707

Call Sign: WH6DIR
Leon W Sims
92-832 Kinohi Pl Apt 8
Kapolei HI 96707

Call Sign: WH7SZ
Michael C Wong
92-324 Kiowao Pl
Kapolei HI 96707

Call Sign: WH7NM
Kenneth R Elton
92 6020 Kohi St
Kapolei HI 96707

Call Sign: NH7YZ
John P Harrison III
91-1146 Kumiuki St
Kapolei HI 96707

Call Sign: WH6CIC
John Canon
92 383 Laaloa St
Kapolei HI 96707

Call Sign: AH6SV

Cameron T Oetjen
92-1019 Lalahi St Apt
12203
Kapolei HI 96707

Call Sign: WH7YO
Elizabeth Ajifu
92-412 Leiole St
Kapolei HI 96707

Call Sign: WL7ACS
Earl L Roemer
92 1125 Liolio Pl
Kapolei HI 96707

Call Sign: WL7ACT
Carol R Roemer
92 1125 Liolio Pl
Kapolei HI 96707

Call Sign: KH7WZ
Donald Lewis
92 661 Makakilo Dr 11
Kapolei HI 96707

Call Sign: WH6USA
Clayton J Deaver
92-739 Makakilo Dr 20
Kapolei HI 96707

Call Sign: WH6WD
Gary A Waters
92-1032 Makakilo Dr 32
Kapolei HI 96707

Call Sign: KG6ZRY
Justin A Harman
92 1014 Makakilo Dr 37
Kapolei HI 96707

Call Sign: WH6CRA
Sam Boon Moore
92-1041 Makakilo Dr 77
Kapolei HI 96707

Call Sign: KH7EY
Robert J Myers
92-1121 Makamai Lp
Kapolei HI 96707

Call Sign: KH7IR
Carla S Myers
92-1121 Makamai Lp
Kapolei HI 96707

Call Sign: KH7IS
Robert A Myers
92-1121 Makamai Lp
Kapolei HI 96707

Call Sign: WH6CDR
Lan K Delos Santos Sr
92 365 Malahuna Pl
Kapolei HI 96707

Call Sign: WH7NU
Ryan S Mc Garry
91 1039 Mamaka St
Kapolei HI 96707

Call Sign: WH6DRJ
Charlene Ann A Sagpao
91-1022 Maulihiwa St
Kapolei HI 96707

Call Sign: WH6UA
Robert L Smith
92-727 Mehani St
Kapolei HI 96706

Call Sign: WH7NT
Barry J Magaoay
92 1200 Mekila St
Kapolei HI 96707

Call Sign: WH7YE
Nelson Kauhi
91-1089 Namahoe St 6H
Kapolei HI 96707

Call Sign: KH6WV
Roger W Rumbaugh
92-756 Newa Pl
Kapolei HI 96707

Call Sign: WH6DWV
Floyd A Reed
92-657 Newa St
Kapolei HI 96707

Call Sign: AH6QS
Glenn M Ah Nee
92 756 Nohopaa St
Kapolei HI 96707

Call Sign: KH7SD
Glenn M Ah Nee
92 756 Nohopaa St
Kapolei HI 96707

Call Sign: WH6AL
Reynold T Hioki
91-1019 Oaniani St
Kapolei HI 96707

Call Sign: N4YSQ
Ronald P Mc Callum
91-821 Oaniani St
Kapolei HI 96707

Call Sign: WH7YF
Keith K Kauhi
91-1004 Owakalena St
Kapolei HI 96707

Call Sign: WH7YG
Francis Kalamau
91-1004 Owakalena St
Kapolei HI 96707

Call Sign: KH6JAS
Duane Luff
91-1089 Paaoloulu Way
Kapolei HI 96707-3101

Call Sign: KB5MTI
Dean S Kozel
91-1096 Paaoloulu Way
Kapolei HI 96707

Call Sign: NH7DV
Joseph K Littlejohn
92-1236 Palahia St
Kapolei HI 96707

Call Sign: KE5FJM
Roland M Zwicky
92-1350 Palahia St
Kapolei HI 96707

Call Sign: KB6CNU
Florence V Coss
92-1175 Palahia St F201
Kapolei HI 96707

Call Sign: KH7WQ
Wendy W Lueder
92 1021 Palailai Pl
Kapolei HI 96707

Call Sign: WH7NR
John A Kapololu
92 683 Palailai St
Kapolei HI 96707

Call Sign: WH7UB
Charles E West
92-890 Palailai St
Kapolei HI 96707

Call Sign: KH7RZ
Anthony E Estaniqui II
92 951 Panama St Ii 35
Kapolei HI 96707

Call Sign: W2IIL
Adam M Bodzioch Jr
92-1143 Panana St 1505
Kapolei HI 96707-3742

Call Sign: KH7AR
David E Markland
91 202 Puahiohio Way
Kapolei HI 96707

Call Sign: WH7OA
Tony T Talo
92 990 Puanihi St
Kapolei HI 96707

Call Sign: WH6CXH
Mark T Yoshinaga
92 991 Puanihi St
Kapolei HI 96707

Call Sign: AH6QD
Felipe A Penullar Jr
92-1189 Pueonani St
Kapolei HI 96707

Call Sign: AH6GA
George E Mc Carty Jr
92-1307 Pueonani St
Kapolei HI 96707

Call Sign: NH6Y
Stephen F O Kelley Sr
298 Saratoga Cir
Kapolei HI 96707

Call Sign: WH6CUW
Diane Wynn G Lamosao
92-1244 Uahanai St
Kapolei HI 96707

Call Sign: NH7IW
Donald C Schomer
92-552 Uhiuala St
Kapolei HI 96707

Call Sign: WH7NQ
Filipo L Ilaoa
91 239 Wahane Pl
Kapolei HI 96707

Call Sign: AH7P
Victor M Ferrer
91-1038 Wahipana St
Kapolei HI 96707

Call Sign: KH6VF
Victor M Ferrer
91-1038 Wahipana St
Kapolei HI 96707

Call Sign: WH6DPF
Victor M Ferrer
91-1038 Wahipana St
Kapolei HI 96707

Call Sign: WH7UU
Charles L Carson
92- 104 Waialii Pl Ste O
922
Kapolei HI 96707

Call Sign: KD7DML
Mildred M Vogan
92100 Waipahe Pl
Kapolei HI 96707

Call Sign: WH7YT
Debra L Graves
92-100 Waipahe Pl
Kapolei HI 96707

Call Sign: WH7XH
Steven Graves
92-100 Waipahe St
Kapolei HI 96707

Call Sign: KH7GF
Ken A Ka Ahanui
Kapolei HI 96707

Call Sign: N6RMQ
Charlie W Craft
Kapolei HI 96707

Call Sign: KH7XO

Paul R Spohn
Kapolei HI 96709

Call Sign: NH7NG
Deborah M Tyrone
Kapolei HI 96709

Call Sign: WH6CNO
Wayne E Fredericks Jr
Kapolei HI 96709

Call Sign: WH7NY
Patrick F Soma
Kapolei HI 96709

FCC Amateur Radio License in Kauai

Call Sign: WH6AVR
Dennis Y Eguchi
Kekaha
Kauai HI 96752

Call Sign: WH7HY
Nobuhisa Hattori
3748 Nawiliwili Rd
Kauai HI 96766

FCC Amateur Radio License in Kaunakakai

Call Sign: WH6QC
Lili A Davis
General Delivery
Kaunakakai HI 96748

Call Sign: WH6UX
Frances L Feeter
Hc 01 Box 311
Kaunakakai HI 96748

Call Sign: WH6UY
James W Feeter
Hc 1 Box 311
Kaunakakai HI 96748

Call Sign: WH7RR
Glenn W Brake
Hc 1 Box 460
Kaunakakai HI 96748

Call Sign: WH6PE
Bradley E Thayne
Hcr 100-51
Kaunakakai HI 96748

Call Sign: WH6OT
Reginald K Kealaiki
Star Route 209
Kaunakakai HI 96748

Call Sign: KH6AAI
Ralph J Faust
Kaunakakai HI 96748

Call Sign: KH6DPK
James Y Shimabukuro
Kaunakakai HI 96748

Call Sign: KH6FS
Takeo Yamashiro
Kaunakakai HI 96748

Call Sign: KH6KW
David J Mc Kinley
Kaunakakai HI 96748

Call Sign: KH7BY
Valerie M Gonzalez
Kaunakakai HI 96748

Call Sign: KH7XW
Robert F Wilt Jr
Kaunakakai HI 96748

Call Sign: KY7W
David J Mc Kinley
Kaunakakai HI 96748

Call Sign: NH6KD

Joyce A M Kainoa
Kaunakakai HI 96748

Call Sign: NH7CW
Bernadine H Bicoy
Kaunakakai HI 96748

Call Sign: NH7U
David J Mc Kinley
Kaunakakai HI 96748

Call Sign: WH6CBN
Lane K Namakaeha Jr
Kaunakakai HI 96748

Call Sign: WH6CBO
Wesley B Afelin
Kaunakakai HI 96748

Call Sign: WH6DCI
Dino Fontes
Kaunakakai HI 96748

Call Sign: WH6IS
Herman K Puaa
Kaunakakai HI 96748

Call Sign: WH6RY
Felix Cabalar Jr
Kaunakakai HI 96748

Call Sign: WH6UZ
James C Williams
Kaunakakai HI 96748

Call Sign: WH6WU
Harry H Hanaoka
Kaunakakai HI 96748

Call Sign: WH6ZI
Donald A Gutierres
Kaunakakai HI 96748

Call Sign: WH6ZJ
Neil P Gonzalez

Kaunakakai HI 96748

Call Sign: WH6ZK
Raquel K Cabalar
Kaunakakai HI 96748

Call Sign: WH7VZ
Agatha L Fontes
Kaunakakai HI 96748

Call Sign: NH6AL
Daryl B Bicoy
Kaunakakai HI 96748-
0691

Call Sign: NH7AB
Daryl B Bicoy
Kaunakakai HI 96748-
0691

Call Sign: K6SAX
Ilse B Borden
Kaunakakai HI 96748-
2190

Call Sign: KA5IZH
Patricia A Lucas
Kaunakakai HI 96748

Call Sign: KH6IL
Louis F Lucas
Kaunakakai HI 96748

Call Sign: WH6BEB
Michael M Donleavey
Kaunakakai HI 96748

Call Sign: WH6KD
Darryl L Johnson Jr
Kaunakakai HI 96748

Call Sign: WH6KH
Peter P Calunod Sr
Kaunakakai HI 96748

Call Sign: WH6OM
Glenn S Izawa
Kaunakakai HI 96748

Call Sign: WH6PF
Donna H Puaa
Kaunakakai HI 96748

Call Sign: WH6PG
Janet D Place
Kaunakakai HI 96748

Call Sign: WH6QE
Keith I Izawa
Kaunakakai HI 96748

Call Sign: WH6RV
Randy R Lite
Kaunakakai HI 96748

Call Sign: WH6RW
Peter D Gonzalez
Kaunakakai HI 96748

Call Sign: WH6RX
Shirley A Calunod
Kaunakakai HI 96748

Call Sign: WH6CDD
Richard N Reed
Kaunakakai HI 96748

Call Sign: WH6CDE
Doris M Reed
Kaunakakai HI 96748

FCC Amateur Radio License in Keaau

Call Sign: AH6OV
Leslie G Whiteley
2053 13 St
Keaau HI 96749-9226

Call Sign: WH6BQ

Roger A L Pflum
Box 747
Keaau HI 96749

Call Sign: AH6MB
Hiroyuki Imoto
Co S Remington
Keaau HI 96749-1222

Call Sign: WH6IK
Kaoru Imoto
Co S Remington
Keaau HI 96749-1222

Call Sign: KZ5AR
Panama Canal Zone
Amateur Radio
Hc 1 - Box 5489
Keaau HI 96749

Call Sign: WH6DIF
Panama Canal Zone
Amateur Radio
Hc 1 - Box 5489
Keaau HI 96749

Call Sign: NH7HH
Patricia E Baji
Hc 1 Box 4686
Keaau HI 96749

Call Sign: KE6EVT
Gregg A Datlof
Hc 1 Box 5280
Keaau HI 96749

Call Sign: WH6DVE
Daniel K Datlof
Hc 1 Box 5280
Keaau HI 96749

Call Sign: WH7FC
Gregg A Datlof
Hc 1 Box 5280
Keaau HI 96749

Call Sign: NH7XA
Robert D Watson
Hc 1 Box 5382
Keaau HI 96749

Call Sign: WH6GM
Jeremy K Watson
Hc 1 Box 5382
Keaau HI 96749

Call Sign: WH6GT
Michelle K Watson
Hc 1 Box 5382
Keaau HI 96749

Call Sign: NH7FY
Barbara H Darling
Hc 1 Box 5489
Keaau HI 96749-9521

Call Sign: NH6HT
Edward H Breen
Hc 2 Box 6637
Keaau HI 96749

Call Sign: KH7ZF
John D Vurich
Hc 3 10035
Keaau HI 96749

Call Sign: KA6YUX
Janet S Luh
Hc 3 11037
Keaau HI 96749

Call Sign: KH6VHF
Icer S Vaughan
Hc 3 Box 10045
Keaau HI 96749-9203

Call Sign: WH7FD
Icer S Vaughan
Hc 3 Box 10045
Keaau HI 96749-9203

Call Sign: KA6VGX
John D Seastrom
Hc 3 Box 11037
Keaau HI 96749

Call Sign: WH6CME
Raymond L Hicks
Hcr 1 Box 4004
Keaau HI 96749

Call Sign: NH7WQ
Wallace W Chun
Hcr 1 Box 5253
Keaau HI 96749-9500

Call Sign: WH7VJ
Isaiah P Aquino
Hc 3 Box 13138
Keaau HI 96749

Call Sign: WH7QA
Alantroy W Alexander
Hcr 1 Box 4089
Keaau HI 96749

Call Sign: AH8AA
Robert Soares
Hcr 1 Box 5338
Keaau HI 96749-9500

Call Sign: KH6AE
Paul A Stoner
Hc 3 Box 13531
Keaau HI 96749

Call Sign: KB7MET
Robert R Fry
Hcr 1 Box 4155
Keaau HI 96749

Call Sign: KH7JR
Kathleen A Braun
Hcr 1 Box 5664
Keaau HI 96749

Call Sign: W3FO
Paul A Stoner
Hc 3 Box 13531
Keaau HI 96749

Call Sign: NH6BE
James K Fry
Hcr 1 Box 4155
Keaau HI 96749

Call Sign: NH7QL
Richard B Mwarey
Hcr 1 Box 5668
Keaau HI 96749

Call Sign: AH7G
Richard S Darling Sr
Hc1 Box 5489
Keaau HI 96749-9521

Call Sign: NH6BG
Christopher K Fry
Hcr 1 Box 4155
Keaau HI 96749

Call Sign: KH7FV
Terry L Lonergan
Hcr 1 Box 5695
Keaau HI 96749

Call Sign: WH6DN
John M Luchau
Hc2 Box 6661
Keaau HI 96749-9326

Call Sign: NH7AL
James K Fry
Hcr 1 Box 4155
Keaau HI 96749

Call Sign: WA2AUI
Stewart D Beckley
Hcr 1 Box 5817
Keaau HI 96749-8400

Call Sign: KH6DD
Paradise Contesters
Hc3 - Box 11046
Keaau HI 96749-9206

Call Sign: NH7AM
Christopher K Fry
Hcr 1 Box 4155
Keaau HI 96749

Call Sign: WH6GP
Mark T Smith
Hcr 11057
Keaau HI 96749

Call Sign: WH6DHJ
Paradise Contesters
Hc3 - Box 11046
Keaau HI 96749-9206

Call Sign: WH6BP
Noah L Garramone
Hcr 1 Box 4618
Keaau HI 96749

Call Sign: KB7NXC
Douglas E Mc Grew
Hcr 2
Keaau HI 96749

Call Sign: WH6CSQ
Eugene T Meseck
Hcr 01 Box 5160
Keaau HI 96749

Call Sign: WH6FF
Ivo A Hanza
Hcr 1 Box 5088
Keaau HI 96749

Call Sign: WH7LM
Arnold G Areola
Hcr 2 ~~Box 6009
Keaau HI 96749

Call Sign: WH7QB
Nancy A Areola
Hcr 2 ~~Box 6009
Keaau HI 96749

Call Sign: WH7FR
Marcus A Hoeflinger
Hcr 2 ~~Box 6445
Keaau HI 96749

Call Sign: WH6CVF
Linn M Avattar
Hcr 2 ~~Box 6478
Keaau HI 96749

Call Sign: AH6HN
Ronald C Phillips
Hcr 2 ~~Box 6637
Keaau HI 96749

Call Sign: NH6OV
Leabert F Langsi
Hcr 2 ~~Box 6830
Keaau HI 96749

Call Sign: N6OUM
Walter S White
Hcr 2 ~~Box 9540
Keaau HI 96749-9317

Call Sign: WH7DD
Douglas M Keown
Hcr 2 ~~Box 9551
Keaau HI 96749

Call Sign: N7UQX
Barbara J Magnuson
Hcr 2 ~~Box 9568
Keaau HI 96749

Call Sign: KH7FN
Jack D Packard
Hcr 2 ~~Box 9594
Keaau HI 96749

Call Sign: AH6NJ
Kelvin L Mc Grew
Hcr 2 ~~Box 9611
Keaau HI 96749

Call Sign: WH6VI
Tanya J Mc Grew
Hcr 2 ~~Box 9611
Keaau HI 96749

Call Sign: W7GMH
Edwin J Miller
Hcr 3 ~Box 10016
Keaau HI 96749-9202

Call Sign: AH6KA
Donald K Muth
Hcr 3 ~Box 10082
Keaau HI 96749

Call Sign: KH6KA
Donald K Muth
Hcr 3 ~Box 10082
Keaau HI 96749

Call Sign: KD6RNC
William B Parry
Hcr 3 ~Box 10086
Keaau HI 96749

Call Sign: KE6AXN
Nancy R Parry
Hcr 3 ~Box 10086
Keaau HI 96749

Call Sign: NH7RQ
William B Parry
Hcr 3 ~Box 10086
Keaau HI 96749

Call Sign: NH7RT
Nancy R Parry
Hcr 3 ~Box 10086
Keaau HI 96749

Call Sign: NH7A
Albert C Crespo
Hcr 3 ~Box 11046
Keaau HI 96749

Call Sign: KH6LC
Lloyd J Cabral
Hcr 3 ~Box 11046
Keaau HI 96749-9206

Call Sign: WH7V
Jacques M Saget
Hcr 3 ~Box 11046
Keaau HI 96749-9206

Call Sign: WH7EJ
James J Devincent
Hcr 3 ~Box 11101
Keaau HI 96749

Call Sign: WH7EH
Mary E Devincent
Hcr 3 ~Box 11101
Keaau HI 96749

Call Sign: KH7E
Wilbur W Carlson Jr
Hcr 3 ~Box 11120 ~15-
2047 ~Manako St
Keaau HI 96749

Call Sign: AH7Y
Charles C Cartwright
Hcr 3 ~Box 13041
Keaau HI 96749-9209

Call Sign: NH7XF
Ward Y Oshiro
Hcr 3 ~Box 13070
Keaau HI 96749

Call Sign: WH7LR
April R Housman
Hcr 3 ~Box 13099

Keaau HI 96749

Call Sign: AH7A
Clarence E Smith
Hcr 3 ~Box 13510
Keaau HI 96749

Call Sign: WH6BY
Alistair K Bostrom
Hcr 3 ~Box 13554
Keaau HI 96749

Call Sign: WH7QE
Lorrie A Diamond
Hcr 3 ~Box 14073
Keaau HI 96749-9229

Call Sign: NH7MT
Rod K Diamond
Hcr 3 ~Box 14073
Keaau HI 96749

Call Sign: NH7MU
Daniel R Diamond
Hcr 3 ~Box 14073
Keaau HI 96749

Call Sign: KH7UU
Brandon P Delima
Hcr 6451
Keaau HI 96749

Call Sign: KC6QQI
Martin W Burs
Hcr1 Box 5177
Keaau HI 96749

Call Sign: WH7FB
Kile O Golden
Hcr2 ~~Box 6839
Keaau HI 96749

Call Sign: WH6DZ
Jean A Stoner
Hcr3 ~Box 13531

Keaau HI 96749

Call Sign: KH6SL
Rudy Kok
17-519 Ipu Aiwaha St
Keaau HI 96749

Call Sign: WH7MJ
Juan A Martines
16-110 Kaiewe Pl
Keaau HI 96749

Call Sign: NH7WP
Brevely Blas
16 1472 Keaau Pahoa Rd
Keaau HI 96749-9103

Call Sign: WH7LP
Frank D Crabtree
16 540 Keaau Pahoa Rd 2
Pmb 172
Keaau HI 96749

Call Sign: WH6CVG
Francis Blas
16-1472 KeaauPahoa Rd
Keaau HI 96749

Call Sign: K6HWK
Elijah Hawk
16-540 KeaauPahoa Rd
Ste 2192
Keaau HI 96749

Call Sign: KB7HWK
Beverly A Hawk
16-540 KeaauPahoa Rd
Ste 2192
Keaau HI 96749

Call Sign: NH7QI
John T Kuroda
16-731 Milo St
Keaau HI 96749

Call Sign: KD4NFW
Chris N Schaab
17-227 Palaai St
Keaau HI 96749

Call Sign: WB7UIJ
Linden E Whitfield
15-1792 Puakalo (30) Ave
Keaau HI 96749

Call Sign: NH6HS
Roy T Hockin
Sr5022
Keaau HI 96749

Call Sign: AH6GE
William H Anger
Keaau HI 96749

Call Sign: KH6BAI
Roy S Blackshear
Keaau HI 96749

Call Sign: KH7BB
Carl W Byck
Keaau HI 96749

Call Sign: KH7FK
Jacqueline J Seaquist
Keaau HI 96749

Call Sign: KH7FM
James Seaquist
Keaau HI 96749

Call Sign: KH7Y
Frederic K Honnold
Keaau HI 96749

Call Sign: N7KZB
Kathleen R Wines
Keaau HI 96749

Call Sign: NH6AW
Janet L Mills

Keaau HI 96749

Call Sign: NH6BH
Stephanie Bath
Keaau HI 96749

Call Sign: NH6FP
Richard G Miner
Keaau HI 96749

Call Sign: NH6WT
Edward P Talaro
Keaau HI 96749

Call Sign: NH7AK
Janet L Mills
Keaau HI 96749

Call Sign: NH7AN
Stephanie Bath
Keaau HI 96749

Call Sign: NH7CT
Norman Paik
Keaau HI 96749

Call Sign: NH7FT
Rosemarie V Punsalan
Keaau HI 96749

Call Sign: NH7GE
Walter K Miller
Keaau HI 96749

Call Sign: NH7JC
Gary F Dalton
Keaau HI 96749

Call Sign: NH7JM
Anjala Dalton
Keaau HI 96749

Call Sign: NH7JN
Adrian A Dalton
Keaau HI 96749

Call Sign: NH7JO
Edward F Dalton
Keaau HI 96749

Call Sign: NH7JP
Gary F Dalton Jr
Keaau HI 96749

Call Sign: NH7UI
James W Ramos
Keaau HI 96749

Call Sign: NH7WX
Patricia J Reiss
Keaau HI 96749

Call Sign: NH7WY
Elston T Takayama
Keaau HI 96749

Call Sign: WH6BIR
Joyce M Carlson
Keaau HI 96749

Call Sign: WH6CSN
Francis Blas Jr
Keaau HI 96749

Call Sign: WH6ID
Ammon K Kaopua
Keaau HI 96749

Call Sign: WH6IM
Mark T Foster
Keaau HI 96749

Call Sign: WH6IV
Jason Kaopua
Keaau HI 96749

Call Sign: WH6LM
Nalani Mills
Keaau HI 96749

Call Sign: WH6XK
David W Harrison
Keaau HI 96749

Call Sign: WH7DI
Inoke J Mills
Keaau HI 96749

Call Sign: WH7DJ
Tiara L Mills
Keaau HI 96749

Call Sign: WH7EI
Karl H Seebruch
Keaau HI 96749

Call Sign: WH7FO
Mark D Ayap
Keaau HI 96749

Call Sign: WH7GN
Manuel Escobedo
Keaau HI 96749

Call Sign: WH7JM
John Aniu Jr
Keaau HI 96749

Call Sign: WH7JS
Brent L Runnells
Keaau HI 96749

Call Sign: WH7VK
Noah D Bath
Keaau HI 96749

Call Sign: WH7VL
Francis Blas III
Keaau HI 96749

Call Sign: WH7VO
George K Kekauoha
Keaau HI 96749

Call Sign: WH7VP

George K Kekauoha Jr
Keaau HI 96749

Call Sign: WH7VS
Aaron M Stephens
Keaau HI 96749

Call Sign: WH7XM
Matthew R Byck
Keaau HI 96749

Call Sign: WH7XN
Carl W Byck
Keaau HI 96749

Call Sign: WJ7G
Gregory M Wines
Keaau HI 96749

Call Sign: AH6J
Robert L Schneider
Keaau HI 96749-0131

Call Sign: KH6QM
Harry S Barnes
Keaau HI 96749-0313

Call Sign: WH6DA
Roy D Bath
Keaau HI 96749-0457

Call Sign: AH6RE
Curtis A Knight
Keaau HI 96749-0536

Call Sign: NH7WV
Beau K Mills
Keaau HI 96749-1201

Call Sign: KH6RZ
Amador Six Meter Dx
Club
Keaau HI 96749-1443

Call Sign: NH6P

Big Island Six Meter Club
Keaau HI 96749-1443

Call Sign: W6YKM
Amador Six Meter Dx
Club
Keaau HI 96749-1443

Call Sign: NH7UW
James E Adams
Keaau HI 96749-1943

Call Sign: NH7WW
Gerald L Reiss
Keaau HI 96749-2184

Call Sign: K1BLP
Gerald G Witham
Keaau HI 96749

Call Sign: KH6ER
Doris M Carlson
Keaau HI 96749

Call Sign: NH6ER
Doris M Carlson
Keaau HI 96749

Call Sign: NH6GG
Daniel D Pierson
Keaau HI 96749

Call Sign: NH6SQ
Michael I Schneider
Keaau HI 96749

Call Sign: WH6BO
James D Crowley
Keaau HI 96749

Call Sign: WH6BZ
Karen M Crowley
Keaau HI 96749

Call Sign: KH6SR

Sheldon T C Remington
Keaau HI 96749-1222

FCC Amateur Radio License in Kealakekua

Call Sign: KH6LI
Richard H Cormack
Box 1241
Kealakekua HI 96750

Call Sign: WH6CZN
Lillian D Ku
82 796 Kamakani St Capt
Cook
Kealakekua HI 96750

Call Sign: NH7TS
Joseph M Crable
81-1244 Konawaena
School Rd
Kealakekua HI 96750

Call Sign: KD6OW
Robert L Vader
Kealakekua HI 96750

Call Sign: KD7LOK
Leo F Robeson
Kealakekua HI 96750

Call Sign: KH7DAH
Joseph M Crable
Kealakekua HI 96750

Call Sign: KH7ID
Mitchell J Tam
Kealakekua HI 96750

Call Sign: KH7TAM
Mitchell J Tam
Kealakekua HI 96750

Call Sign: NH6Q
Jesse E Shaw

Kealakekua HI 96750

Call Sign: WH6WF
Troy T Terazono
Kealakekua HI 96750

Call Sign: WH6WH
Bernard C De Guair
Kealakekua HI 96750

Call Sign: WH6WM
Marnie M Humble
Kealakekua HI 96750

Call Sign: WH6YR
Cathy R Lewis
Kealakekua HI 96750

Call Sign: WH7CM
Thomas S Kaneo
Kealakekua HI 96750

Call Sign: WH7DR
Meleana L Smith
Kealakekua HI 96750

Call Sign: WH7SA
Charles A Ganuelas
Kealakekua HI 96750

Call Sign: KH6BRZ
David Basque
Kealakekua HI 96750

Call Sign: KH6EJV
Leslie G Robinson
Kealakekua HI 96750-
0149

Call Sign: NH7PW
Matthew M Henera Lau
Kealakekua HI 96750-
1596

Call Sign: KH6CIY

Martin J Vitousek
Kealakekua HI 96750

Call Sign: NH6AI
James M Tanaka
Kealakekua HI 96750

Call Sign: WH6HE
Horace T Yanagi Jr
Kealakekua HI 96750

FCC Amateur Radio License in Kealia

Call Sign: WH6KS
Alfred F Darling
Kealia HI 96751-0214

FCC Amateur Radio License in Keauhou

Call Sign: KF7AZ
Howard R Conant
Keauhou HI 96739

Call Sign: N6TYB
Stephanie A Serrell Conant
Keauhou HI 96739

Call Sign: N6XLJ
Bradley G White
Keauhou HI 96739

FCC Amateur Radio License in Kekaha

Call Sign: KH7IM
Robert L Campbell
4535 Amakihi Rd
Kekaha HI 96752

Call Sign: NH7CD
Darline M Rita-Sarmento
7779 Iwipolena Rd
Kekaha HI 96752-0238

Call Sign: NH7ZR
Alfred P Sarmento
7779 Iwipolena Rd`
Kekaha HI 96752-0128

Call Sign: WH6IB
Cathleen M Libal
Pmrf Barking Sands
Kekaha HI 96752

Call Sign: WH6JG
Gayla M Burns
Pmrf Barking Sands
Kekaha HI 96752

Call Sign: WH6ED
James D Libal
1216B Talos Dr Pmrf
Barking Sands
Kekaha HI 96752

Call Sign: AH6SD
Abraham K Nihipali
Kekaha HI 96752

Call Sign: AH6TD
David C Herring
Kekaha HI 96752

Call Sign: K6DCH
David C Herring
Kekaha HI 96752

Call Sign: KC2EKZ
Steven B Handy
Kekaha HI 96752

Call Sign: KH6EZ
Edward M Pagaduan
Kekaha HI 96752

Call Sign: KH7FP
Charles J Haffner
Kekaha HI 96752

Call Sign: KH7S
Alfred Sacramed
Kekaha HI 96752

Call Sign: NH6D
Abraham K Nihipali
Kekaha HI 96752

Call Sign: NH6GD
Darline M Rita
Kekaha HI 96752

Call Sign: NH6RN
Pineapple State Paper
Chasers
Kekaha HI 96752

Call Sign: NH6YE
Dennis B Burns
Kekaha HI 96752

Call Sign: NH7DH
Richard J Teter
Kekaha HI 96752

Call Sign: W7TEN
Richard D Nelson
Kekaha HI 96752

Call Sign: WH6CNQ
Abraham K Nihipali
Kekaha HI 96752

Call Sign: WH6DHO
160 Gab Club
Kekaha HI 96752

Call Sign: WH6DQK
Adrian M Bouche'
Kekaha HI 96752

Call Sign: WH6DTT
Stephanie A Bostick
Kekaha HI 96752

Call Sign: WH6DVL
Dereck K Kaneshiro
Kekaha HI 96752

Call Sign: WH6S
Richard D Nelson
Kekaha HI 96752

Call Sign: WH7SW
Pamela E Thrasher
Kekaha HI 96752

Call Sign: WH7ZE
Erica Fraser
Kekaha HI 96752

Call Sign: WV0Z
Pineapple State Paper
Chasers
Kekaha HI 96752

Call Sign: KH6DRT
Evillo Abreu
Kekaha HI 96752-0486

Call Sign: NH7CS
R Andrew De Laveaga
Kekaha HI 96752-0492

Call Sign: NH6JB
Randall J Hee
Kekaha HI 96752-0627

Call Sign: WH7HV
Timothy J Smith
Kekaha HI 96752-1246

Call Sign: WL7BXJ
Orville F Alwin Jr
Kekaha HI 96752-1300

Call Sign: KH6EH
Gerald B Lingelbaugh
Kekaha HI 96752

Call Sign: KH6HG
Robert R Valencia Sr
Kekaha HI 96752

Call Sign: NH6PP
Efren S Pacol
Kekaha HI 96752

Call Sign: WH6BWH
Val G Balauro Jr
Kekaha HI 96752

Call Sign: WH6GN
Joe R Brown
Kekaha HI 96752

Call Sign: WH6OJ
Dwyane O Clark
Kekaha HI 96752

FCC Amateur Radio License in Kihei

Call Sign: KH7CH
Michael A Dion
1880 A Anapa Pl
Kihei HI 96753-7801

Call Sign: KB5RSJ
Keric A Hill
25 Akeu Pl
Kihei HI 96753

Call Sign: WH7CR
Rachel A Heckscher
2124 Awihi Pl 103
Kihei HI 96753

Call Sign: WH7CP
Eric K Olson
2124 Awihi Pl Apt 103
Kihei HI 96753

Call Sign: WH6DQO

Shawn T Medley
172 E We;Alahap Rd
Kihei HI 96753

Call Sign: NH6HG
David Rand
1690 Halama St
Kihei HI 96753-8051

Call Sign: NH7CM
David Rand
1690 Halama St
Kihei HI 96753-8051

Call Sign: NH7G
David Rand
1690 Halama St
Kihei HI 96753-8051

Call Sign: WH6CBS
Randall C Bell
271 Hapakolu Pl
Kihei HI 96753

Call Sign: KC7KHW
Lis C Richardson
95 Hoohale St
Kihei HI 96753

Call Sign: KE6TJ
Austin H Green
3430 Hookipa Pl
Kihei HI 96753

Call Sign: N6XLB
Kevin L Jarc
33 Hoolalei Way
Kihei HI 96753

Call Sign: WH7AE
Mark T Souza
35 Iliwai Loop
Kihei HI 96753

Call Sign: N1CNQ

Robert E Conlon
41 Iliwai Loop
Kihei HI 96753

Call Sign: N1SHV
Dale L Conlon
41 Iliwai Loop
Kihei HI 96753

Call Sign: WH6CRS
Thomas E Abbott
89 Iliwai Lp
Kihei HI 96753

Call Sign: WH6DJC
Gloria J Chee
587 Kaiola St
Kihei HI 96753

Call Sign: KH6AP
Charles P Reid
618 Kaiola St
Kihei HI 96753

Call Sign: WH6CWE
David R Stevens
2058 Kanoe St 1C
Kihei HI 96753

Call Sign: K9MHO
Peter J Pilecki
2875 Kauhale St
Kihei HI 96753

Call Sign: KH6NT
Francis J Cooper Jr
2904 Kauhale St
Kihei HI 96753

Call Sign: AB4CO
Jacques M Saget
3520 Keahi Pl
Kihei HI 96753

Call Sign: AH6M

Ronald D Pitts
3520 Keahi Pl
Kihei HI 96753

Call Sign: N7PMC
Paolo Cortese
3520 Keahi Pl
Kihei HI 96753

Call Sign: KH7BG
Akihito Matsubara
3520 Keahi Pl
Kihei HI 96753-9211

Call Sign: NH6T
Reginald L Olson
3520 Keahi Pl
Kihei HI 96753

Call Sign: K8DSV
Marc A Grodan
3355 Kehala Dr
Kihei HI 96753

Call Sign: WH7WJ
Peter M Metz
480 Kenolio Rd 18 204
Kihei HI 96753

Call Sign: WH6SD
Edward J Walker
Kihei
Kihei HI 96753

Call Sign: WH6ZZ
Randy Pascua Sr
30 Kuilima Pl
Kihei HI 96753

Call Sign: NH6ZL
John M Marshall
15 Kulanihakoi St 5G
Kihei HI 96753

Call Sign: KG6DSN

Lance C Murphy
225 Kuli Puu St
Kihei HI 96753-7165

Call Sign: KC0NGC
Gregory Bardos
64 Kulipuu St
Kihei HI 96753

Call Sign: KH6AH
Hawaii Internet-Remote
Amateur Radio Club
854 Kumulani Dr
Kihei HI 96753

Call Sign: NH6BN
Donald A Schneider II
609 Kupulau Dr
Kihei HI 96753

Call Sign: KH6IAP
Gary T Henderson
723 Kupulau Dr
Kihei HI 96753

Call Sign: KD4CSV
Donald A Schneider II
1115 Kupulau Dr
Kihei HI 96753

Call Sign: KH7JL
David J Ernisse
5295 L Honoapiilani Rd
C18
Kihei HI 96761

Call Sign: WH6OR
Wayne R Bachman
3545 Lanihou Pl
Kihei HI 96753

Call Sign: KH6REO
Edward W Field
71 Laumaewa Loop
Kihei HI 96753-8257

Call Sign: WH6OP
Donald J Fabozzi II
550 Lipoa Pkwy
Kihei HI 96753

Call Sign: NH7FA
George J Reioux
613 Luana Pl
Kihei HI 96753

Call Sign: N6BMJ
Margaret A Reioux
613 Luana Pl
Kihei HI 96753

Call Sign: N6BMK
Paul J Reioux
613 Luana Pl
Kihei HI 96753

Call Sign: WH6ZP
Dale A Netz
153 Makalauna St
Kihei HI 96753

Call Sign: WH6MI
Bruce B Joiner
3443 Malina Pl
Kihei HI 96753

Call Sign: WH6AS
Daniel A Page Sr
3513 Malina Pl
Kihei HI 96753

Call Sign: AH6MO
Achim Rogmann
C/O K Scheper 1587 N
Alaniu Pl
Kihei HI 96753

Call Sign: K6GSS
John A Hultquist Jr
188 Noe St

Kihei HI 96753

Call Sign: AH7S
Steven C Milewski
279 Ohina Pl
Kihei HI 96753

Call Sign: WH6DWJ
Charnan Carroll
1639 S Alaniu Pl
Kihei HI 96753

Call Sign: WH6MH
Philip J Kirkley
1087 S Kihei Rd
Kihei HI 96753

Call Sign: NH7FB
William B Carpenter
3146 S Kihei Rd
Kihei HI 96753

Call Sign: AH6JT
Michael S Gower
2191 S Kihei Rd 2305
Kihei HI 96753

Call Sign: WA6ECX
Robert E Pursel Jr
2495 S Kihei Rd 254
Kihei HI 96753

Call Sign: KH6FB
Robert E Pursel Jr
2495 S Kihei Rd 254
Kihei HI 96753

Call Sign: W9DOR
Kenneth R Leiser
2387 S Kihei Rd A302
Kihei HI 96753

Call Sign: WH7JP
Abraham R Gladstone

2463 S Kihei Rd Apt
C16303
Kihei HI 96753

Call Sign: WH7MAX
Abraham R Gladstone
2463 S Kihei Rd Apt
C16303
Kihei HI 96753

Call Sign: WA7YET
Michael E Eddy
2575 S Kihei Rd Apt G508
Kihei HI 96753

Call Sign: N6SIW
James L Paul
1450 S Kihei Rd B205
Kihei HI 96753

Call Sign: KF6OF
Carl T Williams
2219 S Kihei Rd B207
Kihei HI 96753

Call Sign: KH6MQ
Donald F Epler
2777 S Kihei Rd K107
Kihei HI 96753

Call Sign: N7KAI
Daniel K Nakooka
851 S Kihei Rd P 206
Kihei HI 96753

Call Sign: WH6DSH
Debra J Brown
1993 S Kihei Rd Ste 205
Kihei HI 96753

Call Sign: WH6CYC
Timoteo Battad Jr
2219 S Kikei A206
Kihei HI 96753

Call Sign: KH6CYC
Timoteo Battad Jr
2219 S Kikei Rd A206
Kihei HI 96753

Call Sign: KC7KBA
Lawrence G Ankrum Jr
1993 So Kihei Rd 605
Kihei HI 96753

Call Sign: KF7OUJ
Hisao Wakatabi
1215 South Kihei Rd Ste
O968
Kihei HI 96753

Call Sign: KH6WH
Hisao Wakatabi
1215 South Kihei Rd Ste
O968
Kihei HI 96753

Call Sign: WH6DSG
Derrick Makekau
305 Uala Pl
Kihei HI 96753

Call Sign: KH6HOD
Bethel R Morris
39 Uilani St
Kihei HI 96753

Call Sign: KH6HOE
Charles R Morris
39 Uilani St
Kihei HI 96753

Call Sign: KH6OA
Robyn M Walters
1299 Uluniu Rd Apt C104
Kihei HI 96753

Call Sign: KE6CSI
Jill Goldman
2837 Umalu Pl

Kihei HI 96753

Call Sign: KD7SME
David G Peterson
140 Uwapo Rd 16 101
Kihei HI 96753

Call Sign: WH6DUC
Richard R Brown
140 Uwapo Rd Unit 25102
Kihei HI 96753

Call Sign: WH6DMH
Catherine A Friendshuh
75 Waiapo St
Kihei HI 96753

Call Sign: KC7TGO
Carmen J Burkhart
3300 Wailea Alanui 37D
Kihei HI 96753

Call Sign: NH6EC
Gregory J Devito
155 Wailer Ike 12
Kihei HI 96753

Call Sign: NH7BK
Gregory J Devito
155 Wailer Ike 12
Kihei HI 96753

Call Sign: WH6COM
Nancy A Baker
140 Walua Pl
Kihei HI 96753

Call Sign: KB6VCP
John R N Walker
Kihei HI 96753

Call Sign: KM4IP
Jon R Galbraith
Kihei HI 96753

Call Sign: WH7NKG
Nicholas K Giaconi
Kihei HI 96753

Call Sign: WH7XQ
Nicholas K Giaconi
Kihei HI 96753

Call Sign: KH7QL
Joseph A Raley
Kihei HI 96753-0767

Call Sign: WH6DCG
Robert Kasca
Kihei HI 96753-2129

Call Sign: AH6MP
John Anthony
Kihei HI 96753

Call Sign: NH7UP
Robert L Robertson
4390 A Kapuna Rd
Kilauea HI 96754

Call Sign: WH7ZD
Charles M Brown
4264 Ala Muku Pl C3
Kilauea HI 96754

Call Sign: KH6PH
Ronald M Burkhart
Box 480
Kilauea HI 96754

Call Sign: WH7ZF
Paul W Marshall
General Delivery
Kilauea HI 96754

Call Sign: KG6QQD
Lloyd V Gardner

4317 Kapuna Rd
Kilauea HI 96754

Call Sign: NH6WA
Brian M Schaefer
4560 Kuawa Rd
Kilauea HI 96754

Call Sign: N7SVP
Shannon J Roselli
Kilauea HI 96754

Call Sign: N7UGX
James D Roselli
Kilauea HI 96754

Call Sign: NH7UQ
Debra S Gochros
Kilauea HI 96754

Call Sign: NH7XC
Tor Chantara
Kilauea HI 96754

Call Sign: WH7SP
John N Pfendler
Kilauea HI 96754

Call Sign: K6ZUP
Eli B Ames
Kilauea HI 96754

Call Sign: WH6GL
Clyde R Lovelace
Kilauea HI 96754

Call Sign: WH6IZ
Soren M Burkhart
Kilauea HI 96754

Call Sign: K6TWA
Clifford R Waeschle
4710 Kahilholo Rd
Kilawea HI 96754-1182

Call Sign: NH7VH
Georges H Foss Jr
Kilawea HI 96754

Call Sign: KH6FMT
John B Dillon
Box 758
Koloa HI 96756

Call Sign: WH6CVS
Gerald J Mc Kenna
3735 Comao Rd
Koloa HI 96756

Call Sign: WH7JW
Lionel R Medeiros
1870 Hoone Rd 821
Koloa HI 96756-9791

Call Sign: WH7JX
Mary E Neudorffer
1870 Hoone Rd 821
Koloa HI 96756-9791

Call Sign: KB6QAZ
Steve A Bojorquez
3323 Kalua Moa Rd
Koloa HI 96756

Call Sign: N6RGK
Bonnie M Bojorquez
3323 Kalua Moa Rd
Koloa HI 96765

Call Sign: KB6KL
Monroe F Richman
1728 Keoniloa Pl
Koloa HI 96756

Call Sign: KH7DV
Walter L Briant
2381 Kipuka St

Koloa HI 96756

Call Sign: KH7M
James R Reid
3465 Lawailoa Ln
Koloa HI 96756

Call Sign: W6KPI
James R Reid
3465 Lawailoa Ln
Koloa HI 96756

Call Sign: WH6DDZ
Hawaii Chapter Quarter
Century Wireless Assoc
3465 Lawailoa Ln
Koloa HI 96756

Call Sign: NH6FJ
Neal J Iseri
5356 Malino Rd
Koloa HI 96756

Call Sign: WH7SJ
Judith R Byce
1951 Muku Pl
Koloa HI 96756

Call Sign: WH7SK
Richard H Byce
1951 Muku Pl
Koloa HI 96756

Call Sign: NH6WJ
Eric S Santiago
3833 Ohu Ohu St
Koloa HI 96756

Call Sign: KF6IVV
Ellis C Brooks
Po Box 127
Koloa HI 96756

Call Sign: WH7JU
Ellis C Brooks

Po Box 127
Koloa HI 96756

Call Sign: WA7LHT
Kitoku Ishiguro
2121 Poipu Rd
Koloa HI 96756

Call Sign: WH6CFU
Charles N K Blake
3140 Poipu Rd
Koloa HI 96756

Call Sign: K5ZAI
Charles W Skelton Jr
2640 Puuholo Rd
Koloa HI 96756

Call Sign: WH7SH
Rodilio V Baring
4206 Upa Rd
Koloa HI 96756

Call Sign: KH6F
Gemi Pascua
3752 Waihohonou Rd
Koloa HI 96756 0675

Call Sign: WL7CT
Deric B Solis
5421 Wailaau Rd
Koloa HI 96756

Call Sign: WH6CFI
Cayetano Gerardo
3606 Wailani Rd
Koloa HI 96756

Call Sign: AH6PX
Ed F De Deo
Koloa HI 96756

Call Sign: AH6TX
Howard S Krawitz
Koloa HI 96756

Call Sign: KE6MG
Gordon H Marron
Koloa HI 96756

Call Sign: WH6DOV
Carrie M Ringering
Koloa HI 96756

Call Sign: WH6DTX
Howard S Krawitz
Koloa HI 96756

Call Sign: WH6TG
Verna H Schoffstall
Koloa HI 96756

Call Sign: WH7OP
Frank D Frazier
Koloa HI 96756

Call Sign: WH7SS
Linda M Ruby
Koloa HI 96756

Call Sign: WH7GM
David K Okinaka
Koloa HI 96756

Call Sign: WH6CCL
Daryl L Gerardo
Koloa HI 96756-1641

Call Sign: AH6AW
Susumu Muraoka
Koloa HI 96756

Call Sign: KH6ENC
169Th Olaa Acwf
Koloa HI 96756

Call Sign: KH6KU
Vance J Pascua
Koloa HI 96756

Call Sign: NH6EP
Gerald P Pascua
Koloa HI 96756

Call Sign: NH6KG
Nora A Masuda
Koloa HI 96756

Call Sign: NH7ZQ
Vance J Pascua
Koloa HI 96756

Call Sign: WH6BLS
Jace P Pascua
Koloa HI 96756

Call Sign: WH6MO
Michael J Schoffstall
Koloa HI 96756

FCC Amateur Radio License in Kona

Call Sign: KH6ANA
Anacleto Heloca Sr
Kealakekua
Kona HI 96750

FCC Amateur Radio License in Kualapuu

Call Sign: WA6OPQ
William K Arthur Jr
Kualapuu HI 96757

Call Sign: WH6IT
Sherman U M Napoleon Jr
Kualapuu HI 96757

Call Sign: WH7WA
Annette E Gorospe
Kualapuu HI 96757

FCC Amateur Radio License in Kula

Call Sign: WH6KW
Darrell S Williams
433 Crater Rd
Kula HI 96790

Call Sign: WH6DRE
Melissa E Hashimoto-
Binkie
461 Hapapa Rd
Kula HI 96790

Call Sign: WH6DSF
Frank B Russell
Hc 1 Box 965
Kula HI 96790

Call Sign: WH6DSI
Miles D Wolbe
12 Hoihoi Pl
Kula HI 96790

Call Sign: NH6UN
Nancy L Leota
755B Kamarciki Rd
Kula HI 96790

Call Sign: KC4VNN
Mark G Ausbeck
1071 Kamehameiki Rd
Kula HI 96790

Call Sign: WA6QQU
Arthur J Konkel Jr
1108 Kau St
Kula HI 96790

Call Sign: KG6FXF
Doreen Key
1495 Kekaulike Ave
Kula HI 96790

Call Sign: N6IJR
Michael L Benner
1495 Kekaulike Ave

Kula HI 96790-8915

Call Sign: KH6VG
David S Carvalho
7345 Kula Highway
Kula HI 96790-9467

Call Sign: WH6SF
Karen L Schneider
204 Kula Hwy
Kula HI 96790

Call Sign: NH6EQ
Tetsuo Tamanaha
136 Kulalani Cir
Kula HI 96790

Call Sign: WH7EP
Robert G Yapp Jr
19 Manu St
Kula HI 96790

Call Sign: WH7AC
Richard C Yust
1287 Middle Rd
Kula HI 96790

Call Sign: KH7CC
Thomas K Worthington
1035 Naalae Rd
Kula HI 96790

Call Sign: NH6Y
Thomas K Worthington
1035 Naalae Rd
Kula HI 96790

Call Sign: KH6BKL
Raymond C Freitas
Rr 2 Box 239
Kula HI 96790

Call Sign: WH6AU
David J Darling
Rr 2 Box 780

Kula HI 96790

Call Sign: WH6BYH
Harry A Fullerton
107 Waimele Way
Kula HI 96790-1180

Call Sign: AH6IU
Harold K Purdy
Kula HI 96790

Call Sign: NH6RK
Norma C Hughes
Kula HI 96790

Call Sign: WH6CTR
Steve K Amy
Kula HI 96790

Call Sign: WH6AT
Michael K Ritter
Kula HI 96790

Call Sign: WH6CTP
Oliver Perz
411 Holopuni Rd
Kulo HI 96790

FCC Amateur Radio License in Kurtistown

Call Sign: AH6KZ
Alexander G Erbe
Kurtistown HI 96760

Call Sign: KD6YF
Trudy V Lindsay
Kurtistown HI 96760

Call Sign: KE7UV
William F Twidale
Kurtistown HI 96760

Call Sign: KE7UW
Maryann Twidale

Kurtistown HI 96760

Call Sign: KH6AF
Hawaii Chapter Qcwa
Kurtistown HI 96760

Call Sign: KH6BMM
Robert M Shimamoto
Kurtistown HI 96760

Call Sign: KH6HHD
Yozo Endo
Kurtistown HI 96760

Call Sign: KH6JAH
Le Vaughn Carter
Kurtistown HI 96760

Call Sign: KH7BP
Todd W Lum
Kurtistown HI 96760

Call Sign: KH7FL
Jerome P Siebenrock
Kurtistown HI 96760

Call Sign: KH7MN
Anthony L Yates
Kurtistown HI 96760

Call Sign: KH7ZJ
Kenneth H Cutting
Kurtistown HI 96760

Call Sign: N6ODT
Robert B Lindsay
Kurtistown HI 96760

Call Sign: NH6DS
Catherine J Mcphee
Kurtistown HI 96760

Call Sign: NH7BI
Catherine J Broyles
Kurtistown HI 96760

Call Sign: NH7WT
Ronald E Lawson
Kurtistown HI 96760

Call Sign: NH7WU
Vanda J Lawson
Kurtistown HI 96760

Call Sign: WH6BI
Le Vaughn Carter
Kurtistown HI 96760

Call Sign: WH6CWK
Timothy A Spellicy
Kurtistown HI 96760

Call Sign: WH6CYU
Sally R Allen
Kurtistown HI 96760

Call Sign: WH6DCC
Chris D Allen
Kurtistown HI 96760

Call Sign: WH6DFS
Puna Amateur Radio Club
Kurtistown HI 96760

Call Sign: WH6DGP
Hawaiian Acres
Emergency Response
Kurtistown HI 96760

Call Sign: WH7VN
Clay Jung
Kurtistown HI 96760

Call Sign: WB4JTT
David G Johnson
Kurtistown HI 96760-0055

Call Sign: KB6EGA
Robert E Gomez
Kurtistown HI 96760-0720

Call Sign: KB9YGQ
Cary V Deringer
Kurtistown HI 96760-0793

Call Sign: WH6LU
Richard S Gardner
Kurtistown HI 96760

Call Sign: WH6OU
Jimmy J Ault
Kurtistown HI 96760

FCC Amateur Radio License in Lahaina

Call Sign: WH6DQZ
Dana D Alonzo-Howeth
180 Awaiku St
Lahaina HI 96761

Call Sign: WH6DJD
Diane L Christofferson
7 Coral Pl
Lahaina HI 96761

Call Sign: WB7UGT
Jeffrey F Wood
658 Front St 126A
Lahaina HI 96761

Call Sign: WH7QH
Anne Mccoy
1034 Front St Apt 219
Lahaina HI 96761

Call Sign: N0UGZ
Kristin A Kennedy
1034 Front St Apt 222
Lahaina HI 96761

Call Sign: WH6CRV
Louise J Lagbas
115 Hamau Pl
Lahaina HI 96761

Call Sign: WH6YF
Barney B Lagbas Jr
115 Hamau Pl
Lahaina HI 96761

Call Sign: WH6YG
Joseph D Kobatake
5170G Hanawai St
Lahaina HI 96761

Call Sign: KB6EVA
Maryanna Waldrup
4955 Hanawai St 5103
Lahaina HI 96761

Call Sign: WH7VA
Marc S Orgish
23 Hua Nai Way
Lahaina HI 96761

Call Sign: K6KDS
Richard L Miller
33 Hui Dr
Lahaina HI 96761

Call Sign: KH7QM
Marcus Coleman
110 Kaanapali Shores Pl
Lahaina HI 96761

Call Sign: WH6BPR
Gary L Kepner
564 Kahena St
Lahaina HI 96761

Call Sign: WH6COA
Bernice K Hokoana
Kauaula Valley
Lahaina HI 96767

Call Sign: WH6COB
John H Hokoana Jr
Kauaula Valley
Lahaina HI 96767

Call Sign: WH6COD
Donella M Hokoana
Kauaula Valley
Lahaina HI 96767

Call Sign: NH7VV
Harald Enko
C/O Sylvia Feeberger 3788
L Honoapiilani Rd C104
Lahaina HI 96761

Call Sign: NH7VW
Alexander Spitzer
C/O Sylvia Feeberger 3788
L Honoapiilani Rd C104
Lahaina HI 96761

Call Sign: KG6ELB
James M O Connor
3350 L Honoapiilani Rd
Ste 215 458
Lahaina HI 96761

Call Sign: WH6VG
Melvin D Waller
51 Loa Pl
Lahaina HI 96761

Call Sign: K3UOC
Michael J Manafo
4790 Lower Hanoapiilani
Rd
Lahaina HI 96761

Call Sign: WH6COE
Rose K Mc Cabe
936 N Niheu St
Lahaina HI 96761

Call Sign: WH6DQN
Tonie A Takeshita
5095 Napilihau St Pmb
323
Lahaina HI 96761

Call Sign: WH2D
Maui Dx Club
5095 Napilihau St Unit
109 B
Lahaina HI 96761

Call Sign: KH6MX
Maui Prep Amateur Radio
Club
5095 Napilihau St Unit
109 B
Lahaina HI 96761

Call Sign: WH6DWY
Maui Prep Amateru Radio
Club
5095 Napilihau St Unit
1098
Lahaina HI 96761

Call Sign: KC6JAE
Gordon J Firestein
186 Paia Pohaku Pl
Lahaina HI 96761-5708

Call Sign: KH6GRV
John O Healey
772 Pauoa St
Lahaina HI 96761

Call Sign: WH7NE
Hilary Spreiter
175 Pualoke Pl Apt 2
Lahaina HI 96761

Call Sign: KH6JJH
John J Helly
50 Puu Anoano St 1504
Lahaina HI 96761

Call Sign: KH7SWT
Steven W Tenney
150 Puukolii Rd 51
Lahaina HI 96761

Call Sign: WH7RT
Steven W Tenney
150 Puukolii Rd 51
Lahaina HI 96761

Call Sign: KH6HTV
James R Andrews
150 Puukolii Rd Condo 55
Lahaina HI 96761

Call Sign: WH6DBH
Mark J Bates
171 Wahikuli Rd
Lahaina HI 96761

Call Sign: N6YKJ
Wilhelm K Weber
216 Wahioli Way
Lahaina HI 96761

Call Sign: NH7PQ
Lashawna J Stringham
843 Wainee 107 Pmb 612
Lahaina HI 96761

Call Sign: WH6PY
John A Kidnay
480 Wainee St
Lahaina HI 96761

Call Sign: NH7FH
Emma S Grubler
Lahaina HI 96761

Call Sign: WB8TBI
Michael J Lawrence
Lahaina HI 96761

Call Sign: WH6DJB
Robert T Romero
Lahaina HI 96761

Call Sign: WH7XU
Barry R Cohn

Lahaina HI 96761

Call Sign: AH2CC
John E Monroe
Lahaina HI 96767

Call Sign: KH2DC
Katherine A Monroe
Lahaina HI 96767

Call Sign: KH6RO
Richard L Miller
Lahaina HI 96767

Call Sign: NH7RF
Jeffrey P Kalbach
Lahaina HI 96767

Call Sign: WH7EZ
Everett J Balmores
Lahaina HI 96761-8138

Call Sign: WH6BZH
Gary L Shipp
Lahaina HI 96761

Call Sign: WH6COY
Hilary Spreiter
Lahaina HI 96761

Call Sign: WH6COZ
Casey Robinson
Lahaina HI 96761

Call Sign: WH6KP
Patrick T Rogers
Lahaina HI 96761

**FCC Amateur Radio
License in Laie**

Call Sign: WH6CXS
Mario S Gancinia
Box 1743 55 220 Kulanui
St

Laie HI 96762

Call Sign: WH6CRJ
Priscilla F Whittaker
Byu H Box 1777
Laie HI 96762

Call Sign: WH6KJ
Tommy K Jessop
Byu H Box 5760
Laie HI 96762

Call Sign: NH6MI
Samuel K Peneku III
Byu Hawaii Box 1729
Laie HI 96762

Call Sign: WH6CUO
Alma D Waddell
Byu Tva 6022
Laie HI 96762

Call Sign: KH7TG
Stephen R Allred
55-491 Iosepa St
Laie HI 96762-1262

Call Sign: K7IHI
Larry A Le Mone
55 474 Kamehameha Hwy
Laie HI 96762

Call Sign: WH6JT
Jason Green
Bx 1429 55220 Kulaui St
Laie HI 96762

Call Sign: WH6PZ
Joseph P Baker
55 457 Moana St
Laie HI 96762-1294

Call Sign: K2VZ
Arima Iwase
55-651 Naniloa Loop

Laie HI 96762

Call Sign: KH6JDU
Izumi Soma
55-651 Naniloa Loop
Laie HI 96762

Call Sign: WH6KK
Willie H Kwansing
55-550 Naniloa Loop Apt
L220
Laie HI 96762

Call Sign: WH6XY
J Perry Christensen
55 550 Naniloa Lp 6153
Laie HI 96762

Call Sign: WH6CUP
Martha L Christensen
55 568 Naniloa Lp 9C
Laie HI 96762

Call Sign: WH7D
J Perry Christensen
55 568 Naniloa Lp 9C
Laie HI 96762

Call Sign: KH6BYU
Northeast Oahu Amat Rad
Group
55-568 Naniloa Lp 9C
Laie HI 96762

Call Sign: WH6AOW
Richard N Dennis
55-098 Naupaka St
Laie HI 96762

Call Sign: W0SGR
Harold E Blubaugh
55-099 Naupaka St
Laie HI 96762

Call Sign: KH7YU

Selina P Unga
55 124 Puuahi St
Laie HI 96762

Call Sign: KH7YV
Ofeina D Unga
55 124 Puuahi St
Laie HI 96762

Call Sign: WH6CUK
Nangkiba R Toaraa
Laie HI 96762

Call Sign: WH6DBN
Jared K L Lau
Laie HI 96762

FCC Amateur Radio License in Lanai City

Call Sign: KH6CED
Cedric P Urpanil Mr.
954 Fraser Ave
Lanai City HI 96763

Call Sign: KH6CPU
Cedric P Urpanil
Lanai City HI 96763

Call Sign: NH7PH
Hilary Lincoln
Lanai City HI 96763

Call Sign: NH7PI
Clarence K Lincoln
Lanai City HI 96763

Call Sign: WH6DUA
Francis R Hashii
Lanai City HI 96763

Call Sign: WH7JI
Cedric P Urpanil
Lanai City HI 96763

Call Sign: WH7TD
John Schaumburg
Lanai City HI 96763

Call Sign: WH7VT
Alton M Aoki
Lanai City HI 96763

Call Sign: WH7VY
Andrew De La Cruz
Lanai City HI 96763

FCC Amateur Radio License in Laupahoehoe

Call Sign: KB6QYH
Maureen E Fontaine
35-175 Kihalani
Homestead Rd
Laupahoehoe HI 96764

Call Sign: KD4GW
Claude R Fontaine Jr
35-175 Kihalani
Homestead Rd
Laupahoehoe HI 96764

Call Sign: KH6MEF
Maureen E Fontaine
35-175 Kihalani
Homestead Rd
Laupahoehoe HI 96764

Call Sign: KH6JRM
Russell R Roberts Jr
Laupahoehoe HI 96764

Call Sign: KH7XS
Big Island Contest Club
Laupahoehoe HI 96764

Call Sign: NH7GB
Bronson S Haunga
Laupahoehoe HI 96764

Call Sign: NH7GD
Laverne K Kaniho
Laupahoehoe HI 96764

Call Sign: NH7GM
Sallee Harrison
Laupahoehoe HI 96764

Call Sign: WH6DHU
Big Island Contest Club
Laupahoehoe HI 96764

Call Sign: WH6DHX
Mauna Kea Contest Club
Laupahoehoe HI 96764

FCC Amateur Radio License in Lawai

Call Sign: AH7P
Edward M Coan
4698E Akemama Rd
Lawai HI 96765

Call Sign: WH6CTV
Elpidio B Cardenas
3815 Kauhale Rd
Lawai HI 96765

Call Sign: KH7DL
Maverline M Gardner
4570 Kui Lei St
Lawai HI 96765

Call Sign: KE6NHI
Jane E Goldsmith
Lawai HI 96765

Call Sign: KH6G
Clarence A Gardner
Lawai HI 96765

Call Sign: KH7CY
Barbara S Coan
Lawai HI 96765

Call Sign: KH7LQ
David F Leong
Lawai HI 96765

Call Sign: KH7LR
Jonathan D Leong
Lawai HI 96765

Call Sign: KH7LS
Janelle A Leong
Lawai HI 96765

Call Sign: KH7LT
Jessica R Leong
Lawai HI 96765

Call Sign: NH6HB
Grace Y Leong
Lawai HI 96765

Call Sign: NH7CK
Grace Y Leong
Lawai HI 96765

Call Sign: NH7CO
Isaac H K Yoshimori
Lawai HI 96765

Call Sign: NH7EE
Myra J Rosare
Lawai HI 96765

Call Sign: NH7TZ
Jane E Goldsmith
Lawai HI 96765

Call Sign: WH6CUU
Michael A Cardenas
Lawai HI 96765

Call Sign: WH6DUX
Heather Prinzing
Lawai HI 96765

Call Sign: WH6DXA
Jeff P Dorough
Lawai HI 96765

Call Sign: WB7NYM
Richard L Hestad
Lawai HI 96765-0646

Call Sign: KH6HY
Alfred L Dickens
Lawai HI 96765-1110

Call Sign: KH7B
Clarence A Gardner
Lawai HI 96765

Call Sign: NH6HY
James L Miller
Lawai HI 96765

Call Sign: NH6VY
Edgar H Takabayashi
Lawai HI 96765

Call Sign: WH6BHD
Alan S Hironaka
Lawai HI 96765

FCC Amateur Radio License in Lawai Kanai

Call Sign: AH6CG
Lawai Amateur Radio
Association
Lawai Kauai HI 96765

Call Sign: NH7RR
Lawai Amateur Radio
Association
Lawai Kauai HI 96765

Call Sign: WH6CCK
Herbert T Miyazaki
Lawai Kauai HI 96765

Call Sign: WH6DGV
Lawai Amateur Radio
Association
Lawai Kauai HI 96765

Call Sign: WH6CCM
Jessie M Miyazaki
Lawai Kauai HI 96765

FCC Amateur Radio License in Lihue

Call Sign: NH7MW
Marvin C Agrade
2775 Aheahe St
Lihue HI 96766

Call Sign: KH6ESN
James S Uemura
3399 Ainakea St
Lihue HI 96766

Call Sign: NH7YS
Tad T Miura
3105 Akahi St
Lihue HI 96766

Call Sign: WH6ADY
Ronald L Victorino Jr
3894 Alala St
Lihue HI 96766

Call Sign: WH6DEO
Midway Atoll Amateur
Radio Club
C/O Lisa King USFWS
Lihue HI 96766-0099

Call Sign: WH6CNB
Deborah J Rudell
2728 Eleki Pl
Lihue HI 96766

Call Sign: KH7GV
James K Zaima Jr

General Delivery
Lihue HI 96766

Call Sign: NH7DI
Carey K Koide
1970 Hanalima St Apt
C105
Lihue HI 96766

Call Sign: WH6DOU
Christian N Ogawa
2090 Hanalima St Apt
Dd204
Lihue HI 96766

Call Sign: WH7HH
Robert W Hansmeier
1970 Hanalima St P205
Lihue HI 96766

Call Sign: WH6AJA
James W Amorin
Hanamaulu Kauai
Lihue HI 96715

Call Sign: KH6EOM
Bernaldo Ulanday Jr
4013 Hoohana St
Lihue HI 96766

Call Sign: KH6BFU
John S Botelho
4313 Hoohana St
Lihue HI 96766

Call Sign: NH6GQ
Barry T Miyasato
2840 Hoolako St
Lihue HI 96766

Call Sign: NH7CI
Barry T Miyasato
2840 Hoolako St
Lihue HI 96766

Call Sign: KH6RB
Dennis E Fukushima
2863 Hoolako St
Lihue HI 96766

Call Sign: WH7TX
Franklin D Kakazu
4396 Hopena St
Lihue HI 98766

Call Sign: KH6BCB
James I Takaki
3183 Iinouye St
Lihue HI 96766-1124

Call Sign: WH6YV
Ryan R Shintani
4290 Kailewa St
Lihue HI 96766

Call Sign: WH6CSH
Cheryl L Nickles
3231 Kalapaki Circle
Lihue HI 96766

Call Sign: WH6CSI
Andrew L Nickles
3231 Kalapaki Circle
Lihue HI 96766

Call Sign: NH7YN
David D Moraes
4560 Kalepa Cir 10
Lihue HI 96766

Call Sign: WB2SQW
John J Culliney Md
2940 Kanani St
Lihue HI 96766

Call Sign: WH6DQJ
Allison A Culliney
2940 Kanani St
Lihue HI 96766

Call Sign: WH7MD
John J Culliney Md
2940 Kanani St
Lihue HI 96766

Call Sign: WH7SN
Kelly M Culliney
2940 Kanani St
Lihue HI 96766

Call Sign: KH6GSS
Bruce H Inouye
2762 Kapena St
Lihue HI 96766

Call Sign: KH7CI
Billy R Richardson
4218 Kaulu Pl
Lihue HI 96766

Call Sign: WH6DGQ
Island School Radio Club
3-1875 Kaumua Lii Hwy
Lihue HI 96766

Call Sign: WH6DNU
Kauai Community College
Amateur Radio Club
Mar-01 Kaumualii Hwy
Lihue HI 96766

Call Sign: WH6DPG
Kauai Community College
Arc
3 1901 Kaumualii Hwy
Lihue HI 96766-9500

Call Sign: NH6GL
Carl D Schroeder
4245 Kole Pl
Lihue HI 96766

Call Sign: WH6DIH
Wilcox Memorial Hospital

Mar-20 Kuhio Highway
Ste B
Lihue HI 96766

Call Sign: WH6WH
Wilcox Memorial Hospital
Mar-20 Kuhio Highway
Ste B
Lihue HI 96766

Call Sign: KC7UJQ
Linda M Beer
3 3400 Kuhio Hwy A 406
Lihue HI 96766

Call Sign: WH7HU
Tom Neal
3 3400 Kuhio Hwy A401
Lihue HI 96766

Call Sign: WH6DTV
Richard F Etzel
3 3400 Kuhio Hwy C209
Lihue HI 96766

Call Sign: N4HSX
Annette C Smith
3 33400 Kuhio Hwy C408
Lihue HI 96766

Call Sign: N4HSW
David M Smith
Mar-00 Kuhio Hwy Sun
Village
Lihue HI 96766

Call Sign: WH6DPB
Shaun V Koide
4145 Mano St
Lihue HI 96766

Call Sign: WH7M
Midway Kure Dx
Foundation

Box 660099 Midway Isl
Stn 40
Lihue HI 96766-0099

Call Sign: NH7DL
Jeanne M Russell
2811 Mokoi St
Lihue HI 96766

Call Sign: WH6DXC
Jason E Nichols
2952 Ohi Ohi St 2
Lihue HI 96766

Call Sign: WH6BTK
John S Yamane
2932 Pikake St
Lihue HI 96766

Call Sign: WH6DOM
Manuel I Garcia
4355 Pohu St
Lihue HI 96766

Call Sign: WH6QT
Jan W Tenbruggencate
2878 Pua Nani St
Lihue HI 96766

Call Sign: WH6DOL
Dennis E Erskine
4121 Rice St 2510
Lihue HI 96766

Call Sign: KH6DLU
Ulderico Abreu
4121 Rice St Apt 207
Lihue HI 96766

Call Sign: AH6SH
Michael R Wheable
Lihue HI 96766

Call Sign: KC6GPY
Michael R Wheable

Lihue HI 96766

Call Sign: KD6VLT
Marshall Mac Cready
Lihue HI 96766

Call Sign: KH6CVJ
Ronald W Middag
Lihue HI 96766

Call Sign: KH6ECE
Kuniaki Shimauchi
Lihue HI 96766

Call Sign: KH6TH
Randy L Baab
Lihue HI 96766

Call Sign: KH7DT
Gavin L Reid
Lihue HI 96766

Call Sign: KH7TU
Kenneth D Thomas
Lihue HI 96766

Call Sign: NH6HR
Hawaiian Radio Dx Group
Lihue HI 96766

Call Sign: NH6JV
Gary M Morita
Lihue HI 96766

Call Sign: NH6SJ
Samuel M Shirai
Lihue HI 96766

Call Sign: NH7CQ
Steven H Schafer
Lihue HI 96766

Call Sign: NH7DF
Lloyd E Carey
Lihue HI 96766

Call Sign: NH7DG
Suzanne M Peters
Lihue HI 96766

Call Sign: NH7RD
Charles K Gazda
Lihue HI 96766

Call Sign: WB6CVJ
Ronald W Middag
Lihue HI 96766

Call Sign: WH6AKP
William N Rapozo
Lihue HI 96766

Call Sign: WH6CDM
Steven J Gates
Lihue HI 96766

Call Sign: WH6CFJ
Teofilo P Tacbian
Lihue HI 96766

Call Sign: WH6DGM
Hawaiian Radio Dx Group
Lihue HI 96766

Call Sign: WH6DOX
Duane A Samiano
Lihue HI 96766

Call Sign: WH6DPA
Sheldon T Chu
Lihue HI 96766

Call Sign: WH6DQP
Craig A Harwell
Lihue HI 96766

Call Sign: WH6EY
John D Martin
Lihue HI 96766

Call Sign: WH6QI
Michael S Kano
Lihue HI 96766

Call Sign: WH7HT
John R Mcintyre
Lihue HI 96766

Call Sign: WH7OO
Darren G Dzurilla
Lihue HI 96766

Call Sign: WH7SI
David W Bown
Lihue HI 96766

Call Sign: WH7SL
Carol J Claunch
Lihue HI 96766

Call Sign: WH7SM
Donald G Claunch
Lihue HI 96766

Call Sign: WH7UY
Darrel M Niitani
Lihue HI 96766

Call Sign: WH7VW
Sean Childers
Lihue HI 96766

Call Sign: WH7WG
Lisa L Kaaihue
Lihue HI 96766

Call Sign: WH7XC
James L Miller
Lihue HI 96766

Call Sign: KH6CZJ
Yoshitomi Kaihara
Lihue HI 96766-5871

Call Sign: WH6AP

Wilfred Espiritu
Lihue HI 96766

Call Sign: WH6CKA
W John Taylor
Lihue HI 96766

Call Sign: WH6GJ
Adlai H Hiraoka
Lihue HI 96766

Call Sign: WH7A
Dennis J Alkire
Lihue HI 96766

FCC Amateur Radio License in MCBH Kaneohe Bay

Call Sign: WH6DVU
J T Nixon
M C B H Kaneohe Bay HI 96863

FCC Amateur Radio License in Makaha

Call Sign: W6ARF
Ronald A Potter
84 510 Farrington Hwy 7
Makaha HI 96792-1950

Call Sign: KH6EZD
Curtis A Russell
84-456 Ikuone Pl
Makaha HI 96792

Call Sign: AH6TE
Thomas A Likos Jr
84 314 Makau St
Makaha HI 96792

Call Sign: WH6CWH
Healing Heart Foundation
Amateur Radio Club

84-683 Upena St
Makaha HI 96792

FCC Amateur Radio License in Makakilo

Call Sign: KH6JIK
Anthony Bessara IV
92 371 Akauka St
Makakilo HI 96707-1138

Call Sign: KH6JEH
Robert D Bessara
92 371 Akaula St
Makakilo HI 96707-1138

Call Sign: KH6JEO
Anthony Bessara III
92-371 Akaula St
Makakilo HI 96707

Call Sign: WH6BLY
Melissa R Bessara
92-371 Akaula St
Makakilo HI 96707

Call Sign: KH6JEJ
Peter L Bessara
92-371 Akaula St
Makakilo HI 96707-1138

Call Sign: WH6BXI
William M Ahkoi Jr
92-443 Akaula St
Makakilo HI 96707

Call Sign: NH6SC
Jerry P Shafer
92-608 Akaula St
Makakilo HI 96707

Call Sign: K4OHF
David M Bolender
92-7049 Elele St 40
Makakilo HI 96707

Call Sign: NH6X
Michio Ogawa
C/O Don N Sakai 92-111
Ho Ina Pl
Makakilo HI 96707

Call Sign: WH6OW
Thomas A Giguere
92-1161 Hoike Way
Makakilo HI 96707

Call Sign: KH7EK
James K Veomett
92 1322 Hunekai St
Makakilo HI 96707

Call Sign: WH6MG
Gregory F Polito
92-1017-56 Makakilo Dr
Makakilo HI 96707

Call Sign: WH6BLC
Roy F Bodnar Jr
92750 Nenelea St
Makakilo HI 96707

Call Sign: WH6KR
Jason F Agcaoili
92-751 Nohona St
Makakilo HI 96707

Call Sign: WH6GA
Donald R Bentz
92-1085 Painiu Pl
Makakilo HI 96707

Call Sign: WH6DK
Kelly A Collins
92-1085 Painiu Pl
Makakilo HI 96707

Call Sign: AH6DC
David L Kirby
92-910 Panana St

Makakilo HI 96707

FCC Amateur Radio License in Makana

Call Sign: NH6CT
Thomas A Likos Jr
84 314 Makau St
Makana HI 96792

Call Sign: WH6DJR
Thomas A Likos Jr
84 314 Makau St
Makana HI 96792

FCC Amateur Radio License in Makawao

Call Sign: NH6H
David H Judd
220 Alalani St
Makawao HI 96768

Call Sign: WH6CDP
Kathleen D Notestone
59 Alapio Pl
Makawao HI 96768

Call Sign: WH6DIZ
Paul K Kaneshiro
38 Alea Pl
Makawao HI 96768

Call Sign: WH6DAP
David F Schlicher
1465 Baldwin Ave
Makawao HI 96768

Call Sign: WH6IH
Mark B Macanas
3491 Burns Pl
Makawao HI 96768

Call Sign: WH6VD
Henry P Vendiola

10 C Ai St
Makawao HI 96768

Call Sign: WH6SC
Thomas J Zaccagnini
51 E Keala Loa
Makawao HI 96768

Call Sign: KH7FY
James L Murray
519 E Olinda Rd
Makawao HI 96768

Call Sign: WH6DMG
Anthony E Balag
123 Ikea Pl
Makawao HI 96768

Call Sign: WH7UL
Edwin C Barrett III
2775 Iolani St
Makawao HI 96768

Call Sign: WH6XE
Keenan K Enfield
438 Kaiaulu Lp
Makawao HI 96768

Call Sign: N0HYA
Terry W Tanner
162 Kapuahi St
Makawao HI 96768

Call Sign: WH6TK
Richard W Clayton
255 Kaualani Dr
Makawao HI 96768

Call Sign: WH6CZE
Wayland D C Kam
798 Kaulona St
Makawao HI 96768

Call Sign: KH6AIQ
Takashi Kamasaki

661 Lea Pl
Makawao HI 96768

Call Sign: KD7HCU
Thatcher E Deane
2860 A Liholani St
Makawao HI 96768

Call Sign: WH7XS
Daryl F Lemm
80 Makani Rd
Makawao HI 96768

Call Sign: WH6DWI
Albert G Fleming
71 Makawao Ave Unit 2
Makawao HI 96768

Call Sign: KH7ZT
Gretchen D Cardoso
745 Onipaa Pl
Makawao HI 96768

Call Sign: KF6LWN
James Mann
P.O. Box 1630
Makawao HI 96768

Call Sign: KF6LYU
Melinda A Mann
P.O. Box 1630
Makawao HI 96768

Call Sign: WH7XW
James Mann
P.O. Box 1630
Makawao HI 96768

Call Sign: KH6HHG
Stanley T Yamato
1078 Ukiu Rd
Makawao HI 96768-1017

Call Sign: AH6SZ
Thatcher E Deane

1091 Ulele St
Makawao HI 96768

Call Sign: KH6XM
Douglas Dragon
Makawao HI 96768

Call Sign: KH7FX
Robert C Murdoch
Makawao HI 96768

Call Sign: NH7ED
Randall J Eneim
Makawao HI 96768

Call Sign: WH6CTQ
Ross S Trivas
Makawao HI 96768

Call Sign: WH6DUB
Amanda L Schaefer
Makawao HI 96768

Call Sign: WH6DUE
Devin Sylva
Makawao HI 96768

Call Sign: WH6NL
Frank Ford
Makawao HI 96768

Call Sign: NH7DT
Annie R Hill
Makawao HI 96768-1648

Call Sign: NH7DS
Barry H Hill
Makawao HI 96768-1648

Call Sign: NH6TE
Perry L Kunin
Makawao HI 96768-1797

Call Sign: WH6GI
Ryan P Resquer

Makawao HI 96769

FCC Amateur Radio License in Maui

Call Sign: AH6OQ
Tatsuo Naito
Haiku
Maui HI 96708

Call Sign: KB5DNY
Altus W Plunkett
2811 Liholani St 12
Pukalani
Maui HI 96768

Call Sign: WH7HL
Ruddy J Bareng
3357 Old Haleakala Hwy
Pukalani
Maui HI 96768

Call Sign: KH6ADR
Kapalua Dx Club
Villa 31B-1 500 Bay Dr
Kapalua
Maui HI 96761

FCC Amateur Radio License in Maunaloa

Call Sign: K9FD
Mervyn D Schweigert
1650 Kaluakoi Rd
Maunaloa HI 96770

Call Sign: KH7C
Mervyn D Schweigert
1650 Kaluakoi Rd
Maunaloa HI 96770

Call Sign: K9FD
Mervyn D Schweigert
Maunaloa HI 96770

Call Sign: K9FD
Mervyn D Schweigert
Maunaloa HI 96770

Call Sign: KE6QQ
Paul J Mullin
Maunaloa HI 96770

Call Sign: KH6JJ
Mervyn D Schweigert
Maunaloa HI 96770

Call Sign: WH6TT
George E Huizinga
Maunaloa HI 96770

Call Sign: WH7QQ
Paul J Mullin
Maunaloa HI 96770

**FCC Amateur Radio
License in Mililani**

Call Sign: WH7ES
Perry K Nihi
94-074 Aaahi Pl
Mililani HI 96789

Call Sign: NH6UW
Alberta T Valdez Ms.
94-295 A'Aahi St
Mililani HI 96789

Call Sign: WH6DMW
Christopher Valdez
95-1002 Aahu St
Mililani HI 96789

Call Sign: NH7WK
Albert A Pascua
95-202 Aelike Pl
Mililani HI 96789

Call Sign: WH6CWT
Stephen S Sung

94 1025 Ahahui Pl
Mililani HI 96789

Call Sign: WH6DND
James L Flynn
95-265 Alaalaa Lp
Mililani HI 96789

Call Sign: WA7HCA
Barry D Nupen
94 463 Alapoai St
Mililani HI 96789

Call Sign: KH6MLD
Michael L Datuin
95-324 Alo Pl
Mililani HI 96789

Call Sign: WH6DUR
Michael L Datuin
95-324 Alo Pl
Mililani HI 96789

Call Sign: NH7OX
Michael A Tamamoto
95-655 Alohilani St
Mililani HI 96789

Call Sign: WH7LJ
Michael C Spencer
94 321 Alula Pl
Mililani HI 96789

Call Sign: KH6JM
Milton Cortez
94-1020 Anania Cir 76
Mililani HI 96789-2046

Call Sign: WH6BZX
Wilfred M Komine
94 412 Anania Dr
Mililani HI 96789

Call Sign: KH6TG
Anthony S Gannon

94-333 Anania Dr Apt 27
Mililani HI 96789

Call Sign: WH6DRY
Anthony S Gannon
94-333 Anania Dr Apt 27
Mililani HI 96789

Call Sign: WH6DTR
Anthony S Gannon
94-333 Anania Dr Apt 27
Mililani HI 96789

Call Sign: WH6DLS
Jason A Taglianetti
94-165 Apele Pl
Mililani HI 96789

Call Sign: AH6QI
Garner C Mihata
95-216 Aua Pl
Mililani HI 96789

Call Sign: WH6DSJ
Stanley R Mull
95-111 Auina St
Mililani HI 96789

Call Sign: WH6DRQ
Dody M Viquelia
95-541 Awiki St
Mililani HI 96789

Call Sign: KA4INK
John A Carr
94-263 Awiwi Pl
Mililani HI 96789-1809

Call Sign: KH7YH
Wayne Y Matsumoto
95 1040 Eulu St
Mililani HI 96789

Call Sign: NH7VM
Richie I Mitsumoto

95-1043 Haakualiki St
Mililani HI 96789

94 370 Hokuili Pl
Mililani HI 96789

95-1035 Hookanahe St
Mililani HI 96789

Call Sign: KH6RM
Joseph F Curado
95-295 Hakupokano Lp
Mililani HI 96789

Call Sign: NH6F
William F Slocomb
94 426 Hokuili St
Mililani HI 96789

Call Sign: NH6K
Robert W Jones
95-1029 Hookowa St
Mililani HI 96789

Call Sign: WH6CGD
Victor K K Pang
95-136 Hamumu Pl
Mililani HI 96789-2868

Call Sign: WH6QJ
Victor G Gustafson
94-233 Hokulewa Loop
Mililani HI 96789-2322

Call Sign: AH6P
Dennis K Yee
95 1078 Hookupu St
Mililani HI 96789

Call Sign: WH6DML
Victor K K Pang
95-136 Hamumu Pl
Mililani HI 96789-2868

Call Sign: WH6FS
Matthew W R Ho
94-421 Hokulewa Pl
Mililani HI 96789

Call Sign: KH7LD
Dennis K Yee
95 1078 Hookupu St
Mililani HI 96789

Call Sign: KH6Y
Robert H Snyder
95-617 Hinalii St
Mililani HI 96789

Call Sign: WH6CES
Florie R Hintze
94-423 Hokuli St
Mililani HI 96789

Call Sign: WH7XI
Michael A Koochi
95-212 Hooni Pl
Mililani HI 96789

Call Sign: KH6JWL
Dale W Goodin
94-470 Hokuala St
Mililani HI 96789

Call Sign: KH7FR
Toby L Clairmont
94 566 Holaniku St
Mililani HI 96789

Call Sign: WH7IF
Dan M Suehiro
94-151 Ihuanu Way
Mililani HI 96789

Call Sign: WH6DKH
Ruth Masuda
4-344 Hokuala St Apt 114
Mililani HI 96789

Call Sign: KH7GC
Susan K Clairmont
94 566 Holaniku St
Mililani HI 96789

Call Sign: NH6SB
David O Jaictin
94-243 Ihumoe Pl
Mililani HI 96789

Call Sign: KH6BTS
Santos Padilla
94 419 Hokuhele Pl
Mililani HI 96789-2341

Call Sign: WH7AI
Richard E Yenke
95-1033 Hololani St
Mililani HI 96789

Call Sign: KH6ILO
James R Swain
95 389 Ikaloa St
Mililani HI 96789

Call Sign: WH6BTH
Estrellita A Padilla
94 419 Hokuhele Pl
Mililani HI 96789-2341

Call Sign: KH7XD
Leland A Nakai
95-1021 Hookanahe St
Mililani HI 96789

Call Sign: NH6LK
Julie A Ariola
95 1023 Kaapeha St 55
Mililani HI 96789

Call Sign: AH7V
Bert Y Ikezawa

Call Sign: NH7VN
Neal P Detwiler

Call Sign: WL7CKD
Ray A Mottley

95-1045 Kahakiki St
Mililani HI 96789

94-174 Kapuahi Pl
Mililani HI 96789

94-256 Keaolani St
Mililani HI 96789

Call Sign: WH7CJ
Jason Fujinaka
95-1069 Kahakiki St
Mililani HI 96789

Call Sign: KH6DM
Timothy L Kolb
94364 Kapuahi St Apt 59
Mililani HI 96789

Call Sign: KH6DAD
Richard D Fewell
94-256 Keaolani St
Mililani HI 96789

Call Sign: NH6YD
Pamela L Fowler
95-322 Kahikinui Ct 230
Mililani HI 96789

Call Sign: WH6CTG
Carrie M Oliveira
94 659 Kauakapuu Loop
Mililani HI 96789

Call Sign: WH7BP
Bryan A Fewell
94-256 Keaolani St
Mililani HI 96789

Call Sign: WH6CRB
John P Newell
95-019 Kahoea St 151
Mililani HI 96789

Call Sign: WA8WNR
John W Camery
94-647 Kauakapuu Loop
Mililani HI 96789-1832

Call Sign: WH7BQ
Richard D Fewell
94-256 Keaolani St
Mililani HI 96789

Call Sign: KH6TB
Melvin H Yoshioka
94 260 Kaholo St
Mililani HI 96789

Call Sign: WH6UQ
Wendy F Nakano
95-735 Kauanomeha Pl
Mililani HI 96789

Call Sign: KH7YJ
Victor B Mattox
94-427 Keaoopua St 160
Mililani HI 96789

Call Sign: WH6DUL
Mario Alvarez
94-405 Kaholo St 93
Mililani HI 96789

Call Sign: WH7GE
Arnold R Schulmeister
95-477 Kaulia Pl
Mililani HI 96789

Call Sign: WH6BXW
Jody A Abalos
94-416 Keaoopua St 53D
Mililani HI 96789

Call Sign: WH6DJZ
Douglas Pang
95-326 Kaloapau St 132
Mililani HI 96789

Call Sign: KH7RS
Richard I Senones
95 161 Kauopae Pl
Mililani HI 96789

Call Sign: NH6QK
Kurt M Yamaguchi
94-416 Keaoopua St 53D
Mililani HI 96789

Call Sign: WH6CJF
Gary K L Von
94-125 Kamaio Pl
Mililani HI 96789

Call Sign: WH6LW
George J Massad
94-430 Kauopua St
Mililani HI 96789

Call Sign: NH6TI
Bruce E West
94 434 Keaoopua St Apt
38A
Mililani HI 96789-2283

Call Sign: WH6JE
Douglas H Kaanehe
95-264 Kaopua Loop
Mililani HI 96789-1245

Call Sign: WH6DRR
Leland M Yagi
94-164 Keaolani St
Mililani HI 96789

Call Sign: WH6CXY
J Martin Pahinui
94 434 Keaoopua St
Apt38B
Mililani HI 96789

Call Sign: WH6DRL
Phyllis H Scott-Clark

Call Sign: KH6BRY
Bryan A Fewell

Call Sign: NH7XQ
Daniel M Buckheit
94-366 Keehuhiwa St
Mililani HI 96789

Call Sign: NH7AJ
Stephen D Fry
94 376 Kiapaakai Pl
Mililani HI 96789

Call Sign: WH6IN
Robin B Perez
94-419 Kilani St
Mililani HI 96789

Call Sign: WH7PB
Ralph E Cruz Jr
95-671 Kilohoku St
Mililani HI 96789

Call Sign: WH6DSU
Shane A Smythe
95-153 Kipapa Dr 534
Mililani HI 96789

Call Sign: AE4MO
Raymond Oropesa
95-169 Kippa Dr Apt12
Mililani HI 96789

Call Sign: AH6TY
Raymond Oropesa
95-169 Kippa Dr Apt12
Mililani HI 96789

Call Sign: WH6DKA
Andrew Padilla
95-1139 Koolani Dr 122
Mililani HI 96789

Call Sign: WH6AAK
Daniel E Slocum
95-1067 Koolani Dr Apt
346
Mililani HI 96789-5998

Call Sign: NH6OL
Victor N Askman
95 455 Kuahelani Ave 102
Mililani HI 96789

Call Sign: NH7RS
Richard F Strimel
94-165 Kuahelani Ave 177
Mililani HI 96789

Call Sign: W5DY
Henry Wilkens III
95-146 Kuahelani Ave Apt
262
Mililani HI 96789

Call Sign: NH6XK
Dean S Frazier
94-567 Kuaie St
Mililani HI 96789

Call Sign: NH6ZI
Reef A Amano
94-583 Kuaie St
Mililani HI 96789

Call Sign: WB2JYW
Nancy E Chun
94-633 Kuaie St
Mililani HI 96789

Call Sign: WH6DNJ
Owen H Matsunaga
95-501 Kuanoni Way
Mililani HI 96789

Call Sign: KH6SK
Stephen S Kawamae
95-1054 Kuauli St 187
Mililani HI 96789

Call Sign: WH6DWT
Stephen S Kawamae
95-1054 Kuauli St 187

Mililani HI 96789

Call Sign: NH6AS
Derek Y Kajihiro
95 1021 Kuauli St Apt 115
Mililani HI 96789-4942

Call Sign: NH7AI
Derek Y Kajihiro
95 1021 Kuauli St Apt 115
Mililani HI 96789-4942

Call Sign: N3VBS
Terry R Howard
94-1049 Lahe St
Mililani HI 96789

Call Sign: NH7VO
Brian K Carvalho
95-1024 Lahui St
Mililani HI 96789

Call Sign: KH6LV
Keith T Nishimura
95 1008 Lalai St
Mililani HI 96789

Call Sign: KH7JF
Erwin M Soares
95 1115 Lalai St
Mililani HI 96789

Call Sign: KH7XI
John J Dorsey
94 427 Lanikuhan Pl
Mililani HI 96789

Call Sign: KH7ET
Geoffrey H Kimak
94-433 Lanikuhana Pl
1120
Mililani HI 96789

Call Sign: NH6C
Philip P Quinn

45-645 Lau Awa St
Mililani HI 96789-2929

Call Sign: WH7QJ
Brian Fukuhara
95-094 Lauaki Pl
Mililani HI 96789

Call Sign: KH7AT
Kevin Y O Kong
95 652 Lauawa St
Mililani HI 96789

Call Sign: NH6DO
Kurtis T Mabe
95 117 Lelewalo St
Mililani HI 96789-3719

Call Sign: NH7BG
Kurtis T Mabe
95 117 Lelewalo St
Mililani HI 96789-3719

Call Sign: WH6KM
Kurtis T Mabe
95 117 Lelewalo St
Mililani HI 96789-3719

Call Sign: KH6CVO
David M Rodrigues
95-1107 Leolani St
Mililani HI 96789

Call Sign: NH6DL
Timothy K Hurley
95-1014 Lokalia St
Mililani HI 96789

Call Sign: KH6TO
Michael M Sato
95-389 Lonomea St
Mililani HI 96789

Call Sign: AH6MF
Kimitaka Kamiya

C/O Ama 95-1050 Maka
Ikai St Ap 23G
Mililani HI 96789

Call Sign: KH6PZ
James M Kataoka
95 1050 Makaikai St Apt
8J
Mililani HI 96789

Call Sign: KH6MO
Noboru Matsunaga
94-116 Makapipipi St
Mililani HI 96789

Call Sign: WH6DCA
Stephen D Fry
95 721 Makaunulau St
Mililani HI 96789

Call Sign: KH6PA
Troy D Griffin Jr
95-730 Makaunulau St
Mililani HI 96789-2832

Call Sign: WH7G
Troy D Griffin Jr
95-730 Makaunulau St
Mililani HI 96789-2832

Call Sign: WH7PA
Troy D Griffin Jr
95-730 Makaunulau St
Mililani HI 96789-2832

Call Sign: NH7VP
Sean R Kamai
94-531 Makohilani St
1023
Mililani HI 96789

Call Sign: NH6AV
Stephen D Fry
94 528 Maukuku Pl
Mililani HI 96789

Call Sign: WH7TL
Thomas D Bookman
94-940 Meheula Parkway
149
Mililani HI 96789

Call Sign: WH7IR
Peter S Fornek
94-755 Meheula Pkwy
13B
Mililani HI 96789

Call Sign: W8DS
Richard F Strimel
94-741 Meheula Pkwy
20C
Mililani HI 96789

Call Sign: WD5FNX
Judy A Strimel
94-741 Meheula Pky 20C
Mililani HI 96789

Call Sign: NH6KW
Vincent T Soeda
95-204 Milia Pl
Mililani HI 96789

Call Sign: KD5TBQ
Thomas D Ferstl
95-100 Moenamanu St 457
Mililani HI 96789

Call Sign: WH7BE
Roland T Coelho
94-548 Mulehn St
Mililani HI 96789

Call Sign: NH7PB
Blaine T Murakami
94-441 Nui St
Mililani HI 96789

Call Sign: WH7CL

Terry S Yonamine
95-205 Pahiku Pl
Mililani HI 96789

Call Sign: KH6EJZ
Christopher G Harrison
95 130 Paia Pl
Mililani HI 96789-2857

Call Sign: WH6CKP
Lynne R Harrison
95 130 Paia Pl
Mililani HI 96789-2857

Call Sign: WH6CBA
Paul P Peterson
95-807 Paikauhale St
Mililani HI 96789

Call Sign: N3TEC
Barbara A Mason
95-894 Paikauhale St
Mililani HI 96789-2879

Call Sign: KH6IIC
Peter A Harada
94-178 Paionia Pl
Mililani HI 96789

Call Sign: KH6JJF
Edith M Harada
94-178 Paionia Pl
Mililani HI 96789

Call Sign: NH6VC
Ann P Scheller
94-108 Puanane Loop
Mililani HI 96789

Call Sign: AH6IM
Daniel W Miyashiro
94-386 Punono St
Mililani HI 96789

Call Sign: NH6RY

Patricia K Miyashiro
94-386 Punono St
Mililani HI 96789

Call Sign: WH6EK
Chris A Akahoshi
95-1021 Ulahea St
Mililani HI 96789

Call Sign: WH6ER
William P Harrington
95-370 Waialpi
Mililani HI 96789

Call Sign: NH7WL
Joseph F Hunkler
95-227 Waikalani Dr A
703
Mililani HI 96789

Call Sign: NH7IU
Kurt A Daniels
95-227 Waikalani Dr A807
Mililani HI 96789

Call Sign: KE2FM
Ronald A Amrhein Sr
95 269 Waikalani Dr C
205
Mililani HI 96789

Call Sign: WH6CPH
Gilbert Cera
95-2044 Waikalani Pl
Mililani HI 96789

Call Sign: WH6CGB
Regan Eltagonde
95-2048 Waikalani Pl Apt
205D
Mililani HI 96789

Call Sign: WH6DRF
Joycelyn D Kea
95-176 Wailawa St

Mililani HI 96789

Call Sign: NH6RX
Wendell W Perry Mr
95 545 Wailoa Loop
Mililani HI 96789-1406

Call Sign: AH6OO
Norman K De Sellem
94-316 Waimaka St
Mililani HI 96789

Call Sign: W5EEK
Norman K De Sellem
94-316 Waimaka St
Mililani HI 96789

Call Sign: KM6VF
Stephen L Osterday
95-255 Waioleka St 78
Mililani HI 96789

Call Sign: WH6CDZ
Dean Y Nakamatsu
95-330 Waioni St
Mililani HI 96789

Call Sign: WH6CEA
Cheryl F Nakamatsu
95-330 Waioni St
Mililani HI 96789

Call Sign: WH6CEB
Avis N Nakamatsu
95-330 Waioni St
Mililani HI 96789

Call Sign: KH6CWM
Joe Y Nakamatsu
95-330 Waloni St
Mililani HI 96789

Call Sign: WH6FW
Paul W Dale
95-107 Wekiu Pl

Mililani HI 96789

Call Sign: WH7SE
Courtney T Britt
95-968 Wikao St Apt
H101
Mililani HI 96789

Call Sign: WH7SF
Maevlyn A Britt
95-968 Wikao St Apt
H101
Mililani HI 96789

Call Sign: NH7NM
Edward R Chavez
95-797 Wikao St B206
Mililani HI 96789

Call Sign: KH7PV
Roy W Dahlin
94 56 Z Kiilani St
Mililani HI 96789

Call Sign: AH6QP
Theresa Hp Kuehu
Mililani HI 96789

Call Sign: KB7QEE
Duane V Stadden
Mililani HI 96789

Call Sign: KH6KD
Michael A Bacon
Mililani HI 96789

Call Sign: KH7LC
Milton Y Migita
Mililani HI 96789

Call Sign: KH7MO
Shelly A Migita
Mililani HI 96789

Call Sign: KH7QZ

Jenny C Migita
Mililani HI 96789

Call Sign: KH7TO
Bethany A Gustavus
Mililani HI 96789

Call Sign: WH6DKU
Dwight T Au
Mililani HI 96789

Call Sign: WH7QN
Yvette P Stalker
Mililani HI 96789

**FCC Amateur Radio
License in Mililani Town**

Call Sign: WH6JC
John Langman
95-174 Alaalaa Loop
Mililani Town HI 96789

Call Sign: WH6BXS
Robert Y Fujimoto Jr
95 1034 C Ainamakua Dr
Mililani Town HI 96789

Call Sign: WH6MV
Michael F Spengel
95-630 Hanile St G101
Mililani Town HI 96789

Call Sign: KH6VN
Douglas S M Fukunaga
94-496 Hokuala
Mililani Town HI 96789

Call Sign: NH6RZ
Raymond E Nawrocki
94-469 Hokuala St
Mililani Town HI 96789

Call Sign: WH6HH
Magdalina V Nawrocki

94-469 Hokuala St
Mililani Town HI 96789

Call Sign: WH6CAV
Melissa A Padilla
94-419 Hokuhele Pl
Mililani Town HI 96789

Call Sign: KH6GFQ
Henry S Yamamoto
94-409 Hokulewa Pl
Mililani Town HI 96789

Call Sign: KH6JOI
Raymond H Hasegawa
95-152 Kahela St
Mililani Town HI 96789

Call Sign: WH6CAB
Tammy K Hasegawa
95-152 Kahela St
Mililani Town HI 96789

Call Sign: KH6PO
Paul W Wolfgang
95-174 Kahela St
Mililani Town HI 96789

Call Sign: KG6SC
Clarence E Takeuchi
95-126 Kuahelani Ave
Mililani Town HI 96789

Call Sign: AH6RD
Rodney D Ching
95 698 Lewanuu St
Mililani Town HI 96789

Call Sign: KH7ZG
Rodney D Ching
95 698 Lewanuu St
Mililani Town HI 96789

Call Sign: WH6NO
Lori S Ikeda

95333 Lonomea
Mililani Town HI 96789

Call Sign: KH7RP
William A Javier
95 230 Waidleka St 37
Mililani Town HI 96789

Call Sign: NH6OF
Arnold K Yamashita
Mililani Town HI 96789

FCC Amateur Radio License in Molokai

Call Sign: WH6CYG
Wayde H Lee
Molokai HI 96748

Call Sign: WH6CHB
David E Robins
Molokai HI 96748

FCC Amateur Radio License in Mountain View

Call Sign: NH6DZ
Susan J Parker
General Delivery
Mountain View HI 96771

Call Sign: NH7BJ
Susan J Parker
General Delivery
Mountain View HI 96771

Call Sign: NH7IQ
Susan J Parker
General Delivery
Mountain View HI 96771

Call Sign: WH7CV
Douglas J Wingate
General Delivery

Mountain View HI 96771

Call Sign: WH7DW
Douglas J Wingate
General Delivery
Mountain View HI 96771

Call Sign: N5DEF
Delilah R Anderson
184065 Maunakea Aloha
Estates
Mountain View HI 96771

Call Sign: KH7WF
Diane N Phillips
Mountain View HI 96771

Call Sign: NH7WO
Philip C Clemmer
Mountain View HI 96771

Call Sign: WH6DI
Donald M Riding
Mountain View HI 96771

Call Sign: WH6HQ
Samuel A Miller
Mountain View HI 96771

Call Sign: WH6JR
Matthew C Clemmer
Mountain View HI 96771

Call Sign: WH6JX
Kenji J Clemmer
Mountain View HI 96771

Call Sign: WH6KY
Phullis Y Clemmer
Mountain View HI 96771

Call Sign: WH6YY
Scott I Uehara
Mountain View HI 96771

Call Sign: WH7VQ
Daniel M Miller
Mountain View HI 96771

Call Sign: KC5KV
Rayburn J Anderson
Mountain View HI 96771

Call Sign: AH6GG
Christopher M Stewart
Mountain View HI 96771

Call Sign: WH7VR
Michael K Miller
Mountain View HI 96771-
0111

Call Sign: KH6FI
Fred N Benardella
Mountain View HI 96771-
0729

Call Sign: WA2HFI
Fred N Benardella
Mountain View HI 96771-
0729

Call Sign: KH7LK
Gerald J Peterson
Mountain View HI 96771-
1294

Call Sign: WH6AE
Alan P Fifield
Mountain View HI 96771

Call Sign: WH6NC
G Neil Merwyn
Mountain View HI 96771

FCC Amateur Radio License in Naalehu

Call Sign: WH6CQN
Cynthia Baji

84 Lokelani St
Naalehu HI 96772

Call Sign: WH6DPI
Joshua Lunz
931206 Southpoint Rd
Naalehu HI 96772

Call Sign: NH7PL
Patrick L Stallcup
Naalehu HI 96772

Call Sign: KB6PKF
Candace A Prairie
Naalehu HI 96772

Call Sign: N6OKZ
Steven R Prairie
Naalehu HI 96772

Call Sign: NH6DU
Charles L Horan
Naalehu HI 96772

Call Sign: NH6LH
Paul N Sears
Naalehu HI 96772

Call Sign: NH7UM
Lowell D Lawton
Naalehu HI 96772

Call Sign: WH6DDU
Jason M Tonini
Naalehu HI 96772

Call Sign: WH6DIU
Bryant D Malepe
Naalehu HI 96772

Call Sign: WH6DPH
Leilani M Desmond
Naalehu HI 96772

Call Sign: WH7DF

Steven P Cunha
Naalehu HI 96772

Call Sign: WH7DP
Ladd K Hashimoto
Naalehu HI 96772

Call Sign: WH7PY
William E Forster
Naalehu HI 96772

Call Sign: WH7SG
Maribel C Julian
Naalehu HI 96772

Call Sign: WH7UX
James E Powell
Naalehu HI 96772

Call Sign: WH7YZ
Tyler P Amaral
Naalehu HI 96772

Call Sign: WH7ZG
William B Oxener
Naalehu HI 96772

Call Sign: WH7ZK
Kamaki S Fujikawa
Naalehu HI 96772

Call Sign: KF6GYM
Jeff A Cathrow
Naalehu HI 96772

Call Sign: NH7JT
Michael L Last
Naalehu HI 96772-0291

Call Sign: WH6DFP
Ross K Esperon Jr
Naalehu HI 96772-0342

Call Sign: KH6CA
Cherub W Akin

Naalehu HI 96772-0652

Call Sign: KH6TA
Thomas A Akin
Naalehu HI 96772-0652

Call Sign: WH6CQG
Joseph Apo
Naalehu HI 96772

Call Sign: KH6DC
Ken K Miyahara
Naalehu HI 96772

Call Sign: WH6HC
Wade K Baji Sr
Naalehu HI 96772

Call Sign: WH6Q
John L Horan
Naalehu HI 96772

FCC Amateur Radio License in Nanakuli

Call Sign: KH6CCV
Michael T Yamanoha
87-288 Maia St
Nanakuli HI 96792

FCC Amateur Radio License in Ninole

Call Sign: AH6FO
Hermanus B Jansen
Ninole HI 96773

Call Sign: AH6V
Jeremy J Storm
Ninole HI 96773

Call Sign: KH7SO
David R Broyles
Ninole HI 96773

Call Sign: WH6DAT
Denise A Foster
Ninole HI 96773

FCC Amateur Radio License in Ocean View

Call Sign: WH6DPK
Wenhui Yang
92-8363 Bamboo Ln
Ocean View HI 96737

Call Sign: NH6ID
Linda F Nelson
92-8489 Bamboo Ln
Ocean View HI 96737

Call Sign: NH6I
Norman B Nelson Jr
92-8489 Bamboo Ln
Ocean View HI 96737-
6072

Call Sign: WH7DO
Justin S Santos
Ocean View HI 96735

Call Sign: AH6BP
Donald H Mc Gwin
Ocean View HI 96737

Call Sign: AH6L
Michael A Linnolt
Ocean View HI 96737

Call Sign: KA1AFJ
Daniel S Durgin
Ocean View HI 96737

Call Sign: KH6AFJ
Daniel S Durgin
Ocean View HI 96737

Call Sign: KH6EL
Earl Laver

Ocean View HI 96737

Call Sign: KH6JQM
Michael J Morrow
Ocean View HI 96737

Call Sign: KH6RC
Randy Vanleeuwen
Ocean View HI 96737

Call Sign: KH6TS
Teddi Stransky
Ocean View HI 96737

Call Sign: KH7RW
Christopher S Freeman
Ocean View HI 96737

Call Sign: NH6WH
Robert G Riechel
Ocean View HI 96737

Call Sign: NH7DQ
Richard Flint
Ocean View HI 96737

Call Sign: NH7FJ
John R Thibadeaux
Ocean View HI 96737

Call Sign: NH7NB
Elizabeth N Kuluwaimaka
Ocean View HI 96737

Call Sign: NH7NV
Dennis J Leiser
Ocean View HI 96737

Call Sign: NH7OG
Robert K C Punihaole
Ocean View HI 96737

Call Sign: NH7OK
Mack D Goddard
Ocean View HI 96737

Call Sign: NH7RP
Stepehn E Graham
Ocean View HI 96737

Call Sign: NH7SC
David E Ward
Ocean View HI 96737

Call Sign: NH7UB
William H Kinney
Ocean View HI 96737

Call Sign: NH7WM
Janice L
Keihanaikukauakahihu
Ocean View HI 96737

Call Sign: NH7XK
Earl Laver
Ocean View HI 96737

Call Sign: WH6CPL
Elizabeth N Kuluwaimaka
Ocean View HI 96737

Call Sign: WH6DPJ
Wenjing Yang
Ocean View HI 96737

Call Sign: WH6FC
Richard O Ward
Ocean View HI 96737

Call Sign: WH6HD
Melvin R Kuluwaimaka Sr
Ocean View HI 96737

Call Sign: WH7BS
Dee P Hawk
Ocean View HI 96737

Call Sign: WH7DM
Randy Vanleeuwen
Ocean View HI 96737

Call Sign: WH7DQ
Rudolph H Kaupu
Ocean View HI 96737

Call Sign: WH7DS
Gary Kastle
Ocean View HI 96737

Call Sign: WH7DT
Ryan M Kastle
Ocean View HI 96737

Call Sign: WH7DU
Mary E Kastle
Ocean View HI 96737

Call Sign: WH7DV
Earl D Kemmer
Ocean View HI 96737

Call Sign: WH7DZ
Anthony R Colombo
Ocean View HI 96737

Call Sign: WH7EA
David H Mc Elhaney
Ocean View HI 96737

Call Sign: WH7EB
Loren H Heck
Ocean View HI 96737

Call Sign: WH7EC
Teddi Stransky
Ocean View HI 96737

Call Sign: WH7ED
Aaron Puou
Ocean View HI 96737

Call Sign: WH7EE
Rell M Woodward
Ocean View HI 96737

Call Sign: WH7EF
George R Hershberger
Ocean View HI 96737

Call Sign: WH7EG
Robert E Barry
Ocean View HI 96737

Call Sign: WH7FE
Linda K Somers
Ocean View HI 96737

Call Sign: WH7FH
Madalyn K Mc White
Lamson
Ocean View HI 96737

Call Sign: WH7FI
Robin L Lamson
Ocean View HI 96737

Call Sign: WH7FK
Anne M Williamson
Ocean View HI 96737

Call Sign: WH7FL
Beverly A Byouk
Ocean View HI 96737

Call Sign: WH7GO
Beatrice L Bowman
Ocean View HI 96737

Call Sign: WH7GP
Natalie A Edgerton
Ocean View HI 96737

Call Sign: WH7GV
Merilyn J Humphrey
Ocean View HI 96737

Call Sign: WH7GWK
Gary Kastle
Ocean View HI 96737

Call Sign: WH7MEK
Mary E Kastle
Ocean View HI 96737

Call Sign: WH7MK
Robert A Pennington
Ocean View HI 96737

Call Sign: WH7OK
Philip E Kuss
Ocean View HI 96737

Call Sign: WH7OL
Linda M Laws-Kuss
Ocean View HI 96737

Call Sign: WH7OM
Hannah G Uribes
Ocean View HI 96737

Call Sign: WH7ON
Evelyn L Thompson
Ocean View HI 96737

Call Sign: WH7QW
Alan G Clark
Ocean View HI 96737

Call Sign: NH7LR
Melvin O Roddenberg
Ocean View HI 96737

Call Sign: WH6BTJ
John S Elhard
Ocean View HI 96737

Call Sign: WH7FF
Kasia M Mayfield
Ocean View HI 96737

Call Sign: WH7FG
Galen R Lutz
Ocean View HI 96737

Call Sign: KH7WG

Karla Gottschalk
Ocean View HI 96737

Call Sign: NH7OI
Dennis R Smith
Ocean View HI 96747

Call Sign: NH7PK
David A Castle
Ocean View HI 96737-
6355

Call Sign: WH7FJ
Israel D Gorali
Ocean View HI 96737-
7135

FCC Amateur Radio
License in Ookala

Call Sign: NH7EA
Kenneth G Urbanozo
Ookala HI 96774

Call Sign: NH7IR
Tyler K Urbanozo
Ookala HI 96774

Call Sign: WH6DIV
June Greenfelder
Ookala HI 96774

Call Sign: WH6MT
Catharine H Perrins
Ookala HI 96774

Call Sign: WH7GZ
June Greenfelder
Ookala HI 96774

Call Sign: WH7HO
John C Greenfelder
Ookala HI 96774

Call Sign: WH7HM

Allen R Perrins Jr
Ookala HI 96774-0041

FCC Amateur Radio
License in Paauilo

Call Sign: KH6JAW
Hawaii Chapter Qcwa
Pob 436
Paauilo HI 96776-0436

Call Sign: NH7UJ
Dex K Alpiche Jr
Paauilo HI 96776

Call Sign: WH6HW
Darrell D Fox
Paauilo HI 96776

Call Sign: WH7RF
David N Jackson
Paauilo HI 96776

Call Sign: KH6CC
Jack N Wheeler
Paauilo HI 96776-0436

Call Sign: NH6EL
Richard R Ynigues
Paauilo HI 96776

Call Sign: NH6FL
William Agustin Sr
Paauilo HI 96776

Call Sign: WH6PO
Richard W Paiva
Paauilo HI 96776

Call Sign: WH6PP
Norma J Paiva
Paauilo HI 96776

FCC Amateur Radio
License in Pahala

Call Sign: AJ0T
Ronald O Ebert
95 1166 Alahaki Rd
Pahala HI 96777-0429

Call Sign: KA0FBB
Nadine R Ebert
95 1166 Alahaki Rd
Pahala HI 96777-0429

Call Sign: KH7EO
Joseph R Villa
Pahala HI 96777

Call Sign: NH7WD
Ted V Blanco
Pahala HI 96777

Call Sign: WH7ZH
Brandy N Borst
Pahala HI 96777

Call Sign: WH6CAL
Christopher J Linden
Pahala HI 96777

Call Sign: WH6EQ
Delaney D Packard
Pahala HI 96777

FCC Amateur Radio
License in Pahoa

Call Sign: KH6GKK
Paul E Bueltmann Jr
16-2251 Ainaloa Dr
Pahoa HI 96778-7555

Call Sign: NH7MK
Seth K Mc Gary
15-2711-B Aweoweo
Pahoa HI 96778

Call Sign: KH7LJ

Thomas T Raffipiy
16-2087 Hanale Dr
Pahoa HI 96778

Call Sign: NH7HV
Daylen K Raffipiy
16-2087 Hanale Dr
Pahoa HI 96778

Call Sign: NH7HO
Gordon K Naehu Jr
152679 Hee St
Pahoa HI 96778

Call Sign: NH7MF
Amy J Naehu
152679 Hee St
Pahoa HI 96778

Call Sign: NH7MG
Micah S K Naehu
152679 Hee St
Pahoa HI 96778

Call Sign: K6CH
William R Darling
13-3431 Hookupu St
Pahoa HI 96778

Call Sign: KH7S
William R Darling
13-3431 Hookupu St
Pahoa HI 96778

Call Sign: N6NHZ
Karen S Darling
13-3431 Hookupu St
Pahoa HI 96778

Call Sign: NH6AA
Karen S Darling
13-3431 Hookupu St
Pahoa HI 96778

Call Sign: NH7AA

William R Darling
13-3431 Hookupu St
Pahoa HI 96778

Call Sign: WA2VIA
Ignatius J Galgan
13-3362 Hookupu St
Pahoa HI 96778

Call Sign: KA6OOJ
Fredericka F Loveless
15-121 Kahakai Blvd
Pahoa HI 96778

Call Sign: KA6OOK
Clarence A Loveless
15-121 Kahakai Blvd
Pahoa HI 96778

Call Sign: AH6I
Milton W Nodacker
15-2741 Kaku St
Pahoa HI 96778

Call Sign: WA7TFE
Milton W Nodacker
15-2741 Kaku St
Pahoa HI 96778

Call Sign: WH7WT
Jean Nodacker
15-2741 Kaku St
Pahoa HI 96778

Call Sign: KH7HI
Peter C Yoes
12-7102 KalapanaKapoho
Rd
Pahoa HI 96778

Call Sign: WH7CB
Peter C Yoes
12-7102 KalapanaKapoho
Rd
Pahoa HI 96778

Call Sign: WH7CU
Elizabeth L Yoes
12-7102 KalapanaKapoho
Rd
Pahoa HI 96778

Call Sign: KD7AJM
Mathew J Rippa
13-3422 Kula St
Pahoa HI 96778

Call Sign: WH6DRW
Mathew J Rippa
13-3422 Kula St
Pahoa HI 96778

Call Sign: KH7ZI
Robin B Williams
15 2681 Kumu St
Pahoa HI 96778

Call Sign: AH6GM
Ernest H Cottingham
15-2681 Kumu St
Pahoa HI 96778

Call Sign: WH7LQ
Kali D Fermantez
13 4044 Lauone St
Pahoa HI 96778

Call Sign: KA6EIR
Jon A Olson
13-631 Leilani Ave
Pahoa HI 96778

Call Sign: K9UBS
Marvin L Dice Jr
14-4736 Malulani Circle
Pahoa HI 96778

Call Sign: KO4RR
Joe M Owen
12 253 Mapuana Ave

Pahoa HI 96778

Call Sign: KH6JHG
Mike R Blankenbecler
13 3364 Moku St
Pahoa HI 96778

Call Sign: WH6HF
David L Powell
13-3507 Moku St
Pahoa HI 96778

Call Sign: NH7HN
Donald G Laa
152701 N Hee St
Pahoa HI 96778

Call Sign: NH7ME
Abraham L Lagadon
15 2688 N Hee St
Pahoa HI 96778

Call Sign: KH6JAW
Maynard V Friend
15 2745 N Kahala St
Pahoa HI 96778

Call Sign: WH6BX
Sean V Krejci
15-2705 N Moi St
Pahoa HI 96728

Call Sign: KH7LM
Beverlin F Gable
15-391 N Puni Makai St
Pahoa HI 96778

Call Sign: AG4DP
Steve C Huff
15-2746 Niuhi
Pahoa HI 96778

Call Sign: NH7OC
Manuel C Lowe
15-2746 Niuhi St

Pahoa HI 96778

Call Sign: KF4GRR
Melinda K Huff
15-2746 Niuhi St
Pahoa HI 96778

Call Sign: KH7ZU
Thomas D Blackburn
133639 Nohea St
Pahoa HI 96778

Call Sign: KD6LSS
Jeffrey W Hartz
13-3421 Nohea St
Pahoa HI 96778

Call Sign: NH7MM
Malissa L Lagadon
15-2688 Nt Hee St
Pahoa HI 96778

Call Sign: NH7MN
Jason T Lagadon
15-2688 Nt Hee St
Pahoa HI 96778

Call Sign: N6IXU
Robert C Blair
12 111 Oliana Dr
Pahoa HI 96778

Call Sign: WH6DVF
Thomas D Hema
13-3489 Oneloa St
Pahoa HI 96778

Call Sign: WH7LO
Thomas M Chittenden
15 624 Puni Mauka Loop
South
Pahoa HI 96778

Call Sign: NH6WS
Marion E Sanford Sr

Rr 1 Box 102
Pahoa HI 96778

Call Sign: NH6VQ
Tracy S Anicas
Rr 2 Box 2309
Pahoa HI 96778

Call Sign: KH6AZQ
George S De Conte
Rr 2 Box 4012
Pahoa HI 96778

Call Sign: NH6GN
James A White
Rr 2 Box 4038
Pahoa HI 96778

Call Sign: WH7UZ
Kasi Jammeh
Rr 2 Box 4500
Pahoa HI 96778

Call Sign: AH6PG
Michael D Halpern
Rr 2 Box 4853
Pahoa HI 96778

Call Sign: AH0AG
Kirk A Sheppard
Rr 2 Box 6274
Pahoa HI 96778

Call Sign: WH6CMN
Paul A Hadik
Rr 2 Box 92
Pahoa HI 96778

Call Sign: AH6SK
Larry G Sell
Rr 3 Box 1117
Pahoa HI 96778

Call Sign: WB0RQL
Larry G Sell

Rr 3 Box 1117
Pahoa HI 96778

Call Sign: WH6DBO
Sharon C Marshall
Rr 3 Box 1173
Pahoa HI 96778

Call Sign: NH7MQ
Gene S Higa
Rr 3 Box 1183
Pahoa HI 96778

Call Sign: WH7ZC
Antonio M Sianez
Rr 3 Box 1203
Pahoa HI 96778

Call Sign: WH6DPO
Marvin H Kitchen
Rr 3 Box 1379
Pahoa HI 96778

Call Sign: WH6DVH
Nancy S Kitchen
Rr 3 Box 1379
Pahoa HI 96778

Call Sign: WH6DVI
Marvin A Kitchen
Rr 3 Box 1379
Pahoa HI 96778

Call Sign: WH6BZT
Wendell O Greenleaf
Rr 3 Box 2251
Pahoa HI 96778

Call Sign: WH7JK
Casey V Francis
Rr 3 Box 81517
Pahoa HI 96778

Call Sign: KC7OKZ
James A Todd

Rr 4 Box 2230
Pahoa HI 96778

Call Sign: WH6AVX
John W Prugh
Rrt 2 Box 78
Pahoa HI 96778

Call Sign: KH7SW
Shirley Watson
16-2051 Silversword Dr
Pahoa HI 96778

Call Sign: WH6DPP
Brent D Watson
16-2051 Silversword Dr
Pahoa HI 96778

Call Sign: WH6DPQ
Shirley Watson
16-2051 Silversword Dr
Pahoa HI 96778

Call Sign: WH7QD
David P Brown
15 2793 So Manalo St
Pahoa HI 96778

Call Sign: WA0FUR
Harrison J Klein
15-2678 Welea St
Pahoa HI 96778-8568

Call Sign: KH7ZV
Joshua K Keliihoomalu
Pahoa HI 96774

Call Sign: AH6LH
Ray F Orloski
Pahoa HI 96778

Call Sign: AH6SY
Thomas C Burnett
Pahoa HI 96778

Call Sign: KE6AHX
Thomas C Burnett
Pahoa HI 96778

Call Sign: KH6RZ
Big Island Six Meter Club
Pahoa HI 96778

Call Sign: KH7BN
Aukai E Sewell
Pahoa HI 96778

Call Sign: KH7N
Thomas C Burnett
Pahoa HI 96778

Call Sign: KH7ZL
Cynthia C Keliihoomalu
Pahoa HI 96778

Call Sign: KH7ZN
Robert P Keliihoomalu Jr
Pahoa HI 96778

Call Sign: KH7ZW
Tiaraerlecia U
Keliihoomalu
Pahoa HI 96778

Call Sign: KL7UB
Thomas R Jacobson
Pahoa HI 96778

Call Sign: NH6BQ
Andrew K Dunn
Pahoa HI 96778

Call Sign: NH6BR
Tiana K Dunn
Pahoa HI 96778

Call Sign: NH6DB
Lehuanani A Angay
Pahoa HI 96778

Call Sign: NH7AS
Andrew K Dunn
Pahoa HI 96778

Call Sign: NH7AT
Tiana K Dunn
Pahoa HI 96778

Call Sign: NH7BC
Lehuanani A Angay
Pahoa HI 96778

Call Sign: NH7HG
Scotty L Aiu
Pahoa HI 96778

Call Sign: NH7MC
Ana Marie D Aiu
Pahoa HI 96778

Call Sign: NH7MI
Keone A Aiu
Pahoa HI 96778

Call Sign: NH7MJ
Bruce R Miller
Pahoa HI 96778

Call Sign: NH7MP
John R Williams
Pahoa HI 96778

Call Sign: NH7NP
Cheriann K Aiu
Pahoa HI 96778

Call Sign: NH7YF
Solomon Singer
Pahoa HI 96778

Call Sign: NH7ZE
Solomon Singer
Pahoa HI 96778

Call Sign: W6YM

Frederic K Honnold
Pahoa HI 96778

Call Sign: WH6CSS
Theodore G Troy
Pahoa HI 96778

Call Sign: WH6DHL
Big Island Six Meter Club
Pahoa HI 96778

Call Sign: WH6DPM
Steven H Jacquier
Pahoa HI 96778

Call Sign: WH6DVG
Greg A Seivert
Pahoa HI 96778

Call Sign: WH6VO
Sydney R Singer
Pahoa HI 96778

Call Sign: WH6XU
Richard A Rimer
Pahoa HI 96778

Call Sign: WH7JT
David A Stowe
Pahoa HI 96778

Call Sign: WH7LL
Davelyn Aniu
Pahoa HI 96778

Call Sign: WH7LN
Ione N Chittenden
Pahoa HI 96778

Call Sign: WH7WH
Tina M Liwai
Pahoa HI 96778

Call Sign: KH7ST
John G Gapp

Pahoa HI 96778-1128

Call Sign: NH7PE
Irene M Kubica
Pahoa HI 96778-1328

Call Sign: NH7PF
Tim Kubica
Pahoa HI 96778-1328

Call Sign: NH6OK
Vernal K Peleiholani
Pahoa HI 96778

Call Sign: NH6TU
Kenneth Gable
Pahoa HI 96778

Call Sign: WH6BHJ
Michael L Smith
Pahoa HI 96778

Call Sign: WH6CGI
David R N Jamieson
Pahoa HI 96778

Call Sign: WH6KF
Dale S Mercier
Pahoa HI 96778

Call Sign: KH6HLP
Equatorial Lights Amateur
Radio Club
Pahoa HI 96778-0511

Call Sign: KH6KFI
Equatorial Lights Amateur
Radio Club
Pahoa HI 96778-0511

Call Sign: W6KFI
California Pacific Amateur
Radio Club
Pahoa HI 96778-0511

Call Sign: W6ZOP
California Pacific Arc
Pahoa HI 96778-0511

Call Sign: NH7ML
Henry M Luis
15-2698 Moi St
Pahua HI 96778

FCC Amateur Radio License in Paia

Call Sign: KH6AH
William J Brown
Box 313
Paia HI 96779

Call Sign: KH6BYS
Clarence M Matsumoto
222 C Haija Hwy
Paia HI 96779

Call Sign: AH6E
Stanley G Goosby
3 Hoe St
Paia HI 96779

Call Sign: KH6BE
Stanley G Goosby
3 Hoe St
Paia HI 96779

Call Sign: KN6BE
Stanley G Goosby
3 Hoe St
Paia HI 96779

Call Sign: WH6EM
Theodore D Baumann
25 Kaiholo Pl
Paia HI 96779

Call Sign: KH7CA
Michael D Langford
37 Kulia Pl

Paia HI 96779

Call Sign: NH6IM
Morrow F Bagda
51 Lana St
Paia HI 96779

Call Sign: NH7QE
Gregory Bardos
54 Lana St
Paia HI 96779

Call Sign: AH6AM
Les S Hieda
39 Meha Pl
Paia HI 96779

Call Sign: KF0VV
Robert R Ramsay
52 Pua Ole St
Paia HI 96779

Call Sign: KH6ST
Robert R Ramsay
52 Pua Ole St
Paia HI 96779

Call Sign: KH7VL
Karl W Hill
Paia HI 96779

Call Sign: WH6CRP
Martin B Kirk
Paia HI 96779

Call Sign: WH6CRQ
Peter Weymouth
Paia HI 96779

Call Sign: WH6CTS
Gail L Klevens
Paia HI 96779

Call Sign: WH6EN
Geoffrey D Cassel

Paia HI 96779-1131

Call Sign: NH6ZH
John D Powell
Paia HI 96779

Call Sign: WH6EO
Armin Engert
Paia HI 96779

Call Sign: WH6RZ
James E Sanders
Paia HI 96779

Call Sign: WH6CGN
Meagan L Johnson
Paia HI 96779

FCC Amateur Radio License in Papaaloa

Call Sign: AH6SL
Robert L Holmes
Papaaloa HI 96780

Call Sign: KH7RQ
Thomas P Carpenter
Papaaloa HI 96780

Call Sign: KH7RU
Kristen M Carpenter
Papaaloa HI 96780

Call Sign: N0EFP
Robert L Holmes
Papaaloa HI 96780

FCC Amateur Radio License in Papaikou

Call Sign: NH7IL
Victoria P I Naboa
27-469 Old Mamalahoa
Hwy
Papaikou HI 96781

Call Sign: KI4IGB
Joel R Cook
27-380 Papaikou Rd
Papaikou HI 96781

Call Sign: NH6BV
Wallace A Ishibashi Jr
Rr 1 Box 135B
Papaikou HI 96781

Call Sign: NH7AU
Wallace A Ishibashi Jr
Rr 1 Box 135B
Papaikou HI 96781

Call Sign: NH7DZ
Wallace A Ishibashi III
Rr 1 Box 135B
Papaikou HI 96781

Call Sign: KH6BEV
Ernest C Luiz
Papaikou HI 96781

Call Sign: KH7BS
James I Patao Jr
Papaikou HI 96781

Call Sign: NH6OW
Jaime C Aguinaldo
Papaikou HI 96781

Call Sign: W6MEF
Walter E Anderson
Papaikou HI 96781

FCC Amateur Radio License in Pearl City

Call Sign: KH7TB
Clifton Qc Lum
2015 Aamanu St
Pearl City HI 96782

Call Sign: KH6BGV
Norman C Freitas
2149 Aamanu St
Pearl City HI 96782

Call Sign: KH6C
James R Proffitt
2024 Aaniu Loop
Pearl City HI 96782-1310

Call Sign: KH6GJO
Margaret B Proffitt
2024 Aaniu Loop
Pearl City HI 96782-1310

Call Sign: KH6IH
William C Carlstrom
2088 Aaniu Loop
Pearl City HI 96782

Call Sign: NH6NP
Mildred E Carlstrom
2088 Aaniu Loop
Pearl City HI 96782

Call Sign: WH6CFC
Clement M K Kamaka
2301 Ahakapu St
Pearl City HI 96782

Call Sign: NH6KY
James W Texeira
2323 Ahakapu St
Pearl City HI 96782

Call Sign: KH6GNS
Gerald F Smith
2359 Ahakapu St
Pearl City HI 96782

Call Sign: WH6BKA
James T Higa
2349 Ahakuka Pl
Pearl City HI 96782

Call Sign: WH6APD
Leo S Nakano
2346 Ahapule St
Pearl City HI 96782

Call Sign: WH6CZK
Trudie L Rosa
1168 Aikoo Pl
Pearl City HI 96782

Call Sign: WH7PE
Jerry R Allsbrook
2290 Akepa St
Pearl City HI 96782

Call Sign: KH7OO
Pacific Contest Club
2514 Akepa St
Pearl City HI 96782

Call Sign: WH6CUZ
Erik K Kang
2217 Akeukeu St
Pearl City HI 96782

Call Sign: NH6ZP
Lester F Sacks
2241 Akeukeu St
Pearl City HI 96782

Call Sign: KH6BTV
Samuel Bohol Sr
2275 Akeukeu St
Pearl City HI 96782

Call Sign: KH6IPQ
Beverly J Braun
2275 Akeukeu St
Pearl City HI 96782

Call Sign: N3WQE
Howard J Bogac
1607 Aloha Ave
Pearl City HI 96782

Call Sign: NH6LN
Michael F Laley
2217 Amikuku Pl
Pearl City HI 96782

Call Sign: NH7WA
Alan K Cardoza
2262 Apoepoe St
Pearl City HI 96782

Call Sign: WH6CJY
Stanley Y Fernandez
2209 Aumakua St
Pearl City HI 96782

Call Sign: WH6APY
Larry T Nakamura
2258 Amokemoke St
Pearl City HI 96782

Call Sign: KH6NYC
Edward W Steffens Sr
2235 Auhuhu St
Pearl City HI 96782-1230

Call Sign: KH6GLC
Clarence E Self
2247 Aumakua St
Pearl City HI 96782-1361

Call Sign: KH6GCM
Jerome H Ongies
2339 Amokemoke St
Pearl City HI 96782

Call Sign: WH6CYW
Edward W Steffens Sr
2235 Auhuhu St
Pearl City HI 96782-1230

Call Sign: AH6QX
Sandra M Pigg
2332 Aumakua St
Pearl City HI 96782

Call Sign: KH2YA
Ruben F Imanil
2313 Amoomoo St
Pearl City HI 96782

Call Sign: KH6FQ
Harold K Nakano
2354 Auhuhu St
Pearl City HI 96782

Call Sign: KH7HC
Sandra M Pigg
2332 Aumakua St
Pearl City HI 96782

Call Sign: KH6YA
Ruben F Imanil
2313 Amoomoo St
Pearl City HI 96782

Call Sign: NH6HA
Richard K Suzuki
2364 Auhuhu St
Pearl City HI 96782

Call Sign: WH7TQ
Adele H Lum
2362 Aumakua St
Pearl City HI 96782

Call Sign: WH7FS
Russell A Borden
2217 Anapanapa St
Pearl City HI 96782

Call Sign: NH6HL
Richelle M Suzuki
2364 Auhuhu St
Pearl City HI 96782

Call Sign: KH6CU
James E Kennedy
2382 Aumakua St
Pearl City HI 96782-1148

Call Sign: WH6DQW
William W Hope Jr
2229 Apaakuma St
Pearl City HI 96782

Call Sign: WH6CEH
Stanton Y Oshiro
2401 Auhuhu St
Pearl City HI 96782

Call Sign: NH6SV
David C Reis
2412 Aumakua St
Pearl City HI 96782

Call Sign: KH6JNV
Maurice M Oshiro
1103 Apoepoe Pl
Pearl City HI 96782

Call Sign: WH6DAS
Floyd F Burns
2408 Auhuhu St
Pearl City HI 96782

Call Sign: NH6NF
Alexander A Birch Jr
2414 Aumakua St
Pearl City HI 96782

Call Sign: NH6ZQ
Jim W Shiets
2211 Apoepoe St
Pearl City HI 96782

Call Sign: KH6HGQ
Priscilla L Villados
2103 Aumakua St
Pearl City HI 96782

Call Sign: WH6BWS
Roxanne W Birch
2414 Aumakua St
Pearl City HI 96782

Call Sign: KH6RC
Seiji Arakaki
2437 Aumakua St
Pearl City HI 96782

Call Sign: KH6JFI
Ronald F Harburg
2457 Aumakua St
Pearl City HI 96782-1047

Call Sign: KH6ER
Peter Y Y Choo Jr
2234 Aupaka St
Pearl City HI 96782

Call Sign: WH7PP
Gordon K Naehu Sr
2281 Aupaka St
Pearl City HI 96782

Call Sign: KH7SY
Eugene B Westgate II
558 B Birch Cir
Pearl City HI 96782

Call Sign: NH6UX
Anthony J Cagalawan
1479 D Kanihi St
Pearl City HI 96782-2000

Call Sign: NH7OE
Cyrilee A Billings
808 Date Dr
Pearl City HI 96782

Call Sign: NH7XX
Patrick J Obado
1799 Hoohai St
Pearl City HI 96782

Call Sign: WH6DJL
Jon G Pharis
2104 Hoohai St
Pearl City HI 96782

Call Sign: NH7ZB
Shane P Correia
2187 Hoohai St
Pearl City HI 96782

Call Sign: WH6CXX
Eric M Nagamine
1651 Hoohalia St
Pearl City HI 96782

Call Sign: WH7BD
Kenika D Lai Hipp
1650 Hoohalike St
Pearl City HI 96782

Call Sign: KF6QZD
Jenee S Odani
1675 Hooheno St
Pearl City HI 96782

Call Sign: AH6HW
Judith A Ching
1675 Hooheno St
Pearl City HI 96782

Call Sign: KH6IJS
Howell F Ching
1675 Hooheno St
Pearl City HI 96782

Call Sign: WH7DN
Richard J Oka
98-1429 Hoohiki St
Pearl City HI 96782

Call Sign: WH7YB
Sean H Mullaney
98-1335 Hoohonua St
Pearl City HI 96782

Call Sign: WH7PO
Dean C Tano
98-1374 Hoohonus St
Pearl City HI 96782

Call Sign: KH6JGE
Alan J Roche
1729 Hoohulu St
Pearl City HI 96782

Call Sign: WH6DQH
Bernice J Herodies
98-459 Hookanike St Unit
61
Pearl City HI 96782

Call Sign: WH6DSV
Bernard R Spaulding
1328 Hookano St
Pearl City HI 96782

Call Sign: AH6LN
Nobutaka Saito
819 Hookena St
Pearl City HI 96782

Call Sign: WH6YZ
William F Mabida
1192B Hoola Pl
Pearl City HI 96782

Call Sign: WH7IP
Brian K Lelepali
1598 Hoolana St
Pearl City HI 96782

Call Sign: KH7CG
Rudy M Pascua Jr
1736 Hoolana St
Pearl City HI 96782

Call Sign: NH6TG
Albert Moniz
1142 Hoolaulea St
Pearl City HI 96782

Call Sign: WH7EL
Ronald S Ikari Jr
1989 Hoolaulea St
Pearl City HI 96782

Call Sign: KH6AOZ
Hidenobu Hiyane
1334 Hoolauna St
Pearl City HI 96782

Call Sign: WH6CRO
Brian E Belcher
1982 Hoolehua St
Pearl City HI 96782

Call Sign: KH7YO
Albert Somera
1269 Hooli Cir
Pearl City HI 96782

Call Sign: WH6MF
Keith A Takeda
98-1462 Hoomahie Loop
Pearl City HI 96782

Call Sign: WH6CNH
Robert T Nakagawa
98-1571 Hoomaike St
Pearl City HI 96782

Call Sign: WH6IX
Jo Anne L Nakagawa
98-1571 Hoomaike St
Pearl City HI 96782

Call Sign: W4YQS
William V Swartz
976 Hoomalimali St
Pearl City HI 96782

Call Sign: WH6DPE
Louise M Kaneshiro
88 Hoomalu St
Pearl City HI 96782

Call Sign: WH6ABJ
Carol S K Lee
267 Hoomalu St
Pearl City HI 96782

Call Sign: WH6AIJ
Albert Garcia
766 Hoomoana St
Pearl City HI 96782

Call Sign: AH6AN
Arnold H Ringler
1570 Hoonipo St
Pearl City HI 96782-2246

Call Sign: WH6BYU
Genji Ono
1442 Kalauipo St
Pearl City HI 96782

Call Sign: KH6BNZ
Tom T Higa
98-232B Kaluamoi Pl
Pearl City HI 96782

Call Sign: WH6HV
Richard D Fewell
1060 Kam Hwy 3601A
Pearl City HI 96782

Call Sign: KH6LH
Dennis D Lai Hipp
1060 Kamehameha Hwy
206A
Pearl City HI 96782-2558

Call Sign: WH6QN
Dennis D Lai Hipp
1060 Kamehameha Hwy
206A
Pearl City HI 96782-2558

Call Sign: AH6CD
Michael A Sonstegard
1060 Kamehameha Hwy
3501B
Pearl City HI 96782

Call Sign: WH7VD

George A Smith
1060 Kamehameha Hwy
Apt 2903A
Pearl City HI 96782

Call Sign: WH7CX
Lorin R Hymas
1060 Kamelameha Hwy
A4404
Pearl City HI 96782

Call Sign: NH6JW
Gene G Marshall
1479 Kanihi St
Pearl City HI 96782

Call Sign: WH6CAP
Donn M Jurich
98-222 Kaulike Dr
Pearl City HI 96782

Call Sign: KH7YX
Roy H Yamamoto
1443 Kaumoli Pl
Pearl City HI 96782-1922

Call Sign: NH6ML
Vernon D Young
1422 Kaumoli St
Pearl City HI 96782

Call Sign: KH6Q
Arnold M Onizuka
1473 Kaumoli St
Pearl City HI 96782

Call Sign: WH6FR
Kenneth K Yamada
1278 Kaweloka St
Pearl City HI 96782

Call Sign: WH6BVX
Eve K O Hannigan
1271 F Kipaipai St
Pearl City HI 96782

Call Sign: WH7OY
Jacob R Sipe
98-1361 Koaheahe Pl 110
Pearl City HI 96782

Call Sign: KH7FG
Michael N Diniega
2307 Komo Mai Dr
Pearl City HI 96782

Call Sign: KH7ERD
Eduardo Dantes
2055 Komo Mai Dr
Pearl City HI 96782

Call Sign: WH6OO
Robert J Wiepert
98-1438C Koaheahe St
Pearl City HI 96782

Call Sign: KH7FF
Joseph N Diniega
2307 Komo Mai Dr
Pearl City HI 96782-1053

Call Sign: WH6UT
Eduardo Dantes
2055 Komo Mai Dr
Pearl City HI 96782

Call Sign: WH6AJY
Takatoshi Mima
1231 Komo Mai Dr
Pearl City HI 96782

Call Sign: WH7GC
Marianne Lewis
2421 Komo Mai Dr
Pearl City HI 96782

Call Sign: WH6MU
Hang T Nguyen
1390 Kuahaka St
Pearl City HI 96782

Call Sign: WH6BJZ
Kyle K Ho
2026 Komo Mai Dr
Pearl City HI 96782

Call Sign: WH6BKE
Brendon K Lee
2435 Komo Mai Dr
Pearl City HI 96782

Call Sign: KH7HT
Jared L Wong
1772 Kuahaka St
Pearl City HI 96782

Call Sign: KH6IEL
Raymond E Thompson
2040 Komo Mai Dr
Pearl City HI 96782-1325

Call Sign: KH6JMI
Benson W K Lee Sr
2435 Komo Mai Dr
Pearl City HI 96782

Call Sign: KH6PK
David M Nashiwa
98-1673 Laauhauahua Pl
Pearl City HI 96782

Call Sign: KH6GQ
Anthony G Di Brogrozcio
2236 Komo Mai Dr
Pearl City HI 96782

Call Sign: KH6JOJ
Ronald S Rabellizsa
2498 Komo Mai Dr
Pearl City HI 96782

Call Sign: KH7UA
Melissa N Richardson
904 B Lahakila Ave
Pearl City HI 96782

Call Sign: WH7DB
Lester Y Tamashiro
2267 Komo Mai Dr
Pearl City HI 96782

Call Sign: NH6YT
Conrado R Basa
2514 Komo Mai Dr
Pearl City HI 96782

Call Sign: KH7PJ
Dale A Esperum Jr
4001 Lanakila Ave
Pearl City HI 96782

Call Sign: KH7YB
William H Gould
2268 Komo Mai Dr
Pearl City HI 96782

Call Sign: WH6DJM
Kevin B Pascual
2519 Komo Mai Dr
Pearl City HI 96782

Call Sign: NH6MQ
Francis W Hall Sr
1841A Lanikeha Pl
Pearl City HI 96782

Call Sign: KH7ED
Serina M Diniega
2307 Komo Mai Dr
Pearl City HI 96782

Call Sign: WH7YD
Daron M Makaiwi
2519 Komo Mai Dr
Pearl City HI 96782

Call Sign: WH6DUJ
Stephen E Griffing
1400 Laniwai Ave
Pearl City HI 96782

Pearl City HI 96782

Pearl City HI 96782

Call Sign: NH6QL
Harumi Kubo
914 Leomele St
Pearl City HI 96782

Call Sign: KH6BBK
Nobuo Nihei
1555 Noelani St
Pearl City HI 96782

Call Sign: KH6XQ
Harry T Arakaki
956 Puu Kula Dr
Pearl City HI 96782

Call Sign: NH6QM
Bob K Kubo
914 Leomele St
Pearl City HI 96782

Call Sign: KH7RKT
Randall K Takaesu
98 817B Noelani St
Pearl City HI 96782

Call Sign: WH7I
Masaharu Nakao
C/O Harry T Arakaki 956
Puu Kula Dr
Pearl City HI 96782

Call Sign: KH6NY
Miles T Hirata
1006 Maiha Cir
Pearl City HI 96782

Call Sign: WH6DNC
Grant Y Oka
98-915 Noelani St
Pearl City HI 96782

Call Sign: WH6OS
Lance Y Isa
833 Second St
Pearl City HI 97682

Call Sign: AH6AC
Dale J Ott
1052 Maiha Cir
Pearl City HI 96782

Call Sign: WH6DJV
Steven K Veray
98-1387 Nola St Apt C
Pearl City HI 96782

Call Sign: KC7IFU
Aldon L Perkins
800 Third St C 165
Pearl City HI 96782-3360

Call Sign: KA7DQX
Alfred W Pool
915 Makamua Pl
Pearl City HI 96782

Call Sign: KH7PK
Joseph A Holtzmann
1663 Paaafna Pl
Pearl City HI 96782-1553

Call Sign: KH6BL
Shigeri Takenaka
96-218 Waiawa Rd 62
Pearl City HI 96782

Call Sign: NH7OZ
Trisha M Hiroshige
1112 Malha Cir
Pearl City HI 96782

Call Sign: KH6VS
Douglas J Fujimoto
1638 Puananala St
Pearl City HI 96782

Call Sign: NH6IY
Della M Bungcayao
96-218 Waiawa Rd 67
Pearl City HI 96782

Call Sign: KH6WI
Haruo Tao
1477 Maluawai St
Pearl City HI 96782

Call Sign: KH6VB
Philip H Okada
723 Puu Hina Pl
Pearl City HI 96782

Call Sign: NH7SO
Virgil G Stephens
96-1408 Waihona Pl
Pearl City HI 96782

Call Sign: KH7QA
Ashley A Kotomori
98 718 Moanalua Rd Ste
158
Pearl City HI 96782

Call Sign: KH6BTD
Benjamin Pataray
773 Puu Hina Pl
Pearl City HI 96782

Call Sign: KA3TUA
Kristine R Carraher
Pearl City HI 96782

Call Sign: NH6NM
Dale Y Sano
1329 Nanakai St

Call Sign: KH6FP
Stuart S Nishimura
1254 Puu Kipa St

Call Sign: KH6DSQ
Bertoldo Salbosa
Pearl City HI 96782

Call Sign: KH6IDB
Philip A Morin
Pearl City HI 96782

Call Sign: KH6JFS
Wendell K Lee
Pearl City HI 96782

Call Sign: KH6ROZ
Rosielyn A De Vera
Pearl City HI 96782

Call Sign: KH7IE
Sam B Cadelinia
Pearl City HI 96782

Call Sign: KH7RS
Robert Villanueva Sr
Pearl City HI 96782

Call Sign: KH7XS
Rosielyn A De Vera
Pearl City HI 96782

Call Sign: NH6JK
Beverly A T Taira
Pearl City HI 96782

Call Sign: NH6RS
Robert Villanueva Sr
Pearl City HI 96782

Call Sign: NQ8Z
Mark A Carraher
Pearl City HI 96782

Call Sign: WH6CMP
John L Altonn
Pearl City HI 96782

**FCC Amateur Radio
License in Pearl Harbor**

Call Sign: KD6BVX

Michael A Coombs
Box 212
Pearl Harbor HI 96860

Call Sign: WH6CSU
Jon P Leger
Sima Box 141
Pearl Harbor HI 96860

**FCC Amateur Radio
License in Pepeekeo**

Call Sign: NH6CB
Benjamin K Tajon
Pepeekeo HI 96783

Call Sign: NH7AW
Benjamin K Tajon
Pepeekeo HI 96783

Call Sign: NH7DY
Sheila R Edler
Pepeekeo HI 96783

Call Sign: NH7GF
Nathan A Tajon
Pepeekeo HI 96783

Call Sign: WH6CWM
Parley I Tajon
Pepeekeo HI 96783

Call Sign: WH7WX
Laney J Azevedo
Pepeekeo HI 96783

Call Sign: WH6CPX
Bill Mince
Pepeekeo HI 96783-0086

Call Sign: KH7MC
Sandra L Tajon
Pepeekeo HI 96783-0311

Call Sign: NH6ET

Ann K Snyder
Pepeekeo HI 96783-0608

Call Sign: WH6KG
Gene C P Chung
Pepeekeo HI 96783

**FCC Amateur Radio
License in Princeville**

Call Sign: WH6DVM
Frances Mead-Messinger
3963 Aloahi Dr
Princeville HI 96722

Call Sign: WH6DVN
Roderick Messinger
3963 Aloalii Dr
Princeville HI 96722

Call Sign: NH7YM
John G Burns
Box 223254
Princeville HI 96722

Call Sign: NH6WG
Leonard Prybutok
3830 Edward Rd
Princeville HI 96722

Call Sign: K0GVS
Benedict A Bohach
4944 Emmalani Dr
Princeville HI 96722

Call Sign: WH6DSC
William E Miller
4215 Kekuahaca Ln
Princeville HI 96722

Call Sign: WD6CHA
Dallas L Brown
4184 Kekuanaoa Ln
Princeville HI 96722

Call Sign: N6QCC
Jack M Law
4146 Liholiho Rd
Princeville HI 96722

Call Sign: KF6VRB
Susan C Nilsen
4836 Moli Pl
Princeville HI 96722-5347

Call Sign: KH6ZQ
Peter W Nilsen
4836 Moli Pl
Princeville HI 96722

Call Sign: KK6ZQ
Peter W Nilsen
4836 Moli Pl
Princeville HI 96722

Call Sign: WH6MN
Richard K Jacobsen
5068 Napookala Circle
Princeville HI 96722

Call Sign: NH7Y
Hartwin E A Weiss
4833 O'U Pl
Princeville HI 96722

Call Sign: WH6DGH
Campbell Kauai Amateur
Radio Club
Pmb 364
Princeville HI 96722-3300

Call Sign: WH6DGJ
Kauai Vhf/Uhf Arc
Pmb 364
Princeville HI 96722-3300

Call Sign: WH6DXD
Franklin D Tobias Sr
3880 Wyllie Rd 11C
Princeville HI 96722

Call Sign: WH7HR
Diana S Bowman
3880 Wyllie Rd Apt 10B
Princeville HI 96722

Call Sign: KH6IAO
Clarence M Ashman
Princeville HI 96722

Call Sign: NH7UV
Ginny Baldwin
Princeville HI 96722

Call Sign: WH6DTU
Bruce S Conrey
Princeville HI 96722

Call Sign: WH7SR
Anthony M Romero
Princeville HI 96722

Call Sign: AE7V
Gilbert A Casiraghi
Princeville HI 96722-3236

Call Sign: NH7UU
Elmer A Snyder
Princeville HI 96722-3375

Call Sign: NH7YO
Daniel D Stricker
Princeville HI 96722-3683

Call Sign: NH7YP
Cheryl A Stricker
Princeville HI 96722-3683

Call Sign: K0JKR
George W Taylor
Princeville HI 96722

**FCC Amateur Radio
License in Puhi**

Call Sign: KH7DW
Ranney J Warburton
Puhi HI 96766

Call Sign: NH6GA
Jacqueline L Ruth
Puhi HI 96766

Call Sign: NH7CA
Jacqueline L Ruth
Puhi HI 96766

Call Sign: AH6KN
Patty L Kaliher
Puhi HI 96766

**FCC Amateur Radio
License in Pukalani**

Call Sign: WH6NQ
Michael P Slattery
2774 Ainalani Dr
Pukalani HI 96768

Call Sign: NH6EE
Roberta U Medeiros
3384 Anuwanu Pl
Pukalani HI 96768

Call Sign: NH7BL
Roberta U Medeiros
3384 Anuwanu Pl
Pukalani HI 96768

Call Sign: WH6CYD
Joseph Medeiros
3384 Anuwanu Pl
Pukalani HI 96768

Call Sign: KH6HA
Arleigh B Hughes
158 Haulani St
Pukalani HI 96768

Call Sign: WH6CRU

David L Welty
328 Hololani St
Pukalani HI 96768

Call Sign: KH6DDT
David A Dunlap
2879 Iholani St
Pukalani HI 96768

Call Sign: WD9DDT
David A Dunlap
2879 Iholani St
Pukalani HI 96768

Call Sign: KH6WS
James T Sato
132 Ikea Pl
Pukalani HI 96768

Call Sign: WH6CS
Charles A Ladley
2634 Iolani St
Pukalani HI 96768

Call Sign: WH6AWE
Wayne K Nishida
2860 Ipolani St
Pukalani HI 96788

Call Sign: AH7B
Luc J Cooman
255 Kaualani
Pukalani HI 96768

Call Sign: KH6SQ
Terrence F Clayton
255 Kaualani
Pukalani HI 96768

Call Sign: AH7ZA
Kaualani Contest Group
255 Kaualani Dr
Pukalani HI 96768

Call Sign: WH6DHD

Kaualani Contest Group
255 Kaualani Dr
Pukalani HI 96768

Call Sign: WH6WX
Charles S Clayton
249 Kavalani Dr
Pukalani HI 96768

Call Sign: WH7AD
Robert J Collum Jr
20 Kuikele Pl
Pukalani HI 96768

Call Sign: KF4OLR
Curtis R Carter
3140 B Liholani St
Pukalani HI 96768

Call Sign: KA5WMF
Robert L Plunkett
2811 Liholani St 12
Pukalani HI 96768

Call Sign: N7KUZ
Dana A Smith
2811 Liholani St 19
Pukalani HI 96768

Call Sign: KH6JEZ
Americo B Carnevale Sr
87 Noho Pl
Pukalani HI 96768

Call Sign: WA3TWA
George N Maeda
2806 Palalani St
Pukalani HI 96768

Call Sign: WH6DAQ
Oran L Marksbury
204 Pukalani St
Pukalani HI 96788

Call Sign: WH7U

Oran L Marksbury
204 Pukalani St
Pukalani HI 96788

Call Sign: WA6ZNI
Joseph L Hargrove
Pukalani HI 96788

Call Sign: WH6BFA
Thomas S Yoshida
Pukalani HI 96788

Call Sign: WH6CUE
James D Soriano
Pukalani HI 96788

Call Sign: WH6DIW
Andrew K Kala
Pukalani HI 96788

Call Sign: WH6DMD
Mimi C Mitchell
Pukalani HI 96788

Call Sign: WH7XO
Nancy L Kala
Pukalani HI 96788

Call Sign: WH7XP
Kim M Ullman-Orestano
Pukalani HI 96788

Call Sign: WH6AV
David J Neto
173 Ikea Pl
Pukalaui HI 96768

Call Sign: WH6CYH
Victoria L Arck
2690 Akalani Loop
Pukulani HI 96793

FCC Amateur Radio License in Puunene

Call Sign: KC5JNZ
Robert E Bray
Puunene HI 96784

Call Sign: NH7FC
William F Schnitzer
Puunene HI 96784

Call Sign: NH6PU
Patrick A Richards Mr
Puunene HI 96784

Call Sign: WH6CV
John H Beaman
Puunene HI 96784

FCC Amateur Radio License in Schofield Barracks

Call Sign: WH6CRL
John M Phillips
C Co 725 Msb Box 671
Schofield Barracks HI 96857

Call Sign: WH6ZA
John E Dickey
Hhc 3D Bde Box 21
Schofield Barracks HI 96857

Call Sign: KE6TKQ
Daniel J Mcnece
703 Mi Bde Box 409
Schofield Barracks HI 96857

FCC Amateur Radio License in Tripler

Call Sign: WH6DIT
Tripler Army Medical Center
1 Jarrett Thite Rd

Tripler HI 96859

FCC Amateur Radio License in Volcano

Call Sign: KC7AXX
Frank E Box Mr
194200 Akakani Rd
Volcano HI 96785-0750

Call Sign: WH6BN
Marc L Swanson
Box 418
Volcano HI 96785

Call Sign: N6SBB
Charles W Ricketts
19-4055 Kalani Honua St
Volcano HI 96785

Call Sign: WH6CPJ
James H Pedersen
19-3950 Keonelehua Rd
Volcano HI 96785

Call Sign: KL7PN
Stephen W Stout
11-2250 Leila St
Volcano HI 96785

Call Sign: AH7H
Richard E Frazier
Volcano HI 96785

Call Sign: AH7NA
Coast To Coast Contest Club
Volcano HI 96785

Call Sign: KA6BPC
James B Moore
Volcano HI 96785

Call Sign: KH6YR
Hot Lava Contest Club

Volcano HI 96785

Call Sign: KH6ZM
Massimo A Zenobi
Volcano HI 96785

Call Sign: KH6ZN
Pu'U O'O Radio Club
Volcano HI 96785

Call Sign: KH7M
Pu'U O'O Radio Club
Volcano HI 96785

Call Sign: KH7TW
Naupaka B Zimmerman
Volcano HI 96785

Call Sign: KJ6SY
Loretta A Ricketts
Volcano HI 96785

Call Sign: NH6YK
Theodore A Brattstrom
Volcano HI 96785

Call Sign: NH6YU
Lisa M King
Volcano HI 96785

Call Sign: NH7LH
Peku L Kapuni Reynolds
Volcano HI 96785

Call Sign: NH7RO
Jeff A Cathrow
Volcano HI 96785

Call Sign: WH6BFM
Su Reed
Volcano HI 96785

Call Sign: WH6CBG
Jeanne M Testa
Volcano HI 96785

Call Sign: WH6CF
Joann Homsany
Volcano HI 96785

Call Sign: WH6CSO
Mark A Forsythe
Volcano HI 96785

Call Sign: WH6DAU
Tad M Wenkam
Volcano HI 96785

Call Sign: WH6DIA
Hot Lava Contest Club
Volcano HI 96785

Call Sign: WH6DIP
Pu'U O'O Radio Club
Volcano HI 96785

Call Sign: WH6DTD
Douglas D Wilson
Volcano HI 96785

Call Sign: WH6DVB
Glenn N Kadota
Volcano HI 96785

Call Sign: WH6DXF
Lydia Meneses
Volcano HI 96785

Call Sign: WH6VU
William O R Stephenson
Volcano HI 96785

Call Sign: WH7DY
Stephen A Macedo
Volcano HI 96785

Call Sign: WH7M
Hot Lava Contest Club
Volcano HI 96785

Call Sign: WH7QF
Alexander J Mac Kenzie
Volcano HI 96785

Call Sign: NH7EX
Halena Kapuni Reynolds
Volcano HI 96785-0071

Call Sign: KH6IMB
Wilfred R Tanigawa
Volcano HI 96785

Call Sign: KH6JY
Northrup H Castle
Volcano HI 96785

Call Sign: NH6XM
John F Gager
Volcano HI 96785

Call Sign: WH6CJ
Gwendolyn N Gager
Volcano HI 96785

FCC Amateur Radio License in Wahiawa

Call Sign: KC5LIR
Suyin G Yau Venable
154 Abbott St 102
Wahiawa HI 96786

Call Sign: WH6ADM
Tom T Oyabu
1045 Aheahe Ave 117
Wahiawa HI 96786

Call Sign: AH6IY
Ronald H Fujimoto
59 California Ave
Wahiawa HI 96786-1507

Call Sign: WH6DMX
Regina M Akhay
85 California Ave

Wahiawa HI 96786

Call Sign: KH7SZ
Duane J Mc Crum
1375 California Ave
Wahiawa HI 96786

Call Sign: KH7PT
Phil Potter
1881 California Ave
Wahiawa HI 96786

Call Sign: KH6JUU
George K Hanzawa
2120 California Ave
Wahiawa HI 96786

Call Sign: NH7AF
Seikichi Uehara
2120 California Ave
Wahiawa HI 96786

Call Sign: WH6TT
Joseph J Halloran
2331 California Ave
Wahiawa HI 96786

Call Sign: WH7GD
Robert T Hasul
500 Center St 2155
Wahiawa HI 96786

Call Sign: NH6PH
Paul R Newhouse Jr
101 Circle Dr
Wahiawa HI 96786

Call Sign: KH7IV
Rossana A Mendoza
241 Circle Mauka St
Wahiawa HI 96786

Call Sign: WH6BZY
John A Curr III

9046C Deborah Sampson
Ct
Wahiawa HI 96786

Call Sign: WH6BNP
Monica A Hampton
4802 E Carpenter St
Wahiawa HI 96786

Call Sign: KH6BW
Andy R Wisler Sr
1822 Eames St
Wahiawa HI 96786-2610

Call Sign: WH6DRG
Lance T Fabian
260-101 Eena Rd
Wahiawa HI 96786

Call Sign: NH6SS
Clayton P Howe
733 Fenander Ave
Wahiawa HI 96786

Call Sign: K7CLC
Curtis L Crutcher
265 Fenander Ave Unit
102
Wahiawa HI 96786

Call Sign: WH6DNO
Jared T Nakata
1826 Glen Ave A
Wahiawa HI 96786

Call Sign: KH6JGF
Robert Torres
3 Halakahiki Pl
Wahiawa HI 96786

Call Sign: KH7IU
Annette A Pascual
6 Halakahiki Pl
Wahiawa HI 96786-1512

Call Sign: WH6COT
Christopher M Hodges
429B Haley Ave
Wahiawa HI 96786

Call Sign: WH6QY
Brian L Mc Clure
4622B Handrich St
Wahiawa HI 96786

Call Sign: WH6CRH
Douglas R Clark
89F Helemano Mr
Wahiawa HI 96786

Call Sign: N7CLW
Ty M Sloan
1328 Hewitt St 101
Wahiawa HI 96786

Call Sign: WH6UK
Keith A Liles
2060B Hikina Ct
Wahiawa HI 96786

Call Sign: AH6DJ
Gary M Watanabe
276 Ilima St
Wahiawa HI 96786-1616

Call Sign: KH7WM
Henry U Nunes
263 Iliwai Dr
Wahiawa HI 96786

Call Sign: KH6GBG
Alfred Z Shimabuku
407 Iliwai Dr
Wahiawa HI 96786-2310

Call Sign: KH6BT
Edward M Matsusaka
Box 905 104 Imaka Pl
Wahiawa HI 96786

Call Sign: WH7ZO
Jared J Chumley
5148 Kaena Ave
Wahiawa HI 96786

Call Sign: KH7XP
Larry T Inouye Jr
15 Kalie St
Wahiawa HI 96786

Call Sign: WH7TT
Edward R Haddock
182 Kaliko Dr
Wahiawa HI 96786

Call Sign: AH6TB
Thomas E Primiano-
Holton
252 Kaliponi St
Wahiawa HI 96786

Call Sign: NH7ZC
Thomas E Primiano-
Holton
252 Kaliponi St
Wahiawa HI 96786

Call Sign: KH7QG
Jamin M Hiebert
535 Kaniahe St
Wahiawa HI 96786

Call Sign: KH7PKK
Peter K Kauahi 4Th
440 Kanoelehua Pl
Wahiawa HI 96786

Call Sign: WH6DMV
Peter K Kauahi 4Th
440 Kanoelehua Pl
Wahiawa HI 96786

Call Sign: KH6DR
Edward S Saito
241 Karsten Dr

Wahiawa HI 96786   Wahiawa HI 96786-1867   Wahiawa HI 96786

Call Sign: KH6JHY   Call Sign: WH6CFV   Call Sign: WH6JM
Jack F Pechous   Eric S Konno   Jimmy M Villamor
247 Karsten Dr   455A Kilani Ave   232 Koa St Apt C9
Wahiawa HI 96786   Wahiawa HI 96786   Wahiawa HI 96786

Call Sign: KH7PR   Call Sign: WH6CFT   Call Sign: WH6WY
Judith C Brown   Mitsuko Konno   Dewayne Williams
266 A Karsteu Dr   455A Kilani Ave   4715B Kole Kole Ave
Wahiawa HI 96786   Wahiawa HI 96786   Wahiawa HI 96786

Call Sign: WH7RY   Call Sign: WH6CFW   Call Sign: KH6JIW
Steven K Stone   Mark K Konno   Nelson O Rose II
314 Kellog St   455A Kilani Ave   149 Kuahiwi Ave Apt 209
Wahiawa HI 96786   Wahiawa HI 96786   Wahiawa HI 96786

Call Sign: KH6BSQ   Call Sign: WH6GZ   Call Sign: WH6PV
Nobuo Takamori   Solomon V Caballero Sr   Bedford Walton
353 Kellog St   250 Kilani Ave 2   1176 Lakeview Cir
Wahiawa HI 96786   Wahiawa HI 96786   Wahiawa HI 96786

Call Sign: AH6OF   Call Sign: WH6HP   Call Sign: KH6JUH
Carl M Matsuura   Daniel A Young   Lewis D Lovitt Sr
1909 Kiekie Pl   206 Kilani Pl   78 B Lakeview Cir
Wahiawa HI 96786   Wahiawa HI 96786   Wahiawa HI 96786

Call Sign: KH6QIP   Call Sign: KH7JA   Call Sign: AH7F
Albert M Matsusaka   Christopher J Hatico   Arthur H Hebben
28 Kilani Ave   1960 Kinipopo St   124 Leilehua Rd
Wahiawa HI 96786   Wahiawa HI 96786   Wahiawa HI 96786

Call Sign: KH6MAC   Call Sign: NH6VA   Call Sign: WH6CRF
Henry A Mcmurray Jr   Joseph L Vierra   Pavel I Pavlov
83 Kilani Ave   414A Koa St Apt A   124 Leilehua Rd
Wahiawa HI 96786   Wahiawa HI 96786-2267   Wahiawa HI 96786

Call Sign: NH7SP   Call Sign: NH2CR   Call Sign: WH6TY
Henry A Mcmurray Jr   Vicente S Malanog   Vassil H R Vatev
83 Kilani Ave   232 Koa St Apt C2   124 Leilehua Rd
Wahiawa HI 96786   Wahiawa HI 96786   Wahiawa HI 96786

Call Sign: NH6A   Call Sign: WH7VM   Call Sign: WH6DCL
Yasuo Konno   Vicente S Malanog   Walter G Koch
455 Kilani Ave   232 Koa St Apt C2   124 Leilehua Rd

Wahiawa HI 96786-2860   Wahiawa HI 96786   Wahiawa HI 96786

Call Sign: WH6DVV   Call Sign: KF4SGA   Call Sign: WH7EV
Fernando Arcayna   Sara L Carlson   Glenn J Hartman
1222 Loko Dr   4544A Mokihana Pl   126 Neff St 206
Wahiawa HI 96786   Wahiawa HI 96786   Wahiawa HI 96786

Call Sign: KH6LK   Call Sign: WH7TI   Call Sign: AE4RM
Kaoru Oshiro   Irene Guerrero   Huston Y Weems Jr
1305 Manua St   196 A Muliwai Ave   358B Okinawa Loop
Wahiawa HI 96786   Wahiawa HI 96786   Wahiawa HI 96786

Call Sign: WH7NV   Call Sign: WH6DWO   Call Sign: WH6CYK
Danica C Palmer   Climer Malanog   Steven H Hadamik
157 Mcandrew St   101 Nanea Ave   276 Olive Ave Apt 6
Wahiawa HI 96786   Wahiawa HI 96786   Wahiawa HI 96786

Call Sign: NH7QR   Call Sign: WH6BWE   Call Sign: NH6YC
Edwin E Chung-Hoon   Donald C Hounsell   Richard E Tutt
64 Miki Miki Pl   945 Neal Ave   One Ihoiho Pl Apt A510
Wahiawa HI 96786   Wahiawa HI 96786   Wahiawa HI 96786

Call Sign: NH6GJ   Call Sign: NH6XE   Call Sign: KC5GAX
Robert W Jones   Gloria I Boag   Richard C Lalone II
1720 Moala Pl   945 Neal Ave   159 Palapalai Circle 101
Wahiawa HI 96786-2504   Wahiawa HI 96786   Wahiawa HI 96786

Call Sign: WH7S   Call Sign: NH6XF   Call Sign: NH7TR
Robert W Jones   Maxwell N Boag   Richard C Lalone II
1720 Moala Pl   945 Neal Ave   159 Palapalai Circle 101
Wahiawa HI 96786-2504   Wahiawa HI 96786   Wahiawa HI 96786

Call Sign: KH6ACD   Call Sign: WH6CPS   Call Sign: WH6BDU
Ernestine L Yee   Lona Juttner   Francis K Kahawai
27 Moe Moe Pl   945 Neal Ave   335-4 Palm St
Wahiawa HI 96786   Wahiawa HI 96786   Wahiawa HI 96786

Call Sign: KH6WU   Call Sign: WH6IY   Call Sign: WH6LV
Charles S Y Yee   Christian Eckhoff   Larry R Murray
27 Moe Moe Pl   945 Neal Ave   134 Plum St
Wahiawa HI 96786   Wahiawa HI 96786   Wahiawa HI 96786

Call Sign: AH6TM   Call Sign: WH6BOU   Call Sign: KH6GMA
Christopher P Carlson   Kevin H Makins   Rolland O Belcher
4544A Mokihana Pl   4-945 Neal Ave   208 Plum St

Wahiawa HI 96786   Wahiawa HI 96786   Wahiawa HI 96786

Call Sign: WH6TV
Gary S Victor
2033 Puu Pl
Wahiawa HI 96786

Call Sign: WH6VY
Glen Mitcham
229 Turner St
Wahiawa HI 96780

Call Sign: NH6CE
June J Sakamoto
1735 Walea St
Wahiawa HI 96786

Call Sign: NH6XD
William M Pardue
215 Rose St
Wahiawa HI 96786

Call Sign: KH6LK
Parry N Medeiros
222 A Turner St
Wahiawa HI 96786

Call Sign: NH6DJ
Kevin H Sakamoto
1735 Walea St
Wahiawa HI 96786-2527

Call Sign: WH6HJ
Edwin M Hiroe
205-1 Rose St
Wahiawa HI 96786

Call Sign: WH7LK
Parry N Medeiros
222 A Turner St
Wahiawa HI 96786

Call Sign: KH7N
Lloyd Becones
1769 Walea Uka Pl
Wahiawa HI 96786

Call Sign: WH6DJK
Peter Bishop
219 B Rose St
Wahiawa HI 96786

Call Sign: WH6DNN
Jared H Medeiros
222 Turner St A
Wahiawa HI 96786

Call Sign: KH7EX
Robert L Wright
55 Walker Ave Apt 29
Wahiawa HI 96786

Call Sign: WH6DNH
Alison J Bishop
219 B Rose St
Wahiawa HI 96786

Call Sign: WH6DNE
Kendra N Medeiros
222 Turner St Apt A
Wahiawa HI 96786

Call Sign: NH7J
Angus J Mac Feeley
1307 Whitmore Ave
Wahiawa HI 96786

Call Sign: WH6DMY
Leonardo S Jamias
1564 Royal Palm Dr
Wahiawa HI 96786

Call Sign: KH6ASH
William L Moore
30 Uluwehi St
Wahiawa HI 96786

Call Sign: WH6CXF
Richard A Schroeder
1830 Wilikina 810
Wahiawa HI 96786

Call Sign: WH6DNP
Robert D Jamias
1564 Royal Palm Dr
Wahiawa HI 96786

Call Sign: WH6BXR
Kenneth W Carver III
Uscg Commsta Honolulu
Wahiawa HI 96786

Call Sign: K4HVD
Everest F Schmidli
298 Wilikina Dr 507
Wahiawa HI 96786

Call Sign: WH6CPI
Paul K Hokoana
1802D Santa Fe St
Wahiawa HI 96786

Call Sign: KH6VI
Nathan E Barrett
176 Wai Ct 101
Wahiawa HI 96786

Call Sign: NH7FF
Robert J Baker
1600 Wilikina Dr C709
Wahiawa HI 96786

Call Sign: NH6QY
Prince J Abdullah
374B Tinian St

Call Sign: WH7VI
Nathan E Barrett
176 Wai Ct 101

Call Sign: KH6EH
Elmer S Bumanglag
Wahiawa HI 96786

Call Sign: KH6JQY
Wallace J Estenes
Wahiawa HI 96786

Call Sign: KH6YJ
Jay J Pasco
Wahiawa HI 96786

Call Sign: KH7NJ
Ruben M Alcoran
Wahiawa HI 96786

Call Sign: NH2IG
Jay J Pasco
Wahiawa HI 96786

Call Sign: NH2JA
Elmer S Bumanglag
Wahiawa HI 96786

Call Sign: NH2JY
Lenny Arlene Pasco
Wahiawa HI 96786

Call Sign: WH6DQI
Domingo V Layugan Jr
Wahiawa HI 96786

Call Sign: WH6VLZ
Lenny Arlene Pasco
Wahiawa HI 96786

Call Sign: WH7GW
Jason D Laponsey
Wahiawa HI 96786

Call Sign: NH2IN
Jimmy Villamor
232 Koa St Apt C9
Wahiwa HI 96786

**FCC Amateur Radio
License in Wai Pahu**

Call Sign: NH6TB
Sidney E Miller
94-743 Kaaka St
Wai Pahu HI 96797

**FCC Amateur Radio
License in Waialua**

Call Sign: KH7PQ
Shawn S Tempesta
68 024 Apuhihi St W106
Waialua HI 96791

Call Sign: WH6PQ
Bruce A Kososki II
67 249A Kahaone Lp
Waialua HI 96791

Call Sign: KH6KB
Leslie A Nunes Sr
67319 Kiapoko Pl
Waialua HI 96791

Call Sign: WH6CJH
Faith F Fraser
67-176 Kuoha St
Waialua HI 96791

Call Sign: WH6AUJ
Glorry A Miura
66-909 Lupenui Pl
Waialua HI 96791

Call Sign: N6EQZ
William T Sommer Sr
67 346 Waialua Beach Rd
Waialua HI 96791

Call Sign: AH6KJ
Gary S Bignami
68-205 Waialua Beach Rd
Waialua HI 96791

Call Sign: KH6HOG
Michael A Holmberg

Waialua HI 96791

Call Sign: WH6AQI
Ubaldo Dicion
Waialua HI 96791

Call Sign: WH6CLI
Rodney S Dicion
Waialua HI 96791

Call Sign: WH6COH
Calvin Q L Wong Jr
Waialua HI 96791

Call Sign: WH6COI
Patricia Wong
Waialua HI 96791

Call Sign: WH6DAM
Mary A Heaney
Waialua HI 96791

Call Sign: WH6DKZ
Matthew A Holmberg
Waialua HI 96791

Call Sign: WH7TH
Michael A Holmberg
Waialua HI 96791

Call Sign: KH6IMM
William L Star
Waialua HI 96791-0626

Call Sign: KH6RU
Restituto C Ulep
Waialua HI 96791

Call Sign: WH6CLH
Monica S Dicion
Waialua HI 96791

Call Sign: WH6CLJ
Juvencio M Ramos
Waialua HI 96791

Call Sign: WH6COG
Edison S Dicion
Waialua HI 96791

**FCC Amateur Radio
License in Waianae**

Call Sign: NH7ZG
Gregory Bardos
84-757 Kiana Pl
Waianae HI 96792

Call Sign: NH6KP
William L Kapaku
89316B Mano Ave
Waianae HI 96792

Call Sign: N6JVJ
Carol K Cunningham
84 687 Ala Mahiku St
135A
Waianae HI 96792-1625

Call Sign: WH7VV
Joseph K Carrero
84-688 Ala Mahiku St
1726
Waianae HI 96792

Call Sign: AH6OU
Joseph E Grimes
84-664 Ala Mahiku St
191B
Waianae HI 96792

Call Sign: NH6LA
Ronald Vea
84 664 Ala Mahiku St
194B
Waianae HI 96792

Call Sign: NH6LV
Mary A Vea

84 664 Ala Mahiku St
194B
Waianae HI 96792

Call Sign: WH6DWX
Mack H Humphery
84 718 Ala Mahiku St 75
C
Waianae HI 96792

Call Sign: NH6OC
Akiyoshi Kuriyama
87-154 Alapaki St
Waianae HI 96792

Call Sign: WH6BBJ
Lynda J Messier
86 126 Analipo Pl
Waianae HI 96792-3001

Call Sign: NH6RD
Virginia Kapaku
89-316 B Mano Ave
Waianae HI 96792

Call Sign: K3MXO
Michael W Tauson
85-933 Bayview St Apt
202
Waianae HI 96792

Call Sign: WH7NK
Noah Bernal
87 221 Bohiohi Pl
Waianae HI 96792

Call Sign: NH6RC
Sherwood K Kaopua
85-140 E Ala Hema St
Waianae HI 96792

Call Sign: WH6PX
Chuck M Toland
85-175 Farrington Hwy
Waianae HI 96792

Call Sign: WH6DBB
Alinna L Figueroa
87 1276 Farrington Hwy
Waianae HI 96792

Call Sign: WH6CJI
Christopher A Freitas Sr
87-1612F Farrington Hwy
Waianae HI 96792

Call Sign: WH6CJM
William N Freitas
87-1612F Farrington Hwy
Waianae HI 96792

Call Sign: WH6CJN
Clarence Freitas Jr
87-1612F Farrington Hwy
Waianae HI 96792

Call Sign: WH7GR
Victor G Greenstein
87-1938 Farrington Hwy
Waianae HI 96792

Call Sign: NH6PE
Samuel P Pae Sr
87-770 Farrington Hwy
Waianae HI 96792

Call Sign: WH6CTE
Adeline A Carlos
94 965 Farrington Hwy
316
Waianae HI 96792

Call Sign: WA6DAP
Evelyn A White
84-265 Farrington Hwy
511
Waianae HI 96792

Call Sign: WH6CWW
Hal C Howard

85-175 Farrington Hwy
A119
Waianae HI 96792

Call Sign: WH6CWX
Deanna L Beery
85-175 Farrington Hwy
A119
Waianae HI 96792

Call Sign: NH2Z
Le Roy A Shaver
84-265 Farrington Hwy
Apt 608
Waianae HI 96792

Call Sign: WH2E
Ann S Shaver
84-265 Farrington Hwy
Apt 608
Waianae HI 96792

Call Sign: K1OSP
Theresa A Moore
84 965 Farrington Hwy
Apt B712A
Waianae HI 96792

Call Sign: NH7GA
Charles D Henley Sr
85 175 Farrington Hwy
Apt C 236
Waianae HI 96792-2821

Call Sign: NH6QQ
Lyle Patric K Bonilla
87-889 Hakeakea St
Waianae HI 96792

Call Sign: WH6BVF
Lambert M Keahi
89-418 Halekala Ave
Waianae HI 96792

Call Sign: KH6IR

Alexander S Andrade Jr
84-963 Hana St
Waianae HI 96792

Call Sign: KH6WB
Alexander S Andrade Sr
84-963 Hana St
Waianae HI 96792

Call Sign: WH6DTE
Alexander S Andrade Sr
84-963 Hana St
Waianae HI 96792

Call Sign: WH7RZ
Alexander S Andrade Jr
84-963 Hana St
Waianae HI 96792

Call Sign: KH7ON
Paulette P Dibibar
87 828 Helekula Way
Waianae HI 96792

Call Sign: WH7NJ
Howard J Abraham
87 190 Helelua St Apt 6
Waianae HI 96792

Call Sign: NH7WJ
Kimberley K Ray
86-041 Hoaha Pl
Waianae HI 96792

Call Sign: WH7NL
Charles R Carroll
86 287 Hokukga Pl
Waianae HI 96792

Call Sign: WH7NO
Herbert Hew Len
86 303 Hokupaa St
Waianae HI 96792

Call Sign: WH6ACO

Peter B Popa
85-945 Imipono St
Waianae HI 96792

Call Sign: WH6PM
George D Bond
86 892 Iniki Pl
Waianae HI 96792

Call Sign: WB9LAS
Melvin R Wininger
85 105 K Ala Akau St
Waianae HI 96792-2345

Call Sign: KH7IC
Chiko Asuncion
87-1025 Kahiwelola St
Waianae HI 96792

Call Sign: WH7ZQ
Jennifer V King
87 1020 Kaipoi St
Waianae HI 96792

Call Sign: NH6OB
Harold L Viela
85 1048 Kepauala St
Waianae HI 96792

Call Sign: NH6LY
Joewella O Viela
85-1045 Kepauala St
Waianae HI 96792

Call Sign: WH6DNT
Gregory Bardos
84-757 Kiana Pl 27C
Waianae HI 96792

Call Sign: NH7OR
Lynn E Wallenhorst
84 102 Kiapa Pl
Waianae HI 96792

Call Sign: KH7UT

Ronald L Wallenhorst
84 102 Kiapa Pl
Waianae HI 96792-1817

Call Sign: NH7OQ
Tadaji E Wallenhorst
84-102 Kiapa Pl
Waianae HI 96792

Call Sign: NH6LX
Lynette L Kekahuna
87-214 Kipaipai Pl
Waianae HI 96792

Call Sign: NH6LZ
Daniel K Kekahuna Sr
87-214 Kipaipai Pl
Waianae HI 96792

Call Sign: NH6RH
Daniel K Kekahuna Jr
87-214 Kipaipai Pl
Waianae HI 96792

Call Sign: KH6QH
Reynold Gomban
87 076 Kulaaupuni St
Waianae HI 96792

Call Sign: WH6CMQ
Richard F Humble Jr
85-1164 Kumaipo St
Waianae HI 96792

Call Sign: WH7NP
Earl H Higa
86 247 Kuwale Rd
Waianae HI 96792

Call Sign: KH6BEN
Walter S Konishi
86-325 Kuwale Rd
Waianae HI 96792

Call Sign: WH7TE

Airleen L Lucero
89-239 Lapeka Ave
Waianae HI 96792

Call Sign: NH6GC
Clifford L Brown
87-211 Laulele St
Waianae HI 96792

Call Sign: WH6CZY
John H N Hanohano
86 204 Leihua St
Waianae HI 96792

Call Sign: WH7WM
Teri K Savaiinaea
86-233 Leileho Pl
Waianae HI 96792

Call Sign: KH6BBC
Virgasun A Sordillia Sr
940 Lemi St
Waianae HI 96786-2008

Call Sign: NH6TZ
Emily M Favinger
87-1698 M Farrington
Hwy
Waianae HI 96792

Call Sign: WH6CJV
Geraldine K Kealoha
Crocker
87-282 Maia St
Waianae HI 96792

Call Sign: AH6A
Donald G Shook
84-036 Makau St
Waianae HI 96792

Call Sign: WH6CGF
Samasoni Save Jr
87-118 Mamoalii Pl
Waianae HI 96792

Call Sign: KE4AKK
Robert A Brown
87-156 Mamoalii Pl
Waianae HI 96792

Call Sign: WH6DJX
Rachael Roe
87-204 Mamoalii Way
Waianae HI 96792

Call Sign: NH6WD
Henry R Balmores
87-175 Manuaihue Pl
Waianae HI 96792

Call Sign: NH6RB
Mark K De Costa
84-643 Manuku St
Waianae HI 96792

Call Sign: NH6TM
Debra E De Costa
84-643 Manuku St
Waianae HI 96792

Call Sign: NH6TY
Gerard K De Costa
84-643 Manuku St
Waianae HI 96794

Call Sign: NH6SP
William A Buck
87-185 Manuliilii Pl
Waianae HI 96792

Call Sign: WA7ESE
William G Albright
87-175 Manuoioi Pl
Waianae HI 96792-3233

Call Sign: WH7OB
Leo Tanielu
87 565 Manuu St
Waianae HI 96792

Call Sign: KH6V
Shigeto Tsuruda
85-915 Midway St
Waianae HI 96792

Call Sign: WH6EP
Joseph H Lewi Jr
87 236 Mikana St
Waianae HI 96792

Call Sign: WH6HB
Vanessa Lewi
87 236 Mikana St
Waianae HI 96792

Call Sign: NH7VK
Carl S Otsuka
87-160 Mikana St
Waianae HI 96792-3727

Call Sign: WH7NW
Douglas L Prather
86 174 Moelua St
Waianae HI 96792

Call Sign: WH6DTO
Norman A Taylor
87-1815 Mohihi St
Waianae HI 96792

Call Sign: WH6ACI
Gabe K Kilakalua Jr
89 440 Mokiawe St
Waianae HI 96792

Call Sign: WH6CGC
Charlotte A Kilakalua
89-440 Mokiawe St
Waianae HI 96762

Call Sign: AH6JM
Kenneth J Thomas
84-915 Moua St
Waianae HI 96792

Call Sign: KC6RYQ
Sherland W Robinson
87-1054 Oheohe
Waianae HI 96792

Call Sign: KH6PD
Robert J Cunningham
87-1062 Oheohe St
Waianae HI 96792-3452

Call Sign: NH7VL
Glin H Nelson
87-238 Ohiohi Pl
Waianae HI 96792

Call Sign: NH7WI
Ruby R Rellin
89-1028 Pikaiolena St
Waianae HI 96792

Call Sign: WH6DKX
Ernest P Perez
851065 Pilikana Way
Waianae HI 96792

Call Sign: NH7DB
Craig A Brumbaugh
85-1053 Pilikana Way
Waianae HI 96792

Call Sign: WH7OC
Tiave R Tiave
89 523 Puakolu St
Waianae HI 96792

Call Sign: WH6BWV
Nolan T Gouveia
86-348 Puhawai Rd
Waianae HI 96792

Call Sign: KH6BRN
Domingo Correa Sr
86-357 Puhawai Rd
Waianae HI 96792

Call Sign: NH6LI
Kenneth L Quilantang Sr
85-417 Pulapula Pl
Waianae HI 96792

Call Sign: KH6FN
Charles S Nakamine
85160 Waianae Valley Rd
Waianae HI 96792

Call Sign: AD6JE
Donna L Malinousky
Waianae HI 96792

Call Sign: KD6IPX
Bruce D Bonbright
Waianae HI 96792

Call Sign: KH6UE
Given K Nakamine
Waianae HI 96792

Call Sign: NH6FC
Jerrol W Booth
Waianae HI 96792

Call Sign: NH6QO
Phillip G Naone Jr
Waianae HI 96792

Call Sign: NH7WG
Bruce D Bonbright
Waianae HI 96792

Call Sign: WH6DJI
William K Akama III
Waianae HI 96792

Call Sign: WH6DTI
Herbert J Godbolt Jr
Waianae HI 96792

Call Sign: WH7NX
Sterling K Robinson

Waianae HI 96792

Call Sign: WH7OE
Robert L Ward
Waianae HI 96792

Call Sign: WH7OG
Marcella A Young
Waianae HI 96792

Call Sign: WH7OH
Ronald A Young
Waianae HI 96792

Call Sign: WH7OI
Sidney A Young
Waianae HI 96792

Call Sign: WH7OJ
Bailey R Young
Waianae HI 96792

Call Sign: WH6CFF
Miles K Carreiro
Waianae HI 96792

Call Sign: WH6CFG
Melford P Kallikea
Waianae HI 96792

Call Sign: WH6COW
Kathleen W O Neill
Waianae HI 96792

FCC Amateur Radio License in Waikoloa

Call Sign: WH6DRU
Paul C Oshiro
68-1755 Alana Pl
Waikoloa HI 96738

Call Sign: WH6DPT
Douglas W Jones
68-3564 Awamoa Pl

Waikoloa HI 96738

Call Sign: KL0UL
Jack Niederkorn
68-3567 Awamoa Way
Waikoloa HI 96738

Call Sign: KH6KN
Kenneth S Noller
68-1747 Ho Ohiki Pl
Waikoloa HI 96738

Call Sign: W6KSN
Kenneth S Noller
68-1747 Ho Ohiki Pl
Waikoloa HI 96738

Call Sign: WD4MLF
Jesse R Maupin
68-3840 Lua Kula St Apt
A204
Waikoloa HI 96738

Call Sign: KC6UQO
Edgardo Vasquez
68-1754 Melia St C120
Waikoloa HI 96738

Call Sign: WH7DG
Edgardo Vasquez
68-1754 Melia St C120
Waikoloa HI 96738

Call Sign: KF6VUT
Harlan D Holmwood
Po Box 383523
Waikoloa HI 96738-3523

Call Sign: K5UN
Gary F Michell
68 1961 Puu Nui St
Waikoloa HI 96738

Call Sign: KH6LL
Gary F Michell

68 1961 Puu Nui St
Waikoloa HI 96738

Call Sign: AH6WX
Victor F Morris Jr
Waikoloa HI 96738

Call Sign: KH6DXX
Dirk Kossenjans
Waikoloa HI 96738

Call Sign: KP4WN
Victor F Morris Jr
Waikoloa HI 96738

Call Sign: WH6CRI
Gerald J Horan
Waikoloa HI 96738

Call Sign: WH6DQT
Dirk Kossenjans
Waikoloa HI 96738

Call Sign: WH6YN
Joseph K Mossman
Waikoloa HI 96738

Call Sign: WH6YS
Erick M Calloway
Waikoloa HI 96738

Call Sign: WH7PG
Jeffrey D Lee
Waikoloa HI 96738

Call Sign: WH7WZ
April K Lee
Waikoloa HI 96738

Call Sign: KH6MN
Eric S Wakely
Waikoloa HI 96738

Call Sign: NH6V
Robert H Van Geen

Waikoloa HI 96738-4561

FCC Amateur Radio License in Wailuku

Call Sign: AH6EE
David M Clothier
449-B Iao Valley Rd
Wailuku HI 96793

Call Sign: WH6CW
Robert T Janis Jr
373 B Lakee Ln
Wailuku HI 96793

Call Sign: WH6DKY
Arthur S Agdeppa Jr
950 Akaiki Pl
Wailuku HI 96793

Call Sign: WH7BC
Monte K Watanabe
959 Akaiki Pl
Wailuku HI 96793

Call Sign: WH7CO
Denn Ko
1586 Alako St
Wailuku HI 96793

Call Sign: WH6DPW
Nestor S Gines
828 Aukai Pl
Wailuku HI 96793

Call Sign: N0KXY
Carol R Kennedy
15 Awela Circle 101
Wailuku HI 96793

Call Sign: WH6BXL
Jeff S Migasato
618 Ciholiho St
Wailuku HI 96793

Call Sign: WH7WE
Holiann Ho
26 Emoloa Pl
Wailuku HI 96793

Call Sign: WH6DNW
John H Cotney Jr
107 Eulu St
Wailuku HI 96793

Call Sign: KH6NQ
Jack L Long
Gen Del
Wailuku HI 96793

Call Sign: N0DQD
Robert J Kennedy
250 Hauoli St Apt 419
Wailuku HI 96793

Call Sign: KH6HE
Alexander Miguel
2115 Hewahewa Pl
Wailuku HI 96793

Call Sign: WH7CN
Jordan Y Nagasako
1360 Hiahia St
Wailuku HI 96793

Call Sign: KH6JVO
Frank L Carlson
408 High St
Wailuku HI 96793

Call Sign: WH7XV
Jeffrey L Marsh
75 Hoauna St
Wailuku HI 96793

Call Sign: WH6CBQ
Gregory P Lussier
270 Hookahi St Ste 207
Wailuku HI 96793

Call Sign: NH6IB
Willard M Eller
673 Kaae Rd
Wailuku HI 96793

Call Sign: KH6JDA
Jeffrey D Amaral
25 Ka'Ale'A Way 11B
Wailuku HI 96793

Call Sign: NH6BO
Jeffrey D Amaral
25 Ka'Ale'A Way 11B
Wailuku HI 96793

Call Sign: WH6ARG
Kristine M Uramato
2132 Kahawai St
Wailuku HI 96793

Call Sign: KH6H
Melvin T Fukunaga
2011 Kahekili Hwy
Wailuku HI 96793

Call Sign: NH7EY
August P Leval
1946 Kaihamu Pl
Wailuku HI 96793

Call Sign: KH6RK
Russell G Phillips
58 Kamahao St
Wailuku HI 96793-8302

Call Sign: WH7PZ
Russell G Phillips
58 Kamahao St
Wailuku HI 96793-8302

Call Sign: AH7RK
Russell G Phillips
58 Kamaha'O St
Wailuku HI 96793-8302

Call Sign: WH6BXG
Scott J Miyashiro
1837 Kaohu St
Wailuku HI 96793

Call Sign: AH6QT
Lucas F Bruno III
341 Lani Cottage B
Wailuku HI 96793

Call Sign: NH6BW
Milton F Yamashiro
1322 Lower Main St A8
Wailuku HI 96793-1942

Call Sign: K5ZYO
Steve G Annis
1235 Kilou Lp
Wailuku HI 96793

Call Sign: KD6CVU
Lucas F Bruno III
341 Lani Cottage B
Wailuku HI 96793

Call Sign: KH6CJJ
Kent R Carlson
2143 Mahinakea St
Wailuku HI 96793

Call Sign: NH7PP
Danny P Ancheta
1387 Kilou Pl
Wailuku HI 96793

Call Sign: KH7SR
Dennis E Baldwin
1876 Launiupoko Pl
Wailuku HI 96793

Call Sign: WH6QM
John C Tucker
1911 Makila Pl
Wailuku HI 96793-2923

Call Sign: KH6JIB
Robbie W Reneau
1876 Koa'E Pl
Wailuku HI 96793

Call Sign: WH6DEP
Stephen R Correa Jr
6 Lehuapueo Pl
Wailuku HI 96793

Call Sign: WH7UW
Gail M Raikes
637 Mapuana Pl
Wailuku HI 96793

Call Sign: KH6HPS
Mary K Allton
2044 Kolo Pl
Wailuku HI 96793

Call Sign: KH6EK
Michael T Sone
314 Liholiho St
Wailuku HI 96793

Call Sign: WH6BZQ
Paul M Pigao
1582 Mill St
Wailuku HI 96793

Call Sign: NH6QE
Edwin J Fernandez
364 Konahea St
Wailuku HI 96793

Call Sign: K5BGG
Fred A Morgan
333 Liholiho St
Wailuku HI 96793

Call Sign: AH6IF
Dean K Tanimoto
311 Nakoa Dr
Wailuku HI 96793

Call Sign: WH7TU
Mark K Oldag
488 Kopaa Pl
Wailuku HI 96793

Call Sign: NH6SI
Matthew C Niles
355 Liholiho St
Wailuku HI 96793

Call Sign: KH6DT
Dean K Tanimoto
311 Nakoa Dr
Wailuku HI 96793

Call Sign: WH6DQM
Marc M Miyakawa
10 Kopi Ln 18204
Wailuku HI 96793

Call Sign: WH6CQU
Jefferson J Niles
355 Liholiho St
Wailuku HI 96793

Call Sign: WB6QPW
James B Mayo
1148 Nakuluai
Wailuku HI 96793

Call Sign: WH7AF
Anna M Foust
45 Kuaiwa 19A
Wailuku HI 96793

Call Sign: KH6FS
Milton F Yamashiro
1322 Lower Main St A8
Wailuku HI 96793-1942

Call Sign: WH7XX
Lars M Gascon
1101 Nakuluai St
Wailuku HI 96793

Call Sign: WH6DJA
Kaipo Kahai
102 Nokekula Loop
Wailuku HI 96793

Call Sign: WH6DPX
Alex T Rosal
676 Nukuwai Pl
Wailuku HI 96793

Call Sign: WH6DOH
Salvador Haban
772 Olena St
Wailuku HI 96793

Call Sign: WH6YE
Marada Decker Jr
324 Oluloa Dr
Wailuku HI 96793

Call Sign: W3GW
Joseph L Gerry Jr
34 Palekaiko Pl
Wailuku HI 96793

Call Sign: KH6AJQ
John M Sakuma
611 Pio Dr
Wailuku HI 96793

Call Sign: WH6DME
Dawn N Hoewaa
663 Pohala St
Wailuku HI 96793

Call Sign: AH6RQ
Joseph J Bommarito
99 Poniu Cir
Wailuku HI 96793

Call Sign: WH7NG
Jason T Kerber
46 Poniu Circle
Wailuku HI 96793

Call Sign: NH6IW
Steven S Fernandez
2136 Puuohala Pl
Wailuku HI 96793

Call Sign: WH6AW
Michael G Capuano
Rr 1 Box 391 500
Wailuku HI 96793

Call Sign: AH6GR
Randal A Leval
275 S Alu Rd
Wailuku HI 96793

Call Sign: NH6FT
Joni T Leval
275 S Alu Rd
Wailuku HI 96793

Call Sign: N7AK
Alvin F Kanda
2252 W Vineyard St
Wailuku HI 96793

Call Sign: KE4QPG
Luis A Rico
Wailuku HI 96793

Call Sign: KH6MM
Marvin M Tanaka
Wailuku HI 96793

Call Sign: KH6NO
Wilmer K F Hew
Wailuku HI 96793

Call Sign: KH6WF
Paul H Matsuda
Wailuku HI 96793

Call Sign: WH6BXP
Stanley S Mori
Wailuku HI 96793

Call Sign: WH6DMI
Kenneth H Hayashida Jr
Wailuku HI 96793

Call Sign: WH6U
Lucas F Bruno III
Wailuku HI 96793

Call Sign: WH7NF
Leslie A Dunn
Wailuku HI 96793

Call Sign: WH7UH
Walter H Pacheco
Wailuku HI 96793

Call Sign: KH6FMS
Larry M Wada
Wailuku HI 96793-0394

Call Sign: KB6QOP
Silvia C Dowling
Wailuku HI 96793

Call Sign: WH6BXX
Stanley S Shigematsu
Wailuku HI 96793

Call Sign: WH6GW
Francis Y Kihara
Wailuku HI 96793

**FCC Amateur Radio
License in Waimanalo**

Call Sign: WH6CXI
Al C Kaopuiki
41-673 Ala Koa St
Waimanalo HI 96795-1802

Call Sign: WH6TR
Victor L Redding
41-060 Ehukai St
Waimanalo HI 96795

Call Sign: KH7IH
Eric K Kim
41 581 Flamingo St
Waimanalo HI 96795

Call Sign: KH7QX
Fagota Tataipu Jr
41 545 Hihimanu St
Waimanalo HI 96795

Call Sign: NH7SQ
Stuart Akagi
41-240 Hihimanu St
Waimanalo HI 96795

Call Sign: KA7CZH
Ronald D Trautwein
41-016 Hilu St
Waimanalo HI 96795

Call Sign: KH6GJZ
John J Radovich Sr
41-023 Hinalea St
Waimanalo HI 96795-1611

Call Sign: WH6SP
Robert H Johnson
41-030 Hinalea St
Waimanalo HI 96795

Call Sign: KH7ZZ
Eugene M Garcia Jr
41-228 Huli St
Waimanalo HI 96795

Call Sign: WH6CIU
Brandon K Lopez
41-1649 Humuka Loop
Waimanalo HI 96795

Call Sign: WH6CIV
Kyle K A Lopez
41-1649 Humuka Loop
Waimanalo HI 96795

Call Sign: WH6CIX
Blaise M Lopez Jr
41-1649 Humuka Loop
Waimanalo HI 96795

Call Sign: WH6BZV
Chad K L Kahunahana
41-635 Inoaole St
Waimanalo HI 96795

Call Sign: KH7PI
Lance C Wong
41 711 Kaaumoand Pl
Waimanalo HI 96795

Call Sign: KH6CXP
Franklin K Baker Jr
41-702 Kalanianaole
Waimanalo HI 96795

Call Sign: WH6CIS
Bruce K Mossman
41-1014 Kalanianaole
Hwy
Waimanalo HI 96795

Call Sign: WH6CIT
Christopher D Kaufmann
41-1014 Kalanianaole
Hwy
Waimanalo HI 96795

Call Sign: NH7VS
Morgan Parker
41-1698 Kalanianaole
Hwy
Waimanalo HI 96795

Call Sign: NH7YR
Jennifer A Crummer
41-927 Kalanianaole Hwy
Waimanalo HI 96795

Call Sign: KH6IKE
Isaac Kaopua Jr

41-238 Kauholokahiki St
Waimanalo HI 96795

Call Sign: WH7LZ
Isaac Kaopua Jr
41-238 Kauholokahiki St
Waimanalo HI 96795

Call Sign: AH6LL
Lovell K Ka'Opua Sr
41-265 Kauholokahiki St
Waimanalo HI 96795

Call Sign: KH6LOL
Lovell K Ka'Opua Sr
41-265 Kauholokahiki St
Waimanalo HI 96795

Call Sign: WH7UG
Lovell K Ka'Opua
41-265 Kauholokahiki St
57
Waimanalo HI 96795

Call Sign: NH6UV
Gabriel B Ferolino
41-1420 Kuhimana St
Waimanalo HI 96795

Call Sign: KH7HQ
Rana Mae M Rarang
41 1441 Kuhimana St
Waimanalo HI 96785

Call Sign: WH6BZF
Lawrence De Costa Jr
41-727H Kumuhaw St
Waimanalo HI 96795

Call Sign: AH6QE
Alfred A Rivera
41 749 Kumuhau St
Waimanalo HI 96795

Call Sign: WH6QG

Kenneth Lesperance
41-755 Kumuhau St
Waimanalo HI 96795

Call Sign: WH6DQX
Kristine G Lesperance
41-755A Kumuhau St
Waimanalo HI 96795

Call Sign: WH6UH
Ramona M Visnak
41-963 Laumilo
Waimanalo HI 96795

Call Sign: WH6G
Howard H Welfeld
41 1010 Laumilo St
Waimanalo HI 96795

Call Sign: AH6DI
Albert L Brown
41-932 Laumilo St
Waimanalo HI 96795

Call Sign: KH6MB
Joseph M Barr
41-863A Laumilo St
Waimanalo HI 96795

Call Sign: KH6CB
James A Awana Jr
41-838 Mahiku Pl
Waimanalo HI 96795

Call Sign: NH7RX
James A Awana Jr
41-838 Mahiku Pl
Waimanalo HI 96795

Call Sign: WH6CJJ
James K Kealohanui
41-524 Poalima St Apt 218
Waimanalo HI 96795

Call Sign: WH6II

Timothy R Guild
Sea Life Park
Waimanalo HI 96795

Call Sign: WH6DQA
Amy E Bauchens
Waimanalo HI 96795

Call Sign: WH6CZT
Rose Marie M Norton
Waimanalo HI 96795-0110

Call Sign: NH6RR
Carl W Engleman
Waimanalo HI 96795

Call Sign: WH6CIR
Rene G Cabamongan
Waimanalo HI 96795

FCC Amateur Radio License in Waimea

Call Sign: AH8H
George A Talbot
4569 Makeke Rd
Waimea HI 96796-1199

Call Sign: KF6VI
John W Gill
4740 Waimea Canyon Dr
Waimea HI 96796

Call Sign: AH6TA
Wendy E Albertson
Waimea HI 96796

Call Sign: KH6JRY
Elizabeth S Ikehara
Waimea HI 96796

Call Sign: NH7UH
Scott K Yamase
Waimea HI 96796

Call Sign: WH6BEA
Albert M Yamane
Waimea HI 96796

Call Sign: WH6DVP
Joseph M Wyckoff
Waimea HI 96796

Call Sign: WH7SU
Robert T Tanita
Waimea HI 96796

Call Sign: WH7TZ
Wendy E Albertson
Waimea HI 96796

Call Sign: NH6JA
Michael A Madrid
Waimea HI 96796-0821

Call Sign: WH6CGT
Daryl H Date
Waimea HI 96796

Call Sign: WH6MQ
Alan M B H Chun
Waimea HI 96796

Call Sign: WH6CMY
Martin P Hittle
84-754 Ala Mahiku Dr
51B
Wainae HI 96792

FCC Amateur Radio License in Waipaho

Call Sign: KH7LP
Stan T Yamamoto
94 225 A Kahuamo Pl
Waipahu HI 96797

Call Sign: KH7CJ
Thomas M Yamada
94-1139 Akeu Pl

Waipahu HI 96797

Waipahu HI 96797

Waipahu HI 96797

Call Sign: KH6QU
Terence Reis
94 211 Anapau Pl
Waipahu HI 96797

Call Sign: KH7OZ
Cheryl N Galapon
94 1104 Halelehua St
Waipahu HI 96797

Call Sign: NH2BW
Robert Villanueva Sr
94 1035 Hohola St
Waipahu HI 96706

Call Sign: WH6AYN
John R Wheat Jr
94-1001 Awalai St
Waipahu HI 96797

Call Sign: NH6UY
Patrick B Guerin
94-395 Hamau St
Waipahu HI 96797

Call Sign: NH2BX
Robert Villanueva Jr
94 1035 Hohola St
Waipahu HI 96797

Call Sign: WH6DRC
Dwayne M Fedalizo
94-408 Awamoi St
Waipahu HI 96797

Call Sign: WH7VF
Cleve E Florendo
94322 Hanawai Circle
Waipahu HI 96797

Call Sign: KH6OC
Richard T Sakamoto Jr
94 1036 Hohola St
Waipahu HI 96797

Call Sign: WH6DKL
Gayle Igarashi
94-995 Awamoku Pl
Waipahu HI 96797

Call Sign: KH7IW
Noli M Tomas
94 1285 Hene St
Waipahu HI 96797

Call Sign: WH6BPQ
Russell G Nobriga
94-583 Honowai St
Waipahu HI 96797

Call Sign: KH6FF
David K Apo
94 998 C Eleu St
Waipahu HI 96797

Call Sign: KH6IW
Francis H Anzai
94-478 Hepia Pl
Waipahu HI 96797

Call Sign: NH6XV
Basilio Demecilio
94-593 Honowai St
Waipahu HI 96797

Call Sign: KH6DNY
Danilo Arreola
94 1083 Hahana St
Waipahu HI 96797

Call Sign: WH6AAM
Ronald L S Yurong Sr
94-532 Hiahia Loop
Waipahu HI 96797

Call Sign: KH6BO
Bernard S Hamada
94-1098 Hoomakoa St
Waipahu HI 96797

Call Sign: NH2JC
Danilo Arreola
94 1083 Hahana St
Waipahu HI 96797

Call Sign: KH6DJE
Etsuo Mansho
94-1334 Hiana Pl
Waipahu HI 96797

Call Sign: NH6ZS
Gregory Amancio
94-1107 Huakai St
Waipahu HI 96797

Call Sign: WH7YC
Ted L Mokiao
94-1037 Halekapio St
Waipahu HI 96797

Call Sign: WH6DJJ
Philip K Yee
94-457 Hiapaiole Loop
Waipahu HI 96797

Call Sign: KH7RX
Stuart M Miyasato
94-102 Hulahe St
Waipahu HI 96797

Call Sign: KH7NL
Leo U Galapon Jr
94 1104 Halelehua St

Call Sign: KH7JN
Teresita T Torres
94 1278 Hiapaiole Pl

Call Sign: WH6AQQ
Richard J Keopuhiwa
94-718 Ka Aoki Pl

Waipahu HI 96797

Waipahu HI 96797

Waipahu HI 96797

Call Sign: KD4VAI
David P Montague
94 1088 Kaaholo St
Waipahu HI 96797

Call Sign: WH6DVW
Thomas P Chang
94-1010 Kaeele St
Waipahu HI 96797

Call Sign: KH7NV
Aljacob C Banas
94 1203 Kahuanvi St
Waipahu HI 96797

Call Sign: NH7OF
Timothy W Billings
94 937 Kaaholo St
Waipahu HI 96797

Call Sign: WH6CUA
Mary A Yago
94 1185 Kahuahale St
Waipahu HI 96797

Call Sign: KH6JQD
James J Fernando
94-280 Kahuawai St
Waipahu HI 96797

Call Sign: KH7RI
William W Silva Jr
94 751 Kaaka St
Waipahu HI 96797

Call Sign: NH6KZ
Rudy A Topinio
94-1153 Kahuahale St
Waipahu HI 96797

Call Sign: KH7HJ
John N Reeves Jr
94-597 Kaiewa St
Waipahu HI 96797-1248

Call Sign: KH6XB
Mark D Vidinha
94-667 Kaaka St
Waipahu HI 96797

Call Sign: KH6OJ
Dionicio R Mabute
94-345 Kahuahele
Waipahu HI 96797

Call Sign: AL7RQ
Robert M Harrison
94-204 Kaiholena Pl
Waipahu HI 96797

Call Sign: WH7UD
Mark D Vidinha
94-667 Kaaka St
Waipahu HI 96797

Call Sign: NH6QJ
Dionicio R Mabute
94-345 Kahuahele
Waipahu HI 96797

Call Sign: WH6DWC
Alfred K Orion
94-730 Kalae St
Waipahu HI 96797

Call Sign: WH7XB
Mark D Vidinha
94-667 Kaaka St
Waipahu HI 96797

Call Sign: KH7JP
Elena D Mabute
94 345 Kahuahele St
Waipahu HI 96797

Call Sign: KH6VI
Diana A Tom
94-757 Kalae St
Waipahu HI 96797

Call Sign: WH7XJ
Louella K Vidinha
94-667 Kaaka St
Waipahu HI 96797

Call Sign: KH7NW
Johnele Mabute
94 345 Kahuahele St
Waipahu HI 96797

Call Sign: WH6DTJ
Armando Gonzalez
94-474 Kalukalu St
Waipahu HI 96797

Call Sign: WH6FX
David B Akana
94-777 Kaaka St
Waipahu HI 96797

Call Sign: KH7OS
Lily K Toyama
94 228 Kahualii St
Waipahu HI 96797

Call Sign: NH6S
Alan G Asakura
94-979 Kau'Olu Pl Unit
1205
Waipahu HI 96797

Call Sign: KH6JEI
Derek M Fukunaga
94-1005 Kaamea St

Call Sign: KH6BXY
Otis S Nakamura
94-1470 Kahualoa St

Call Sign: NH6KV
Steven M Sano

94 1001B Kikepa St
Waipahu HI 96797

Call Sign: WH7AO
Maria I P Danao
94-1021 Koliana St
Waipahu HI 96797

Call Sign: WD6FAF
Charles Grandjean Iv
94-420 Kuahui St
Waipahu HI 96797-4532

Call Sign: WH6PI
James E Gripp Jr
94-1378 Kuleua Loop C
Waipahu HI 96797

Call Sign: AH6FY
Scott Van Inwagen
94-159 Kupuna Loop
Waipahu HI 96797

Call Sign: WH7GQ
Ernest W Burnett
94-439 Kupuna Loop
Waipahu HI 96797

Call Sign: WH6PU
George F Burnett
94-439 Kupuna Lp
Waipahu HI 96797

Call Sign: KB0ZKZ
Artur O Czepczynski
94 592 Kupuohi St Apt G
Waipahu HI 96797

Call Sign: KH6OGO
Robt A Schultz
94-1002 Lauwi Pl
Waipahu HI 96789

Call Sign: WB9OGO
Robert A Schultz

94-1002 Lauwi Pl
Waipahu HI 96789

Call Sign: NH6KX
Clifford Y Suwa
94 846 Lelepua Pl 22D
Waipahu HI 96797

Call Sign: WH6DB
Brayson K L Chang
94-844C Lelepua St
Waipahu HI 96797

Call Sign: WH6NJ
Sondra N Onaka
94-844C Lelepua St
Waipahu HI 96797

Call Sign: KH7UP
Roel P Llego
94 246 Leoku St F 213
Waipahu HI 96797

Call Sign: KH7VA
Miguel R Diwa
94 246 Leoku St F 213
Waipahu HI 96797

Call Sign: KH7TS
Norman D Delossantos
94 246 Leoku St F213
Waipahu HI 96797

Call Sign: WH6CVX
Sherwin M Bactat
94-066 Leolua St Apt 102
Waipahu HI 96797-1807

Call Sign: KC0ELJ
Timo Schroeder
94-871 Leomana Way
Waipahu HI 96797-4015

Call Sign: WH6DL
George H Crozier

94-207 Loaa St
Waipahu HI 96797

Call Sign: KH6HJA
Crawford F Sullivan
94-516 Loaa St
Waipahu HI 96797

Call Sign: WH6QX
Gloria Heberling
94-201 Lumiaina Pl E104
Waipahu HI 96797

Call Sign: WH6CSL
William Cristea
94-646 Lumiaina St Aa102
Waipahu HI 96797

Call Sign: KH7WL
Federico P Ader Jr
94 517 Lumiaina St K106
Waipahu HI 96797

Call Sign: WH6DMS
Curtis L Kanahele
94 640 Lumiauau St A 2
Waipahu HI 96797

Call Sign: KC4TJB
Donald W Toews
94-530 Lumiauau St D 104
Waipahu HI 96797

Call Sign: NH6RA
Mark E Deiner
94 824 Lumiauau St Dd 104
Waipahu HI 96797

Call Sign: KH6DF
Duane K Fujiwara
94 828 Lumiauau St L103
Waipahu HI 96797

Call Sign: WH7ZM

Thomas M Boller
94-824 Lumiauau St U201
Waipahu HI 96797

Call Sign: KH6IHK
Dale E Hood
94-1036 Lumihoahu St
Waipahu HI 96797

Call Sign: N6YJG
Dennis G Cayabyab
94-870 Lumihoahu St
Waipahu HI 96797-3924

Call Sign: KH6MZ
John R Raymond
94-987 Lumihoahu St
Waipahu HI 96797-1030

Call Sign: KH6IAH
Bernard R Dier
94 1108 Lumikula St
Waipahu HI 96797-3939

Call Sign: NH6RS
Frederick Debebar
94-1096 Lumikula St
Waipahu HI 96797

Call Sign: WH6WA
Joe R Hollars
94 765 Meahale St
Waipahu HI 96797

Call Sign: WH6CQK
Daniel Q Vuong
94-1128 Mohalu St
Waipahu HI 96797

Call Sign: NH6AG
Ronald H Takaki
94-1139 Mopua Loop J3
Waipahu HI 96797

Call Sign: KB6YZX

Stanley H Hiraoka
94 209 Na Auao Pl
Waipahu HI 96797

Call Sign: WH7ZW
Brandon K Yamamoto
94 653 Nakili Pl
Waipahu HI 96797

Call Sign: KH6MK
Melvin K Koizumi
94-1099 Nawele St
Waipahu HI 96797

Call Sign: KQ6EB
Melvin K Koizumi
94-1099 Nawele St
Waipahu HI 96797

Call Sign: WH6CEO
Ray H Nakashima
94-1173 Noheaiki St
Waipahu HI 96797

Call Sign: WH6DCS
Neil J Washer
94 1052 Ohilau Pl
Waipahu HI 96797-4245

Call Sign: NH7YC
Vanessa D Kennison
94 1046 Oli Pl Unit H 1
Waipahu HI 96797

Call Sign: WH6BUR
Christopher D Yim
94-413 Opaha St
Waipahu HI 96797

Call Sign: WH6CYS
Patrick L Hamlow
94-406 Opeha St
Waipahu HI 96797-4513

Call Sign: NH6VV

Calvin C M Yee
94-411 Opeha St
Waipahu HI 96797

Call Sign: WH6UL
Sarah Pendleton
94-411 Opeha St
Waipahu HI 96797

Call Sign: KH2YI
Mark Fajardo
94 1038 Paiwa Pl
Waipahu HI 96797

Call Sign: WH7AS
Emmanuel S Sales Sr
94-227 Paiwa St
Waipahu HI 96797

Call Sign: WH7AU
Juanito B Barbosa
94-227 Paiwa St
Waipahu HI 96797

Call Sign: KH7IG
Jeshurun T Cacatian
94 019 Poailani Cir
Waipahu HI 96797-3207

Call Sign: NH7JG
Samuel A Taeu Jr
94 1491 Pokeo St
Waipahu HI 96797

Call Sign: KH6JH
Arden B Warren
94-1430 Polani St 31U
Waipahu HI 96797

Call Sign: WH6DLZ
Frederick B Pack
94-1139 Polinahe Pl
Waipahu HI 96797

Call Sign: WH6DKR

Christopher A Crabtree
94-204 Pouhana Loop
Waipahu HI 96797

Call Sign: WH6DNQ
Peter S Chan
94-1132 Pulai St
Waipahu HI 96797

Call Sign: WH6DKK
Thomas King
94-1005 Pupuhi St
Waipahu HI 96797

Call Sign: KH6BLD
Yeisei Asato
94 270 Pupukoae St
Waipahu HI 96797

Call Sign: WH6BUO
Romulo M Manansala
94-303 Pupuole St
Waipahu HI 96797

Call Sign: WH7TB
William J Swain
94-105 Pupupuhi St 5
Waipahu HI 96797

Call Sign: WH6ET
Brian H Kitaoka
94-1052 Waiolina St
Waipahu HI 96797

Call Sign: AH6B
Louis S Shiraishi
94 - 286 Waipahu St
Waipahu HI 96797

Call Sign: WH7EQ
Louis S Shiraishi
94 - 286 Waipahu St
Waipahu HI 96797

Call Sign: WH7ER

Gavin A Shiraishi
94- 286 Waipahu St
Waipahu HI 96797

Call Sign: WH6DJY
Ruby R Real Layos
94-1562 Waipahu St
Waipahu HI 96797

Call Sign: KH6BL
Lyn K T Shiraishi
94-286 Waipahu St
Waipahu HI 96797

Call Sign: WH7FW
Lyn K T Shiraishi
94-286 Waipahu St
Waipahu HI 96797

Call Sign: WH7GK
Celeste K N Shiraishi
94-286 Waipahu St
Waipahu HI 96797

Call Sign: NH6UC
Rodney S Sedeno
94-207 Waipahu St Apt
192
Waipahu HI 96797

Call Sign: KH7RJ
Darren S Dew
Waipahu HI 96797

Call Sign: WH7FT
Robert D Data
Waipahu HI 96797

Call Sign: WH6CLL
Barrientos N Baltazar
94-365 Kahualena St
Waipahy HI 96797

**FCC Amateur Radio
License in Wake Atoll**

Call Sign: AH6TI
Ricky A Martin
Satcom
Wake Atoll HI 96898

Call Sign: KZ5DX
Ricky A Martin
Satcom
Wake Atoll HI 96898

**FCC Amateur Radio
License in Wake Island**

Call Sign: WA2YUN
Colin C Bradley
Wake Island HI 96898-
0096

**FCC Amateur Radio
License in Wamanalo**

Call Sign: AH6FD
Richard A Richman
Wamanalo HI 96795